W9-BVU-853

Acclaim for Ray Oldenburg
and *The Great Good Place*

"Ray Oldenburg is inspirational. He is the first to recognize and articulate the importance of the greeting place (third place) for the well-being of the individual and society at large."

—Ron Sher, President, Terranomics Development
and founder, Third Place Books, Seattle, Washington

"A day doesn't go by that I don't refer to Ray Oldenburg's *The Great Good Place*. At a time when all great, good independent bookstores everywhere are under siege, we're fortunate that Mr. Oldenburg has articulated our message so clearly."

—Mitchell Kaplan, owner, Books & Books, Miami, Florida

"*The Great Good Place* has put into words and focus what I've been doing all my life, from the barbershop I remember as a child to the bookstore I now own. My goal at Horizon Books is to provide that third place in which people can "hang out." Ray Oldenburg has defined those good places while still recognizing the magical chemistry they require. *The Great Good Place* is a book to read, to recommend, and to quote."

—Victor W. Herman, owner, Horizon Books, with locations
in Traverse City, Petoskey, and Cadillac, Michigan

"The great value of this book is that Mr. Oldenburg has given us an insightful and extremely useful new lens through which to look at a familiar problem..."

—*New York Times Book Review*

"This wonderful and utterly important book verifies our need for fun through conversation in "great good places." Oldenburg writes passionately of our country's current and urgent problems resulting from our ever-increasing social isolation and provides us with a very simple solution. America must read and react to this rational common-sense solution to salving our stressed lives. And our government needs to promote, permit, and zone responsible neighborhood hospitality, recognizing the value of "a vital informal life."

—Lynne Breaux, owner, Tunnicliff's Tavern, Washington, D.C.

"Well-written, informative, and often entertaining."

—*Newark Star-Ledger*

THE
GREAT
GOOD
PLACE

CAFÉS, COFFEE SHOPS, BOOKSTORES, BARS, HAIR SALONS, AND OTHER HANGOUTS AT THE HEART OF A COMMUNITY

RAY OLDENBURG

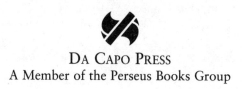

DA CAPO PRESS
A Member of the Perseus Books Group

Cataloging-in-Publication data for this book is available from the Library of Congress.
ISBN: 978-1-56924-681-8

Published by Da Capo Press
A Member of the Perseus Books Group
www.dacapopress.com

Da Capo Press books are available at special discounts for bulk purchases in the
U.S. by corporations, institutions, and other organizations. For more information,
please contact the Special Markets Department at the Perseus Books Group, 2300
Chestnut Street, Suite 200, Philadelphia, PA 19103, or call (800) 810-4145, ext.
5000, or e-mail special.markets@perseusbooks.com.

LSC-C

20 19 18

*To Judith and our
children Jennie, Maren, and Carl*

The pleasure of our lives, for which the pain of our births and our deaths is acceptable, is in the ways of other men and our association with them: not always in their whole souls, their whole hearts, their whole minds, but in their own everyday corrections of the turbulence of their human existences. Can these not also be the subject of our art and our literature?

HENRY FAIRLEE

But aside from friends, there must also be a Place. I suppose that this is the Great Good Place that every man carries in his heart. . . .

PETE HAMILL

A community life exists when one can go daily to a given location at a given time and see many of the people one knows.

PHILIP SLATER

George Dane: I know what I call it . . ."The Great Good Place."
The Brother: I've put it myself a little differently . . . "The Great Want Met."
George Dane: Ah, yes—that's it!

from "The Great Good Place" by HENRY JAMES

Contents

Preface

MY INTEREST IN those happy gathering places that a community may contain, those "homes away from home" where unrelated people relate, is almost as old as I am. Children, I suspect, are instinctively attuned to the climate of human relations around them and experience an inner joy and serenity, a feeling that all is well when the adults in their lives relax and laugh in one another's company. That, at least, was my reaction. Perhaps it was that winter evening during my fifth year, when the older cousins took me along to our town's skating rink and deposited me amid the joyful and animated little crowd in its warming shack, that I first drank the joys of blissful public congregation. I have never since lost my appetite for it.

Subsequent training in sociology helped me to understand that when the good citizens of a community find places to spend pleasurable hours with one another for no specific or obvious purpose, there *is* purpose to such association. Further, the most important of the purposes or functions served by informal public gathering places cannot be supplied by any other agencies in the society. All great cultures have had a vital informal public life and, necessarily, they evolved their own popular versions of those places that played host to it.

To comprehend the importance of the informal public life of our society is to become concerned for its future. Currently and for some time now, the course of urban growth and development in the United States has been hostile to an informal public life; we are failing to provide either suitable or sufficient gathering places necessary for it. The grass roots of our democracy are correspondingly weaker than in the past, and our individual lives are not as rich. Thus, it is always with a sense of urgency that I write and speak on this subject.

I began to take an active professional interest in the topic about ten years ago. I first aired my perspective at a regional sociology convention in 1977. In 1980, a colleague and I collaborated on an article written in the popular vein that was subsequently reprinted in at least nine other periodicals and books. In 1983, we published a longer, more scholarly version in a professional journal. Audience responses were gratifying, but there was also frustration in attempting to make the case within the brief space that articles permit. For the past six years, I've wrestled with a book-length treatment, which this topic surely deserves. After a series of abortive beginnings, it became clear to me that I would not be content to write only for other sociologists nor would I wish to offer solely a description, which good sociology often is.

I wanted to make the case for the informal public life and the Great Good Places essential to it. There is an urgency implicit in the broad-scale destruction of these kinds of places in the United States; we are inadequately equipped even to defend the *idea* of them. The importance of informal meeting places is not deeply ingrained in our young culture, nor is the citizen suitably fortified for a rational argument in their behalf. Even those who would intuitively understand and endorse everything I have to say (and they are many) have too little verbal ammunition. In a world increasingly rationalized and managed, there must be an effective vocabulary and set of rationales to promote anything that is to survive. I can but hope that this effort will contribute to what will have to become a popular understanding of the necessity of a vital informal public life.

I have declined the pose and language of scientific reporting and mean to promote the Great Good Places of society as much as analyze them. Like an attorney-at-law, I am defending a most worthy client who may be facing oblivion and doing so in a language the jury can understand. The jury is middle class, educated, and possessed of choices as to where and how to live. It is capable of making judgments on the matter here put before it and of acting on those judgments. Like the crafty lawyer, I've tried to tailor my anecdotes and illustrations so as to strike chords of response among this panel.

Only the truth will serve my client's interests, and my decision to forego a scientific report assumes no license to play fast and loose with the facts. Several measures were employed in the attempt to represent the phenomena under discussion as they appear in the real world. In identifying the essential characteristics of informal public gathering places and their effect upon the individual and society, I made certain that each conclusion corresponded with my own considerable field experiences; that each of them had been observed and reported by others; and that each had been held up to criticism in the lecture hall. Also, a decision was made to add six chapters of "real life" illustration (Chapters 5 through 10), all of which confirm the basic constructions within the earlier chapters. Finally, time was on my side. In the early years of effort on the subject, many facts seem incompatible with my emerging impression of third places. It is a human tendency to want to discard or discredit, or simply "forget" uncomfortable facts. They are, however, friends in disguise. They are clues to a deeper understanding of the problem that confronts an investigator, but it takes time to fit the stubborn pieces into the puzzle. By current standards of scholarly production, I spent too much time on this project. Such was the nature of my subject, however, that the extra time turned out to be my best methodological technique.

Social scientists who choose to make use of this volume may recognize a familiar structure beneath its plain English and special pleading. The first section of the book is devoted to the creation of an ideal typical core setting of informal public life against which concrete examples may be compared. The second section offers a variety of cultural and historical (real) examples based on the best and, at times, the only accounts available to us. These afford some, and I think significant, substantiation and testing of the ideal type. The final section is devoted to issues relating to informal public life and, though my colleagues are likely to disagree with my positions or the fact that I took positions, they are not likely to dispute the relevance of the issues I've raised.

The considerable amount of fieldwork associated with this effort followed procedures associated with comparative analysis or those used to generate grounded theory. In keeping with that approach, I made use of supplemental data wherever I could find it.

Those wishing to read another author's version of the third place thesis are directed to Phillipe Ariès' paper entitled "The Family and the City," which appeared in *Daedalus* in the spring issue of 1977. Therein, one need only interpret the Frenchman Ariès' café in a generic sense. I stumbled across Ariès' essay toward the end of my own work and reflected on that timing. Though an early reading of his paper would have hastened the development of my own broader perspective, I was spared the inherent pessimism in his analysis.

The bulk of social scientific writing in the area of informal public gathering places consists of ethnographic descriptions that await integration into more abstract and analytical efforts addressing the place and function of these centers of the informal public life of the society. Sociologists may ask themselves why so little has been done in this area since Georg Simmel's brief essay on sociability over half a century ago.

Finally, I would suggest to colleagues that the possibilities for cross-cultural research into the quality of informal public life seem exciting. The most useful and pertinent data are always within the public domain, and the invitation to foreign travel should require little encouragement. Whether the present effort serves to guide such efforts or merely encourage them makes no difference. The important thing is that this research be conducted, if only to help our nation reinstitute the kind of human association essential to all democracies.

Preface to the
Second Edition

AS THE ORIGINAL preface accomplishes the usual purpose of such prolusions, the second affords the author the luxury of choice. Though it is tempting to recount the many and varied experiences, the rich flow of correspondence, and the kindred spirits met as a result of the publication of *The Great Good Place* six years ago, the space allotted here may be more usefully employed.

This second preface is devoted to those readers who have more than a passing interest in the concerns this book addresses. It is primarily for those who wish to learn more and do more in behalf of community, public conversation, and civicism. It is for those who believe in a public life and the need to restore it.

Two brief additions will be developed here, both of which should enhance the utility of the book. First, I will make suggestions for additional reading. Second, I will offer a checklist of the various community-building functions of "great good places" which may be quickly reviewed and assessed against the strengths and deficiencies of any particular neighborhood or municipality. Some of these are developed at greater length in the text proper; some are introduced here for the first time.

In the brief period since *The Great Good Place* was published, many books have appeared with similar themes. America seems to be undergoing a massive reassessment. In the simplest terms, we got where we wanted to go but now we aren't happy about where we are. We have become a suburban nation—the only one in the world. Our migration from both the inner cities and the rural hinterland was, as Lewis Mumford once put it, "a collective effort to live a private life." We aimed for comfort and well-stocked homes and freedom from uncomfortable interaction and the obligations of citizenship. We succeeded.

As if to seal our fate, zoning ordinances were copied and enforced all over the land, prohibiting the stuff of community from intrusion into residential areas. In the subdivisions of post-World War II America, there is nothing to walk to and no place to gather. The physical staging virtually ensures immunity from community.

The preferred and ubiquitous mode of urban development is hostile to both walking and talking. In walking, people become part of their terrain; they meet others; they become custodians of their neighborhoods. In talking, people get to know one another; they find and create their common interests and realize the collective abilities essential to community and democracy.

It is from this perspective, this sense of the terrible costs of suburban development as we've managed it, that much of my reading and writing takes direction. Before publication of this book, I found my kindred spirits almost entirely in the books they wrote, and I am pleased to report that the present decade is witness to an increasing number of volumes having to do with our subject.

My recommendations for additional reading are subjective and incomplete. They consist of the men and women who have had most influence on me and whose books, regardless of publication date, seem to me to have great contemporary relevance.

I could start with none other than Jane Jacobs' *The Death and Life of Great American Cities.* For all the consternation she caused within architectural and planning circles, she has done a tremendous service for us all. One marvels at both the depth and quantity of her insights. Well within the Jacobs' tradition and appearing the same year as my contribution was Roberta Gratz's *The Living City.* Gratz's book contrasts grass roots successes at rebuilding neighborhoods with the disasters wrought by "urban renewal."

Victor Gruen's *The Heart of Our Cities* is still a book worth not only owning but using as a reference work for all aspects of urban and neighborhood development. Gruen is the man who conceived and planned our nation's first covered shopping mall. He came to reject the designation, "father of malling" because his plan was stripped down to commercialism only. He had envisioned a true community center.

Another volume I've nearly worn out is a brief and very readable little book by Wolf Von Eckardt entitled *Back to the Drawing Board*. Like Gruen, Von Eckardt is an advocate of citizen participation in planning and well understands that that can happen only at the neighborhood level.

The best description I've found on what we can learn from the old world is Bernard Rudofsky's *Streets for People;* a richly illustrated and detailed volume on the architectural requirements of a thriving public life. It is fittingly dedicated to "The Unknown Pedestrian" and not one of its scores of illustrations bears any resemblance to our subdivisions.

What almost amounts to a new genre of books are those appearing in response to the "places rated" volumes appearing in the 1980s. Those earlier books ranked cities according to comparative numerical data on health, crime, education, etc. Recognizing that strict adherence to such criteria could lead one to take up residence in "Anywhere, USA," more recent authors have intruded a most relevant question: But is it an interesting place to live?

Mark Cramer's *Funkytowns USA* and Terry Pindell's *A Good Place to Live* are welcome conrasts to the census-based, scoresheet analyses. Pindell treats the dozen or so best places in the U.S. that he's ever heard about in considerable depth. And he writes well; one almost feels as though he or she has been along on the trips. Cramer's "Funkytowns" covers many more towns and cities and, as one reviewer suggested, it should be placed in the glove compartments of all rental cars.

Philip Langdon's *A Better Place to Live* is a painstaking examination of how to "retrofit" American suburbs and when we come to the necessary matter of re-writing the building and zoning codes, this book should be one of the primers. Peter Katz's *The New Urbanism* details and illustrates two dozen developments and re-developments. It represents our architects' best attempts at recreating community. A closing essay (an Afterword) by Vince Scully deserves careful attention.

Recently appearing and already in its second printing is Richard Sexton's *Parallel Utopias* which looks deeply into the thinking behind, and execution of, two notable attempts at creating community today. Seaside, Florida (based on an urban model despite its location) and Sea Ranch, California (based on the model of a rural community) are closely examined. Sexton is a first-rate photographer who illustrates as well as he explains in this book.

A volume which catches everyone's attention when, on my trips, I show it around is David Sucher's *City Comforts*. Contained herein are many suggestions, all photographically-illustrated, as to "minor surgery" and modest additions which combine to make life out in the public domain more enticing, more comfortable, and more livable.

The expert in this sort of thing, of course, is William H. Whyte, and if his larger tome *City* seems a bit formidable, the small and highly illustrated *The Social Life of Small Urban Spaces* will certainly seduce the reader into more of Whyte's research which has been done with exceeding care. Many urban centers have been revitalized in adherence to what Whyte has been able to report.

The political importance of "great good places" is wonderfully documented in a book by Sara Evans and Harry Boyte entitled *Free Spaces*. The writers argue convincingly that such places became much more important after industrialization separated home and the workplace and that they serve to preserve the peoples' democracy against the growing control of both government and the corporations.

Christopher Lasch's *The Revolt of the Elites* discusses the "civic arts" and the art of argument in addition to its main theme—that America's professional and managerial elites have little interest in the broad middle class of our society and have weak ties to nation and place. Their interest in a global economy and their "tourist's attitude" toward place give us cause to both regret and combat the control they have over the rest of us.

As public life is populated with strangers more than ever before; as strangers frighten us more than ever before; and as communities nonetheless depend upon the successful integration of strangers, books about them are also recommended. Lyn Lofland's *A World of Strangers* has become a modern classic. Michael Ignatieff's *The Needs of Strangers* is thought-provoking, and Parker Palmer's *The Company of Strangers* is a pleasure to read.

Before moving to the second part of this preface, there is another kind of reading, just now gathering momentum, that will be of special interest to those concerned with public life. I refer to "civic journalism," or "community journalism," or "citizen journalism," as it is variously called. Though its precise goals and *modus operandi* are still being debated, there is a general consensus that greater citizen involvment is the *desideratum*.

Readers may expect that newspapers will encourage citizen participation in most aspects of community development; that more "level" heads will be invited to present more rational and moderate discussion; that reporting will go beyond mere events and present developments against a background of trends and patterns. Developments and proposals will increasingly be presented in context. Newspapers are expected to be less in league with politicians and the business community than in the past, and more with a citizenry which is trying to "live good lives in good cities."

The reasons for this shift in print journalism are many. Suffice it to note here that there is reason to rejoice in the fact that one of our institutions is moving away from the professional elitism which ill-serves the citizens of a democracy. As newspapers begin to speak more to ordinary citizens, so also will they more often listen to them.

As indicated, the remainder of this discussion will be devoted to the community-building functions which "great good places" typically perform. Most often I refer to such places as "third places" (after home, first, and workplace, second) and these are informal public gathering places. These places serve community best to the extent that they are *inclusive* and *local*.

The first and most important function of third places is that of uniting the neighborhood. In many communities, the post office served this function well when everyone had a mailbox there; when everybody had to walk or drive to it; and it was kept open, by law, twenty-four hours a day. Though there was no seating, it was a place where people met and conversed, at least briefly, with one another.

Drug stores also brought nearly everyone into contact with everyone else in the course of the average week or month. They did this because they offered so many things, beyond pharmaceuticals, that people needed. Also, they typically enjoyed a good (central) location in the town or neighborhood.

Places such as these, which serve virtually everybody, soon create an environment in which everybody knows just about everybody. In most cases, it cannot be said that everyone, or even a majority, will *like* everybody else. It is, however, important to know everyone, to know how they variously add to and subtract from the general welfare; to know what they can contribute in the face of various problems or crises, and to learn to be at ease with everyone in the neighborhood irrespective of how one *feels* about them. A third place is a "mixer."

Assimilation is a function to which third places are well-suited. They serve as "Ports of Entry" for visitors and as places where newcomers may be introduced to many of their predecessors. Andres Duany jokes about the man who spent two days trying to find the resident of a subdivision. His anecdote points up the fact that our postwar residential areas are extremely hostile to strangers, outsiders, and new residents of the area. The streets are typically vacant and there are no local commercial establishments where one might stop to get directions.

There is considerable irony here. Once America became the high mobility society it now is, with about twenty percent of the population changing residence every year, one might have thought that neighborhoods would have been designed so that people could be integrated quickly and easily. What actually happened, however, was quite the opposite. The more people moved about, or were moved about by the companies that employed them, the more difficult it became to penetrate the nation's residential areas.

The hardships involved, and they are many, are not incurred by the newcomers alone. The city and the neighborhood suffer as well when there is a failure to integrate newcomers and enlist their good services to the betterment of community life.

A one-visit Welcome Wagon is a poor substitute for the friendly tavern or coffee-counter where one is *always* welcome. The "neutral ground" (space upon which one is not burdened by the role of host or guest) of third places offers the great ease of association so important to community life. People may come and go just when they please and are beholden to no one. Eventually one meets or otherwise learns about everyone in the neighborhood.

In this respect, third places also serve as "sorting areas." The broad scale association which they provide ultimately leads to the stuff of "sociometrics." That is, people find that they very much like certain people and dislike others. They find people with similar interests, and they find people whose interests aren't similar but are interesting nonetheless. Third places often serve to bring together for the first time, people who will create other forms of association later on.

In true communities there are collective accomplishments. People work together and cooperate with one another to do things which individuals cannot do alone. Though much of this kind of effort is informal, it nonetheless requires a general understanding of who can do what; of the skills, abilities and attitudes of those in the neighborhood. Third places serve to sort people according to their potential usefullness in collective undertakings.

Related to this is the third place's function as a staging area. In time of local crisis, people typically find it necessary to help themselves as much or more than they are helped by municipal agencies. Severe storms and other crises often require a gathering and mobilization of local citizens for the purpose of helping one another. But where? In the aftermath of hurricane Andrew in South Florida not long ago, many people emerged from the destruction feeling that need to gather with others to find out how severe and extensive the damage; to find out what was being done; to see how they could help and/or get help—but for most there was no place to assemble. Careful zoning had denied these people their "third places."

Third places also provide those whom Jane Jacobs called "public characters." These are people who know everybody in the neighborhood and who care about the neighborhood. These are usually store owners or operators who "keep an eye" on what's happening in the neighborhood. These are the people who alert parents about what their kids sometimes "get into" before it is necessary for the police to do so. These are also the people likely to give newcomers their first welcome to the area.

Suburban zoning has replaced "public characters" with the retailers and their employees in the malls and out on the strips. The chains in which these people work thrive by killing off local commercial establishments, and the people who operate the chains do nothing for the community in the way that "public characters" do.

In the negatively-zoned subdivision, there rarely emerges a "public character," for the means by which people might come to know everyone are absent. If the developer's habit of calling a house a "home" is something of a stretch, it doesn't compare with that of calling a subdivision a "community," for that is precisely what it is *not*.

Among the noblest of third place functions, rarely realized anywhere anymore, is that of bringing youth and adults together in relaxed enjoyment. The rampant hostility and misunderstanding between the generations, adult estrangement from and fear of youth, the increasing violence among youth—these and youth-related problems all have a common genesis and it is the increasing segregation of youth from adults in American society.

Raising children was easier when the parents got a lot of help from others in the neighborhood who knew the kids and not only kept an eye on them but generally enjoyed having them around. The ways in which older and younger generations teased, cajoled, chided and amused one another have almost passed from memory now, as have the lessons learned, the examples set, and the local figures admired.

With so many mothers now absent from the home, it is all the more regrettable that the family is so weakly connected (if connected at all) to the other people in the neighborhood. Where third places exist within residential neighborhoods, and are claimed by all, they remain among the very few places where the generations still enjoy one another's company.

Third places serve the elderly as well. It is unfortunate that so many old and retired people find it desireable to make a final migration to some "senior citizen community." It is regrettable that the areas in which they worked and raised children have so little to offer them, so few means of keeping them connected to neighborhood and community.

This book has no chapter on the elderly and the retired. There was the constraint of length and I opted for a chapter on children based on my reasoning that children are ill-equipped and weakly positioned to speak for themselves.

There should be a chapter on the older generation, of course, and not just for their sake. Third places are typically places of business and their slow periods benefit from retired people who can fill the booths and chairs when others are at work or in school. Furthermore, retired people are generally more sociable and more civilized. No longer grubbing for a living, they come to place more value on good conversation, on enjoying people just for the company they offer.

It escapes me right now, who first wrote that urban planning which meets the needs of children and the elderly will be nice for everybody, but truer words are rarely written. Several years ago, I participated in an "Evaluation Study" of a program for retired people in a Minnesota town of barely 7,000 people. The program was contained, for the most part, in the basements of two of the town's larger churches.

Participation was modest in this program and enthusiasm was not high. I was there a full three days and couldn't figure out the purpose, though everyone I talked with insisted that something important was being done "for the elderly." The fourth day began with a meeting in the conference room of the town's largest bank. When the meeting adjourned, I held back and stepped in front of our host as he was about to leave. With just the two of us present, I confronted him with, "What the heck is this all about?" Taken off guard, he blurted, "Well, we had to get them off the street." The important thing being done "for" the elderly was getting them out of the way much as they did with the homeless when Atlanta hosted the Olympics.

These older folks, of course, had looked forward to sitting along the sidewalks in fair weather and to lingering at the lunch and coffee shops and taverns. Here were people most intent upon enjoying community; who now had time to enjoy communal association. The "boosters" however, were intent on denying them these rewards. There was no appreciation of that which the oldest generation contributes to communities which provide a place for them.

Third places provide a means for retired people to remain in contact with those still working and, in the best instances, for the oldest generation to associate with the youngest.

The plight of the elderly and those on fixed incomes generally, points up another important function of third places and it is that performed by all "mutual aid societies." In the convivial atmosphere of third places, people get to know one another and to like one another and then to care for one another. When people care for one another, they take an interest in their welfare; and this is a vastly superior form of welfare than that obtained by governmental programs. It is based on mutual consent, genuine empathy, and real understanding of peoples' situations. Nobody is a "case."

Third place regulars "do for one another," as they would for blood relatives and old friends. They give things they no longer need; they loan items they still want; they do what they can to relieve hardship when it befalls "one of the gang." When someone doesn't "show" for a couple of days, somebody goes around to check on them.

The financial benefits in all of this are considerable. Somebody in the group fixes lawn-mowers. Someone else can handle plumbing and appliances, or knows who does it at considerable savings. Money-saving advice is forthcoming from somebody in the group who has confronted a given problem earlier on. Sometimes, alas, when the group's collective resources are found wanting, the individual is advised, "Get out your pocketbook." Often, however, that is not necessary.

It was in the first "Crocodile Dundee" movie, I believe, that our protagonist was surprised to hear that somebody paid a psychiatrist to listen to his or her troubles. "That's what mates are for!" was, I think, his response. The group support inherent in third place camaraderie, I'm convinced, also saves many people the expense of a "professional caregiver."

This union of friends suggests another function of the third place. An individual can have many friends and engage them often *only* if there is a place he or she can visit daily and which plays host to their meetings.

Friends met in numbers create something of a festive mood for all. Interaction is relatively easy as one is required to contribute only his or her "share" of the time. Laughter is frequent where many friends gather. In their company, the competitive successes and the enervating stresses of the mundane world are "put on hold."

Amid this lengthy enumeration of third place functions, it may be well to point out that the fundamental motivation for this kind of belonging is neither personal advantage nor civic duty. The basic motivation; that which draws people back time and again is *fun*. It is a lamentable fact that so many Americans, when they see the "gang" heavily engaged in "solving the problems of the world" consider them merely to be frivolously wasting time.

The "fun" function of third places is better seen, perhaps, as the entertainment function. That entertainment has deteriorated almost entirely into an industry in the United States is a great pity. We take it passively; we take it in isolation; and we frequently find it boring.

In third places, the entertainment is provided by the people themselves. The sustaining activity is conversation which is variously passionate and light-hearted, serious and witty, informative and silly. And in the course of it, acquaintances become personalities and personalities become true characters—unique in the whole world and each adding richness to our lives.

The major alternative to participatory entertainment is television which really isn't interesting enough to garner all the blame heaped upon it. The critics usually overlook the lack of alternatives to this medium. How many Americans having "surfed" all the channels and, bored by it all, wouldn't like to slip on a jacket and walk down to the corner and have a cold one with the neighbors? Ah, but we've made sure there's nothing on the corner but another private residence . . . indeed, nothing at all within easy walking distance.

We might remind ourselves of the essence of the so-called *joie de vivre* ("joy in living") cultures. That essence is their ability to entertain themselves in an abundance of public places where they may do so daily and at little cost and no discomfort. We may sneer at their simple ways; at their lack of technological gadgetry; and at the fact that their dwellings are more humble than ours. But when all is said and done—they enjoyed life and gave human relationships higher priority than making a buck.

America's growing problem of automobile congestion suggests a related function of third places—where *locally* situated. A third place to which one may walk allows people to "get out of the house" without getting into a car and contributing to traffic congestion. Unfortunately, our census takers log only the commuting use of our roadways. Even casual attention to local driving conditions will reveal that our roads are crowded during most daylight hours and not just at "rush" hours.

Though we live in as large and as well-stocked houses as we can afford, there is frequent need to escape from them. The only real means for most is by car and the only realistic escapes for most is the malls and the strips where they are expected to spend their consumer dollars. Americans spend three to four times as much time shopping as Europeans and much, if not most, of the difference has to do with a lack of alternatives. We have denied ourselves the means of friendly and cost-free association in our neighborhoods. In any total analysis, Walmart and McDonalds are much more expensive than we might imagine.

At the risk of sounding mystical, I will contend that nothing contributes as much to one's sense of belonging to a community as much as "membership" in a third place. It does more than membership in a dozen formal organizations. Why this should be so is not entirely mysterious. It has to do with surviving and, indeed, *thriving* in a "fair game" atmosphere.

Whereas formal organizations typically bring together the like-minded and similarly-interested, third places are highly inclusive by comparison. By "fair game," we mean that in such places the individual may be approached by anyone and is expected to give-and-take in conversation with civility and good humor. Many people find this daunting and many fans of the internet are those who find the communication it affords much "safer."

Those who manage to "get on with one and all" count it a matter of pride, both for themselves and for the group itself. They often marvel at the "strange collection" of people with whom they have found a joyful place. This feeling of belonging probably impresses itself upon those who have third places more so now than in the past. Not only is postwar housing more privatized, it is also more segregated than earlier. Most people these days don't grow up in a "vertical community" but in one narrowly segregated by income and demographics. Their residential experience is based on a thin, horizontal slice of society. Third places, for those who have them nowadays, must seem wonderfully inclusive indeed.

Three more functions of third places seem to me worthy of introduction here, and these are not less important as might be indicated by their late mention. Third places are political fora of great importance. In many countries the emergent solidarity of labor owed strictly to the profusion of cafés in which the workers discussed their common problems, realized their collective strength, and planned their strikes and other strategies. Though many credit an "enlightened" congress with the anti-segregation laws of the sixties, none of it would have happened but for prior assembly in black churches all over the South.

It is not difficult to understand why coffeehouses came under attack by government leaders in England, in Scandinavia, and in Saudi Arabia at various points in history. It was in the coffeehouses where people congregated and often, in their discussions, found fault with the countries' rulers.

Survey after survey finds political literacy low in America. People don't know who serves in the president's cabinet; they don't know who their representatives are; they wouldn't sign our Bill of Rights if presented to them as a petition, etc., etc. As Christopher Lasch recently remarked: Why should they know these things? Why should anyone gather information they never get to use? At a more basic level what these surveys show is a lack of involving discussion and that, in turn, suggests that we've lost many, if not most, of our third places—the political forum of the common man.

Third places also serve as intellectual fora. Politics is not the only important subject discussed in third places. Philosophy, geography, urban development, psychology, history and a great many others are entertained. Everyone is, to some degree, an intellectual and third place regulars more so than most because they air their notions in front of critics.

Unfortunately, we too often think of intellectualism in bookish terms or as belonging to those with credentials. Almost everyone, however, reflects upon life and society's problems. Self-appointed elites may deride "cracker barrel philosophy" but the very term suggests that "ordinary" people think and that they do so in company with their fellow man.

To the outsider, the notion that third place regulars "think alike" is often a tempting summary, but it is wrong. "Membership" in third place groups depends upon coming to terms with people who, on certain subjects, are "out of their minds"—which is to say one doesn't agree with them. Membership also means that sometimes, one's pet ideas don't go over with the group. They don't agree. Unlike that association based on ideology or "political correctness," or scapegoating, one's ideas don't "cost you" in third place gatherings. One's acceptance in such circles depends one's character and one's ability to liven the group—but not on specific notions. One intrudes an idea and the others may nod, or groan, or frown, or laugh but nothing is lost. It's all rather like a good classroom.

Finally, third places may serve as offices. In some kinds of transactions, it is better that neither party be on his or her "home ground" but in some neutral corner, preferably a comfortable and informal one. I was amused, a few years ago, that some of the teachers in a school system resented the fact that the principal spent a portion of almost every day at a local restaurant. He seemed, in their eyes, to be taking advantage of his office. In fact, however, he met a good many parents in that restaurant; parents who didn't have to dress up and spend time waiting in his outer office. He met parents whom he might not have seen otherwise.

Some people are most "locatable" in their third places. It's the only place they are certain to visit on any given day and consequently, it's the best place to "catch" them. I have noticed in the academic world, that many of us maintain contact with those who've retired from the system, not on the campus, but in those third places we both visit.

The third place as "office" is more popular in many other cultures than in the United States where a bureaucratic mentality is more pervasive. In the near and far east, many entrepreneurs are too poor to own offices of their own and use public eating or drinking places, even stating so on their business cards. In Ireland, where everybody deemed to have good sense frequents the pubs, pubs quite naturally are often used as informal offices. It is a practice to be encouraged if for no other reason than the equality it establishes between the parties.

That concludes this account of third place functions which I have offered to enhance the reader's understanding of their potential for community building and which groups may use in considering which of these functions seem important to their neighborhoods and where said functions might be performed.

I should like to close with a nod to those who disagree with that which I seem to be promoting, and indeed am. There are those who "like their privacy" and who consider neighborhoods in which people know one another to be something of an anachronism.

The breed is not new. Even before shopping became a way of life and long before television and other modes of home entertainment became popular, there were people who felt the same way. In my hometown, back in the forties and fifties, when Main Street was lively and filled with people all day long; when we had an abundance of places, both indoors and out, to enjoy one another's company, there were those who never did. And when our little town of about 700 played host to some 10,000 a day during festival time, those same people never took part—not in the preparation, nor the enjoyment.

This, we must understand, is as it should be. The first requirement of a good community is that one need not be a member of it. Public life, civicism, a vital community—these concepts are lost on many and it is surprising that they are not lost on more of us. As I indicated at the outset, this escape from community has been our collective goal for the past several decades.

The response to such people should be polite but firm. They have the right not to assume the responsibilities of a community life; the option not to expend the time and energy that the restoration of public life will require. But it ill behooves them to attempt to frustrate the rest of us in the name of "progress" or whatever rationale they embrace in defense of their life style preferences. Those who choose not to participate always have that choice but those of us who yearn for a public life and for life on the streets of our neighborhoods have been deprived. And we, I think, have the better case.

Ray Oldenburg
Pensacola, Florida
October 1, 1996

Introduction

GREAT CIVILIZATIONS, like great cities, share a common feature. Evolving within them and crucial to their growth and refinement are distinctive informal public gathering places. These become as much a part of the urban landscape as of the citizen's daily life and, invariably, they come to dominate the image of the city. Thus, its profusion of sidewalk cafés seems to *be* Paris, just as the forum dominates one's mental picture of classic Rome. The soul of London resides in her many pubs; that of Florence in its teeming *piazzas*. Vienna's presence is seen and felt most within those eternal coffeehouses encircled within her *Ringstrasse*. The grocery store-become-pub at which the Irish family does its entertaining, the *bier garten* that is father to more formal German organizations, and the Japanese teahouse whose ceremonies are the model for an entire way of life, all represent fundamental institutions of mediation between the individual and the larger society.

In cities blessed with their own characteristic form of these Great Good Places, the stranger feels at home—nay, *is* at home—whereas in cities without them, even the native does not feel at home. Where urban growth proceeds with no indigenous version of a public gathering place proliferated along the way and integral in the lives of the people, the promise of the city is denied. Without such places, the urban area fails to nourish the kinds of relationships and the diversity of human contact that are the essence of the city. Deprived of these settings, people remain lonely within their crowds. The only predictable social consequence of technological advancement is that they will grow ever more apart from one another.

America does not rank well on the dimension of her informal public life and less well now than in the past. Increasingly, her citizens are encouraged to find their relaxation, entertainment, companionship, even safety, almost entirely within the privacy of homes that have become more a retreat from society than a connection to it.

In their kind and number, there has been a marked decline in gathering places near enough to people's homes to afford the easy access and familiar faces necessary to a vital informal public life. The course of urban development in America is pushing the individual toward that line separating proud independence from pitiable isolation, for it affords insufficient opportunity and encouragement to voluntary human contact. Daily life amid the new urban sprawl is like a grammar school without its recess periods, like incurring the aches and pains of a softball game without the fun of getting together for a few beers afterward. Both the joys of relaxing with people and the social solidarity that results from it are disappearing for want of settings that make them possible.

In its organization, as in its style, this book is intended to make a case for those core settings of the informal public life that are essential to good towns and great cities. The initial chapter elaborates the problem of a deficient informal public life and argues for the cultivation of third places as the solution to that problem. The discussion beyond is divided into three major sections devoted, respectively, to the *essence* of the third place, then to *examples* of it, and finally, to *issues* surrounding this failing and forgotten institution.

In the first section, effort is devoted to an intriguing and rewarding task. I've simply asked what the culturally and historically different versions of popular and numerous informal public gathering places *have in common*. Proceeding from the stage to the action that takes place upon it, I describe the social, psychological, and political consequences attaching to regular involvement in the informal public life of the society. Again, I am struck by the similarities that persist across time and culture and am fortified in the conviction that the core settings of informal public life are as uniformly essential as they are outwardly variable.

The second part offers examples of the third place as it has evolved in our culture and in others. I look first at the German-American lager beer garden of the last century, that model of peaceful coexistence and happy association that America needed but ultimately rejected. "Main

Street" describes the energetic informal public life of small-town America in prewar days, our most successful homegrown example. Also included in this section are detailed descriptions of the English pub, the French bistro, the American tavern, and the coffeehouses of England and Vienna. Each concrete example confirms the third place model and offers lessons of its own.

The final section is devoted to issues that impinge upon the character and fate of the informal public life of our society. Chapter 11 examines the urban environment in which an informal public life takes hold or is thwarted. It reveals many of the factors responsible for the paradoxical condition that frustrates us: urban development is currently ruinous to the city. Chapter 12 begins with recognition of the fact that third places are and always have been in the sexist tradition and examines the informal public life in the context of the relations between the sexes. The thirteenth chapter focuses on children, who may ultimately suffer most in a world lacking the experiences and amenities associated with a safe, rich, colorful, and interesting informal public life.

The final chapter bases its optimism on certain lessons that urban Americans are learning as they try to adapt to an environment as grossly unsuited to the good life as it is to good relations among those who share that environment. Hope lies not with the expert or the official but with those who use the environment built for them and find it wanting.

Ray Oldenburg
Pensacola, Florida

Acknowledgments

OVER THE COURSE of this project's development, I've incurred debts to many generous and helpful individuals. Apart from those identified here, I'm indebted to many who read portions of early manuscripts and encouraged the effort and to many more with whom I've discussed aspects of the general subject.

The following people have had a direct hand in contributing to or otherwise shaping the content of this effort, and I am pleased to acknowledge their help. Janice Autenrieth, Audrey Cleland, Frank DeMoss, Kitty Elliott, Michael Galley, Danielle Malone, and George Neal supplied firsthand illustrative material. Mr. and Mrs. Don McGuire helped me reconstruct Main Street in River Park as it was constituted in 1940. Tom Richey and John Jarvis supplied me with useful items extracted from the broad range of their reading.

The staff of the John C. Pace Library was helpful and congenial beyond the call of duty throughout the frequent and varied use I made of that institution's facilities. My dear friend and colleague, Dennis Brissett, with whom I collaborated on earlier efforts, made helpful suggestions in structuring the second and third chapters. Dr. Bernadette Grant offered useful comments on those portions of the manuscript dealing with women's reactions to various aspects of informal public life.

Special thanks are owed to those who labored over the emerging text. Jim Servies, in his final months as director of the John C. Pace Library, found time—much of it on airplanes and in waiting rooms—to do a stylistic editing of most of the book's chapters. Thanks to his efforts, a better flow of words is contained within fewer pages. Seymour Kurtz,

xxxii   *Acknowledgments*

in his role as the publisher's reader, made useful suggestions throughout, and most of them have been incorporated into the final product.

Final shaping of the manuscript was greatly simplified by the efforts of Connie Works, a fine lady and virtuoso on the word processor. My association with the publisher was as pleasant as it was professional, thanks to Laura Greeney, the development editor assigned to this project.

Finally, I must acknowledge one who is no longer among us. Don Martindale passed away while the project was in progress. He was mentor and friend, a renowned and prolific scholar, and a gentleman within an academic world that contains far too few of them. It was his encouragement, more than anyone else's, that sustained my efforts at research outside the mainstream.

PART I

CHAPTER I

The Problem of Place in America

A number of recent American writings indicate that the nostalgia for the small town need not be construed as directed toward the town itself: it is rather a "quest for community" (as Robert Nisbet puts it)—a nostalgia for a compassable and integral living unit. The critical question is not whether the small town can be rehabilitated in the image of its earlier strength and growth—for clearly it cannot—but whether American life will be able to evolve any other integral community to replace it. This is what I call the problem of place in America, and unless it is somehow resolved, American life will become more jangled and fragmented than it is, and American personality will continue to be unquiet and unfulfilled.

> MAX LERNER
> *America as a Civilization*
> 1957

THE ENSUING YEARS have confirmed Lerner's diagnosis. The problem of place in America has not been resolved and life *has* become more jangled and fragmented. No new form of integral community has been found; the small town has yet to greet its replacement. And Americans are not a contented people.

What may have seemed like the new form of community—the automobile suburb—multiplied rapidly after World War II. Thirteen million plus returning veterans qualified for single-family dwellings requiring no down payments in the new developments. In building and equipping these millions of new private domains, American industry found a major alternative to military production and companionate marriages appeared to have found ideal nesting places. But we did not live happily ever after.

Life in the subdivision may have satisfied the combat veteran's longing for a safe, orderly, and quiet haven, but it rarely offered the sense of place and belonging that had rooted his parents and grandparents. Houses alone do not a community make, and the typical subdivision proved hostile to the emergence of any structure or space utilization beyond the uniform houses and streets that characterized it.

Like all-residential city blocks, observed one student of the American condition, the suburb is "merely a base from which the individual reaches out to the scattered components of social existence."[1] Though proclaimed as offering the best of both rural and urban life, the automobile suburb had the effect of fragmenting the individual's world. As one observer wrote: "A man works in one place, sleeps in another, shops somewhere else, finds pleasure or companionship where he can, and cares about none of these places."

The typical suburban home is easy to leave behind as its occupants move to another. What people cherish most in them can be taken along in the move. There are no sad farewells at the local taverns or the corner store because there are no local taverns or corner stores. Indeed, there is often more encouragement to leave a given subdivision than to stay in it, for neither the homes nor the neighborhoods are equipped to see families or individuals through the cycle of life. Each is designed for families of particular sizes, incomes, and ages. There is little sense of place and even less opportunity to put down roots.

Transplanted Europeans are acutely aware of the lack of a community life in our residential areas. We recently talked with an outgoing lady who had lived in many countries and was used to adapting to local ways. The problem of place in America had become her problem as well:

> After four years here, I still feel more of a foreigner than in any other place in the world I have been. People here are proud to live in a "good" area, but to us these so-called desirable areas are like prisons. There is no contact between the various households, we rarely see the neighbors and certainly do not know any of them. In Luxembourg, however, we would frequently stroll down to one of the local cafés in the evening, and there pass a very congenial few hours in the company of the local fireman, dentist, bank employee or whoever happened to be there at the time.

There is no pleasure to be had in driving to a sleazy, dark bar where one keeps strictly to one's self and becomes fearful if approached by some drunk.

Sounding the same note, Kenneth Harris has commented on one of the things British people miss most in the United States. It is some reasonable approximation of the village inn or local pub; our neighborhoods do not have it. Harris comments: "The American does not walk around to the local two or three times a week with his wife or with his son, to have his pint, chat with the neighbors, and then walk home. He does not take out the dog last thing every night, and break his journey with a quick one at the Crown."[2]

The contrast in cultures is keenly felt by those who enjoy a dual residence in Europe and America. Victor Gruen and his wife have a large place in Los Angeles and a small one in Vienna. He finds that: "In Los Angeles we are hesitant to leave our sheltered home in order to visit friends or to participate in cultural or entertainment events because every such outing involves a major investment of time and nervous strain in driving long distances."[3] But, he says, the European experience is much different: "In Vienna, we are persuaded to go out often because we are within easy walking distance of two concert halls, the opera, a number of theatres, and a variety of restaurants, cafés, and shops. Seeing old friends does not have to be a prearranged affair as in Los Angeles, and more often than not, one bumps into them on the street or in a café." The Gruens have a hundred times more residential space in America but give the impression that they don't enjoy it half as much as their little corner of Vienna.

But one needn't call upon foreign visitors to point up the shortcomings of the suburban experiment. As a setting for marriage and family life, it has given those institutions a bad name. By the 1960s, a picture had emerged of the suburban housewife as "bored, isolated, and preoccupied with material things."[4] The suburban wife without a car to escape in epitomized the experience of being alone in America.[5] Those who could afford it compensated for the loneliness, isolation, and lack of community with the "frantic scheduling syndrome" as described by a counselor in the northeastern region of the United States:

The loneliness I'm most familiar with in my job is that of wives and mothers of small children who are dumped in the suburbs and whose husbands are commuters . . . I see a lot of generalized loneliness, but I think that in well-to-do communities they cover it up with a wealth of frantic activity. That's the reason tennis has gotten so big. They all go out and play tennis.[6]

A majority of the former stay-at-home wives are now in the labor force. As both father and mother gain some semblance of a community life via their daily escapes from the subdivision, children are even more cut off from ties with adults. Home offers less and the neighborhood offers nothing for the typical suburban adolescent. The situation in the early seventies as described by Richard Sennett is worsening:

> In the past ten years, many middle-class children have tried to break out of the communities, the schools and the homes that their parents have spent so much of their own lives creating. If any one feeling can be said to run through the diverse groups and life-styles of the youth movements, it is a feeling that these middle-class communities of the parents were like pens, like cages keeping the youth from being free and alive. The source of the feeling lies in the perception that while these middle-class environments are secure and orderly regimes, people suffocate there for lack of the new, the unexpected, the diverse in their lives.[7]

The adolescent houseguest, I would suggest, is probably the best and quickest test of the vitality of a neighborhood; the visiting teenager in the subdivision soon acts like an animal in a cage. He or she paces, looks unhappy and uncomfortable, and by the second day is putting heavy pressure on the parents to leave. There is no place to which they can escape and join their own kind. There is nothing for them to do on their own. There is nothing in the surroundings but the houses of strangers and nobody on the streets. Adults make a more successful adjustment, largely because they demand less. But few at any age find vitality in the housing developments. David Riesman, an esteemed elder statesman among social scientists, once attempted to describe the import of suburbia upon most of those who live there. "There would seem," he wrote, "to be an aimlessness, a pervasive low-keyed unpleasure."[8] The word he seemed averse to using is *boring*. A teenager would not have had to struggle for the right phrasing.

Their failure to solve the problem of place in America and to provide a community life for their inhabitants has not effectively discouraged the growth of the postwar suburbs. To the contrary, there have emerged new generations of suburban development in which there is even less life outside the houses than before. Why does failure succeed? Dolores Hayden supplies part of the answer when she observes that Americans have substituted the vision of the ideal home for that of the ideal city.[9] The purchase of the even larger home on the even larger lot in the even more lifeless neighborhood is not so much a matter of joining community as retreating from it. Encouraged by a continuing decline in the civilities and amenities of the public or shared environment, people invest more hopes in their private acreage. They proceed as though a house can substitute for a community if only it is spacious enough, entertaining enough, comfortable enough, splendid enough—and suitably isolated from that common horde that politicians still refer to as our "fellow Americans."

Observers disagree about the reasons for the growing estrangement between the family and the city in American society.[10] Richard Sennett, whose research spans several generations, argues that as soon as an American family became middle class and could afford to do something about its fear of the outside world and its confusions, it drew in upon itself, and "in America, unlike France or Germany, the urban middle-class shunned public forms of social life like cafés and banquet halls."[11] Philippe Ariès, who also knows his history, counters with the argument that modern urban development has killed the essential relationships that once made a city and, as a consequence, "the role of the family overexpanded like a hypertrophied cell" trying to take up the slack.[12]

In some countries, television broadcasting is suspended one night a week so that people will not abandon the habit of getting out of their homes and maintaining contact with one another. This tactic would probably not work in America. Sennett would argue that the middle-class family, given its assessment of the public domain, would stay at home anyway. Ariès would argue that most would stay home for want of places to get together with their friends and neighbors. As Richard Goodwin declared, "there is virtually no place where neighbors can anticipate unplanned meetings—no pub or corner store or park."[13] The bright spot in this dispute is that the same set of remedies would cure both the family and the city of major ills.

Meantime, new generations are encouraged to shun a community

life in favor of a highly privatized one and to set personal aggrandizement above public good. The attitudes may be learned from parents
but they are also learned in each generation's experiences. The modest
housing developments, those *un*exclusive suburbs from which middle-
class people graduate as they grow older and more affluent, teach their
residents that future hopes for a good life are pretty much confined to
one's house and yard. Community life amid tract housing is a disap-
pointing experience. The space within the development has been
equipped and staged for isolated family living and little else. The
processes by which potential friends might find one another and by
which friendships not suited to the home might be nurtured outside it
are severely thwarted by the limited features and facilities of the modern suburb.

The housing development's lack of informal social centers or informal public gathering places puts people too much at the mercy of their
closest neighbors. The small town taught us that people's best friends
and favorite companions rarely lived right next door to one another.
Why should it be any different in the automobile suburbs? What are
the odds, given that a hundred households are within easy walking
distance, that one is most likely to hit it off with the people next door?
Small! Yet, the closest neighbors are the ones with whom friendships
are most likely to be attempted, for how does one even find out enough
about someone a block and a half away to justify an introduction?

What opportunity is there for two men who both enjoy shooting,
fishing, or flying to get together and gab if their families are not
compatible? Where do people entertain and enjoy one another if, for
whatever reason, they are not comfortable in one another's homes?
Where do people have a chance to get to know one another casually and
without commitment before deciding whether to involve other family
members in their relationship? Tract housing offers no such places.

Getting together with neighbors in the development entails considerable hosting efforts, and it depends upon continuing good relationships between households and their members. In the usual course of
things, these relationships are easily strained or ruptured. Having been
lately formed and built on little, they are not easy to mend. Worse,
some of the few good friends will move and are not easily replaced. In
time, the overtures toward friendship, neighborliness, and a semblance
of community hardly seem worth the effort.

In the Absence of an Informal Public Life

We have noted Sennett's observation that middle-class Americans are not like their French or German counterparts. Americans do not make daily visits to sidewalk cafés or banquet halls. We do not have that third realm of satisfaction and social cohesion beyond the portals of home and work that for others is an essential element of the good life. Our comings and goings are more restricted to the home and work settings, and those two spheres have become preemptive. Multitudes shuttle back and forth between the "womb" and the "rat race" in a constricted pattern of daily life that easily generates the familiar desire to "get away from it all."

A two-stop model of daily routine is becoming fixed in our habits as the urban environment affords less opportunity for public relaxation. Our most familiar gathering centers are disappearing rapidly. The proportion of beer and spirits consumed in public places has declined from about 90 percent of the total in the late 1940s to about 30 percent today.[14] There's been a similar decline in the number of neighborhood taverns in which those beverages are sold. For those who avoid alcoholic refreshments and prefer the drugstore soda fountain across the street, the situation has gotten even worse. By the 1960s, it was clear that the soda fountain and the lunch counter no longer had a place in "the balanced drug store."[15] "In this day of heavy unionization and rising minimum wages for unskilled help, the traditional soda fountain should be thrown out," advised an expert on drugstore management. And so it has been. The new kinds of places emphasize fast service, not slow and easy relaxation.

In the absence of an informal public life, people's expectations toward work and family life have escalated beyond the capacity of those institutions to meet them. Domestic and work relationships are pressed to supply all that is wanting and much that is missing in the constricted life-styles of those without community. The resulting strain on work and family institutions is glaringly evident. In the measure of its disorganization and deterioration, the middle-class family of today resembles the low-income family of the 1960s.[16] The United States now leads the world in the rate of divorce among its population. Fatherless children comprise the fastest-growing segment of the infant population. The strains that have eroded the traditional family configuration have given rise to alternate life-styles, and though their appearance suggests the luxury of choice, none are as satisfactory as was the traditional family when embedded in a supporting community.

It is estimated that American industry loses from $50 billion to $75 billion annually due to absenteeism, company-paid medical expenses, and lost productivity.[17] Stress in the lives of the workers is a major cause of these industrial losses. Two-thirds of the visits to family physicians in the United States are prompted by stress-related problems.[18] "Our mode of life," says one medical practitioner, "is emerging as today's principal cause of illness."[19] Writes Claudia Wallis, "It is a sorry sign of the times that the three best-selling drugs in the country are an ulcer medication (Tagamet), a hypertension drug (Inderal), and a tranquilizer (Valium)."[20]

In the absence of an informal public life, Americans are denied those means of relieving stress that serve other cultures so effectively. We seem not to realize that the means of relieving stress can just as easily be built into an urban environment as those features which produce stress. To our considerable misfortune, the pleasures of the city have been largely reduced to consumerism. We don't much enjoy our cities because they're not very enjoyable. The mode of urban life that has become our principal cause of illness resembles a pressure cooker without its essential safety valve. Our urban environment is like an engine that runs hot because it was designed without a cooling system.

Unfortunately, opinion leans toward the view that the causes of stress are social but the cures are individual. It is widely assumed that high levels of stress are an unavoidable condition of modern life, that these are built into the social system, and that one must get outside the system in order to gain relief. Even our efforts at entertaining and being entertained tend toward the competitive and stressful. We come dangerously close to the notion that one "gets sick" in the world beyond one's domicile and one "gets well" by retreating from it. Thus, while Germans relax amid the rousing company of the *bier garten* or the French recuperate in their animated little bistros, Americans turn to massaging, meditating, jogging, hot-tubbing, or escape fiction. While others take full advantage of their freedom to associate, we glorify our freedom *not* to associate.

In the absence of an informal public life, living becomes more expensive. Where the means and facilities for relaxation and leisure are not publicly shared, they become the objects of private ownership and consumption. In the United States, about two-thirds of the GNP is based on personal consumption expenditures. That category, observes Goodwin, contains "the alienated substance of mankind."[21] Some four *trillion* dollars spent for individual aggrandizement represents a powerful divisive force indeed. In our society, insists one expert on the subject, leisure has been perverted into consumption.[22] An aggressive, driving force behind this perversion is advertising, which conditions "our drive to consume and to own whatever industry produces."[23]

Paragons of self-righteousness, advertisers promulgate the notion that society would languish in a state of inertia but for their efforts. "Nothing happens until somebody sells something," they love to say. That may be true enough within a strictly commercial world (and for them, what else is there?) but the development of an informal public life depends upon people finding and enjoying one another outside the cash nexus. Advertising, in its ideology and effects, is the enemy of an informal public life. It breeds alienation. It convinces people that the good life can be individually purchased. In the place of the shared camaraderie of people who see themselves as equals, the ideology of advertising substitutes competitive acquisition. It is the difference between loving people for what they are and envying them for what they own. It is no coincidence that cultures with a highly developed informal public life have a disdain for advertising.[24]

The tremendous advantage enjoyed by societies with a well-developed informal public life is that, within them, poverty carries few burdens other than that of having to live a rather Spartan existence. But there is no stigma and little deprivation of experience. There is an engaging and sustaining public life to supplement and complement home and work routines. For those on tight budgets who live in some degree of austerity, it compensates for the lack of things owned privately. For the affluent, it offers much that money can't buy.

The American middle-class life-style is an exceedingly expensive one—especially when measured against the satisfaction it yields. The paucity of collective rituals and unplanned social gatherings puts a formidable burden upon the individual to overcome the social isolation that threatens. Where there are homes without a connection to community, where houses are located in areas devoid of congenial meeting places, the enemy called boredom is ever at the gate. Much money must be spent to compensate for the sterility of the surrounding environment. Home decoration and redecoration becomes a never-ending process as people depend upon new wallpaper or furniture arrangements to add zest to their lives. Like the bored and idle rich, they look to new clothing fashions for the same purpose and buy new wardrobes well before the old ones are past service. A lively round of after-dinner conversation isn't as simple as a walk to the corner pub—one has to host the dinner.

The home entertainment industry thrives in the dearth of the informal public life among the American middle class. Demand for all manner of electronic gadgetry to substitute vicarious watching and listening for more direct involvement is high. Little expense is spared in the installation of sound and video systems, VCRs, cable connections, or that current version of heaven on earth for the socially exiled—the satellite dish. So great is the demand for electronic entertainment that it cannot be met with quality programming. Those who create for this insatiable demand must rely on formula and imitation.

Everyone old enough to drive finds it necessary to make frequent escapes from the private compound located amid hundreds of other private compounds. To do so, each needs a car, and that car is a means of conveyance as privatized and antisocial as the neighborhoods themselves. Fords and "Chevys" now cost from ten to fifteen thousand dollars, and the additional expenses of maintaining, insuring, and fueling them constitute major expenditures for most families. Worse, each drives his or her own car. About the only need that suburbanites can satisfy by means of an easy walk is that which impels them toward their bathroom.

In the absence of an informal public life, industry must also compensate for the missing opportunity for social relaxation. When the settings for casual socializing are not provided in the neighborhoods, people compensate in the workplace. Coffee breaks are more than mere rest periods; they are depended upon more for sociable human contact than physical relaxation. These and other "time-outs" are extended. Lunch hours often afford a sufficient amount of reveling to render the remainder of the working day ineffectual. The distinction between work-related communications and "shooting the breeze" becomes blurred. Once-clear parameters separating work from play become confused. The individual finds that neither work nor play are as satisfying as they should be.

The problem of place in America manifests itself in a sorely deficient informal public life. The structure of shared experience beyond that offered by family, job, and passive consumerism is small and dwindling. The essential group experience is being replaced by the exaggerated self-consciousness of individuals. American life-styles, for all the material acquisition and the seeking after comforts and pleasures, are plagued by boredom, loneliness, alienation, and a high price tag. America can point to many areas where she has made progress, but in the area of informal public life she has lost ground and continues to lose it.

Unlike many frontiers, that of the informal public life does not remain benign as it awaits development. It does not become easier to tame as technology evolves, as governmental bureaus and agencies multiply, or as population grows. It does not yield to the mere passage of time and a policy of letting the chips fall where they may as development proceeds in other realms of urban life. To the contrary, neglect of the informal public life can make a jungle of what had been a garden while, at the same time, diminishing the ability of people to cultivate it.

In the sustained absence of a healthy and vigorous informal public life, the citizenry may quite literally forget how to create one. A facilitating public etiquette consisting of rituals necessary to the meeting, greeting, and enjoyment of strangers is not much in evidence in the United States. It is replaced by a set of strategies designed to avoid contact with people in public, by devices intended to preserve the individual's circle of privacy against any stranger who might violate it. Urban sophistication is deteriorating into such matters as knowing who is safe on whose "turf," learning to minimize expression and bodily contact when in public, and other survival skills required in a world devoid of the amenities. Lyn Lofland notes that the 1962 edition of Amy Vanderbilt's *New Complete Book of Etiquette* "contains not a single reference to proper behavior in the world of strangers."[25] The cosmopolitan promise of our cities is diminished. Its ecumenic spirit fades with our ever-increasing retreat into privacy.

Toward a Solution: The Third Place

Though none can prescribe the total solution to the problem of place in America, it is possible to describe some important elements that any solution will have to include. Certain basic requirements of an informal public life do not change, nor does a healthy society advance beyond them. To the extent that a thriving informal public life belongs to a society's past, so do the best of its days, and prospects for the future should be cause for considerable concern.

Towns and cities that afford their populations an engaging public life are easy to identify. What urban sociologists refer to as their interstitial spaces are filled with people. The streets and sidewalks, parks and squares, parkways and boulevards are being used by people sitting, standing, and walking. Prominent public space is not reserved for that well-dressed, middle-class crowd that is welcomed at today's shopping malls. The elderly and poor, the ragged and infirm, are interspersed among those looking and doing well. The full spectrum of local humanity is represented. Most of the streets are as much the domain of the pedestrian as of the motorist. The typical street can still accommodate a full-sized perambulator and still encourages a new mother's outing with her baby. Places to sit are abundant. Children play in the streets. The general scene is much as the set director for a movie would arrange it to show life in a wholesome and thriving town or city neighborhood.

Beyond the impression that a human scale has been preserved in the architecture, however, or that the cars haven't defeated the pedestrians in the battle for the streets, or that the pace of life suggests gentler and less complicated times, the picture doesn't reveal the *dynamics* needed to produce an engaging informal public life. The secret of a society at peace with itself is not revealed in the panoramic view but in examination of the average citizen's situation.

The examples set by societies that have solved the problem of place and those set by the small towns and vital neighborhoods of our past suggest that daily life, in order to be relaxed and fulfilling, must find its balance in three realms of experience. One is domestic, a second is gainful or productive, and the third is inclusively sociable, offering both the basis of community and the celebration of it. Each of these realms of human experience is built on associations and relationships appropriate to it; each has its own physically separate and distinct places; each must have its measure of autonomy from the others.

What the panoramic view of the vital city fails to reveal is that the third realm of experience is as distinct a place as home or office. The informal public life only seems amorphous and scattered; in reality, it is highly focused. It emerges and is sustained in *core settings*. Where the problem of place has been solved, a generous proliferation of core settings of informal public life is sufficient to the needs of the people.

Pierre Salinger was asked how he liked living in France and how he would compare it with life in the United States. His response was that he likes France where, he said, everyone is more relaxed. In America, there's a lot of pressure. The French, of course, have solved the problem of place. The Frenchman's daily life sits firmly on a tripod consisting of home, place of work, and another setting where friends are engaged during the midday and evening *aperitif* hours, if not earlier and later. In the United States, the middle classes particularly are attempting a balancing act on a bipod consisting of home and work. That alienation, boredom, and stress are endemic among us is not surprising. For most of us, a third of life is either deficient or absent altogether, and the other two-thirds cannot be successfully integrated into a whole.

Before the core settings of an informal public life can be restored to the urban landscape and reestablished in daily life, it will be necessary to articulate their nature and benefit. It will not suffice to describe them in a mystical or romanticized way such as might warm the hearts of those already convinced. Rather, the core settings of the informal public life must be analyzed and discussed in terms comprehensible to these rational and individualistic outlooks dominant in American thought. We must dissect, talk in terms of specific payoffs, and reduce special experiences to common labels. We must, urgently, begin to defend these Great Good Places against the unbelieving and the antagonistic and do so in terms clear to all.

The object of our focus—the core settings of the informal public life—begs for a simpler label. Common parlance offers few possibilities and none that combine brevity with objectivity and an appeal to common sense. There is the term *hangout*, but its connotation is negative and the word conjures up images of the joint or dive. Though we refer to the meeting places of the lowly as hangouts, we rarely apply the term to yacht clubs or oak-paneled bars, the "hangouts" of the "better people." We have nothing as respectable as the French *rendez-vous* to refer to a public meeting place or a setting in which friends get together away from the confines of home and work. The American language reflects the American reality—in vocabulary as in fact the core settings of an informal public life are underdeveloped.

For want of a suitable existing term, we introduce our own: the third place will hereafter be used to signify what we have called "the core settings of informal public life." The third place is a generic designation for a great variety of public places that host the regular, voluntary, informal, and happily anticipated gatherings of individuals beyond the realms of home and work. The term will serve well. It is neutral, brief, and facile. It underscores the significance of the tripod and the relative importance of its three legs. Thus, the first place is the home—the most important place of all. It is the first regular and predictable environment of the growing child and the one that will have greater effect upon his or her development. It will harbor individuals long before the workplace is interested in them and well after the world of work casts them aside. The second place is the work setting, which reduces the individual to a single, productive role. It fosters competition and motivates people to rise above their fellow creatures. But it also provides the means to a living, improves the material quality of life, and structures endless hours of time for a majority who could not structure it on their own.

Before industrialization, the first and second places were one. Industrialization separated the place of work from the place of residence, removing productive work from the home and making it remote in distance, morality, and spirit from family life. What we now call the third place existed long before this separation, and so our term is a concession to the sweeping effects of the Industrial Revolution and its division of life into private and public spheres.

The ranking of the three places corresponds with individual dependence upon them. We need a home even though we may not work, and most of us need to work more than we need to gather with our friends and neighbors. The ranking holds, also, with respect to the demands upon the individual's time. Typically, the individual spends more time at home than at work and more at work than in a third place. In importance, in claims on time and loyalty, in space allocated, and in social recognition, the ranking is appropriate.

In some countries, the third place is more closely ranked with the others. In Ireland, France, or Greece, the core settings of informal public life rank a *strong* third in the lives of the people. In the United States, third places rank a weak third with perhaps the majority lacking a third place and denying that it has any real importance.

The prominence of third places varies with cultural setting and historical era. In preliterate societies, the third place was actually foremost, being the grandest structure in the village and commanding the central location. They were the men's houses, the earliest ancestors of those grand, elegant, and pretentious clubs eventually to appear along London's Pall Mall. In both Greek and Roman society, prevailing values dictated that the *agora* and the *forum* should be great, central institutions; that homes should be simple and unpretentious; that the architecture of cities should assert the worth of the public and civic individual over the private and domestic one. Few means to lure and invite citizens into public gatherings were overlooked. The forums, colosseums, theaters, and ampitheaters were grand structures, and admission to them was free.

Third places have never since been as prominent. Attempts at elegance and grand scale continued to be made but with far less impact. Many cultures evolved public baths on a grand scale. Victorian gin palaces were elegant (especially when contrasted to the squalor that surrounded them). The winter gardens and palm gardens built in some of our northern cities in the previous century included many large and imposing structures. In modern times, however, third places survive without much prominence or elegance.

Where third places remain vital in the lives of people today, it is far more because they are prolific than prominent. The geographic expansion of the cities and their growing diversity of quarters, or distinct neighborhoods, necessitated the shift. The proliferation of smaller establishments kept them at the human scale and available to all in the face of increasing urbanization.

In the newer American communities, however, third places are neither prominent nor prolific. They are largely prohibited. Upon an urban landscape increasingly hostile to and devoid of informal gathering places, one may encounter people rather pathetically trying to find some spot in which to relax and enjoy each other's company.

Sometimes three or four pickups are parked under the shade near a convenience store as their owners drink beers that may be purchased but not consumed inside. If the habit ever really catches on, laws will be passed to stop it. Along the strips, youths sometimes gather in or near their cars in the parking lots of hamburger franchises. It's the best they can manage, for they aren't allowed to loiter inside. One may encounter a group of women in a laundromat, socializing while doing the laundry chores. One encounters parents who have assumed the expense of adding a room to the house or converting the garage to a recreation room so that, within neighborhoods that offer them nothing, their children might have a decent place to spend time with their friends. Sometimes too, youth will develop a special attachment to a patch of woods not yet bulldozed away in the relentless spread of the suburbs. In such a place they enjoy relief from the confining over-familiarity of their tract houses and the monotonous streets.

American planners and developers have shown a great disdain for those earlier arrangements in which there was life beyond home and work. They have condemned the neighborhood tavern and disallowed a suburban version. They have failed to provide modern counterparts of once-familiar gathering places. The gristmill or grain elevator, soda fountains, malt shops, candy stores, and cigar stores—places that did not reduce a human being to a mere customer, have not been replaced. Meantime, the planners and developers continue to add to the rows of regimented loneliness in neighborhoods so sterile as to cry out for something as modest as a central mail drop or a little coffee counter at which those in the area might discover one another.

Americans are now confronted with that condition about which the crusty old arch-conservative Edmund Burke warned us when he said that the bonds of community are broken at great peril for they are not easily replaced. Indeed, we face the enormous task of making "the mess that is urban America" suitably hospitable to the requirements of gregarious, social animals.[26] Before motivation or wisdom is adequate to the task, however, we shall need to understand exactly what it is that an informal public life can contribute to both national and individual life. Therein lies the purpose of this book.

Successful exposition demands that some statement of a problem precede a discussion of its solution. Hence, I've begun on sour and unpleasant notes and will find it necessary to sound them again. I would have preferred it otherwise. It is the solution that intrigues and delights. It is my hope that the discussion of life in the third place will have a similar effect upon the reader, just as I hope that the reader will allow the bias that now and then prompts me to substitute Great Good Place for third place. I am confident that those readers who have a third place will not object.

CHAPTER 2

The Character
of Third Places

THIRD PLACES the world over share common and essential features. As one's investigations cross the boundaries of time and culture, the kinship of the Arabian coffeehouse, the German *bierstube*, the Italian *taberna*, the old country store of the American frontier, and the ghetto bar reveals itself. As one approaches each example, determined to describe it in its own right, an increasingly familiar pattern emerges. The eternal sameness of the third place overshadows the variations in its outward appearance and seems unaffected by the wide differences in cultural attitudes toward the typical gathering places of informal public life. The beer joint in which the middle-class American takes no pride can be as much a third place as the proud Viennese coffeehouse. It is a fortunate aspect of the third place that its capacity to serve the human need for communion does not much depend upon the capacity of a nation to comprehend its virtues.

The wonder is that so little attention has been paid to the benefits attaching to the third place. It is curious that its features and inner workings have remained virtually undescribed in this present age when they are so sorely needed and when any number of lesser substitutes are described in tiresome detail. Volumes are written on sensitivity and encounter groups, on meditation and exotic rituals for attaining states of relaxation and transcendence, on jogging and massaging. But the third place, the people's own remedy for stress, loneliness, and alienation, seems easy to ignore.

With few exceptions, however, it has always been thus. Rare is the chronicler who has done justice to those gathering places where community is most alive and people are most themselves. The tradition is the opposite; it is one of understatement and oversight. Joseph Addison, the great essayist, gave the faintest praise to the third places of his time and seems to have set an example for doing so. London's eighteenth-century coffeehouses provided the stage and forum for Addison's efforts and fired the greatest era of letters England would ever see. And there was far more to them than suggested by Addison's remarks: "When men are thus knit together, by a Love of Society, not a Spirit of Faction, and don't meet to censure or annoy those that are absent, but to enjoy one another: When they are thus combined for their own improvement, or for the Good of others, or at least to relax themselves from the Business of the Day, by an innocent and cheerful conversation, there may be something very useful in these little Institutions and Establishments."[1]

The only "useful something" that the typical observer seems able to report consists of the escape or time out from life's duties and drudgeries that third places are said to offer. Joseph Wechsberg, for example, suggests that the coffeehouses of Vienna afford the common man "his haven and island of tranquility, his reading room and gambling hall, his sounding board and grumbling hall. There at least he is safe from nagging wife and unruly children, monotonous radios and barking dogs, tough bosses and impatient creditors."[2] H. L. Mencken offered the same limited view of the places on our side of the Atlantic, describing the respectable Baltimore tavern of his day as "a quiet refuge" and a "hospital asylum from life and its cares."[3]

But there is far more than escape and relief from stress involved in regular visits to a third place. There is more than shelter against the raindrops of life's tedium and more than a breather on the sidelines of the rat race to be had amid the company of a third place. Its real merits do not depend upon being harried by life, afflicted by stress, or needing time out from gainful activities. The escape theme is not erroneous in substance but in emphasis; it focuses too much upon conditions external to the third place and too little upon experiences and relationships afforded there and nowhere else.

Though characterizations of the third place as a mere haven of escape from home and work are inadequate, they do possess a virtue—they invite *comparison*. The escape theme suggests a world of difference between the corner tavern and the family apartment a block away, between morning coffee in the bungalow and that with the gang at the local bakery. The contrast is sharp and will be revealed. The *raison d'etre* of the third place rests upon its differences from the other settings of daily life and can best be understood by comparison with them. In examining these differences, it will not serve to misrepresent the home, shop, or office in order to put a better light on public gathering places. But, if at times I might lapse in my objectivity, I take solace in the fact that public opinion in America and the weight of our myths and prejudices have never done justice to third places and the kind of association so essential to our freedom and contentment.

On Neutral Ground

The individual may have many friends, a rich variety among them, and opportunity to engage many of them daily *only* if people do not get uncomfortably tangled in one another's lives. Friends can be numerous and often met only if they may easily join and depart one another's company. This otherwise obvious fact of social life is often obscured by the seeming contradiction that surrounds it—we need a good deal of immunity from those whose company we like best. Or, as the sociologist Richard Sennett put it, "people can be sociable only when they have some protection from each other."[4]

In a book showing how to bring life back to American cities, Jane Jacobs stresses the contradiction surrounding most friendships and the consequent need to provide places for them. Cities, she observed, are full of people with whom contact is significant, useful, and enjoyable, but "you don't want them in your hair and they do not want you in theirs either."[5] If friendships and other informal acquaintances are limited to those suitable for private life, she says, the city becomes stultified. So, one might add, does the social life of the individual.

In order for the city and its neighborhoods to offer the rich and varied association that is their promise and their potential, there must be *neutral ground* upon which people may gather. There must be places where individuals may come and go as they please, in which none are required to play host, and in which all feel at home and comfortable. If there is no neutral ground in the neighborhoods where people live, association outside the home will be impoverished. Many, perhaps most, neighbors will never meet, to say nothing of associate, for there is no place for them to do so. Where neutral ground is available it makes possible far more informal, even intimate, relations among people than could be entertained in the home.

Social reformers as a rule, and planners all too commonly, ignore the importance of neutral ground and the kinds of relationships, interactions, and activities to which it plays host. Reformers have never liked seeing people hanging around on street corners, store porches, front stoops, bars, candy stores, or other public areas. They find loitering deplorable and assume that if people had better private areas they would not waste time in public ones. It would make as much sense, as Jane Jacobs points out, to argue that people wouldn't show up at testimonial banquets if they had wives who could cook for them at home.[6] The banquet table and coffee counter bring people together in an intimate and private social fashion—people who would not otherwise meet in that way. Both settings (street corner and banquet hall) are public and neutral, and both are important to the unity of neighborhoods, cities, and societies.

If we valued fraternity as much as independence, and democracy as much as free enterprise, our zoning codes would not enforce the social isolation that plagues our modern neighborhoods, but would require some form of public gathering place every block or two. We may one day rediscover the wisdom of James Oglethorpe who laid out Savannah such that her citizens lived close to public gathering areas. Indeed, he did so with such compelling effect that Sherman, in his destructive march to the sea, spared Savannah alone.

The Third Place Is a Leveler

Levelers was the name given to an extreme left-wing political party that emerged under Charles I and expired shortly afterward under Cromwell. The goal of the party was the abolition of all differences of position or rank that existed among men. By the middle of the seventeenth century, the term came to be applied much more broadly in England, referring to anything "which reduces men to an equality."[7] For example, the newly established coffeehouses of that period, one of unprecedented democracy among the English, were commonly referred to as levelers, as were the people who frequented them and who relished the new intimacy made possible by the decay of the old feudal order.

Precursors of the renowned English clubs, those early coffeehouses were enthusiastically democratic in the conduct and composition of their habitués. As one of the more articulate among them recorded, "As you have a hodge-podge of Drinks, such too is your company, for each man seems a Leveller, and ranks and files himself as he lists, without regard to degrees or order; so that oft you may see a silly Fop, and a wonder Justice, a griping-Rock, and a grave Citizen, a worthy Lawyer, and an errant Pickpocket, a Reverend Noncomformist, and a canting Mountebank; all blended together, to compose an Oglio of Impertinence."[8] Quite suddenly, each man had become an agent of England's newfound unity. His territory was the coffeehouse, which provided the neutral ground upon which men discovered one another apart from the classes and ranks that had earlier divided them.

A place that is a leveler is, by its nature, an inclusive place. It is accessible to the general public and does not set formal criteria of membership and exclusion. There is a tendency for individuals to select their associates, friends, and intimates from among those closest to them in social rank. Third places, however, serve to *expand* possibilities, whereas formal associations tend to narrow and restrict them. Third places counter the tendency to be restrictive in the enjoyment of others by being open to all and by laying emphasis on qualities not confined to status distinctions current in the society. Within third places, the charm and flavor of one's personality, irrespective of his or her station in life, is what counts. In the third place, people may make blissful substitutions in the rosters of their associations, adding those they genuinely enjoy and admire to those less-preferred individuals that fate has put at their side in the workplace or even, perhaps, in their family.

Further, a place that is a leveler also permits the individual to know workmates in a different and fuller aspect than is possible in the workplace. The great bulk of human association finds individuals related to one another for some objective purpose. It casts them, as sociologists say, in roles, and though the roles we play provide us with our more sustaining matrices of human association, these tend to submerge personality and the inherent joys of being together with others to some external purpose. In contrast, what Georg Simmel referred to as "pure sociability" is precisely the occasion in which people get together for no other purpose, higher or lower, than for the "joy, vivacity, and relief" of engaging their personalities beyond the contexts of purpose, duty, or role.[9] As Simmel insisted, this unique occasion provides the most democratic experience people can have and allows them to be more fully themselves, for it is salutary in such situations that all shed their social uniforms and insignia and reveal more of what lies beneath or beyond them.

Necessarily, a transformation must occur as one passes through the portals of a third place. Worldly status claims must be checked at the door in order that all within may be equals. The surrender of outward status, or leveling, that transforms those who own delivery trucks and those who drive them into equals, is rewarded by acceptance on more humane and less transitory grounds. Leveling is a joy and relief to those of higher and lower status in the mundane world. Those who, on the outside, command deference and attention by the sheer weight of their position find themselves in the third place enjoined, embraced, accepted, and enjoyed where conventional status counts for little. They are accepted just for themselves and on terms not subject to the vicissitudes of political or economic life.

Similarly, those not high on the totems of accomplishment or popularity are enjoined, accepted, embraced, and enjoyed despite their "failings" in their career or the marketplace. There is more to the individual than his or her status indicates, and to have recognition of that fact shared by persons beyond the small circle of the family is indeed a joy and relief. It is the best of all anodynes for soothing the irritation of material deprivation. Even poverty loses much of its sting when communities can offer the settings and occasions where the disadvantaged can be accepted as equals. Pure sociability confirms the more and the less successful and is surely a comfort to both. Unlike the status-guarding of the family and the czarist mentality of those who control corporations, the third place recognizes and implements the value of "downward" association in an uplifting manner.

Worldly status is not the only aspect of the individual that must not intrude into third place association. Personal problems and moodiness must be set aside as well. Just as others in such settings claim immunity from the personal worries and fears of individuals, so may they, for the time being at least, relegate them to a blessed state of irrelevance. The temper and tenor of the third place is upbeat; it is cheerful. The purpose is to enjoy the company of one's fellow human beings and to delight in the novelty of their character—not to wallow in pity over misfortunes.

The transformations in passing from the world of mundane care to the magic of the third place is often visibly manifest in the individual. Within the space of a few hours, individuals may drag themselves into their homes—frowning, fatigued, hunched over—only to stride into their favorite club or tavern a few hours later with a broad grin and an erect posture. Richard West followed one of New York's "pretty people" from his limousine on the street, up the steps, and into the interior of Club 21, observing that "by the time Marvin had walked through the opened set of doors and stood in the lobby, his features softened. The frown was gone, the bluster of importance had ebbed away and had been left at the curb. He felt the old magic welling up."[10]

In Michael Daly's tragic account of young Peter MacPartland (a "perfect" son from a "perfect" family) who was accused of murdering his father, there is mention of a place, perhaps the only place, in which MacPartland ever found relief from the constant struggling and competition that characterized his life. On Monday evenings, a friend would go with him to Rudy's, a working-class tavern, to watch "Monday Night Football." "It was Yale invading a working-class bar," said the friend. "It was like his first freedom of any kind. He thought it was the neatest place in the world."[11] Mere escape can be found in many forms and does not begin to account for transformations such as these.

Conversation Is the Main Activity

Neutral ground provides the place, and leveling sets the stage for the cardinal and sustaining activity of third places everywhere. That activity is conversation. Nothing more clearly indicates a third place than that the talk there is good; that it is lively, scintillating, colorful, and engaging. The joys of association in third places may initially be marked by smiles and twinkling eyes, by hand-shaking and back-slapping, but they proceed and are maintained in pleasurable and entertaining conversation.

A comparison of cultures readily reveals that the popularity of conversation in a society is closely related to the popularity of third places. In the 1970s, the economist Tibor Scitovsky introduced statistical data confirming what others had observed casually.[12] The rate of pub visitation in England or café visitation in France is high and corresponds to an obvious fondness for sociable conversation. American tourists, Scitovsky notes, "are usually struck and often morally shocked by the much more leisurely and frivolous attitude toward life of just about all foreigners, manifest by the tremendous amount of idle talk they engage in, on promenades and park benches, in cafés, sandwich shops, lobbies, doorways, and wherever people congregate." And, in the pubs and cafés, Scitovsky goes on to report, "socializing rather than drinking is clearly most people's main occupation."

American men of letters often reveal an envy of those societies in which conversation is more highly regarded than here, and usually recognize the link between activity and setting. Emerson, in his essay on "Table Talk," discussed the importance of great cities in representing the power and genius of a nation.[13] He focused on Paris, which dominated for so long and to such an extent as to influence the whole of Europe. After listing the many areas in which that city had become the "social center of the world," he concluded that its "supreme merit is that it is the city of conversation and cafés."

In a popular essay on "The American Condition," Richard Goodwin invited readers to contrast the rush hour in our major cities with the close of the working day in Renaissance Italy: "Now at Florence, when the air is red with the summer sunset and the campaniles begin to sound vespers and the day's work is done, everyone collects in the piazzas. The steps of Santa Maria del Fiore swarm with men of every rank and every class; artisans, merchants, teachers, artists, doctors, technicians, poets, scholars. A thousand minds, a thousand arguments; a lively intermingling of questions, problems, news of the latest happening, jokes; an inexhaustible play of language and thought, a vibrant curiosity; the changeable temper of a thousand spirits by whom every object of discussion is broken into an infinity of sense and significations—all these spring into being, and then are spent. And this is the pleasure of the Florentine public."[14]

The judgment regarding conversation in our society is usually twofold: we don't value it and we're not good at it. "If it has not value," complained Wordsworth, "good, lively talk is often contemptuously dismissed as talking for talking's sake."[15] As to our skills, Tibor Scitovsky noted that our gambit for a chat is "halfhearted and . . . we have failed to develop the locale and the facilities for idle talk. We lack the stuff of which conversations are made."[16] In our low estimation of idle talk, we Americans have correctly assessed the worth of much of what we hear. It is witless, trite, self-centered, and unreflective.

If conversation is not just the main attraction but the sine qua non of the third place, it must be better there and, indeed, it is. Within its circles, the art of conversation is preserved against its decline in the larger spheres, and evidence of this claim is abundant.

Initially, one may note a remarkable compliance with the rules of conversation as compared to their abuse almost everywhere else. Many champions of the art of conversation have stated its simple rules. Henry Sedgwick does so in a straightforward manner.[17] In essence, his rules are: 1) Remain silent your share of the time (more rather than less). 2) Be attentive while others are talking. 3) Say what you think but be careful not to hurt others' feelings. 4) Avoid topics not of general interest. 5) Say little or nothing about yourself personally, but talk about others there assembled. 6) Avoid trying to instruct. 7) Speak in as low a voice as will allow others to hear.

The rules, it will be seen, fit the democratic order, or the leveling, that prevails in third places. Everyone seems to talk just the right amount, and all are expected to contribute. Pure sociability is as much subject to good and proper form as any other kind of association, and this conversational style embodies that form. Quite unlike those corporate realms wherein status dictates who may speak, and when and how much, and who may use levity and against which targets, the third place draws in like manner from everyone there assembled. Even the sharper wits must refrain from dominating conversation, for all are there to hold forth as well as to listen.

By emphasizing style over vocabulary, third place conversation also complements the leveling process. In the course of his investigations into English working-class club life, Brian Jackson was struck by the eloquence of common working people when they spoke in familiar and comfortable environments.[18] He was surprised to hear working people speak with the "verve and panache" of Shakespearian actors. I observed much the same artistry among farmers and other workers in Midwestern communities who could recite, dramatically, verse after verse of poetry, reduce local cockalorums to their just proportions, or argue against school consolidation in a moving and eloquent style.

In Santa Barbara there is a tavern called The English Department, which is operated by a man who was banished from the English department at the local university for reasons that august body never saw fit to share with him. He'd spent most of his adult life listening to talk. He had listened in seminars, classrooms, offices, and hallways of various English departments. But the tavern, he found, was better; it was *living*. "Listen to these people," he said of his customers. "Have you ever heard a place filled like this? . . . And they're all interested in what they're saying. There's genuine inquiry here."[19] In a moment of candor, a past president of a professional association in one of the social sciences told an audience that it had been his experience that most academic departments effectively "rob their students of their Mother wit." The owner of The English Department had made the same discovery. In contrast, third places are veritable gymnasiums of Mother wit.

The conversational superiority of the third place is also evident in the harm that the bore can there inflict. Those who carry the despicable reputation of being a bore have not earned it at home or in the work setting proper, but almost exclusively in those places and occasions given to sociability. Where people expect more of conversation they are accordingly repulsed by those who abuse it, whether by killing a topic with inappropriate remarks or by talking more than their share of the time. Characteristically, bores talk more loudly than others, substituting both volume and verbosity for wit and substance. Their failure at getting the effect they desire only serves to increase their demands upon the patience of the group. Conversation is a lively game, but the bore hogs the ball, unable to score but unwilling to pass it to others.

Bores are the scourge of sociability and a curse upon the "clubbable." In regard to them, John Timbs, a prolific chronicler of English club life, once cited the advice of a seasoned and knowledgeable member: "Above all, a club should be large. Every club must have its bores; but in a large club you can get out of their way."[20] To have one or more bores as "official brothers" is a grizzly prospect, and one suggesting an additional advantage of inclusive and informal places over the formal and exclusive club. Escape is so much easier.

Conversation's improved quality within the third place is also suggested by its temper. It is more spirited than elsewhere, less inhibited and more eagerly pursued. Compared to the speech in other realms, it is more dramatic and more often attended by laughter and the exercise of wit. The character of the talk has a transcending effect, which Emerson once illustrated by an episode involving two companies of stagecoach riders *en route* to Paris. One group failed to strike up any conversation, while the other quickly became engrossed in it. "The first, on their arrival, had rueful accidents to relate, a terrific thunderstorm, danger, and fear and gloom, to the whole company. The others heard these particulars with surprise—the storm, the mud, the danger. They knew nothing of these; they had forgotten earth; they had breathed a higher air."[21] Third place conversation is typically engrossing. Consciousness of conditions and time often slips away amid its lively flow.

Whatever interrupts conversation's lively flow is ruinous to a third place, be it the bore, a horde of barbaric college students, or mechanical or electronic gadgetry. Most common among these is the noise that passes for music, though it must be understood that when conversation is to be savored, even Mozart is noise if played too loudly. In America, particularly, many public establishments reverberate with music played so loudly that enjoyable conversation is impossible. Why the management chooses to override normal conversation by twenty decibels is not always obvious. It may be to lend the illusion of life among a listless and fragmented assembly, to attract a particular kind of clientele, because management has learned that people tend to drink more and faster when subjected to loud noise, or simply because the one in charge likes it that way. In any case, the potential for a third place can be eliminated with the flip of a switch, for whatever inhibits conversation will drive those who delight in it to search for another setting.

As there are agencies and activities that interfere with conversation, so there are those that aid and encourage it. Third places often incorporate these activities and may even emerge around them. To be more precise, conversation is a *game* that mixes well with many other games according to the manner in which they are played. In the clubs where I watch others play gin rummy, for example, it is a rare card that is played without comment and rarer still is the hand dealt without some terrible judgment being leveled at the dealer. The game and conversation move along in lively fashion, the talk enhancing the card game, the card game giving eternal stimulation to the talk. Jackson's observations in the clubs of the working-class English confirm this. "Much time," he recorded, "is given over to playing games. Cribbage and dominoes mean endless conversation and by-the-way evaluation of personalities. Spectators are never quiet, and every stage of the game stimulates comment—mostly on the characteristics of the players rather than the play; their slyness, slowness, quickness, meanness, allusions to long-remembered incidents in club history."[22]

Not all games stimulate conversation and kibitizing; hence, not all games complement third place association. A room full of individuals intent upon video games is not a third place, nor is a subdued lounge in which couples are quietly staring at backgammon boards. Amateur pool blends well into third place activity generally, providing that personality is not entirely sacrificed to technical skill or the game reduced to the singular matter of who wins. Above all, it is the latitude that personality enjoys at each and every turn that makes the difference.

The social potential of games was nicely illustrated in Laurence Wylie's account of life in the little French village of Peyranne. Wylie had noted the various ways in which the popular game of *boules* was played in front of the local café. "The wit, humor, sarcasm, the insults, the oaths, the logic, the experimental demonstration, and the ability to dramatize a situation gave the game its essential interest."[23] When those features of play are present, the game of *boules*—a relatively simple one—becomes a full-fledged and spirited social as well as sporting event. On the other hand, "Spectators will ignore a game being played by men who are physically skilled but who are unable to dramatize their game, and they will crowd around a game played by men who do not play very well but who are witty, dramatic, shrewd, in their ability to outwit their opponents. Those most popular players, of course, are those who combine skill with such wit."

To comprehend the nature of the third place is to recognize that though the cue stick may be put up or the pasteboards returned to their box, the game goes on. It is a game that, as Sedgwick observed, "requires two and gains in richness and variety if there are four or five more . . . it exercises the intelligence and the heart, it calls on memory and the imagination, it has all the interest derived from uncertainty and unexpectedness, it demands self-restraint, self-mastery, effort, quickness—in short, all the qualities that make a game exciting."[24] The game is conversation and the third place is its home court.

Accessibility and Accommodation

Third places that render the best and fullest service are those to which one may go alone at almost any time of the day or evening with assurance that acquaintances will be there. To have such a place available whenever the demons of loneliness or boredom strike or when the pressures and frustrations of the day call for relaxation amid good company is a powerful resource. Where they exist, such places attest to the bonds between people. "A community life exists," says the sociologist Philip Slater, "when one can go daily to a given location and see many of the people he knows."[25]

That seemingly simple requirement of community has become elusive. Beyond the workplace (which, presumably, Slater did not mean to include), only a modest proportion of middle-class Americans can lay claim to such a place. Our evolving habitat has become increasingly hostile to them. Their dwindling number at home, seen against their profusion in many other countries, points up the importance of the accessibility of third places. Access to them must be *easy* if they are to survive and serve, and the ease with which one may visit a third place is a matter of both time and location.

Traditionally, third places have kept long hours. England's early coffeehouses were open sixteen hours a day, and most of our coffee-and-doughnut places are open around the clock. Taverns typically serve from about nine in the morning until the wee hours of the following morning, unless the law decrees otherwise. In many retail stores, the coffee counters are open well before the rest of the store. Most establishments that serve as third places are accessible during both the on and off hours of the day.

It must be thus, for the third place accommodates people only when they are released from their responsibilities elsewhere. The basic institutions—home, work, school—make prior claims that cannot be ignored. Third places must stand ready to serve people's needs for sociability and relaxation in the intervals before, between, and after their mandatory appearances elsewhere.

Those who have third places exhibit regularity in their visits to them, but it is not that punctual and unfailing kind shown in deference to the job or family. The timing is loose, days are missed, some visits are brief, etc. Viewed from the vantage point of the establishment, there is a fluidity in arrivals and departures and an inconsistency of membership at any given hour or day. Correspondingly, the activity that goes on in third places is largely unplanned, unscheduled, unorganized, and unstructured. Here, however, is the charm. It is just these deviations from the middle-class penchant for organization that give the third place much of its character and allure and that allow it to offer a radical departure from the routines of home and work.

As important as timing, and closely related to it, is the location of third places. Where informal gathering places are far removed from one's residence, their appeal fades, for two reasons. Getting there is inconvenient, and one is not likely to know the patrons.

The importance of proximate locations is illustrated by the typical English pub. Though in the one instance its accessibility has been sharply curtailed by laws that cut its normal hours of operation in half, it has nonetheless thrived because of its physical accessibility. The clue is in the name; pubs are called locals and every one of them is somebody's local. Because so many pubs are situated among the homes of those who use them, people are there frequently, both because they are accessible and because their patrons are guaranteed the company of friendly and familiar faces. Across the English Channel sociable use of the public domain is also high, as is the availability of gathering places. Each neighborhood, if not each block, has its café and, as in England, these have served to bring the residents into frequent and friendly contact with one another.

Where third places are prolific across the urban topography, people may indulge their social instincts as they prefer. Some will never frequent these places. Others will do so rarely. Some will go only in the company of others. Many will come and go as individuals.

The Regulars

The lure of a third place depends only secondarily upon seating capacity, variety of beverages served, availability of parking, prices, or other features. What attracts the regular visitor to a third place is supplied not by management but by the fellow customers. The third place is just so much space unless the right people are there to make it come alive, and they are the regulars. It is the regulars who give the place its character and who assure that on any given visit some of the gang will be there.

Third places are dominated by their regulars but not necessarily in a numerical sense. It is the regulars, whatever their number on any given occasion, who feel at home in a place and set the tone of conviviality. It is the regulars whose mood and manner provide the infectious and contagious style of interaction and whose acceptance of new faces is crucial. The host's welcome, though important, is not the one that really matters; the welcome and acceptance extended on the other side of the bar-counter invites the newcomer to the world of third place association.

The importance of a regular crowd is demonstrated every day throughout America in licensed drinking establishments that *don't* have a loyal patronage. The patrons sit spaced apart from one another. Many appear to be hunching over some invisible lead ball of misery sitting on their laps. They peel labels off beer bottles. They study advertising messages on matchbooks. They watch afternoon television as though it were of compelling interest. The scene is reminiscent of the "end of the world ambience" described by Henry Miller in his depressing description of American "joints."[26] There is an atmosphere of lethargy, if not genuine despair. Most of the hapless patrons, one may be sure, enter not only to have a drink but also to find the cheer that ought to be drink's companion. Seeking to gain respite from loneliness or boredom, they manage only to intensify those feelings by their inability to get anything going with one another. They are doomed, almost always, for if silence is not immediately broken by strangers, it is rarely broken at all. This dismal scene is not found in third places or among those who have third places. Those who become regulars need never confront it.

Every regular was once a newcomer, and the acceptance of new-comers is essential to the sustained vitality of the third place. Acceptance into the circle is not difficult, but it is not automatic either. Much of what is involved may be learned by observing the order of welcome to third places. Most enthusiastically greeted is the returning prodigal, the individual who had earlier been a loyal and accepted regular but whom circumstances had, in more recent months, kept away. This individual is perhaps the only one likely to get more than his democratic share of attention. After all, he's been away and there is much to ask and tell him. Next in order of welcome is the regular making his anticipated appearance. The gang was counting on his arrival and greets him accordingly. He is followed by the stranger or newcomer who enters in the company of another regular. Then come strangers in pairs and, at the bottom of the order, is the lone stranger, whose acceptance will take the longest.

Yet, it is the lone stranger who is most apt to become a regular. What he must do is establish trust. More than anything else, it is the element of trust that dictates the strength of the welcome. Strangers accompanied by regulars are vouched for. Strangers in pairs seem all right to one another at least and usually engage in such talk as will further attest to their acceptability. The lone stranger, however, has little to back him up. Though it is in the nature of inclusive groups to welcome new players to the game of conversation, it is also in their nature to want to know and trust those with whom they are talking. Since public life in America is relatively devoid of those connecting rituals that in other cultures serve to ensure the introductions of strangers, the order of welcome is doubly important.

How, then, does the lone stranger become a part of the group? It is not difficult, but it takes time because of the kind of trust that must be established. It is not the kind of trust on which banks base credit ratings or that between combat soldiers whose lives depend on each other. It's more like the trust among youngsters playing unsupervised sandlot baseball. Those who show up regularly and play a fairly decent game become the regulars. Similarly, the third place gang need only know that the newcomer is a decent sort, capable of giving and taking in conversation according to the modes of civility and mutual respect that hold sway among them, and the group needs some assurance that the new face is going to become a familiar one. This kind of trust grows with each visit. Mainly, one simply keeps reappearing and tries not to be obnoxious. Of these two requirements for admission or acceptance, regularity of attendance is clearly the more important.

Viewed from the newcomer's vantage point, third place groups often seem more homogeneous and closed to outsiders than they are. Those not yet a part of them seldom suspect their abundant capacity to accept variety into their ranks. Elijah Anderson was able to write a penetrating analysis of a black third place because this middle-class university student was accepted by the regular and relatively uneducated company of a lower-class ghetto bar.[27] In England, the public bar within the multiroomed public house is reserved for working-class patrons and is off limits to the well-dressed who can afford the fancier rooms. But, as one observer reports, "Once you have been in a few times you can go whenever you like."[28] Such examples are indicative of the character of inclusive places where the membership takes as much delight in admitting unlikely members as exclusive places do in making certain that newcomers meet proper and narrow qualifications.

A Low Profile

As a physical structure, the third place is typically plain. In some cases, it falls a bit short of plain. One of the reasons it is difficult to convince some people of the importance of the third place is that so many of them have an appearance that suggests otherwise. Third places are unimpressive looking for the most part. They are not, with few exceptions, advertised; they are not elegant. In cultures where mass advertising prevails and appearance is valued over substance, the third place is all the more likely *not* to impress the uninitiated.

Several factors contribute to the characteristic homeliness of third places. First, and recalling Emerson's observation, there are no temples built to friendship. Third places, that is, are not constructed as such. Rather, establishments built for other purposes are commandeered by those seeking a place where they can linger in good company. Usually, it is the older place that invites this kind of takeover. Newer places are more wedded to the purposes for which they were built. Maximum profits are expected and not from a group of hangers-on. Newer places also tend to emerge in prime locations with the expectation of capitalizing on a high volume of transient customers. Newer places are also more likely to be chain establishments with policies and personnel that discourage hanging out. Even the new tavern is not nearly as likely to become a third place as an older one, suggesting that there is more involved than the purpose for which such places are built.

Plainness, or homeliness, is also the "protective coloration" of many third places. Not having that shiny bright appearance of the franchise establishment, third places do not attract a high volume of strangers or transient customers. They fall short of the middle-class preference for cleanliness and modernity. A place that looks a bit seedy will usually repel the transient middle-class customer away from home and protect those inside from numerous intrusions by one-time visitors. And, if it's a male third place in which women are not welcome, a definite seediness still goes a long way toward repelling the female customer. Many otherwise worn and aging structures, I should point out, are kept meticulously clean by owners devoted to the comfort and pleasure of their customers. It is the first impression of the place that is at issue here.

Plainness, especially on the inside of third places, also serves to discourage pretention among those who gather there. A nonpretentious decor corresponds with and encourages leveling and the abandonment of social pretense. It is part of a broader fabric of nonpretention, which also includes the manner of dress. Regulars of third places do not go home and dress up. Rather, they come as they are. If one of them should arrive overdressed, a good bit of ribbing, not admiration or envy, will be his desert. In the third place, the "visuals" that surround individuals do not upstage them.

The plainness and modesty surrounding the third place is entirely fitting and probably could not be otherwise. Where there is the slightest bit of fanfare, people become self-conscious. Some will be inhibited by shyness; others will succumb to pretention. When people consider the establishment the "in" place to be seen, commercialism will reign. When that happens, an establishment may survive; it may even thrive, but it will cease to be a third place.

Finally, the low visual profile typical of third places parallels the low profile they have in the minds of those who frequent them. To the regular, though he or she may draw full benefit from them, third places are an ordinary part of a daily routine. The best attitude toward the third place is that it merely be an expected part of life. The contributions that third places make in the lives of people depend upon their incorporation into the everyday stream of existence.

The Mood Is Playful

The persistent mood of the third place is a playful one. Those who would keep conversation serious for more than a minute are almost certainly doomed to failure. Every topic and speaker is a potential trapeze for the exercise and display of wit. Sometimes the playful spirit is obvious, as when the group is laughing and boisterous; other times it will be subtle. Whether pronounced or low key, however, the playful spirit is of utmost importance. Here joy and acceptance reign over anxiety and alienation. This is the magical element that warms the insider and reminds the outsider that he or she is not part of the magic circle, even though seated but a few feet away. When the regulars are at play, the outsider may certainly know neither the characters nor the rules by which they take one another lightly. The unmistakable mark of acceptance into the company of third place regulars is not that of being taken seriously, but that of being included in the play forms of their association.

Johan Huizinga, grand scholar of play, would have recognized the playground character of the third place, for it was clear to him that play occurs in a place apart. Play has its playgrounds—"forbidden spots, isolated, hedged round, hallowed, within which special rules obtain. All are temporary worlds within the ordinary world, dedicated to the performance of an act apart."[29]

The magic of playgrounds is seductive. Having been part of the play, the individual is drawn to where it took place. Not every game of marbles, Huizinga conceded, leads to the founding of a club, but the tendency is there. Why? Because the "feeling of being 'apart together' in an exceptional situation, of sharing something important, or mutually withdrawing from the rest of the world and rejecting the usual norms, retains its magic beyond the duration of the individual game. The club pertains to play as the hat to the head."[30] Many couples are certain to have known the feeling to which Huizinga alludes. They experience it when, in the course of many social events that are duller than they should be, a magic time occurs. It may be an impromptu gathering with no set activity at which everyone stays longer than intended because they are enjoying themselves and hate to leave. The urge to return, recreate, and recapture the experience is there. Invariably the suggestion is made, "Let's do this again!" The third place exists because of that urge.

A Home Away from Home

If such establishments as the neighborhood tavern were nearly as bad as generations of wives have claimed them to be, few of the ladies should have found much reason to be concerned. The evil houses would have fallen of their own foul and unredeeming character. In fact, however, third places compete with the home on many of its own terms and often emerge the winner. One suspects that it is the similarity that a third place bears to a comfortable home and not its differences that poses the greater threat. Aye, there's the rub—the third place is often more homelike than home.

Using the first and second definitions of *home* (according to my Webster's), the third place does not qualify, being neither 1) the "family's place of residence" or 2) that "social unit formed by a family living together." But the third definition of home as offering "a congenial environment" is more apt to apply to the average third place than the average family residence. The domestic circle can endure without congeniality, but a third place cannot. Indeed, many family nests are brutish places where intimacy exists without even a smattering of civility.

Obviously, there is a great deal of difference between the private residence and the third place. Homes are private settings; third places are public. Homes are mostly characterized by heterosocial relations; third places most often host people of the same sex. Homes provide for a great variety of activities, third places far fewer. Largely, the third place is what the home is not, yet, there clearly exists enough similarity to invite comparison.

Seeking traits of "homeness," I chanced upon a volume by the psychologist David Seamon. He set forth five criteria against which "homes away from home" can be assessed. Seamon's illustrative comments are confined to the private residence. Clearly, he did not anticipate a comparison such as this; that makes his criteria particularly useful and not biased toward public places.[31]

The home *roots* us, begins Seamon; it provides a physical center around which we organize our comings and goings. Those who have a third place will find the criterion applies. As a self-employed individual once told me with regard to his coffeeshop, "Other than home, this is the only place where I know I'm going to be every day at about the same time." If the individual has a third place, the place also "has him." In America, the third place does not root individuals as tightly as, say, in France, but it roots them nonetheless. Those who regularly visit third places expect to see familiar faces. Absences are quickly noted, and those present query one another about an absent member.

The third place cannot enforce the regularity of appearance of the individual, as can home or work. A woman from Arizona related to me an account of her third place while she was a single working woman in Chicago. It illustrates the expectations that emerge among third place regulars. She and several others had become friends out of the mutual accessibility and appeal offered by a corner drugstore and its short-order food service. "The store was more home than where we all lived," she said, "in the resident hotels, apartments, YWCA, or whatever. If one of the group missed a day, that was all right. If we didn't see someone for two days, someone went to check to make sure the person was all right."[32]

For most Americans, third places do not substitute for home to the extent that hers had. In some cases, however, they root them even more so. Matthew Dumont, an East Coast psychiatrist, once went "underground" to study a place he dubbed the Star Tavern, in a blighted area of his city. There he found that the bartender and his tavern were meeting the needs of homeless men far better than the local health and welfare agencies. The Star was not a home away from home for those men. It *was* home.[33]

Seamon's second criterion of "at-homeness" is appropriation, or a sense of possession and control over a setting that need not entail actual ownership. Those who claim a third place typically refer to it in the first person possessive ("Rudy's is our hangout"), and they behave there much as if they did own the place.

When visiting another's home, one is bound to feel a bit like an intruder no matter how cordial the host, whereas the third place engenders a different feeling. The latter setting is a public place, and the regular is not an outsider. Further, just as a mother realizes her contribution to the family, regulars realize their contributions to the sociable group. They are members in good and full standing, a part of the group that *makes* the place.

Often, the regular is extended privileges and proprietary rights denied transient or casual customers. A special place may be reserved, formally or informally, for the "friends of the house." Access through doors not normally used by the public may be granted. Free use of the house phone may be permitted. But whether tangible benefits and privileges accrue or not, appropriation increases with familiarity. The more people visit a place, use it, and become, themselves, a part of it, the more it is theirs.

Third, contends Seamon, homes are places where individuals are regenerated or restored. Here, one must readily concede that third places are not recommended for the physically ill or exhausted. The home, if not the hospital, is required for them. But, in terms of the regeneration of the spirit, of unwinding, or of "letting one's hair down"—in terms of *social* regeneration—the third place is ideally suited. Many a dutiful wife and mother will confess that she feels most at home with her close friends at some comfortable snuggery apart from her home and family.

The fourth theme of "at-homeness" is the feeling of being at ease or the "freedom to be." It involves the active expression of personality, the assertion of oneself within an environment. In the home, observes Seamon, this freedom is manifest in the choice and arrangement of furniture and other decor. In the third place, it is exhibited in conversation, joking, teasing, horseplay, and other expressive behaviors. In either case, it is a matter of leaving one's mark, of being associated with a place even when one is not there.

Finally, there is *warmth*. It is the least tangible of the five qualities Seamon associates with "at-homeness," and it is not found in all homes. Warmth emerges out of friendliness, support, and mutual concern. It radiates from the combination of cheerfulness and companionship, and it enhances the sense of being alive. On this account, the score is lopsided in favor of the third place for, although homes can exist without warmth, the third place cannot. While homes provide much that is necessary apart from warmth and friendliness, these are central to third place association that would quickly dissolve without them.

Seamon makes much of the relationship between the warmth of a room or other space and the use it gets. Unused places feel cold and unshared places lack warmth. Seamon is also aware of the sharp rise in "primary" or one-person households in the United States and wonders what impact the loss of warmth has on those individuals and on society. I share a similar concern over the decline of warmth-radiating third places in America's towns and cities, and I'd hazard a guess at the effect of this loss. Colder people!

Summary

Third places exist on neutral ground and serve to level their guests to a condition of social equality. Within these places, conversation is the primary activity and the major vehicle for the display and appreciation of human personality and individuality. Third places are taken for granted and most have a low profile. Since the formal institutions of society make stronger claims on the individual, third places are normally open in the off hours, as well as at other times. The character of a third place is determined most of all by its regular clientele and is marked by a playful mood, which contrasts with people's more serious involvement in other spheres. Though a radically different kind of setting from the home, the third place is remarkably similar to a good home in the psychological comfort and support that it extends.

Such are the characteristics of third places that appear to be universal and essential to a vital informal public life. I've noted each of them in turn without attempting to describe any net effects that these several characteristics may combine to produce. I turn my attention now to such effects.

CHAPTER 3

The Personal Benefits

PRECIOUS AND UNIQUE benefits accrue to those who regularly attend third places and who value those forms of social intercourse found there. The leveling, primacy of conversation, certainty of meeting friends, looseness of structure, and eternal reign of the imp of fun all combine to set the stage for experiences unlikely to be found elsewhere. These benefits also derive from the sociable and conversational skills cultivated and exercised within the third place.

The benefits of participation both delight and sustain the individual, and the worth of the third place is most often counted in personal terms. Yet, even those profits of participation that seem most personal are never wholly so, for whatever improves social creatures improves their relations with others. What the third place contributes to the whole person may be counted a boon to all.

In detailing the gains attending third place involvement, I shall not elaborate those that are pecuniary in nature, although these may often be substantial. As surely as people develop a fondness for one another and meet regularly, they will give one another things, loan tools, books, and other objects, give of their time and labor on occasion, and tell one another about useful sources of goods and services. I have no doubt but that third places figure heavily in what we've come to call the underground economy. But however much a mutual-aid society such a group may become, the pecuniary benefits are secondary. Help, advice, and financial savings are incidental and do not account for the formation of third place circles or their sustaining appeal.

The essential and pervasive rewards attending third place involvement include novelty (which is characteristically in short supply in industrialized, urbanized, and bureaucratized societies), perspective (or a healthy mental outlook), spiritual tonic (or the daily pick-me-up attending third place visits), and friends by the set (or the advantages of regularly engaging friends in *numbers* rather than singly). There may be other benefits to the individual and many would no doubt claim them, but the aforementioned are universal and abundantly evident within all third places.

Novelty

Those distant ancestors who hunted and fished in order to sustain life found ample novelty in those pursuits. They confronted hardship but never boredom. Our own work conditions contrast sharply with those of the hunters and gatherers, and we are not strangers to drudgery or boredom. Most work is highly routine and too narrowly focused to bring many of the individual's talents into play, nor does it afford the exhilaration of the out-of-doors.

Yet, though work is often dull and routine, research suggests that it affords more novelty and stimulation than Americans generally enjoy when they depart the workplace.[1] Particularly in America, the usual activities that occupy the individual's leisure time are not highly valued, require little skill, and, increasingly, fail to keep us from being bored. As technological gains give us more residual time, the low-skill standbys such as recreational driving, shopping, or watching TV become increasingly inadequate in supplying the measure of novelty we require. Garage sales become popular as we try to supplement the limited novelty in the malls. VCRs and satellite dishes are in demand as we try to squeeze additional novelty out of the television set.

In his book on our "joyless economy," Tibor Scitovsky suggests that, due to our Puritan tradition, Americans do not recognize the tremendous human need for novelty.[2] Consequently, we do not cultivate those interests and skills so useful in its pursuit. Compared to Europeans, Scitovsky reports, we are more concerned with seeking comfort and less concerned with going into the world to seek stimulation.

Scitovsky's analysis could explain why many Americans have largely restricted daily life to the domains of home and work. Unfortunately, both the first and second places have evolved into closely contained worlds within which regularity and routine are closely tied to the success of their respective functioning. Both have constant populations, and when life is all but contained within them, some people are encountered too often and others too infrequently. Association loses diversity and people come to expect too much from too few people in a duality of settings in which surprise, adventure, risk, and excitement are alien commodities.

The dullness of this routine easily begets a dullness of personality. Pete Hamill saw the connection and remarked on the clear differences among his own acquaintances: "The most stopped-up, intellectually constipated, and unhappy men I know are those who work all day and go straight home to eat, watch TV, and sleep. There is no special period of the day reserved for the company of other men, no private experiences outside of work and marriage. They have jobs and they have homes but they don't have a place to hang out."[3]

Lackluster colleagues may not be the worst consequence of the lack of novelty in daily life. Drug use in the United States exceeds that of all other nations of the world combined and, to some degree, is a matter of compensating for the lack of stimulation derived from the social and physical environment by substituting internal chemical stimulation. Too, criminologists have become aware that the novelty and excitement of crime contrasts sharply with walking the straight path and may account for much of its appeal.

The third place has three distinct characteristics that promote novelty or stimulation within. First, it harbors a diverse population. In comparison with home and work associations, which tend to cloister people among their own kind, the inclusive third place brings the individual into close, personal, and animated contact with fellow human beings who also happen to teach school, distribute pharmaceutical products, paint houses, sell office equipment, or write for the local newspaper. The habitué of the typical third place thus enjoys a richness of human contact that is denied the timid, the bigoted, the pretentious, and others who choose to insulate themselves from human variety.

Third place regulars are aware of the ecumenical breadth of their associations. One of the good feelings they experience is that stemming from the realization that they are accepted and liked by people from many different walks of life. Individuals may belong to several formal organizations but if they have a third place it is apt to make them feel more a part of the community than those other memberships.

As previously indicated, novelty is also inherent in the lack of scheduling and organization, looseness of structure, and fluidity in the composition of those in attendance at the third place. A resulting uncertainty surrounds each visit. Who among the regulars will be there? Will there be newcomers? Will someone not seen in a long while show up? Will one of the gang bring a friend or relative along?

That excitement is typically evident in the manner with which the third place is approached by its regulars. It is a lively step that carries them from auto to entrance; it is an eager, anticipating eye that appraises the assembly within. The manner of approach differs from that at home or work. In those settings, one knows who is going to be there. One knows how quickly perfunctory greetings will give way to routine. The difference in approaching one setting as against the other is not a question, as spouses are prone to fear, of where the heart is; it is more the promise of something pleasantly novel amid the more usual contexts of duty and routine that lightens one's steps when approaching the third place.

As the third place constituency is more varied, so also is its agenda of conversational topics. At home and work, topics of conversation have little novelty and points of view vary hardly at all. To have a good talk at home usually means a serious discussion, not an entertaining one; it is a conversation that resolves some marital or financial problem. Indeed, to have an entertaining conversation at home usually requires the addition of outsiders. Good conversation becomes the host's and hostess's reward for the effort and expense put into drinks and dinner.

In third places, the agenda of conversation is not dominated by the mundane matters of home maintenance, children's braces, who's going to take one child here and the other one there, and the like, nor by that tether that repeatedly brings workplace talk back to the office or shop. Novelty in third place conversation is lent by the predictable changes but unpredictable direction that it always takes. What trivia will be dredged up from the past and what outlandish speculations made about the future? Who will drag in a tidbit of gossip and how reliable and how spicy will it be? What cases shall this court of universal appeals try on any given day and what judgments shall its judges render? Will the tone be argumentative or agreeable? Will one nod in sympathetic accord or stare incredulously at the author of some asinine pronouncement? Will one be amused, challenged, or merely reinforced in one's prejudices? All of these, certainly.

Finally, and most importantly, novelty in the third place emerges out of the collective ability of that assembly to create it. Indeed, the extent of mutual stimulation that the third place provides is itself novel. England's Mass Observation team came to this conclusion early in their study of that country's pubs just prior to World War II.[4] The pub, they found, "is the only kind of public building used by large numbers of ordinary people where their thoughts and actions are *not* being in some way arranged for them; in the other kinds of public buildings they are the audiences, watchers of political, religious, dramatic, cinematic, instructional, or athletic spectacles. But within the four walls of the pub, once a man has bought or been bought his glass of beer, he has entered an environment in which he is participator rather than spectator." In our own Midwest, Marshall Clinard made the same discovery. Large numbers of solid citizens, he found, preferred the tavern over the church as embodying the kind of association and involvement they valued most highly.[5]

The most satisfying and beneficial diversions are those that invite participation that is both social and active. These two components combine to elevate the quality of experience. The individual puts more into and gets more out of baseball, for example, by playing it than by sitting in the stands watching. But it is better to watch at the park than to watch the limited and remote version that television offers. Also, it is better to play the game as a team member than as a prima donna; better to sit with someone in the stands than to watch alone and better, even, to watch a televised game with someone than to watch alone. We enhance most experiences in these two ways—by increasing the directness of our involvement in an activity and by increasing our social involvement. It is lamentable that even as much work now requires so little initiative, many should choose diversions that require even less.

Conversation's role can hardly be overestimated. Novelty draws on the generous mix of social backgrounds of the people attracted to the typical third place. It is mightily encouraged by a setting that leaves entertainment to the customers who tailor the act to those in attendance and who never give the same performance twice. But the potential for novelty is lost and all comes to naught if there is no mutual stimulation.

The uncomfortable quiet in many American bars gives mute testimony to the importance of conversational skill.

Scitovsky reminds us that conversation is a skill one must first acquire to learn of its benefits.[6] Those who have learned and who know tend to seek the facilitating atmosphere of the third place. The stimulation we seek is always based on a mix of the new and the familiar. Thus, the novelty of the third place emerges against a familiar backdrop of regular characters and the way they can be counted on to react to things. Each individual keeps a dossier on the others, a mental list of mentionables that will surely get a rise out of this one or set that one off.

The third place is largely a world of its own making, fashioned by talk and quite independent of the institutional order of the larger society. If the world of the third place is far less consequential than the larger one, its regulars find abundant compensation in the fact that it is a more decent one, more in love with people for their own sake, and, hour for hour, a great deal more fun.

Perspective

Mental health depends upon the degree of harmony between the organism and its environment and, for most of us, this translates into harmonious relations with other people. An isolated desert prospector or a deep woods hermit may get along nicely with little or no human association, but they are not subject to the tensions of group life. To the extent that people live within the web of society, their environment is occupied and controlled by others and the quality of relations with them reflects the health of individuals and society.

The structure of the urban, industrialized society is not conducive to good human relations. Its high degree of specialization brutalizes many of the relationships people have with one another. The resulting compartmentalization, as Seldon Bacon expressed it, leaves individuals ignorant of the "interests, ideas, habits, problems, likes and dislikes" of those not in their own group. And, "in a complex, specialized, stratified society, we are continually in situations where we are dependent on others, and the others do not seem to care much about us."[7] This condition increases the incidence of aggression-provoking situations while at the same time rendering the expression of aggression evermore dangerous.

In our world, one's perspective on humanity is easily distorted. The sum total of an individual's contacts with other people, firsthand and through the media, can lead to cynicism. Amid the plethora of disquieting news programs, "garbage can" detective shows, uncaring neighbors, malicious neighborhood children, rising crime rates, the failures of the justice system, traffic congestion, inflation, a preoccupation with the grubbing of the marketplace, and isolation from old friends and relatives, it is often difficult to retain a favorable view of humanity.

There is much to discourage association, and association is all the more important because of those conditions. Indeed, those who retreat from close human contact may become dangerous people. Mass murderers, to take an extreme example, commonly exhibit a loner profile. Such people eschew affiliation and nurse their pathological views apart from the observations, the objections, and support of reasonable and decent people. They may exhibit the charm often associated with the psychopath, but they do not have the kinds of relationships that the third place offers.

The elderly illustrate the need for contact less dramatically but more commonly. Many of them are starved for association. When left too much alone, the aged often develop irrational fears. The caller who does not speak when the phone is answered ceases to be merely an impolite individual who's dialed a wrong number and becomes a potential thief finding out if anyone is home—calculating the best time to strike. Or the mind, too much out of touch with others, may begin to dredge up past injuries, decades old, and to dwell upon them and magnify them to the point where sleep is all but impossible. Usually, in these cases, the elderly "come back to normal" soon after association is resumed through visits with relatives, friends, or anyone willing to talk with them.

Younger, more active individuals might never consider chatting with and getting to know a bus driver, a mail carrier, a newspaper deliverer, or a convenience store clerk, but the elderly, who cannot be selective, often pursue such relationships eagerly. Those too old to drive lose that immunity from close neighbors that middle-class America appears to enjoy. Unable to get about as they once did, unable to keep contacts afar, they take a renewed interest in those living and working close by. Not being able to count on human association, having to exert themselves to maintain it, the elderly recognize the importance of association and communication more clearly and urgently than the rest of us. Keeping in touch with people, they too often find, makes all the difference between relative tranquility on the one hand and confronting the demons of isolation on the other.

But mental health and a positive outlook on life demand more than a minimal amount of contact and communication. Much as the body requires a balanced intake, so does the mind. The irritations of modern life call for a counterbalancing kind of experience—for human association that is both pleasurable and gratifying *because* of the presence of others. That people are the source of most of life's joys and pleasures as well as its frustrations and anxieties is a lesson learned through experience. Our good times are mainly contained within and made possible by durable social relationships. Encouragement of self-help outside of regular social contexts is of dubious value, and therapies that regard all social relationships as stressful or threatening may ultimately be harmful. People help themselves most by cultivating the right kinds of social relationships and giving them their due. The average middle-class American would appear to agree with this assessment, but errs in drawing the social circle too small.

The third place contributes to a healthy perspective by combining pleasure with association in a wide group and affording the collective wisdom of its members. John Mortimer's character Rumpole surely has a legion of real-life counterparts, and his situation is illustrative. In one episode, Rumpole is doing his utmost to discourage the impending marriage of his friend. He proceeds to describe that which the friend is placing in jeopardy: "Those peaceful moments of the day. Those hours we spend with a bottle of Chateau Fleet Street, from 5:30 on, in Pomeroy's Wine Bar. That wonderful oasis of peace that lies between the battle of the Bailey and the horrors of Home Life."[8]

Pomeroy's Wine Bar is his third place, which permits Rumpole a blessed interlude between hostile judges and "she-who-must-be-obeyed." His home life hardly seems horrible but the reader can, nonetheless, appreciate the mentality and the bearing of she-who-must-be-obeyed and agree that it calls for just that antidote that Pomeroy's provides. Deprived of it, Rumpole would pine as much for his home life, just as it is, as he does for his oasis of peace. Without undue generosity, one may even insist that Rumpole made no mistake in the mate-selection process. He married a fine lady and most probably would do so again. What Rumpole is keenly aware of, however, is the limitation of the arrangement, the relationship—the institution of marriage. It is that, far more than the character of that fine person who is his fellow prisoner, which must not be allowed to become all consuming because it alone is not sufficient to one's emotional, intellectual, and sociable life.

In the neighborhood taverns of American society, men often refer to their wives as "the old lady" or "the wife," and though males tend to sympathize with other males as to the more trying aspects of marriage (as do females with other females), there is generally no disparagement of wives or the institution of marriage. Rather, the language and attitude in such places are basically cautionary, reminding the individual not to overly glorify marriage or to expect too much from it. The key is to keep one's involvements in perspective.

A similar attitude, a debunking one, is typically held toward work in third place conservation. Kenneth Rexroth found that the men of the lower Appalachian region used the word *scissorbill* and applied it with great contempt.[9] To them, a scissorbill is a hick, a working person so naive as to believe that the boss has the worker's best interests at heart. The majority who use the term are not labor organizers, nor are they cynical or apathetic about work. They are saying to fellow working people, as to spouses, "Hang on to your dignity. Don't make unrealistic demands on life."

For all the persiflage, silliness, unresolved arguments, joking, and banter of third places, an outlook on life is asserted there and, because it evolves from a disinterest impossible in home and work settings, it is a particularly valuable one. Emerson expressed it well when he wrote that life is neither critical nor intellectual, but *sturdy*.[10] Individuals may complain, proclaim, and philosophize, but most of all, they persevere. It is the collective wisdom of the denizens of third places that individuals persevere best when they do not make egoistic and unrealistic demands upon life and those about them. In such circles, a wisdom compatible with experience dominates over any vision at odds with it.

That healthy outlook on life nurtured by the third place owes much to the humor and laughter generated within. Laughter, the experts tell us, is beneficial; it is therapeutic. In such case, the third place is surely a therapy center on that basis alone. With respect to both the frequency of laughter and the content that prompts it, the therapeutic influence is evident.

The home and the workplace, and certainly the public thoroughfares that we trod with sullen countenance, typically do not ring with laughter. Third places do. Some forgotten wag once dubbed the insane asylum a laughing academy and not only was the reference inaccurate and inappropriate, he overlooked the real laughing academies, which are the third places of the land. Their inhabitants laugh more, hour for hour, than in any other setting save some in which formal entertainment is provided. It has been noted that the average American laughs about fifteen times per day.[11] Fifteen times an *hour* would be a conservative estimate for those in a third place on one of its lesser days. I was not surprised to find, in a recent study of all the taverns in a small Midwestern city, that the more a given tavern met other criteria associated with third places, the more laughter rang within it.[12]

What gives rise to this laughter? Though jokes are sometimes exchanged, dependence upon them is slight. The joke or gag is more the outsider's gambit, the device of the drummer or traveling salesperson, historically, who knew the power of laughter but not the lore that prompted it locally. The joke is a second-hand form of humor, and many who love to laugh don't care for jokes at all. The joke depends on contrived situations and humor based on little tricks played upon the mind and emotions. Further, most people don't tell jokes well and, within third places, the average person never comes as close to being a bore as when telling a joke.

The regulars are far more appreciative of flesh-and-blood humor or that involving real people and real situations. Reality—the more immediate the better—is the mother lode of content from which an endless amount of humor and laughter are extracted. Unlike the joke that is put to death by its own punch line, humor based on real situations and people goes on and on. One humorous remark sparks another as the assembly warms to its topic and, often, the ludicrous content applies with painful accuracy to the very people who do the laughing.

Though it may be trite to suggest the importance of being able to laugh at oneself and the heavy business of life, the ability is lacking in many. Through humor we turn the tables on the frustrations, deprivations, and pretensions that afflict our daily existence. As Jacob Levine recently expressed it: "The humorous attitude is . . . a state of mind. In that state, man reasserts his invulnerability and refuses to submit to threat or fear. Again, Freud put it best: 'Humor is not resigned; it is rebellious. It signifies not only the triumph of the ego but also the pleasure principle, which is able to assert itself against the unkindness of the real circumstance.' "[13]

Much humor within third places plays on a characteristic *im*politeness, which really communicates affection. It does so with humor and has the advantage of credibility in a world where so much politeness is pro forma. To illustrate, one of the standard forms of recognition given by one who has just entered a third place and spotted a crony is an announcement to the effect that "If I'd known you were here, I'd have kept on going." This may be followed by a rather pointed interrogation. "Don't you ever do any work?" "She kick you out again?" "Can't you find anyone else to bother?" And to the host or hostess, "Why do you keep letting him in here?" "What kind of a place are you running?" "Ever think about the rest of us?" None of this, of course, would be vocalized were not others present to hear.

Much is communicated by these personalized excursions into low humor. The victim and the assailant have known each other for sometime. Their relationship is not fragile. An invitation to a duel of wits has been extended. A fraternity exists here. Love me, love my pal. Lighten up lads, I'm here to enjoy myself. Join in!

Ordinary rudeness offends its victims. In the third place, much of the talk sounds like rudeness and gains its effect from doing so, but is calculated to delight and communicate the strength of fraternal bonds. When, to take another example, one individual disagrees with what another has said, how should he respond? In the more controlled and subdued settings of everyday life, he who disagrees may pretend not to have heard. Or, he may counter with a calm and reasoned argument. Maybe he will grow sullen and show disapproval of the speaker. In the third place, however, he is likely to respond with an enthusiastic pounce—"You're out of your mind! Let me straighten you out on the facts of life."

The outsider may be shocked to find that no insult was intended and none was taken. That kind of give and take can only occur among people who have learned that their camaraderie counts far more than their moral speculations and pet prejudices. Such affectionate assaults on one another only lend spice to discussions; they do not raise dark questions as to the worth or acceptability of the speakers. That a third place regular occasionally talks as though he were "crazy as hell" is an endearing trait, not an ominous and threatening one.

I would not wish to leave the impression, however, that third place humor is always without any real sting. For individuals who need training in the matter of laughing at themselves, the third place is akin to Parris Island. The membership *will* take note of emerging bald spots and pot bellies never referred to in more tactful circles. The third place crowd is quick to pick up on matters that anger or frustrate an individual, and these will be mentioned not once, but again and again. The group has an uncanny feel for getting a rise out of its various members. All this is beneficial. The individual learns that he'd better be able to laugh at himself before others do, for then the barbs lose their sting, as do the realities that prompt them.

Though third place humor often has a sting, it is not mean. The membership is genuinely fond of most of the objects of its apparent derision; it laughs *with* more than it laughs *at*. But even in laughing at the individual and in his presence, the group is expressing its liking for him. Those who realize this and come to enjoy it have graduated to a higher level of social life; they draw strength from that which other people fear.

The binding and liberating power of humor is recognized in scientific circles but not always fully understood. The humor value of the third place may best be seen by contrasting it with a hypothetical place proposed at a symposium titled "Humor as a Form of Therapy" held in not-so-merry-old-England. One of the presenters suggested that "Laughter could be the human experience which binds neighborhoods together if an appropriate chamber were constructed. . . . A new building, a possible design of which was discussed, could stimulate laughter and reduce anomie—the feeling of the effect of diminishing national and neighborhood consciousness—to a major degree. Some form of community center seems to be a social need. A Laughter Center, specially designed to optimize reception of jokes. . . ."[14]

One quakes at the prospect. Envision the scenario—a committee of architects, psychologists, and gag-writers design the essential features of such a setting. Then a host of these "laughter chambers" are cloned, like fast-food outlets, in every neighborhood in England. As if by magic, lost communities are regained and a sense of national purpose is restored among all those who giggle in unison at the canned material.

The flaw, of course, lies in the assumption that humor would have to be provided; that people are no longer capable of seeing humor in their own lives. The solution offered is part of—an extension of—the very problem of human alienation it purports to remedy. The solution ignores the content of humor, requiring only that people stand or sit next to one another to do their laughing, and ignores the fact that it is not as much laughter as the content of the humor that precedes it that is significant. By laughing *at* one another as well as with one another people gain their sense of belonging and new reserves of strength that no staged performance or exposure to canned humor can provide. It is ironic that such an out-of-touch proposal should have originated in the land of the pub.

Spiritual Tonic

The effect of the third place is to raise participants' spirits, and it is an effect that never totally fades. Third place interaction is a matter of "making other peoples' day" even as they make one's own in a situation where everyone gains. The experience represents, as Henry Sedgwick said of good conversation, the perfect union of egoism and altruism. People enjoy the third place interlude and are left feeling better about themselves afterward for having received and bestowed the warm acceptance that is its hallmark. Individuals who start their day in a friendly coffee circle will never have a totally bad day and have already developed a degree of immunity from the mean-spirited and unhappy people that the second place often harbors.

The mood surrounding a third place varies, with the result that noise level is not a reliable indication of vitality. There is, however, an emotional tenor common to third place crowds no matter how loudly it may be registered. That preeminent student of human sociability, Georg Simmel, suggested three words which, when taken together, might convey its quality. His choices were joy, vivacity, and relief.[15] Joy is the emotion evoked by well-being; vivacity suggests that the tempo is lively; and relief implies a release from duty or the breaking of monotony.

If Simmel's description too much suggests the puppy let off its leash; if it doesn't seem to capture the quieter moments of social relaxation that also characterize third place association, there is another term that does. Third places are also *Gemütlich*. No other language includes a word as effective in communicating the coziness and diffusing friendliness of certain settings as German. What *Gemütlichkeit* may lack in exuberance, it makes up for in the strong neighborly imperative that it captures. It suggests an expansive and inclusive attitude of the mind and inclination of the spirit that welcomes all ages, sexes, and nationalities. It carries an obligation of helping others feel at home as well as doing so oneself. A *Gemütlich* setting is inviting to human beings—all of them.

Our concern, however, is not so much with the degree of effervescence in the third place spirit as with factors that combine to make such places almost always pleasant and enjoyable. Third places are upbeat for the individual even though his or her day may not have gone well. When George Malko did a piece on the Biltmore Bar in New York City some years ago, he asked the man who ran it if he could tell what kind of day his customers had had by the way they acted in the bar. "It's hard to tell," said the man, "When business is bad, a big businessman comes into a bar to forget. And when business is good, he comes in to enjoy."[16] As was suggested earlier, it is characteristic of a third place that personal problems are checked at the door by those who enter.

Third places also remain upbeat because of the limited way in which the participants are related. Most of the regulars in a third place have a unique and special status with regard to one another. It is special in that such people have neither the blandness of strangers nor that other kind of blandness, which takes the zest out of relationships between even the most favorably matched people when too much time is spent together, when too much is known, too many problems are shared, and too much is taken for granted. Many among the regulars of a third place are like Emerson's "commended stranger" who represents humanity anew, who offers a new mirror in which to view ourselves, and who thus breathes life into our conversation. In the presence of the commended stranger, wrote Emerson, "We talk better than we are wont. We have the nimblest fancy, a richer memory, our dumb devil has taken leave for a time. For long hours, we can continue a series of sincere, graceful, rich communications, drawn from the oldest, secretest experience, so that those who sit by, of our kinsfolk and acquaintance, shall feel a lively surprise at our unusual power."[17]

The magic of commended strangers fades as one comes to know them better. They are fallible. They have problems and weaknesses like everyone else and, as their luster fades, so does their ability to inspire our wit, memory, and imagination. The third place, however, retards that fading process, and it does so by keeping the lives of most of its regulars disentangled. One individual may enjoy the company of others at a mutual haunt for years without ever having seen their spouses; never having visited their homes or the places where they work; never having seen them against the duller backdrop of their existence on the "outside." Many a third place regular represents conversationally and sociably what the mistress represents sexually. Much of the lure and continuing allure of the mistress rests in the fact that only pleasure is involved. There is no rising from bed to face the myriad problems that husband and wife must share and that contaminates their lives and their regard for one another. Third places surely contain many of these "mistresses of conversation," people who meet one another only to share good times and scintillating activities and with whom good times and scintillation thus come to be associated. Out of the tacit agreement not to share too much, the excitement attaching to the commended stranger is preserved among third place regulars. What, after all, are such incidentals as home and family and job when the nature of life itself, the course of the world in modern times, or the booted ball that cost a victory in last night's game are on the agenda?

Third places remain upbeat because those who enjoy them ration the time they spend there. They leave when or before the magic begins to fade. One of the reasons why the home and the place of work are not as fondly anticipated is because people must often remain in them when they would rather be elsewhere. That is rarely the case in third places. One or two beers or one or two cups of coffee and the average individual usually departs. There is no duty to stay in such a place beyond its ability to provide satisfaction. Those who spend too much time in the third place are often the dullest and least appreciated people there. In the taverns, for example, one will often find seated at the end of the bar a thin and pale individual whom no one joins in conversation—a "malt worm" is the term used by the English. He's among the most regular but least appreciated individuals in the place. He's regular in attendance but he's not a "regular guy." He's long since lost that edge that makes people interesting, an edge that is honed by confrontation with life on the outside.

Third place association is upbeat because of the freedom of expression that it encourages. It is a freedom from the obligations of social roles and the styles and demeanor with which those roles must be played. Here, individuals may uncork that which other situations require them to bottle up. The timidity which the workplace imposes upon those with families to support does not extend to the third place. Here one may bellow like a street preacher or wail like a new widow, boast with gusto or assume the authoritarian pomp of a high court judge.

Even the pose of adulthood may be abandoned. Grown men and women may taunt, tease, leer, and giggle in the manner of mischievous schoolchildren. Both men and women, in the secure and liberating presence of understanding cronies, may behave in such a way as would seem alien to their spouses and children who know them as far more reserved and serious people. Release from the airs and aura of responsibility and its attendant mood of sobriety, when coupled with the company of appreciative fellow-sufferers, is a heady tonic. The whole catalog of "Things Gone Wrong with Spouses" or the long litany of "Episodes and Habits That Temper the Love of Children" can be reviewed under the lens of humor and with detachment. In such instances, people turn the tables on the frustrations and deprivations of daily life, and they take delight in doing so.

Amateurism is encouraged in third places and this, also, lends to the joys of association there. Life on the outside, the whole set of social roles the average individual plays, is inadequate to the expressive needs of a vital human being. The mundane world subdues us, especially the modern urban one, which dislikes idiosyncrasies and will not tolerate "characters." It encourages us to be image-conscious and self-conscious. It prefers a "cool" individual, and "cool" individuals don't kick up their heels. We may not put a rose between our teeth and dance the fandango at the supermarket. We may not do the buck-and-wing out of the boss's office or while being ushered to our seat at a restaurant. We may not sing our favorite ballads while waiting in line at the movie theater. It is not safe to render our classic imitation of the boss's "yes man" at the office water cooler. Where, then, does one do such things?

Popular opinion suggests that one doesn't do them at all. The latitude for spirited expression in modern society is lessened. People are made nervous by it. The public pays no attention to the young man walking along with a radio blaring near his ear nowadays, but let him sing—let him make his own music—and they're apt to frown at him. Nor are we supposed to get excited about things or, if we do, we aren't supposed to show it. The "world out there" doesn't want us to call a son-of-a-bitch by his well-deserved name. It doesn't want men to dance together or gather in the local parks and sing in harmony 'round kegs of beer. That which, in a less constricted but better ordered society, is emblematic of peace and goodwill, is likely to be regarded as disturbing the peace in our own. If there are speeches to be delivered, leave them to the office-seekers. If there is any bellowing to be done, leave it to the fundamentalist preachers. The average person, popular opinion suggests, ought to be content with a little singing in the shower and with taking low-voiced snipes at his or her spouse across the breakfast table. But for people with spirit (or who need spirit), this is too stifling and vapid. Those among us who, in everyday life, are not singers, dancers, poets, orators, psychologists, comedians, sages, impressionists, pool hustlers, hams, or heroes may become them in the third place. There the stage is available and it's a wonderful stage, for the audience appreciates the actor no matter how bad the act. What more encouragement does amateurism need?

In my experience, those who have a third place are usually disdainful of the private, invitational cocktail party, which has become far too much a substitute for third place association among the upper segments of the broad middle class in America. This and the "Happy Hour" have earned their dubious reputations precisely because they fail their claimed purpose. Such gatherings are usually anything but exuberant or relaxing. Part of the problem with cocktail parties has to do with their physical setting. The home is designed, built, and appointed as a quiet and restful place. It is the repository of many fragile family possessions. It appeals to genteel dignity more than to uninhibited gaiety. Each of its members and each of its guests understands that the carpeting, wallpaper, appliances, furniture, and fixtures are to be treated with care. The home, in short, is not a place to let loose. But that is only part of the problem.

At the usual cocktail party, there aren't enough comfortable seats for all the guests; thus no one is supposed to sit. Etiquette against drinking while standing is set aside in favor of a routine in which one is expected to stand and talk to first one individual, couple, or small group and then tactfully move on to the next. When all combinations and permutations have been exhausted—when all have done their duty—guests are free to leave. Scintillating conversation is prized, and it is the fervent hope of the host and hostess that they will have master-minded a successful guest list and provided the occasion for it. But conversation must stop short of spirited orations and boisterous argument. The cocktail party is an enforced routine that has evolved in such a way as to disguise its own failure. In so doing, it precludes any hope of a jolly good time.

For fuller expression (to say nothing of *relaxation*), a third place is required. It is remarkable that the great majority of people, when given the latitude for fuller expression, do not become vulgar. The form of sociability and the rules governing its expression seem, in third places, to hold up in the face of increasing numbers and revelry. It is to the credit of those assembled that they can raise their spirits to an upper limit without raising hell at the same time. The denizens of the third place satisfy their needs for spirited social intercourse regularly, and because they do it often, their indulgences are not frenzied and remain within bounds. They achieve levels of exuberance refreshingly beyond that offered by life on the outside and they do so without courting disaster.

Friends by the Set

It is a fact of social life that the number, kind, and availability of friends depend upon *where* one may engage them. If our dependence upon place in this regard is not always understood, it is because our closest and dearest friends may be granted special rights to enter our homes and lives almost at will. Few people, however, can be allowed such privileges if privacy is to be preserved and individuals are to maintain control over their lives and relationships. Involved here is the "paradox of sociability." Simply stated, one must have protection from those with whom one would enjoy sociable relations.[18] One can't have them bursting into one's home or one's place of work or even have them around when one wishes they were not. The average individual may regularly engage a host of friends only if he or she can be free of them whenever that freedom is necessary or desired. Of course, there must also be freedom *to* engage friends easily if a generous number of active friendships are to be maintained.

It is this paradox of sociability that encourages a proliferation of third places, of convenient gathering sites, wherever human beings have settled. Only where planning or zoning disallows them do they fail to appear as a natural manifestation of people's need to have readily accessible meeting places that may be visited and departed from at will. Where third places are not provided, the individual's active friendships are greatly diminished, as is the ease with which he or she can make contact with friends. Such is typically the case in the newer automobile suburbs where zoning regulations disallow those kinds of establishments elsewhere appropriated as gathering spots. Within developments containing nothing but homes, residents are confronted with an unhappy choice: they may either open their homes to frequent and unbidden intrusions by friends or they may sharply curtail informal socializing. Usually, and with good reason, they opt for privacy. The home after all, must be kept as a sanctum sanctorum of privacy, rest, and recuperation, and it must be thus preserved for all members of the family.

As many an urbanite and suburbanite has learned, having an extensive network of friends is no guarantee against loneliness. Nor does membership in voluntary associations, the "instant communities" of our mobile society, ensure against social isolation and attendant feelings of boredom and alienation. The network of friends has no unity and no home base. One's many friends may offer no more than sporadic and unreliable accessibility. The voluntary organizations offer true group affiliation and they have a home base, but what they offer is available only at scheduled times. And, in many of them, interest tends to be confined to the mutual problems and concerns of parents without partners, the work of the church, the playing and analyzing of bridge games, and so on. What urban life increasingly fails to provide, and what is so much missed, is convenient and open-ended socializing—places where individuals can go without aim or arrangement and be greeted by people who know them and know how to enjoy a little time off.

But how worthwhile are the friends one enjoys in a third place? Are they no more, perhaps, than the "casual companions" described by the psychiatrist and psychologist Ignace Lepp as content to "amuse themselves together" but who do little to help the individual reach his or her potential in life? Are they such lesser entities as Harry Carmichael, in one of his mystery novels, referred to as mere "pub pals"? "That kind of friendship," said Carmichael's hero, "flourishes only in the atmosphere of licensed premises. Take it outside into the real world and it just withers away."[19] The idea that settings reserved for relaxation and sociability and the people met within them are somehow less than real is fairly common in both lay and professional thinking. Why some are inclined to honor life's drudgery and the companions to it while discounting the finer associations to which we treat ourselves when free to do so is curious. The question ought not to be which friends are best but what are the benefits derived from the various kinds of friends one may have.

Before assessing pub or coffee shop pals apart from "closer" friends, it should be recognized that some are both. Some of the friends found within the third place have extensive contact and involvement beyond it and a given third place may, for them, be little more than an incidental host to a relationship formed elsewhere and engaged in many places. We once imagined that the third place might have had its beginnings under just such circumstances. It may have been that men who hunted together in order to survive in prehistoric times eventually found much to admire in one another and wished to further their association. That hunch seems plausible in light of what still goes on in the workplace. Those we admire at work and who seem to be "good people" are those we invite to grab a beer after work to get to know them.

Another qualifier should be added before comparing types of friendships. Those who disparage "pub pals" as lesser or "not real" friends often disregard constraints upon the individual that restrict the wider enjoyment of friendship. That many friends are engaged only in third places is not always a matter of choice. Many such friendships would be brought home but for the other members of the family, especially the spouse. Jiggs never hesitated to bring the gang from Dinty Moore's home when Maggie was away. The problem was her characteristic omnipresence. She was a mighty force in containing Jigg's friendships within the tavern. One of the great pluses in friendship is that it exists outside the social structure. It is a relationship not limited by family, work, church, or any other "justifying" organizational tie. But, just as surely as friendships may be independent of those settings, they must have some *place* to be nourished.

Let us focus on friends of the third place who, by a tacit and mutual agreement, meet only there. What are they worth amid the variety of human associations one may have? How do they compare with the more individualized forms of friendship, which correspond more to common notions of what friendship is and seem more to suit our needs?

Third place friendships, first of all, complement more intimate relations. Those who study human loneliness generally agree that the individual needs intimate relationships and that he or she also needs affiliation. To affiliate is to be a member of some club, group, or organization. The tie is to the group more than to any of its individual members. There is a great difference between intimacy and affiliation, and there is no substituting one for the other. We need both. Lacking intimacy, affiliation becomes little more than a means of dulling the sense of emptiness in our lives. Lacking affiliation, intimacy becomes overburdened even as it risks the dullness of restricted human contact.

Third places are forms of affiliation, and friends there come in "sets." Among those who have given allegiance to a third place, the regulars usually happen to be friends. Exceptions are few, for the company encourages harmony among all who gather in the name of sociability; further, the sources of human division are "left outside." Everyone is the friend of everyone else, and the membership requirements are exceedingly modest. What this means is that the individual with a third place has a host of friends that are not limited by the narrowness of personal choice. Many who acquire a third place would not have believed, at the outset, that many of the others there would make good friends. They would never have chosen them individually and would not have them at all but for the fact that they "came with the set." Third place friendships thus have a breadth and variety typically greater than that found in other forms of friendship. To the sum of the individual's experiences is added a richness that accrues not because of personal choice but because personal choice takes a back seat. Third places thus counter the inbreeding of sociability along social class and occupational lines, which the family and workplace encourages.

Within the informal group affiliation that third places offer, there is no dependence upon any particular friend. No single individual makes the third place what it is. It is only necessary that some familiar faces be present at this locus of affiliation as particular individuals come and go. Friends engaged on this basis do not burden and disappoint one another, as is often the case with individualized friendships. These friends need not wait for one another nor arrange their meetings. They do not cancel plans or complicate them, as individual friends often do. This is, in short, a more reliable form of friendship than can be maintained between two people who must mesh their personal schedules. There is a Chinese proverb that holds that "a humble friend in the same village is better than sixteen influential brothers in the Royal Palace." That epigram is a tribute to one of the most important characteristics that friends may possess—availability. Even the best of personal friends are often unavailable. One of the great advantages of the informal affiliation of the third place is the routine, daily steadiness of the friendly association it affords.

Places that host group affiliation allow friends to meet and interact with one another in generous numbers, and there is a certain magic to those numbers. Friends met collectively have effects upon one another that do not result when the company is not gathered and its members meet one another individually. Experts who have looked at these numbers from the perspective of mental health have made several pertinent observations.[20] First, "the larger the group, the more 'socializing' there is, and the greater the pressure to avoid all topics of conversation which might lead to argument or disharmony." Also, large groups prove to be less emotionally demanding for the individual participant, even as their greater number enhances the feeling of acceptance in the individual. The result: "This package of status and 'belongingness' without the demand for individual emotional output is perhaps what makes large group activity most conducive to mental health."[21] The assembly of friends engenders a "high" within the individual that cannot be duplicated when members of the company are met singly. To be enthusiastically welcomed into such an assembly, to be acknowledged and greeted by people from different walks of life, does considerable good for the individual's self-esteem.

In his recent book on dwelling among friends, Claude Fischer begins by tempering enthusiasms for friendships and social support networks generally.[22] They are a mixed blessing. Helpful neighbors can also be pests. Friends who hold your hand when you need it may also hold out their hand for financial help and strain the relationship in doing so. There are costs involved in maintaining the kinds of friendship relations to which many are now restricted. The birth of a baby, a divorce, a change of residence, a change in one's values, or any number of factors can cause friendships to lose their value. Modern society multiples the impediments to friendship and forces people to a cost accounting where it should not have to be applied.

What modern society is losing in its failure to proliferate third places is that *easier* version of friendship and congeniality that results from casual and informal affiliation. As a complement to friendships with strain built into them, there ought to be those in which people meet only to enjoy one another, with an immunity from the costs and impositions that other kinds of friendships entail. What is needed is that optimal staging of selves and sociability that the third place offers and that guarantees that the price of friendship will be rock bottom even while those assembled are in a most enjoyable state. Those who discount this kind of affiliation and this "lesser" form of friendship in favor of more demanding relationships do us no service. Some of the joys and blessings of being alive ought to be as easily achieved as a stroll down to the place on the corner—but there does have to be a place on the corner!

CHAPTER 4

The Greater Good

FROM THE OTHER side of the breakfast table, a former colleague gave me the first reaction to my third place thesis. For a long time he pored over the draft with interest and apparent approval. Suddenly he erupted in anger. I was then accused of promoting a way of life in which the masses spend their time lounging about coffeehouses or taverns while all hope of a better world crumbles about them. People, he argued, would be far better advised to join political action groups than waste their time in the manner I was advocating. I was unable to determine what prompted his displeasure. He had misjudged the third place; yet, he was hardly alone in doing so and his objection merits a response in its own terms.

The Political Role

If Americans generally find it difficult to appreciate the political value of third places, it is partly because of the great freedom of association that Americans enjoy. In totalitarian societies, the leadership is keenly aware of the political potential of informal gathering places and actively discourages them. I recall from childhood days some old-timers of German descent discussing Hitler's ban against the assembly of more than three persons on the street corners of German towns and cities. A colleague who recently traveled through the Soviet Union remarked on the fear Russians have of expressing themselves, even in informal gatherings. The most open expression she noted was what took place at roadside when the touring buses stopped in open country and men and women went into the bushes on opposite sides of the road in lieu of visiting restrooms.

Manuela Hoelterhoff visited Dresden, East Germany, in 1983, and later wrote "the miserableness of the cuisine and the scarcity of restaurants are largely intentional, and only partly a function of the German palette or the absence of high quality food. Cafes, in which people might linger for more than one hour discussing the horrors of the day, are potentially the breeding grounds of dissent; best keep them at a minimum. In Dresden, the asocial underpinning of communist society becomes crystal clear."[1]

In Hungary, just prior to 1954, the government encouraged a revival of traditional farmers' reading circles where peasants might discuss their mutual problems. At first the people were timid and reluctant to participate in these gatherings but in time they did. The ensuing discussions were critical of the regime and it was not long before the Communist newspapers proclaimed such groups to be centers of local resistance. They were discontinued. In retrospect, the revival of the discussion groups turned out to be a deliberate ruse designed to lure the peasants to staged elections, after which they were decreed to have no legitimate purpose.[2]

Sweden's rulers banned the drinking of coffee in the eighteenth century. Officialdom was convinced that the coffeehouses were "dens of subversion where malcontents planned revolts." Several members of the medical profession were coerced into giving "scientific" medical testimony to the effect that coffee was injurious to the human body.[3] Free assembly, at its most spontaneous and informal levels of occurrence—a right seemingly so basic that our Constitution does not spell it out—is anathema to fascist rule.

Just as third places run counter to the type of political control exercised in totalitarian societies, so they are essential to the political processes of a democracy. There can be no better example of this than offered by our own dear land for, as much as the mere idea may upbraid the sensitivities of some, our democracy had its origins in the local taverns of the revolutionary era. More than anywhere else in colonial America, the taverns offered a democratic forum. There protest gelled into action and the organization of the revolution and of the society to follow were agreed upon. Within them, as the historians Carl and Jesse Bridenbaugh put it, "there existed that full and free interplay of spontaneous and responsible group association which appears to be a necessary condition of a healthy social order."[4] Much abused, characteristically undervalued, the tavern furnished the "requisite machinery" for a new social and political order.

Sam Warner examined the taverns of Philadelphia at that crucial time and concluded that, "Then, as now, each one had its own crowd of regulars and thus each constituted an informal community cell of the city. Out of the meetings of the regulars at the neighborhood tavern came much of the commonplace community development which preceded the Revolution and later proved to be essential to the governance of the city and the management of the ward. Regular meetings of friends, of men of common occupations, led to clubs of all kinds and of every degree of formality from regular billiard sessions to fire companies and political juntos. Benjamin Franklin and the many community innovations of his junto showed the potential of these informal tavern groups. They provided the underlying social fabric of the town, and when the Revolution began made it possible to gather militia companies quickly, to form effective committees of correspondence and of inspection, and to organize and to manage mass town meetings."[5]

Throughout most of our history, the taverns also served to bring the voting constituency into contact with its elected officials and with local business leaders as well. Of the eighteenth-century public houses, Warner reports that they "opened out to all the life of the street and . . . did not shield the leaders of the town from contact with the life that surrounded them."[6] Fred Holmes noted the same accountability in nineteenth-century Madison, Wisconsin, where "Many of the legislators, whose biennial salary was five hundred dollars in those days, also availed themselves of the saloon's free lunches. At mealtime they hurried over to Wirka's or Genske's, where a free lunch of cold meats, fish, and relishes awaited them, all to be had with a nickel glass of beer. No lobbyists hung about the Capitol corridors in those days awaiting the opportunity to invite the unsuspecting legislator to a pancake breakfast or a steak dinner."[7]

The early political life of Grover Cleveland illustrates the role that the third place played in political accountability. It was a time when ordinary citizens could reach an official almost as easily as the special interest groups that now dominate political life. As Allan Nevins' account reveals, the saloon was the meeting ground between the elected and the electorate: "Buffalo of the seventies was a democratic community, and no man could be sheriff in such a city without knowing many different kinds of people. In saloons like Louis Goetz's or Gillick's, Cleveland chatted with everybody. He liked to play pinochle, poker, and a card game called 'sixty-six.' Another saloon where he might be found was The Shades, at Main and Swan near his office, where the patrons drew their own liquor from barrels and kegs picturesquely ranged about the wall, for there was no bar, and made their own change from a peck of loose silver on the table. Still another was Bass's. In general, it was food, not drink, that drew Cleveland to a saloon, as it drew other professional and business men."[8]

Was it growth and progress or special interests that eventually separated politicians from the bulk of their constituency? Warner traced the pattern of change in the city of Philadelphia, which as a small town had not experienced the limitations of those merchants' centers that came later in the form of the exchanges, the Chamber of Commerce, and the gentlemen clubs. "These later gatherings," wrote Warner, "were either meeting places of specialists and thereby encouraged only the brokers' or downtown merchants' view of the city, or they were closed organizations which directed their members' attention inward toward the sociability of the group."[9] Ushered away from the informal gathering places of ordinary citizens by those with greater means and special interests, American politicians became insulated from the electorate. The spatial design of our centers of government accentuated the problem. As the architect Victor Gruen has observed, we construct "civic centers that are concentration camps for bureaucrats, who are thus prevented from mingling with common folks." That, suggests Gruen, "may explain why they lose their touch with and understanding of the problems of the latter."[10]

Today's politicians maintain contact with their constituency through the media. Major elections and much of politics generally have become largely a television phenomenon. Television takes the place of active participation and weakens the local grass-roots structure; political influence increasingly shifts to remote sources of power and manipulation.[11] The Pulitzer Prize-winning historian and advisor to presidents, James M. Burns, has expressed alarm over the limitations of television and the abuses of it that threaten to make a shambles of the democratic process. Personalities now overshadow issues. Candidates need no longer be party leaders or even able to work with the party leaders. Elections are treated like horse races by a media that often ignores important issues. Worst of all, leadership personalism is taking over and the process is unlikely to produce effective leadership. The remedy? Burns was able to point to it clearly and without need of elaboration: "A basic solution to this grave tendency will be to reinvigorate local leadership, family participation, civic organizations."[12]

The need for face-to-face grass-roots participation in the political process is essential in a democracy. Television has obscured that need, but it has not obviated it. Even if the media were as professional, ethical, objective, and infallible as those who live off it like to claim, it could serve but a limited role in the political life of a democracy. Its speed, its efficiency, and the breadth of its audience are features as valuable to despotism as to democracy. What the tavern offered long before television or newspapers was a source of news *along with* the opportunity to question, protest, sound out, supplement, and form opinion locally and collectively. And these active and individual forms of participation are essential to a government of the people. An efficient home-delivery media system, in contrast, tends to make shut-ins of otherwise healthy individuals; the more people receive news in isolation, the more they become susceptible to manipulation by those who control the media.

For all the hold television takes of specific groups and individuals, it never gives them any attention. Mass media do not and cannot extend to that small corner of the world in which most of us live. As Winston Kirby remarked of those individuals who have grown up with television, "the product of the TV age does not identify with his city or apparently any city. He is a product of this, his planet, or as McLuhan says, the global village."[13] Global matters are important, of course, but so are local matters, and the media are simply incapable of anything approaching adequate local coverage. We live in the "hole" of an "informational doughnut."[14] We are better informed about a school bus accident in a South American country than of the actions of a local city council, which will have far greater impact upon our lives. Many Americans bemoan the disappearance of local, associational communities. One of several reasons for their disappearance is the fact that such communities have no reality in the media, even as the media increasingly define what is real. People live in their respective neighborhoods, developments, or subdivisions for years and those areas are rarely, if ever, mentioned on television. It is as though we don't live anywhere, or at least anywhere that matters.

Reinvigoration or restoration of grass-roots political involvement is essential, and the reestablishment of the gathering places necessary to it is just as essential. It will not be as easy. During the same period in which television rose to prominence, we were busy building communities devoid of those places where grass roots can take hold. These are the suburbs, which Robert Goldston described as denying civicism by their very nature. "Suburbia," he wrote, "offers almost no facilities for accidental encounters or for collective meetings; social participation beyond the narrow range of family and friends is limited to the passive receipt of goods, information, and entertainment from impersonal and isolated sources."[15]

Thus, the official edicts and policies of despots are not the only means of shutting down the casual meetings of friends and neighbors essential to the democratic process. In the United States, we unwittingly accomplish the same end through the combination of mass construction technologies, zoning ordinances, and unimaginative planning. If developers intentionally built communities without local gathering places and good sidewalks leading to them from every home, and did so for the purpose of inhibiting the political processes of the society, we would call it treason. Is the result any less negative without the intent?

In a recent plea for the promotion of what he calls "civic intelligence" in America's schools, David Mathews[16] reminds his reader that the word *idiot* comes to us from the ancient Greeks, who equated privacy with stupidity. Idiots were those who only understood their private worlds and failed to comprehend their connection to the encompassing social order. And how does one avoid becoming or remaining an idiot? Primarily through frequent engagement in the most basic of all political activities—*talk*. It is clear that the main activity of the third place is essential to the containment of idiocy. Mathews writes:

> Good political talk creates and reflects an "enlarged mentality." It is where we recognize the connectedness of things—and our own connectedness. It is where we develop the capacity to understand the structure and functioning of the *whole* social body, which is the capacity to govern

ourselves democratically. . . . Good political talk is also where we discover what is common amidst our differences.

The Habit of Association

Third places play a broader role than that involving the political processes of a community. They have been parent to other forms of community affiliation and association that eventually coexist with them. The right of free assembly, wrote de Tocqueville, "is the most natural privilege of man."[17] How that right is exercised and implemented is not widely understood or appreciated. Free assembly does not begin, as so many writers on the subject seem to assume, with formally organized associations. It does not begin in the Labor Temple. It does not begin in fraternal orders, reading circles, parent-teacher associations, or town halls. Those bodies are drawn from a prior habit of association nurtured in third places.

In eighteenth-century America, the habit of association was engendered in the ordinaries, or the inns and taverns of the towns and along the waysides between the towns. It was fostered in gristmills and gunshops; in printers' offices and blacksmith shops. The old country store provided the daily haunt for many a second-generation settler. To the stores and restaurants that hosted informal association were later added ice cream parlors, pool halls, and the big saloons. Schools and post offices were often the centers of public gathering. Emerging towns and cities were variously rich or poor in such informal village centers. Those that lacked them had little or no social life as a result.

In his work on rural America, Newell Sims pointed to the importance of open and inclusive association as central to the formation of community. The problem, always, was that of overcoming the extreme individualism or associational poverty engendered by the farmers' mode of existence. Sparse settlement and independent economic pursuit discouraged the socializing process and retarded the development of casual association out of which mutual sympathy and the art of conversation arise. Where inclusive third places were absent, "the most vital phase of social life" was missing. "That deficiency . . . is the lack of essential community itself."[18]

Organization, Sims discovered, was an advanced stage in the development of community and "before it can arise and be maintained the substance of community must be present."[19] The habit of association must be well established before people accept offices and submit themselves to the bylaws of formal organizations. The failing, so often, was that although the farmers were much alike in their thinking and even more alike in the practical problems they faced, they tended to live in isolation from one another. "Mutual confidence, sympathies, enthusiasms, purposes, and understandings" were largely left unestablished and a "true group mind through the interplay of individual minds" could not evolve.[20] What was everywhere needed was association of the simplest kind—"that of casual, incidental, informal, and temporary meeting for the purpose of extending and deepening acquaintance."[21]

Rural life hindered the tendency to socialize. It wasn't that the American farmer lacked the social instinct or had any less of it than anyone else. It was that the conditions of rural life and, often, that of local clergymen, operated against its realization in the social habits of the people. In Clermont, Ohio, for example, a survey conducted in 1914 showed the clergy's stand on the following social activities: Sunday baseball (100 percent against), movies (65 percent against), dancing (90 percent against), playing cards (97 percent against), pool halls (85 percent against), and the annual circuses (48 percent against). Only tennis, croquet, and agricultural fairs received general approval.[22]

A similar investigation was sponsored by the Presbyterian church in Marshall and Boone counties in Indiana, in 1911. There it was found that the churches faltered or flourished as a function of the broader social life of the community. Eighty percent of the churches were strenuously opposed to social activities, even those sponsored by the church itself. What social life existed was centered in the villages; in the majority of them, there was little or none. Churches were weakest in membership and enthusiasm in precisely those villages that lacked informal gathering places and there, also, was where saloons of the unsavory kind took advantage of the void in wholesome play, recreation, and informal association. The prevailing attitude of the clergy was that social life would not save anyone. One parson voiced the typical view, declaring that "what the churches need is not social life but more spiritual life."[23]

The authors of that report concluded with some irony that the churches were strongest where the lodges were strongest and that "both are expressions of the same spirit of fraternity and sociability." Two clear conclusions were drawn: "(1) Community social life is necessary to healthy religious life, and (2) If the church is going to succeed it must recognize the social needs of the community and assume its share of the leadership in social activities."[24] Perhaps the strongest indictment that can be made against the Puritanism and Protestantism of developing America is that, far too often, they sought to ensure the life of the church at the expense of the life of the community.

Rural sociologists were uniquely positioned to perceive the essence of community and the basic mechanisms and processes that made it possible. Their insights developed out of a great deal of looking at what was *not* there. What was missing is clearly indicated in one of Galpin's passages: "The first plain necessity is for every farm family to extend its personal acquaintance and connections from its own dooryard out to every home in the neighborhood, and then out to every home in the community. This must be a settled policy for social preservation, a sacred determination, a sort of semi-religious principle in every home, neighborhood, and community. In village and city daily pressure brings contact. In the country, rational procedure must take the place of pressure. This places rural acquaintance-making of a large-scale character on the same high moral level with the great idealism which moves men when bare economic compulsion is wanting."[25]

The habit of association comes easier in the city, but it does come automatically. Affiliations stemming from family membership and employment are not, of themselves, adequate to either community or grass-roots democracy. There must be places in which people can find and sort one another out across the barriers of social difference. There must be places akin to the colonial tavern visited by Alexander Hamilton, which offered, as he later recorded, "a genuine social solvent with a very mixed company of different nations and religions.[26] There were Scots, English, Dutch, Germans, and Irish; there were Roman Catholics, Seventh daymen, Moravians, Anabaptists, and one Jew" gathered in a "great hall stocked with flies." The public house attracted the widest variety of loosely-knit regulars and "from them developed an amazing number of social clubs of a more carefully organized type."[27]

A century later, immigrant Germans fashioned a collective life in Milwaukee in much the same way. Their lager beer gardens attracted and welcomed all who cared to frequent them and out of that initial and informal socializing emerged the reading circles, shooting clubs, choral groups, bands, fraternities, home guards, volunteer fire departments, and other organizations that lent substance and fabric to the life of the community and to the lives of its members. Theirs was a particularly clear and successful example of how a community emerges among individual families. It showed how the habit of association must initially be encouraged on the most inclusive basis possible.

There are many among us who give countless hours of passive attention to the television set, who are content to watch one "L.O.P." (Least Objectionable Program) after another, and who nonetheless insist that time spent in a tavern or coffee shop is wasted. Those who *provide* television programming certainly know better. Time after time, in the face of labor strikes or high unemployment, the television crews find their way into the taverns of Pittsburgh or Detroit to report on the mood and outlook of the working person. The media folk know full well that it is in such places that workers come to understandings about the role of management and government and, as well, the postures of their own unions. It is in such places, more than any others, where the democratic process survives. It is in the local diner, tavern, or coffee shop that those who face common problems find their common ground, give substance and articulation to group sentiment, and offer social support to one another.

An Agency of Control and a Force for Good

Third places, especially those dispensing alcoholic beverages, have rarely been recognized as agencies of social control and forces for good in American community life. Indeed, the more puritanical the society or the greater the push to maximize the productivity of its labor force, the dimmer the view of hanging out and the places that encourage it. With the loss of close community life and the parallel emergence of genuinely corrosive forces, however, the role of the third place may be better appreciated.

In the late 1930s, before *mass society* and *mass media* became commonplace terms, a team of English researchers contemplated the effects of those forces upon community life with concern and apprehension.[28] Their exhaustive study of Worktown, a city of 180,000 in the north of England, was completed just before the war broke out. By that time, it had become clear that local sources of influence over the life of the individual were on the wane. "Is life worth living?" rhetorically asked the authors of the study, not as much concerned with the answer as who supplied it. "A hundred years ago the main answers were in a man's heart, his wife's body, the parish church, or the local pub." But that was a hundred years ago. By 1940, the *Daily Mirror*, football pools, radio, and other forms of mass communication were supplying the answers.

The content of the new influences was suspect and the investigators realized their strength, particularly among the young. It was clear that those profiting from them had little or no concern about the nature of these influences. Communities had suddenly become vulnerable to subtle but highly pervasive forces and their effects on attitude and behavior.

Over many centuries, communities had refined and made highly effective those means of controlling local influences, but means of controlling the newer external ones were almost nonexistent. For example, an enormous amount of red tape might be thrown in the way of a pub owner wanting to stay open later than usual on Coronation Day. Meanwhile, a national newspaper could put a falsified, deliberately slanted and misleading story in the hands of millions and few would ever know. "The newer institutions," wrote the investigators, "are simply out for profits, and they have a pretty well free hand."[29]

The situation is familiar. In the United States, municipal officials can intimidate any tavern owner, close any park, declare establishments undesirable and put them off limits, and clean up their towns as election time approaches. Whether "for real" or "for show," local control over local influences can be effective. But the same officials and agencies who come down hard on local influences stand impotent in the face of the mass media. Programming objectionable to millions of parents continues to be shown on television, while experts dryly and endlessly debate the effect—those experts, too, are remote from the life of the community.

Recently, a woman in our neighborhood interrupted a group of preteen boys playing baseball in the park. The boys were producing a loud and steady stream of the foulest imaginable language, and the lady asked them to cool it. The youngsters had adopted the vocabulary of many premier media entertainers—Robin Williams, Eddie Murphy,

Buddy Hackett, Richard Pryor, George Carlin, and a host of younger wits who are foul-mouthing their way to stardom.

Not only is the mass media free from local control, it also creates a new kind of celebrity that bears little resemblance to the heroes of old. The typical media celebrity rejects responsibility for elevating standards. To the contrary, he or she is more likely than the ordinary soul to get divorced, have accidents, get involved in fights, and use controlled substances while giving the impression that it is chic and sophisticated to do so.

The best counter to the harmful and alien influence that the media too often represents are face-to-face groups in which people participate in discussions of what is important to them and how to preserve it. And here, perhaps, is where the media does its greatest damage. The delivered newspaper and the piped-in voices of radio and television encourage people to stay in their homes. Time spent in isolation is time lost to affiliation. The media is geared to isolated consumers while isolating them all the more.

Having lived with the ubiquitous media for several decades now, we may at least begin to appreciate what remains of local gathering places in a new light. It has not been our inclination to put the tavern or teen hangout in the same league with the church, scout troop, or 4-H club. Earlier they seemed polar opposites. In retrospect, it may be seen that malt shops and corner beer joints were also agencies of control. Though foul language may have been heard in the tavern, it was pretty much confined there by people who would have been repulsed to find it in the media, nor was it as bad as one hears on television today. The mother of the 1930s or 40s may not have approved of her son's spending so much time at the corner drugstore, but she knew where he was, knew that adults were around, and knew nothing "really bad" would happen there. How many mothers would welcome such a place today? The impatient wife, too, was likely to know exactly where her husband was dawdling on the way home from work, but it was usually a little irritation she suffered and nothing worse. Both parents and spouses have become increasingly concerned about keeping tabs on family members as the gulf between the privacy of the home and the public domain widens. The places that remain to attract people outside their homes are rarely local and are removed from the control of family members.

The third place, where it remains, exercises its measure of control in community life. Within its walls and among its membership, moreover, an even more positive effect may be noted. The third place is a force for good. It affords its habitués the opportunity for more decent human relations than prevail outside, and it is their habit to take advantage of that opportunity.

Though the regular company of the third place is composed of peers, *it is* there, as elsewhere, some are more equal than others. Those to whom an extra bit of deference is extended embody the same characteristics. They are not the glad-handers or the joke-tellers or those most dutiful in attendance. They are honest, tactful, and considerate. They can be trusted. In their presence, others know where they stand. They are worth knowing and others are comfortable with them. In my considerable experience with a progression of third places encompassing all age groups, I have found this facet of them to be invariable—the cream rises!

Much of the refreshing appeal of the third place derives from the fact that within its circle, the "right people are put at the top" symbolically. In work organizations, many considerations determine who winds up in positions of leadership. Virtue has little to do with it. *Asperius nihil est humili cum surgit in altum* complained many a Roman ("Nothing is more annoying than a low man raised to a high place"), and as many Americans as Romans have suffered that sting. I doubt that many compare the more esteemed of the third place with those in charge of the workplace, but the differences are no doubt felt and contribute to the mystical lure of the Great Good Place. In the third place, right prevails and whatever hint of a hierarchy exists is predicated upon human decency.

As a black graduate student attending the University of Chicago, Elijah Anderson gained admittance to the inner circle of regulars at Jelly's, a bar and liquor store located in Chicago's south side.[30] The black ghetto bar was not held in high regard, even in its own neighborhood. Yet, to gain admittance to its inner circle one had to be regularly employed, treat other people "right," be of strong character, be of "some 'count" (rather than "no 'count" like a pusher), and be worthwhile to have around. Virtue counted for most just where outsiders would have least suspected. "Their system of values," Anderson concluded, "might be summed up in one word—'decency.' "[31] For the men who made a home-away-from-home there, Jelly's offered a "chance to be." Wrote Anderson:

> Other settings, especially those identified with the wider society, with its strange, impersonal standards and evaluations, are not nearly as important for gaining a sense of personal self-worth as are the settings attended by friends and other neighborhood people.[32]

One of the oft-repeated tragedies of the times is that white urban planners remove these important settings from the neighborhoods of the have-nots of society and can only imagine that they have done the people a favor.

In that society apart afforded by the Great Good Place there exists a link between virtue reflected and deference paid not found in the external world. As a friend of mine once put it: "Each working day I must enter a world of titles and pretensions and concealed motivations. Now I make sure that I visit another kind of world and every day if possible—one of nicknames and the gentle ribbing that deflates pretension. And you know, since I started doing that my days are altogether much more pleasant and 'they' don't get to me half as much as they used to."

Promotion of decency in the third place is not limited to it. The regulars are not likely to do any of those things roundly disapproved at the coffee counter. Many items of proper and improper behavior are reviewed in the countless hours and open agenda of rambling third place conversations. A dim view is taken of people who let their property become an eyesore, of that less-than-human breed who would litter a parking lot with a used paper diaper, of the ethical moron who would look for a pretext to sue somebody in pursuit of unearned and undeserved money, or of someone guilty of not meeting parental duties or responsibilities. One cannot long be a member of the inner circle without having acquired an additional conscience. For those who rely on their third place, the question, "What would the guys think about this?" attends every ethical and moral decision that must be made, large or small, and the decisions are made more clearly and favorably because of it.

Third places are a force for decency both within and beyond the happy groups who gather at them. They bring out the best in people as though it were a requirement of belonging. Since those gathered may have a beer in hand or may appear to be "escaping" work and family duties at a coffee counter, however, the good is easily overlooked—even by the individuals involved. The third place promotes more decency without proclaiming it than many organizations that publicly claim to be the embodiment of the virtues.

Fun with the Lid Kept on

I recently chatted with a practicing psychiatrist all too familiar with wife-beating. He lamented the decline of the neighborhood tavern in which he felt men could "let off steam" and not have to "take everything out on their wives." He was convinced that much of the irrational aggression and violence of the wife-beater is due to the lack of safety valves such as the lively tavern once offered to a far greater proportion of the population than it does today.

My suspicion is that a good tavern keeps "steam" from building up more than it provides a means to "blow it off," but there seems ample evidence to support both views. The ethnologist is likely to argue that there is a need to "let off steam" and to do so collectively. Attention to the collective rituals among the world's many cultures soon reveals the prevalence of all manner of wanton reveling. Celebrations are institutionalized in the form of feasts, festivals, junkets, religious holidays, saturnalian binges, organized drinking bouts—even licentious orgies, in some instances.

It is characteristic of such events that everyday norms and decorum are ignored; that the spirit of revelry affects all and not just the few; that the madness is manifest in public and not privately, and not casually, but with a serious intensity. Further, indications are that such behavior serves a purpose.

The sustaining habits and morals of a society are not endangered by these mad periods. Quite the opposite. The members of the community, in associating this behavior with special occasions, are mindful of the contrast between it and the decorum to be observed at other times. Social systems are also moral systems, which control, repress, and to a degree, oppress their members. The feast or holiday allows relief from normal restraints while at the same time reinforcing their observance generally. What is permitted in revelry is not permitted at other times.

Also, far more than the routines of daily life, the collective revelry of festival periods is an expression of social cohesion. As indulgences climb, so does the feeling of belonging to a community. It is never so great to be Irish as on St. Patrick's Day. How many among us "help" the Irish celebrate because our own traditions of revelry have been lost?

In simpler and more unified societies, people engage in revelry according to a well-established calendar, and they revel together. All anticipate such events and take part in them. No one considers participation optional. But in the complex industrial society people follow individual schedules. They work different shifts, observe different holidays, and take vacations at different times. National holidays are passively observed by many and are largely ignored by many others. In the United States, the Christmas–New Year period apparently produces as much depression as great, good fun. If people "take to the streets," it is with their credit cards and not their horns and flasks.

Amid the sociological individualism of industrial societies, people are left to celebrate largely on their own. While a small percentage are free to revel at any time, the great majority go about their everyday routines. The traditions that once set the occasions, sites, and limits of celebrations have faded. Contemporary reveling does not often serve the functions of unifying and integrating community and society, nor does it reinforce normative behavior. All that remains is a psychological urge to "bust loose" now and then.

We see this antisocial remnant of what had been functional and solidifying revelry in the fighting and other hell-raising typical in many bars and cabarets. We see it in the slam-dancing done to punk rock. We see it, even, in the form of ghetto riots, which offer an opportunity to "let loose" amid the grinding boredom of poverty in the American city. We see it growing in the nation's sport arenas, where there is cause for alarm in the growing propensity to violence. By the late 1970s, the Red Sox organization found it necessary to employ some twenty football players to circulate among the fans and either "settle down" the more troublesome ones or physically eject them from the park, and those men are kept busy.[33]

People will act up and act out whether or not their towns and cities provide ritualized occasions for it; the less revelry is ritualized, the more unpredictable and dangerous it becomes. The imperative is to contain such behavior, and in so doing, restore its positive functions. Can the third place meet this imperative, as our psychiatrist friend believed? To some extent it does, and to a much larger extent it would if third places were more numerous, more accessible, and better integrated into American life.

A good example of the kind of third place well designed for revelry was the old-fashioned, all-male, beer-only taverns generously scattered throughout Canada before the brasseries began offering quieter, more genteel competition. The taverns combined immodest beer consumption with loud conversation. Most of the seating was at large tables, where noisy arguments, yelling, and shouting were encouraged. These were places men went to "whoop it up." But there were clearly understood limits. The patrons remained seated. They were not allowed along the bar. All ordering was through male waiters old enough to have been around and big enough to play the bouncer. Profanity was not allowed. Drunks were promptly evicted. The crowd was local and the individuals who comprised it reveled in familiar company, providing additional measure of control that friends can exercise. There were no gimmicks to draw customers. Beer and boisterousness, the one lending to the other, were the simple but adequate ingredients in the revelry of traditional Canadian beer taverns.

In comparison with contemporary U.S. taverns and their patrons, the Canadians stayed longer, drank more, and "lived it up" with greater gusto—but they also caused less trouble. Their revelry was controlled. The need to let off steam was satisfied within set limits, which were understood and appreciated and did not dampen the reveler's spirits.

The average third place hardly matches the traditional Canadian tavern in boisterousness. However, the volume of vocal output is but one among many ingredients in revelry, and all third places offer many of the others. All lend the strength of numbers. All allow an escape from routine within a space permitting relaxation and gaiety. The lower intensity of celebration is compensated for by the frequency with which it is indulged; what most third places lack in madness, they make up for in being part of the rhythm of daily life. Best of all, the third place lends itself well to modern urban life. It fits in with the scheduled life and the compartmentalization of space according to activity or function.

Outposts on the Public Domain

In the United States we are losing control over the public domain and forfeiting many of its uses. Each new "Age of Confinement," as Grady Clay puts it, is a matter of intentional policy, and these policies have as effectively removed third places from the public domain as they have beggars, peddlers, tramps, kids, old people, strollers, and loungers.[34] This is a crucial matter and one given serious attention in the final section of this book. Here, I would like simply to suggest the importance of third places in securing the public domain for the use and enjoyment of decent people.

One of the clear consequences of policies antagonistic to the social and recreational use of the urban public domain is the loss of the monitoring function performed by responsible and law-abiding citizens. It is the ordinary citizen who tips the balance toward a safe public domain for the policing agencies of a free society are not adequate to the task. It is the substantial numbers of average people who provide the "natural surveillance" necessary to the control of street life.[35] The sidewalk cafés or *terrasses* of Paris are, thus, not only primary centers of the average Parisian's enjoyment of informal public life, they also represent some ten thousand outposts at which millions of ordinary people keep unconscious vigil even while enjoying their city.

Americans, generally, have been conditioned to an attitude toward public space and places that says, "This is not mine. I have no responsibility for this. The city pays people to take care of this." The attitude corresponds with the dearth of amenities now characterizing our public domain generally. Those with a third place out there somewhere, however, take a different view. They expect to be able to walk to and from their place or park their cars nearby and not worry about them. They expect their haunt and its environs to be safe and reasonably well kept. An unsavory incident at or near the establishment will have its patrons up in arms and demanding remedy. Further, as Oscar Newman points out, the more people define an area as theirs, the more active they become in monitoring what goes on in and around it. Out of frequent visits and the familiarity resulting from them, people develop a sense of what is normal behavior for an area and, knowing what to expect, they more actively enforce those norms themselves.[36] Those who imagine that a neighborhood is improved by ridding it of an old-time diner or corner tavern would do well to recognize that several dozen policemen's aides are lost with it.

An Accurate Representation?

Experiences with previous audiences suggest that a few essential matters regarding the third place be made as clear as possible. I have admitted my bias—I am *for* the third place; I am convinced that the association met within is good for society and individuals. This bias is bound to arouse some healthy skepticism, particularly among those who do not have a third place. At this point, the generic description of the features and virtues of the third place has been completed and qualifications are now in order.

I am sometimes accused of presenting a sanitized version of the third place. A few critics have reminded me that Adolf Hitler's use of the beer hall had little to do with warmth and companionship, and that neighborhood taverns have abetted the antidemocratic operation of big city political machines such as Tammany Hall.

At the risk of sounding disingenuous, I would insist that any third place is pretty much as I've described it, or it is not a third place. The description presented in the initial chapters is not derived from speculation. It is built from observations, my own and those of others. Thus, it is not sanitized from life but based on careful observation of it.

Certainly, the characterization does not fit the majority of establishments that otherwise *might* have become third places. Looking again to taverns, as the skeptic usually does, I would be the first to suggest that the average one is more likely *not* to be a third place than to be one. Many unwholesome things may attract people to such places. What distinguishes the third place is that decency and good cheer consistently prevail. The regulars know it and this is what brings them back.

Two additional points should be clarified. The third place is not a universal remedy for all social and personal ills, nor will the kind of association it offers appeal to everyone. As to the positive consequences of third place association to the individual and communal life, I have been conservative, having limited discussion to benefits that are direct and rather easily observed once inside the world of the third place.

As to the limited appeal of the third place, even in societies like France and England, which give the third place the status it deserves, not everyone flocks to it. Only slightly more than half of the men in those countries visit the café or pub with any regularity.[37] In small town America, where everybody "knows everybody" and third places are accessible to all, many do not frequent them. It is probably good that some stay away. Third place association is not a matter of sitting around and wasting time, as its critics often like to imagine. There must be a fondness for other people that extends beyond the confines of one's social kind and skill at conversation. The addition of dour-faced people who couldn't contribute and who'd rather be elsewhere would hardly improve things.

As in the best of times and the best of places, the third place should simply be an option. Our urban topography presently favors those who prefer to be alone, to stay in their homes, or to restrict their outings to relatively exclusive settings. It is the adventuresome, gregarious, and "clubbable" types who are being short-changed by the course urban development has taken in our society. And these are the people upon whom some semblance of a community life most depends.

PART II

CHAPTER 5

The German-American Lager Beer Gardens

"SOCIAL LIFE TODAY," wrote the Wisconsin historian Fred Holmes, "offers few meeting places like the old German saloon. Compared with it, the modern tavern is an arrogant pretender."[1] In their saloons and even more so in their lager beer gardens, the immigrants from Germany set an example of controlling the use of the alcoholic beverage and literally building communities around its tempered use. Our history records no finer example of the successful third place than the German-American lager beer garden. In reflecting upon it, I recall that the man who wrote that "nothing is more hopeless than a scheme of merriment" was an Englishman and not a German.[2] The German immigrant had the formula for merriment. It was so successful that it could be implemented daily without danger, disruption, or risk of failure.

The character of the lager beer garden grew out of a combination of factors. Among these, the demographics of immigration played an important part. German immigration, particularly after 1840, was as diverse as it was extensive. It was not dominated by a laboring class or any other social strata. Many "walks of life" had to be incorporated and unified into the communities established in the new land. At their basic, informal, and most pervasive levels, the sociable gathering places of these new Americans were *inclusive*.

The old-world traditions that the immigrants brought with them also played a vital role. In the main, they were those of a broad, urban middle class brought up in the enlightenment cities of Germany—a tradition with rich patterns of associational life. The lager beer garden was imported, as were the *turnen* or gymnastic clubs, shooting clubs, singing societies, chess clubs, drama clubs, fraternities, intellectual, cultural, and educational societies, and all manner of voluntary associations.

Beyond the chemistry inherent in the flow of immigrants and the traditions they brought with them were two important aspects of the life-view of the Germans that governed their collective behavior. These were a passion for order and the realization that informal socializing lay at the base of a viable community life. The lager beer garden became the parent form of association out of which the more formally organized activities would emerge. In order for the beer garden to play this important role, it had to have a unifying effect and never a disruptive one. It is not surprising, then, that the typical Yankee saloon left a great deal to be desired.

A German immigrant to Milwaukee described the latter in a letter to relatives in the Old Country written in 1846: "You can't stand around," he complained, "you get neither a bench nor chair, just drink your schnapps and then go."[3] There were other things amiss. The Yankees had the dangerous habit of buying rounds or treating. Treating may have posed a threat to the frugal German's pocketbook, but more than that, it threatened order. It undermined control over alcoholic intake, for among those buying rounds for one another it is the fastest drinker who sets the pace. All others are pressed to drink at a rate exceeding their personal inclinations. Against this habit, the Germans would establish the "Dutch treat" or the habit of each paying for his own beer and ordering at a pace controlled by the individual drinker.

In the Yankee saloon, the drinks were too strong. The English and Welsh had established the first breweries, but their products were much too potent. In the Irish saloons whiskey was the staple, behavior was rough, and those were anything but family places. Wherever the Germans settled in number and the locale was suitable for the growing of hops, there emerged German breweries and, shortly thereafter, a profusion of German saloons and lager beer gardens. Against the romanticized notion that the Germans, above all, demand fine-tasting beer is the historic fact that they paid even more attention to its alcoholic content.

That the Germans valued reduced potency above taste was amply attested to by Junius Browne, who wrote of the lager beer gardens in New York City in the 1870s: "The question, 'Will lager beer intoxicate?' first arose, I believe, on this island, and, very naturally, too, considering the quality of the manufactured article. I have sometimes wondered, however, could there be any question about it, so inferior in every respect is the beer made and sold in the Metropolis. It is un-doubtedly the worst in the United States—weak, insipid, unwhole-some, and unpalatable; but incapable of intoxication, I should judge, even if a man could hold enough to float the Dunderberg. It is impossi-ble to get a good glass of beer in New York, and persons who have not drunk it in the West have no idea what poor stuff is here called by the name."[4]

Alvin Harlow's account of Cincinnati during the same period sug-gests that the quality of the beer improved as one went west: "Some old-timers will tell you that John Hauch brewed the best beer in Cincinnati in the long ago, and he was as particular as any vintner of Rheims or Epernay as to his processes and handling. Along with many other connoisseurs, he shook his head when beer began to be bottled in the '70s; beer should always be kept in wood. He demanded that saloonkeepers who handled his beer should keep it in cellar coolness and handle it gently. His drivers were not permitted to drag a keg off the wagon and let it thump down on a pad on the sidewalk; it must be lifted carefully and lowered into the cellar with equal care."[5]

The Germans clearly held standards of taste with respect to their national beverage. The sorry state of early New York beer, drunk under the pretense that it was good, as Browne suggested, serves only to show the greater importance they attached to temperance in drinking. Bad as early New York beer might have been, they would not turn to the "strong stuff." The attitude was exemplified in Harlow's account of the goings-on during Cincinnati's fest of the Sangerbund in the summer of 1856: "In the afternoon we noticed a few cases of exhilaration, but none of that brutal intoxication which is too common in large gatherings of the Anglo-Saxon race. The comparatively unstimulating beverages in which they indulge has something to do with this, but the practice of taking all ages and sexes to these meetings has more. It should be said that nothing stronger than beer might be sold at German outings. Once, when an outsider tried stealthily to purvey hard liquor, his bottles were seized and broken by the managers."[6]

The lessons on drinking had been learned and refined into tradition in the Old Country and their importance was evident to the objective traveler. One such was the Englishwoman Violet Hunt, who contrasted public drinking establishments in Germany with those of her native England around the turn of the century. Her descriptions abundantly suggest what the German-Americans sought to establish across the Atlantic: "on a certain summer afternoon a troop of orderly, sober, decent, suave, and gentle persons of all ages and sexes were sitting on freshly-raked gravel, at little tables covered all with red-chequered table-cloths and coffee-cups and glasses on them. Their children sat beside them, and their dogs crouched at their feet or circulated about the feet of other clients. Birds hopped about under the tables, picking up crumbs which these gentle people from time to time cast to them. There they sat, stolidly, composedly, as if butter wouldn't melt in their mouths, gulping down grosse Hellers and kleiner Dunklers, and more and more of them, with no diminution of their holy calm. Their dogs did not quarrel, the birds still hopped about their toes in utter confidence; everyone was sure that no chairs would be hurriedly pushed aside or angry words flout the sweet air they were taking in, amid smoke of cigars or pipes, and the soft breath of human converse. And discreet wives, with their children of all ages to think about, kept an eye on the sun and saw that it was declining. When they thought it was time, they folded up their fancy work, wrapped up the remainder of their buns, shook the crumbs off their children's bibs and folded them up likewise, and turned their eyes westward to where the gilded spires of Hildesheim seem to point them to their homes. Then men got up and shook themselves, and paid. There was in them plenty of beer, but not the least bit of harm in the world."[7]

Ms. Hunt, after observing this demonstration of humankind's mastery over demon drink, leapt to the announcement that it couldn't happen in England. There, she said, such ugly sights and sounds would follow two hours of drinking that the government would find justification for barring children from such places. In her native England, with all its "strenuous temperance and protective liquor laws" there were no places comparable to the German beer garden: "Any place of call in England which permitted itself to be as attractive as any of these would undoubtedly lose its license. Government morality would soon be on its hind legs at once lest vice should masquerade as health, joy as beauty. It carefully penalizes joy and merry-making by the enforcement of due ugliness in every place where this habit is permitted to be indulged."[8]

Much of the difference, Ms. Hunt insisted, was due to the drink: "German beer is not in the least like, in strength, in quality, or maturing, to the stuff which notoriously wrecks the Englishman's peace of mind, his pocket, and his home. It is not heady, it is diluted; it is not drugged or doctored, and it is kept properly."[9]

Junius Browne also observed the German festive tradition in all its implications from his vantage points among the innumerable lager beer gardens of old New York: "The drinking of the Germans . . . is free from the vices of Americans. The Germans indulge in their lager rationally, even when they seem to carry indulgence to excess. They do not squander their means; they do not waste their time; they do not quarrel; they do not fight; they do not ruin their own hopes and the happiness of those who love them, as do we of hotter blood, finer fibre, and intenser organism. They take lager as we do oxygen into our lungs—appearing to live and thrive upon it. Beer is one of the social virtues; Gambrinus a patron saint of every family—the protecting deity of every well-regulated household. The Germans combine domesticity with their dissipation—it is that to them literally—taking with them to the saloon or garden their wives and sisters and sweethearts, often their children, who are a check to any excesses or impropriety, and with whom they depart at a seemly hour, overflowing with beer and *bonhommie*, possessed of those two indispensables of peace— an easy mind and a perfect digestion."[10]

The passion for order conquered alcohol and its use. Yet, for the saloon and beer garden to become an integral part of community life, *cost* also had to be controlled. The Yankee proprietor and host has always had a keen sense of his fellow citizen's needs for release and diversion and had a knack for capitalizing on it. The German-American, on the other hand, demanded public places where costs were low and loitering and idleness were encouraged. Only if those conditions obtained could the saloon and beer garden become the universal gathering places of the citizenry.

The success of the German-American places caught Browne's attention as he observed New York's Bowery area in its finer days: "With all their industry, and economy, and thrift, the Germans find ample leisure to enjoy themselves, and at little cost. Their pleasures are never expensive. They can obtain more for $1 than an American for $10, and can, and do, grow rich upon what our people throw away."[11] German effectiveness in holding down the cost of public enjoyment was also noted by Holmes in the Milwaukee scene: "Throughout the Gay Nineties beer was cheap, the tax on it being negligible. Indeed, it was not until 1944 that the five-cent glass of beer became scarce in Milwaukee. During the late nineties there were four saloons on the southwest corner of State and Third Streets which sold two beers for a nickel and provided an elaborate free lunch of roast beef, baked ham, sausage, baked beans, vegetables, salads, bread and butter, and other appetizing foods. Two men with but a nickel between them could each enjoy a substantial meal and a mammoth beer."[12] Holmes also pointed to the larger implications: "The early Poor Man's Club solved an important social-economic problem. In a time when capital was needed for the building of homes and the promotion of commercial and industrial activities, it provided recreation and social intercourse for almost nothing."[13]

The German immigrants well understood that informal public gathering places were too important to the life of the community to cripple them by prohibitive pricing. Kathleen Conzen's accounts of Milwaukee's establishments are similar to those of Holmes: "By 1860 the best of Milwaukee's taverns offered beer that was both good and cheap, food which was often free, stimulating conversation, music, perhaps a singing host. . . . The first of Milwaukee's many outdoor beer gardens opened on the northeast side near the river in the summer of 1843. It offered 'well-cultivated flowers, extensive promenades, rustic bowers, and a beautiful view from Tivoli Hill,' as well as a German brass band providing music one afternoon and evening a week, all for a 25¢ admission fee."[14]

Nowadays, the term *lese majesty*, or treason, invokes an image of someone selling secrets to the Russians. German-American immigrants, however, had a much keener and broader sense of it. To them, the manager who overcharged for a public concert or the "roughs" who destroyed a picnic by fighting were engaging in treason as well. Anything that threatened the tranquility and full enjoyment of community life alerted their sensibilities. To them, the social order declined, as Richard O'Connor astutely observed, not by major rifts at its core, but by disorders tolerated at the fringes.[15] To them, the enemy spy and the ticket scalper were of the same ilk. A low and permissive cost for the public consumption of food, drink, and music (primarily) was essential to community and the establishment of solid relations with neighbors.

Orderly behavior and minimal expense were crucial to the ultimate inclusiveness and accommodation of the beer gardens. Everyone had to be allowed to participate lest those places fail in their purpose. The lager beer gardens were there for the children, women, and non-Germans also, and social class was largely forgotten. What was strictly German or could not be shared with outsiders was protected within the family. As Richard O'Connor put it: "In their homes, the Germans tended to keep the family circle, but when the bungs were tapped out and the wine uncorked all nationalities were invited to join in the singing, dancing, drinking, and feasting."[16]

In the Atlantic Garden, which had been one of New York's most celebrated beer gardens, inclusiveness was the essence. Browne reports: "The Atlantic is the most cosmopolitan place of entertainment in the City; for, though the greater part of its patrons are Germans, every other nationality is represented there. French, Irish, Spaniards, Italians, Portuguese, even Chinamen and Indians, may be seen through the violet atmosphere of the famous Atlantic. . . ."[17] The Atlantic was a grand pavilion capable of holding twenty-five hundred people. It was the best the immigrant Germans could offer—and they offered it to one and all.

Inclusiveness was central to the coveted atmosphere of the lager beer garden. It was a garden in a double sense—in addition to the greenery, human relationships and goodwill were cultivated. The atmosphere in which this is accomplished most effectively has a name well understood in the German language. It is *Gemütlichkeit*. What is *Gemütlich* is warm and friendly. It is cozy and inviting. Of all the failings of the Yankee saloon, its lack of *Gemütlichkeit* was undoubtedly the greatest. Such places were for the brawlers and those determined to get drunk, but not for a man and his family nor for those who measured their enjoyment by the pleasure on others' faces.

True *Gemütlichkeit*, an atmosphere in which community and neighborliness is realized and celebrated, could not be based upon exclusion. It could not shut out ages, sexes, classes, or nationalities. By its nature, it must include them and, this above all, the lager beer gardens managed. A German in Cincinnati, for example, might prosper and buy a house "up on the hill," but, as Harlow records: "such people did not disassociate themselves from their fellow countrymen in the Trans-Rhenish area, as downtown newspapers liked to call it; they returned there to the beer halls and restaurants, the numerous clubs and societies—political, literary, musical, athletic—for their relaxation and exercise."[18]

Harlow also records an incident in which a visiting professor from Harvard was introduced to beer garden *Gemütlichkeit* by a friend: "With Escher, I found my way to the society of Germans in Cincinnati, a most interesting group of men, from whom I had much enlargement. Some of the ablest of these men were accustomed to meet at a beer hall in the part of town north of the canal. There were many of these men of quality. . . . These were strong men; their talk made a great impression on me and their personal quality did much to lift me to a higher level of ideals than any of our people supplied."[19]

The frequent discovery of native Americans that there were those in their midst who could create places in which the divisions of the mundane world were overcome was indeed heady stuff. Harlow quotes a Cincinnati reporter who had been invited to a party given by the German Workman's Society in 1869: "The fellowship was contagious; everybody was affected by it. We must not omit the children, from babies up to men in second childhood. Little girls, as many as wanted to dance among the elders, looked for all the world like grown people seen through a spy-glass with the big end to the eye. Everybody was intent upon making everybody else as happy as could be. We commend this example to other people, not better, but more pretentious."[20]

Another newspaper man was present at a German concert and wrote of the socializing that followed: "The air is comforting with the fragrance of hops, coffee, and tobacco. Combined with the music of Suppe and Strauss it induces a benign expansiveness in which one feels like taking the world to one's bosom, even including Old Petrus Grimm, who sits alone at a table with his dour eyes fastened on his beer mug. Petrus is the neighborhood bear, and everybody blames his bitterness on a blighted troth in the Old Country, though it is more likely due to liver and gout."[21]

The inclusiveness at the core of *Gemütlichkeit* was duly noted by Fred Holmes, who sought to correct the error made when people referred to

Wisconsin's lager beer saloons as "poor man's clubs": "the term Poor Man's Club is something of a misnomer, for the saloon attracted not only the daily worker, but his employer and the business and professional men of the community, many of whom were men with wealth. What the term implied, of course, was that the saloon's clientele was not drawn from the highbrow or social-register class. . . . The Poor Man's Club was born of men's desire, conscious or unconscious, for friendly relations with their neighbors. It existed without formal organization, recorded membership, officers, or funds for planned activities. No class cleavages were recognized, characteristic as these were of German society . . . in the popular gathering places—the Schlitz Palm Garden, Schlitz Park, the Milwaukee Garden, Heiser's—the measuring stick of wealth and family prestige was not applied. Rich and poor, artist and laborer, scholar and illiterate all mingled as a single family united by the bonds of homeland and community tastes."[22]

The inclusive or "leveling" character of the lager beer garden was most obvious in the more palatial establishments. Holmes provides a description of the world-famous Schlitz Palm Garden, the most notable indoor "palm gardens."[23] Boasting high, vaulted ceilings, stained-glass windows, rich oil paintings, a pipe organ, and lush palms throughout, it, too, was a "poor man's club." It was policy to make the poor feel as welcome as the rich; social distinctions were not compatible with *Gemütlichkeit*.

The splendor of the place and the quality of the entertainment it provided were not seen as cause for raising prices. Thirty to fifty barrels of beer were dispensed at five cents a glass daily, and free lunches, as in any other saloon in Milwaukee at that time, were standard fare. Concerts were conducted on Sunday and everyone was welcome.[24]

The mixing of nationalities, presence of women, comingling of the rich and poor, and frequent instances in which three generations had fun together at the same time and in the same place—these were the more striking signs of inclusiveness. There are other dimensions of inclusiveness, however, and these include the availability of public gathering places and the general frequency of their use. On both counts, the phenomenon of the lager beer garden was extensive.

Browne estimated that Manhattan alone had three to four thousand lager beer gardens, "not to mention their superabundance in Jersey-

City, Hoboken, Brooklyn, Hudson-City, Weehawken, and every other point within easy striking distance of the Metropolis by rail and steam."[25] And the pattern of profuse growth was similar in Buffalo, Cincinnati, Milwaukee (dubbed the Haupstadt of *Gemütlichkeit*), St. Louis, Chicago, and outer San Francisco.

As Browne observed: "These establishments are of all sizes and kinds, from the little hole in the corner, with one table and two chairs, to such extensive concerns as the Atlantic Garden, in the Bowery, and Hamilton and Lyon Parks, in the vicinity of Harlem."[26]

A lager beer garden differs from a saloon in that the latter has a lengthy bar or bar-counter, which constitutes its focal point of sociable gathering, while in the former tables and chairs are prominent. The term *garden* came into vogue because of the German preference for the summertime version of the beer-drinking institution. Beer, apparently, "went best" with music and fresh air. In many respects, the colossal structures such as the German Winter Garden and the Atlantic Garden were attempts to capture the expansiveness of the out-of-doors park in the cold of winter. In the majority of places, perhaps, reality strained the concept of a garden. In surveying the range of places that went by the name in nineteenth-century New York, Browne concluded that "The difference between a lager-beer saloon and a lager-beer garden among our German fellow citizens is very slight; the garden, for the most part, being a creation of the brain. To the Teutonic fancy, a hole in the roof, a fir-tree in a tub, and a sickly vine or two in a box, creeping feebly upward unto death, constitute a garden."[27]

The large and elegant gardens of the day may be viewed as the precursors of America's contemporary theme parks. Atlantic Garden had, for example, an enormous front bar and many smaller ones. But it also contained a shooting gallery, billiards rooms, bowling alleys, an orchestrion which played daily, and multiple bands which played in the evenings. Many people attended nightly. The outdoor parks of Milwaukee supplied a similar diversity of entertainment. These offered many pavilions and picnic areas, carousels, and long, open-air tables scattered everywhere. Pabst Park sported a fifteen-hundred-foot roller coaster, a Katzenjammer Fun Palace, Wild West shows, and daily concerts during the summer season. Schlitz Park occupied eight acres atop a local Milwaukee hill and had a large pagoda from which visitors could see the entire city. It offered a concert hall with a capacity of five thousand, a menagerie, winter dance hall, bowling alleys, and a large restaurant. Interspersed throughout were shady walks, fountains, and flower beds. At night, thirty-two electric lights, five hundred colored glass globes, and thousands of gas flames lent "grand splendor" to the whole place.[28] Admittance was usually twenty-five cents, which was not a small amount of money for many in those days. The fee was necessary to compensate for the large number of freeloaders those parks attracted.

Many nations of the Old World contributed large numbers to the immigrant flow that peopled the United States, but few among the diverse nationalities actively promoted forms of sociable ethnic mixing essential to the democratic "melting pot." The Jews were consistent antiassimilationists, and the Greeks confined public socializing largely to their own coffee shops. The Scandinavians, Italians, and Poles catered to their own kind, and only the Irish and Germans emerged as "universalists," along with some older Americans no longer reliant upon ethnic ties.[29] The difference between the Irish bar and the German beer garden as focal points of public gathering and interethnic mixing, however, was almost literally the difference between day and night. Whereas "the Irish bar tended to be dimly illuminated, the lighting in the German place was as bright as daylight," and the "German saloon was as much a family institution as the Irish bar was a man's world."[30] Though unescorted women were not welcome in the German places, the entire family was, children included. German saloons and beer gardens typically escaped the chronic American indictment against the barroom. Extremely little crime was associated with them. In fact, German saloonkeepers were often trusted above banks for the safekeeping of one's savings. Even its critics had to admit that the German saloon had a stabilizing influence on the family.

Yet it was the Irish model that eventually prevailed. America adapted itself only to the German national beverage; it kept the beer and dropped most of the amenities with which the Germans had surrounded it. The nation never seemed able to allow the concept of a *good* tavern, and people who cannot envisage good taverns are doomed to have lesser ones.

Perhaps the most irksome aspect of lager beer gardens and the German saloons was that they were most appreciated, enjoyed, and populated on Sundays. From the culture of the enlightenment cities,

the German immigrants brought with them the institution of the
"Continental" Sunday. Germans were accustomed to finding their relaxation and the restoration of their soul in the form of picnic outings,
concerts, *scheutzen fests*, gymnastics, choral singing and, above all, the
rich and boisterous association afforded by the lager beer establishments. The serenity of the German's life-style depended in large measure upon such forms of relaxation; the German riots, such as occurred
in Chicago, stemmed from attempts to shut down typical Sunday
activities. Unfortunately, the dominant modes of religious thought in
America imposed idleness apart from work, particularly on Sundays.

A German newspaper editor, Karl Griesinger, spent several years in
America during those critical times. He was appalled by the boredom
and idleness of the Yankee Sundays and discerned a simple economic
motive beneath all the righteous ranting about "keeping the Sabbath."
American churches were not built by government or any form of
taxation. They depended upon voluntary giving. Giving, in turn,
depended upon attendance and membership. Average preachers were
fighting for their lives as well as for God. Anything that competed with
the church, particularly on Sundays, was threatening not only to the
"kingdom" but also to the poor preacher's livelihood.[31]

Griesinger's analysis was as clear as it was singular: "Clergymen in
America must then defend themselves to the last, like other businessmen; they must meet competition and build up a trade, and it's their
own fault if their income is not large enough. Now is it clear why
heaven and hell are moved to drive the people to the churches, and why
attendance is more common here than anywhere else in the world? It is
an element of high fashion and good manners, and woe unto him who
takes a stand against manners and fashion. Better to commit a slight
forgery than to miss a Sunday in church.

"But then, what else could the Americans do on the sacred Sunday?
Boredom alone would bring them there! 'Six days shalt thou labor and
on the seventh shalt thou rest.' Reasonable men have understood this to
mean that Sunday should be a day for the relaxation of body and soul.
The Americans have arranged matters, however, so that the rest of
Sunday is the rest of the tomb. And they have enacted laws that make
this arrangement compulsory for all.

"On Sunday no train moves, except for the most essential official
business; no omnibus is in service, no steamer when it possibly can

help it. All business places are closed, and restaurants may not open under threat of severe penalties. A gravelike quiet must prevail, says the law, and you may buy neither bread, nor milk, nor cigars, without violating the law. Theaters, bowling alleys, pleasant excursions—God keep you from ever dreaming such things! Be grateful that you are allowed in winter to build a fire and cook a warm supper. People who make such laws must be half crazy!"[32]

History, Griesinger would have been pleased to know, bore him out. Most American churches now sponsor sociable activities for the same reason they once prohibited them, even on Sunday! It is difficult to judge the ultimate effect on the character of Americans of religious views that denied the opportunity to balance competitive relations with those allowing a spirited and joyful association with their fellow creatures. German-Americans, however, held fast against the conditions that produced the dourness of the typical Yankee. They did so, at least, until time ran out. Eventually the combination of W.C.T.U. morality, the bigotry of the Know Nothing party, two wars with Germany, and the willingness of German-Americans to assimilate relegated the lager beer garden and the life-style built around it to the past.

It is disheartening to observe the hollow forms and shoddy imitations of the lager beer garden *Gemütlichkeit*, which are about all that remain today. Some years back, we visited a Midwestern theme park. After paying an immodest parking fee, we were charged nine dollars each for the adults in the party and eight dollars for each child. Inasmuch as there was virtually nothing there for adults, it might have been appropriate to let them in free and give them a beer on the house for the trouble they had taken to transport the children to the park. The most common activity in the park is standing in line; everybody spends most of their time doing that. The beer garden offers one brand only; it's served in waxed-paper cups and is overpriced. On what appeared to be only a moderately busy day, we stood in line for half an hour to get our choice of a bratwurst or a hot dog. People don't go there nightly, as was the case with lager beer gardens of old. One visit per summer is enough for some; one every five years is adequate for others. But for many, I suspect, one visit in a lifetime is more than enough.

A few summers ago, an annual lodge picnic was held in one of the parks of a small city. It was spirited and well attended. Many who had been there said they had a great time, and they talked about it for days, even weeks, afterward. Within the context of that wonderful time, however, several things occurred that might give pause. There were injuries incurred during a softball game, including two broken bones. There were wives upset about the attention their husbands paid to other women. There were husbands upset about wives who reciprocated. For these and other reasons, many couples were not on good terms for quite awhile afterward. There were many bad hangovers the day following the picnic. Equipment and personal possessions were broken or lost. The food and drink consumed ran up a formidable bill.

One may surmise that those folks weren't civilized, or contrarily, that they had a pretty good time. It may appear that they were overdue for such an outing and, understandably, went overboard when the chance for celebration finally came. Those are speculations, but what is clear beyond speculation is that a gathering *of that kind* cannot take place often. The bodies can't afford it. The pocketbooks can't afford it. The marriages can't afford it. By way of contrast, the controlled and inexpensive revelry of the lager beer gardens—all those good times at little expense and no disruption—meant that they could be indulged frequently. And they were. The German-Americans, in addition to inventing innumerable excuses for their own fests, helped the Italians honor Orsini with parade and feast and made a bigger deal of Washington's Birthday and the Fourth of July than the native Yankee.

In Dixie, there's a small community originally settled by German-American farmers. In recent years, and with the uncritical assistance of area newspapers, the locals have been sponsoring a sausage festival. Thousands descend upon the little hamlet, beckoned by a nostalgic spirit, to enjoy an old-style German fest. What sounds from afar like a little German band is, alas, a record played over and over through a public address system. There is no band and there are no costumes. The central area of the celebration is taken up for the most part with booths and tables at which locals offer garage sale items at retail store prices. Among them are few real collectibles and absolutely no deals. Center-stage is dominated by those too poor or timid to become genuine retailers and who hope to peddle their junk to those in a festive mood.

Local craft-hobbiests hawk amateurish pottery, useless objects made of wood and glistening with heavy layers of epoxy, and garish crochet work. There is a petting zoo for the children. Fortunately, as it turns out, it is not free, and the cost of admission is sufficient to keep many children away. Later in the afternoon and early evening, many parents take their children for medical attention for the bites by the fleas, lice, and ticks, which cover the animals.

The beer is not easy to get. One stands in line for tickets and then in another line to trade the tickets in for beer. The beer is served in waxed cups, and the prices are inflated. The food is passable but short of "lip smackin'." To get a plate of it, one stands in line for nearly an hour. All along the streets leading to the festival area are garage and yard sales. Where once small-town America took pride in playing host at its annual celebrations, there is now a new attitude. An ever-increasing number of townsfolk preoccupy themselves with how to get their share of the money involved.

The assessment of this sausage festival would be misleading if I failed to point out that it continues to be a success in terms of its repeated ability to draw crowds. Why? Several factors seem to account for the unmerited popularity of the festival. Most of the visitors, and particularly those under fifty years of age, have only those powers of discernment that experience has provided. Bluntly put, they have not witnessed better community festivities organized at the grass-roots level. Parking is free and there is no staggering admittance charge, as confronts the visitor to the theme parks, World's Fair, or Disney Kingdoms. Many undoubtedly find the event a welcome contrast to the slickness of the corporately-managed theme parks in which people are moved, stacked, and set in line with all due efficiency.

I have indulged in a few comparisons in order to emphasize what America lost in rejecting the example of the lager beer gardens. Ultimately, however, it is not appropriate to compare a contrivance with an institution. It is not accurate to compare an annual oddity, such as the sausage festival, with lager beer gardens, which were once an integral part of a prevailing life-style. An occasional celebration, no matter how well planned, cannot offer what accrues from regular association and participation.

The German-American lager beer garden represents the model, par excellence, of the third place. It was the bedrock for informal and encompassing social participation out of which friendships were formed and interests were matched. Those who came to meet and know one another in the happy informality of the beer gardens went on to form drama clubs, turnen, debating societies, singing groups, rifle clubs, home guards, volunteer fire departments, fraternities, and associations dedicated to social refinement. It was the basis of community. Though organized around drinking, it was, as O'Connor observed, "as respectable as the corner grocery store."[33] Unlike the Yankee saloon, which inspired so many temperance hymns and which promoted the image of Little Nel vainly searching for her father amid a throng of drunken barroom revelers, the beer garden was a unifying force in family life, not a divisive one. The beer garden balanced the competition of the American economic system with steady doses of fraternity; it balanced the inequalities of social life by welcoming all to its circle of amenities on an equal basis. The German-American seemed to know, more than others, the imperatives of people's basic social nature—for one to be happy, others must be happy too. They set the tripod of the first, second, and third places on rough new terrain. Doing so lent stability to their lives and civility to the neighborhoods in which they settled.

CHAPTER 6

Main Street

RIVER PARK WAS typical of small American towns of the era that came to a close at the end of World War II. The old, young, and everyone in between claimed its Main Street as their own; it accommodated and unified them all. Outdoors and in, third place association was frequent and diffuse along its short reach. The desire for a break in routine, to catch up on the gossip, or merely to have something to do was as easily satisfied as a stroll uptown.

The population of River Park was 720 in 1940. The town is located in the upper Midwest, along a river that meanders through the rich agricultural area of southern Minnesota. At that time, the quality of the local roads was not conducive to frequent travel away from the community. The major highway near the town was narrow and dangerous; hills, dips, and sharp curves marked almost every mile of it, for it was constructed when road-makers followed natural contours rather than leveling them. The secondary roads were dusty and rough in dry weather. In the spring, many became soft and often impassible, but the dry summer months turned them into jolting "washboards." In traveling these stretches, the local wits advised, one would do well to place a corn cob between one's teeth in order to "keep from biting your tongue off." The new "blacktop" roads had begun to appear but were few in number.

Television had not yet made its appearance, and the average home was not much of an entertainment center. That fact, coupled with the difficulty of automobile travel, left the members of the community reliant upon one another as sources of novelty, diversity, and entertainment. Here, as in small-town America generally during this period, human company remained the major and almost exclusive means to those necessary embellishments of daily life. In talking with one another and in appreciating one another's antics, escapades, accomplishments, and misfortunes, people's days were made interesting.

Personalities were rich—not always admirable, of course, but rich—as they always tend to be when the pace and focus of daily life allow their fuller appreciation. The community offered the setting Robert Traver had in mind when he wrote of the latitude for personal expression and the savoring of it that small towns afford: "It is inevitable that the development of 'characters' should reach its fullest flower in the smaller communities of America. I have already dilated on my profound distaste for large cities—and I think one of the contributing causes to this enthusiastic loathing of mine is the sad, numbing realization that our big cities are filled with any number of starved and thwarted 'characters' who, because of the huge, blind fury of city living, must forever bottle up a free expression of their individualism, their love for living, to become one with the trampling mob. . . ."[1] River Park was not wanting for "characters" nor, no doubt, was any small town of that period.

Insight into the quality of town life that prevailed in River Park is found in the fact that the practical joke was common. Today the practical joke seems malicious and pointless in most corners of the land. We may prefer to think that we have progressed beyond it, but the fact is that our relationships have become too tenuous and uncertain to risk tampering with them. The practical joke comes into its own only when its victim is well and widely known, when people are intensely interested in one another, and where social ties between people are not fragile. The ruses perpetrated by River Park's inhabitants upon one another were often downright ingenious in conception, and the more successful ones became part of conversational lore for years afterward. Nowadays, practical jokes survive amid the close bonds of combat units, professional ball teams, and closely-knit work groups. In River Park, the same kind of closeness that characterizes such special groups today prevailed throughout the wider community.

A Human Scale

Beyond those aforementioned conditions that kept the local citizens pretty much confined to the immediate locale and encouraged people to get out of their houses, the character of third place association in River Park owed much to the size of the community. The town was within the ranges of population size and physical space that many experts consider ideal.[2] Among adults, everyone knew everyone else on sight, by voice, by reputation, and by the reputation of the individual's family. The size of the community was compatible with the limits of human memory.

It was also compatible with the capacity of the eyes and legs. Anyone could walk to any point within the town and cover a distance of no more than six or seven blocks. No resident had to walk more than four blocks to reach Main Street. Everything the town had to offer was accessible on foot. Main Street was not too long to exceed the capacity of the eyes to recognize human beings along its fullest extent. The population of the town and the places within it were a manageable picture puzzle, which the child could assemble, place by place and face by face, completing it before he or she completed school.

With its population of 720, small by many standards, River Park was nonetheless well above the calculated minimal figure necessary to provide the "convivial society" or to "fulfill the companionship function to the fullest."[3] It was large enough to meet companionship needs but small enough to avoid division. There was some poverty in River Park and everyone lived close to it; it was not an alien, stigmatic thing. There were many bachelors and spinsters, but they were well integrated into the social life of the community such that the "unpaired" were not excluded from the general goings-on. The underlying hostility between Protestants and Catholics (there had been a religious "war" early in the history of the town) did not result in open divisions and did not contaminate the youth of the community, for the most part.

As to the dimensions of Main Street, one could say with some generosity that the town was five blocks in length. But that impression must be shortened. Small-town blocks are not as long as their large-city counterparts, and in River Park most of the commercial establishments on Main Street were contained within an expanse of less than three blocks. All but a few of the business establishments of the community were located in close proximity to one another along Main Street. There were forty of them, located about equally on the north and south sides of the street. Commercially, it was a one-street town, and a short one at that.

The Atmosphere of Main Street

I remarked, initially, that third place association was *diffuse* along the course of River Park's Main Street. By that I mean that it was not confined, as tends to be the case in large urban areas, to a particular bar and grill, coffee shop, or the like. In River Park informal socializing spilled out into the street and into places of commerce that would not tolerate it in large cities. It is for this reason that Main Street was almost as much a third place as any of the sites along it.

Evidence of that general condition was abundant. To begin with, the term *uptown* was used far more often than any particular destination within it. Whether people lived east or west of Main Street, whether north or south of its central intersection, they all spoke of going uptown. Uptown was an entity, a unified place more similar among its parts than different, and to go uptown, aside from doing an errand or going to a specific destination, was to engage those one encountered in social intercourse. Rarely, in those days, did anyone just buy groceries or pick up mail at the post office.

That the social component in frequenting Main Street was strong could be detected in the manner in which people walked along it. Their pedestrian demeanor was quite unlike that so typically observed among their metropolitan counterparts, who tend to walk the downtown streets rapidly, averting their eyes from those they meet going in the other direction and displaying a preoccupied, almost sullen countenance. Indeed, what is taken as the fast pace of urban life, as judged from the scurrying of big-city pedestrians, is often no more than the typical walking behavior of people who don't wish to engage others with whom they share the sidewalks. In the manner described, urbanites signal that they are dedicatedly "going someplace" and are "in a hurry to get there." That is inference; however, all that such a manner of walking makes clear without inference is that those who do it do *not* intend to engage passersby in social acknowledgment, greeting, or conversation.

In River Park, people walked slowly and with open and expectant faces. They were amenable to stopping and exchanging greetings, and they expected to do so. Pedestrians knew those they encountered and were obliged to speak and, beyond that obligation, there was always the likelihood that something of interest or amusement might ensue from stopping and gabbing for a couple of minutes. This is not to suggest that everybody was genuinely fond of everybody else. Some exchanged only curt greetings, but almost everyone could count on at least that much. When two people were on the outs, one might cross the street to avoid meeting the other. This amused others who saw and knew what was happening.

The more gregarious or less busy citizen might take an hour to negotiate one block of Main Street, for there were always a good many people walking or lounging along it during daylight hours. It was not just a matter of whom one might meet coming out of a store or walking in the other direction, for one could chat with the elderly and retired who sat along the store front steps and benches provided by many of the business establishments. The old-timers liked nothing better than to talk with the more active people of the community and keep up on things.

If one were to visit River Park today, one would see quite a different place from that which existed in 1940. The streets would be relatively isolated. In that earlier time, there was a perennial joke about rolling up the streets at ten in the evening. By the same token, the townsfolk might well leave them rolled up today. The people are largely gone from the street now, as are the physical amenities that earlier accommodated them. The architecture of Main Street has changed noticeably. The earlier storefronts featured large windows and the majority of them had outdoor seating, in most cases integral to their architecture. Wide steps and Kasota stone slabs that flanked the entrances were heavily used by those who found them cool places to sit in the summer. Other establishments provided wooden benches, one on either side of a central entrance. Large windows and the encouragement to lounge at the portals combined to unify indoors and out and to encourage a "life of the street" as well. That outdoor seating is all but gone now. The new storefronts are tight against the street and their much smaller windows allow little seeing in or seeing out. Though contemporary merchants may still encourage a bit of loafing in and around their places of business, the revised architecture does not.

The out-of-doors hospitality of River Park in that earlier time was limited to the warmer months of the year. During those times, however, it was an obvious phenomenon. In fair weather, a citizen deciding to spend a few hours uptown in the evening often did so without entering any of the business establishments. It was the habit of people to engage one another where they happened to meet, and this often meant congregating at street corners, leaning against lamp posts or parked cars, or sitting on the benches so abundantly provided.

The diffuse character of third place association was also evidenced by its intrusion into business establishments neither built nor intended for that purpose. Loafing and "shooting the breeze" were not confined to the taverns, cafes, and soda fountains. The two produce establishments offered ample seating on egg crates and feed sacks, if nowhere else, and encouraged idle visitors. One of the town's two doctors' offices had a waiting room often occupied by a group of wise-cracking young ne'er-do-wells whom the doctor had taken under his wing. On many days, half the trade in any of the three local barber shops never spent a dime, but merely stopped in to swap fish stories, glance through the latest magazines, and enjoy the sweep of a large electric fan and the pleasant tonsorial odors.

The accommodating posture of the River Park merchants was not a matter of benevolence towards loafers and hangers-on. Unlike the big-city merchant, they had no real choice of clientele. Success in business meant catering to all those who entered their establishments. To offend a nonpaying customer or a miserly one was to risk losing his or her trade and that of the customer's friends. To do so repeatedly was to fail in business. Also, business was slow, often as not, and company was welcome when no customers were present. Usually there was space for those gathered only to visit and pass the time of day, even when customers appeared. Since merchant, customer, and hangers-on all knew one another, and since hangers-on had been trained from childhood in the "etiquette" of loafing in places of business, there were few problems. As a hanger-on, one did not butt in when business was being conducted and one did not interfere with the movement of customers. Also, one helped out. Many of the local boys learned the art of egg candling and helped out when the need arose or just for fun. They also helped load the trucks, stack boxes, and showed their strength by lifting and piling sacked feed. Many a storekeeper enlisted the strong arms of youth without hesitation when a job needed doing.

The children of River Park learned quickly about the times and places along Main Street during which, and in which, they were welcome to hang around. The nine o'clock curfew was obeyed. The post office could be entered at any time by anyone. The bank could never be entered unless the youths were accompanied by parents. Youngsters learned that they could not loiter in the cafés during meal-times but were usually welcome to do so in the slow periods. Thus, on a Saturday afternoon, after one and before five o'clock, a couple of eight-year-old boys might be found in the corner booth of a local restaurant playing poker. In the pot might be deeds and mortgages with crayoned green and black borders and thousands of dollars in play money. They might be drinking cream soda or Pepsi (or anything else that made a pretend whiskey) from shot glasses—courtesy of the house. The booth was not needed; the boys behaved themselves. Cap pistols placed on the table to "keep the game honest" were never fired. The youngsters kept the place from being a tomb in the off hours. Everyone was content with such situations. (How many parents can get such baby-sitting nowadays?) Then, too, twenty cents over the counter was better than none at all.

Most of all, though, the children liked being out of doors in the daylight hours along Main Street. They and the old-timers had pri-mary license to the sidewalk benches during working hours, for those of the in-between ages were not supposed to loaf during working hours. The outdoor seating along Main Street was the major setting, and about the only one, in which the town's oldest generation freely and enthusiastically associated with its youngest.

Of the forty commercial establishments along Main Street, nineteen regularly encouraged hanging around and visiting. The professional offices and the busy grocery stores were the major exceptions to a general atmosphere that combined sociability with business. River Park was thus a community in which a formally designated social center was not necessary. Even the lack of a pool hall, movie theater, and bowling alley produced no real deprivation and no efforts to secure such places of diversion. The people of River Park, at least up until 1940, had retained the ability to amuse and entertain one another without much need of commercialized diversions. As a direct result, the associational community and habits of cooperation were strong.

The Focal Point

Though something of a third place atmosphere prevailed along the entirety of Main Street, there were also important nuclei of more focused gatherings. Chief among these was Bertram's Drug Store. Bertram's bore a striking similarity to Clifford's Drug Store as described by Roger Barker and his associates in their well-known study of "Midwest," a Kansas town having (coincidentally) the same population as River Park.[4] Similar investigations by Robert Bechtel identified, in one case, the front steps of a local inn and, in another, an unplanned lounge at an Aircraft Control and Warning Station in Alaska.[5] Barker referred to such places as "core settings," whereas Bechtel called them behavioral "focal points."

By their definition, a core setting in a neighborhood or community is that place where one is more likely than anywhe.e else to encounter any given resident of the community. It caters to the greatest variety of local residents and has the greatest number of customers if it is a place of business. It is the place where most gossip is heard and the place where most people can go to find out what's going on in the community. It, in the common vernacular, is "where the action is."

Bertram's Drug Store met all the criteria that Bechtel identifies as necessary for such places. It was centrally located and equally accessible to all; important functions were located in or near it; it allowed people to do *nothing*. Located on a corner of the town's central intersection, it was the place where most motorists "passing through" stopped, if they stopped at all. It was the place where most people went to purchase small gifts. It was the place where people bought magazines to which they did not subscribe. It was the place to buy out-of-town newspapers. It sold comic books and paperback novels. Bus tickets were obtained there and the Greyhounds picked up and dropped off passengers near its front door. It carried a goodly assortment of fireworks and cap pistols during weeks prior to the "Fourth."

The youngsters played cribbage and canasta or pinochle by the hour in booths opposite the soda fountain. The men played poker in a small back room. In the summer, a horseshoes area in back of the store was popular, and the boys of the town frequently played with the men since a foursome of adults was not easy to assemble during working hours.

But the core of this core setting was the soda fountain. It was unoccupied only rarely, and never after school let out. T. R. Young was right, I think, when he spoke of the soda fountain as a special place: "In small-town America, the ice cream parlor provided a place to *be* (or learn to be) a particular kind of social self. . . . Thinking about the places in the modern city where an adequate self-structure might develop, one remains puzzled. Whatever else it does, the city is not geared to that particular task."⁶ Young's meaning may be somewhat elusive but his conclusion seems entirely correct. Without question, the drugstore was the most preferred third place or hangout of the youth of River Park.

A female correspondent who had known a similar place in Ohio implored me to devote a special chapter to the subject. She even supplied a title: "In Praise of Neighborhood Drugstores—The Old-Time Ones with Soda Fountains, Bars Without the Booze." She described its meaning to her: "I grew up in Ohio in a small, industrial town just outside Akron; I was born in 1933. Long before I started to school, my dad would take me along on his every-evening walk 'down to the corner' for a coke. It was a ritual.

"During the course of the years, the owners changed; one pharmacist selling out, another coming in. But the soda fountain remained. It functioned as the gathering place for the neighborhood men who didn't frequent the bar across the street. Neighborhood women came in, made purchases, and went out. The men gathered to talk. I was usually the only child, sitting on the high stool, sipping a cherry coke, or a lemon coke, happy to be there with my dad.

"The adult I've become has often looked back upon the 'corner' as a strong formative force in my life. I can't be quite certain, but I believe it was there that I very early became aware that the world was much wider than Barkerton, Ohio; that there was a city, state, and national government; that what happened in government affected people's lives; and that people participated in government. I suspect that it was all those conversations overheard at the drugstore that made me feel comfortable with conversations about ideas, and at home with man-talk as well as with woman-talk over the kitchen tables of the neighborhood. I suspect that it was 'at the corner' that the roots were planted for a lifetime interest in politics, economics, and philosophy (none of which were part of the world of home), but which were the core of this third place.

"This morning I was feeling grateful for the experiences of 'the corner' that preceded those of the schoolroom. This morning's gratitude evolved into this afternoon's sorrow; my lament for all the children who will never be able to experience what I experienced. Most fathers would not take a girl-child into a bar, if that is where they now go for the man-talk of the third place."[7]

Certainly, Bertram's soda fountain was also coeducational. It was the place of business in which it was all right for girls to "hang around." The soda fountain, indeed, has given all the precedent and knowledge we need to provide for youthful third places. Some time ago, at one of those holiday gatherings of the clan, a relative was describing to me the problems with the teenagers in his community. The community in question had grown up around new mining technology and didn't have any places for kids to hang out that older traditions supply elsewhere. The man complained that the youth of the community were a "bunch of ingrates." They did not appreciate the special hangout that had recently been constructed for them.

After listening to his lament, I asked him two questions: Was the place right smack in the center of town—right in the middle of things? And, "Do the adults go there, too?" The answer in both instances was no. The place was "especially" for the youngsters and nobody wanted such a place right in the middle of town. As in so many cases nowadays involving both the very old and the young, the desire is to set them aside. The old accept their lot more gracefully. The young resent their undeserved shunning by the community, and they have ways of showing it.

Even after the adolescents of River Park became old enough to feel comfortable on their own in the town's 3.2 joints, they never really gave up the drugstore. It was never a place just for the younger kids. In the summer months, the wide expanse of the original Kasota stone steps were festooned with boys, who left just enough space for customers to enter. Out front they engaged in horseplay, watched the local comings and goings, and waited for the opportunity to catch a ride with a boy or girl who had been able to borrow the family car. Inside they were permitted to read comic books without buying them, to carve their initials in the wooden booths, and to "cut up" within limits. The store's owner well calculated that the nickel-and-dime trade of the youth, given its sizable and unfailing volume, was worth the minor disturbances. For the kids, Bertram's was the heart of the community.

The adults never complained about the presence of the children. Bertram's belonged to everybody. Its soda fountain was heavily used by adults, who sat side by side with the youngsters and made no attempt to reserve any portion of it for themselves. Many of the adults avoided the drinking establishments, even though such places served food and offered only the "lightweight" 3.2 beer. The farmers were particularly sensitive about drinking establishments; some of them relaxed their self-imposed bans on Saturday night, although many of them never did. They were combating the stigma of the "saloon farmer." It was duly noted that those local area farmers who spent a good deal of time in the saloons were first in line to claim disaster benefits when the local river overflowed its banks. For most in town from the farm and for those who lived in town and shared a disdain for the drinking establishments, the drugstore's soda fountain was a "bar without the booze."

Other Third Places

Though Bertram's was the town's focal point for those of all ages, there were a variety of lesser locations that lent a rich choice of company and activity. The fact that many locals and farmers from the area did not frequent drinking establishments did not detract from their vitality. In 1940, River Park supported three liquor stores (on and off sale) and five 3.2 joints (four of which served meals and were often referred to as cafés).

With the singular exception of one 3.2 joint favored by the Irish amateur pugilists of the area and dubbed the "Bucket of Blood," these establishments were usually tame. The 3.2 joints were important in the transition of youth to adult status. Both boys and girls, by the time they reached junior and senior high school age, would visit them frequently in the late afternoon and early evening. It was to such places that the high school basketball players migrated after their games to bask in glory. It was in the booths that young couples "going together" spent a lot of time talking, without spending much money. Jukebox selections generally favored the younger crowd. It was here, also, that youth were indoctrinated into the mild forms of gambling such as went on in the community. The pinball machines in some of the places paid off when high scores were attained; the games of cribbage, gin rummy, or pinochle were sometimes played with small bets on the side; punch boards were ever present with an enticing grand prize (such as a nickel-plated .22 rifle) displayed on the back bar. Most of the places had a dice cup at the bar, and the bartenders rolled against the customers for drinks whenever requested. Always, there was a tempered indulgence in the games and there were no problems with youthful gambling. An adult or two might become genuinely addicted to the slot machines located in the liquor stores, but youth were banned from playing the one-armed bandits.

The town had one lodge and by 1940 it was minimally active. It was a fraternal order steeped in secrets, and everyone was content to let the whole matter be as secret as possible, for the simple reason that its members never did anything worth talking about. The vital civic associations of the community were the Volunteer Fire Department and the Boosters' Club, usually in that order. Beyond those, the term *club* was humorously applied to two kinds of gatherings totally devoid of any formal organization. One was the sunshine club, which grew out of the desire of retired males to watch and comment upon the activities of Main Street and the fact that the merchants along Main Street provided ample outdoor seating that allowed them to do just that. It was called a sunshine club because its members usually shifted from one side of the street to the other during the course of the day to remain under the sun's warming rays.

There was also the liars club, a label applied to the routine gathering of a group of elderly males in the town's Express Office. Main Street was located about a mile from the railway station, and the Express Office was connected to the railway express service by means of a dray truck. At night the office was used for social purposes. The old-timers were a fairly select group; not just any old man was accepted to the ranks and given his special place around the wood stove. As a third place, it came alive shortly after the supper hour and marked its best attendance in the winter months when domestic claustrophobia became more acute. Its members were bona fide cronies who had known one another as children, who had taken wives well before togetherness became part of the bargain, and who met like elite peers to discuss changing times with a degree of smugness the elderly hardly display anymore.

The only location that might have competed with the drugstore as a community focal point was the post office. Mail was not delivered to business establishments or residences, and everyone had to make a daily trip to the post office to pick it up. It was a meeting place and, although no seating existed within, there was space to stand and talk. It was always open and, in 1940, it still had its huge plate glass window, which allowed anyone inside to be seen. On winter nights, it was a place to stop and warm oneself before trodding home.

The several third place locations along Main Street varied considerably in the tone and temper of diversion that they allowed. In the post office and the express office, as in the casual conversing that went on in many of the business establishments, things were relatively subdued. The 3.2 joints were a bit more lively, and the liquor stores were downright boisterous. At any given time, River Park could offer about as much revelry as any of its citizens desired. On Saturday nights, everything was more up-tempo than usual.

Whether it was quiet talk or foot-stomping and hoots of loud laughter, all of River Park's third places and its Main Street, generally, were active—at least until that hour when "they rolled up the streets." The key, I have no doubt, to the *sustained* level of activity lay in the fact that the great majority of persons who visited the places along Main Street and who did so with a desire for company in mind, *did so alone.* It is this characteristic that modern communities fail to achieve and that is so much missed in modern life. Those who have found a place where they can stop in as lone individuals and find association and camaraderie awaiting them are indeed as rare as they are fortunate. Most of us have to go *with* friends to a place in order to have someone to talk to when we get there. We must plan, we must make arrangements, we must try to establish a set time as well as a set place in order to regularize whatever third association we can claim. In small towns like River Park, before home entertainment and fast highways took or kept people elsewhere, the lone individual could find company and diversion virtually without effort. It was the casual and effortless satisfaction of the social instinct that allowed the River Parks of that time to keep boredom at bay.

But times have changed. The streets of River Park are largely devoid of people now and one can walk the whole of Main Street, up one side and down the other, without hearing laughter from any of its doorways and without speaking to anyone in the course of that walk. No one is sitting beside the doorways, because the seating has been removed. The old and the young don't amuse one another along the Main Street sidewalks anymore. There are few windows left to look into and see life on the inside, and little of interest to see if you're on the inside looking out.

The town has given up its once renowned annual celebration. The locals usually say it's because nobody, including the county sheriff, could control the gang of motorcycle punks who came in the latter years to spoil other people's good times. In fact, however, the decline began earlier. The old-timers, who had once worked hard and selflessly to create the food and festivities, were replaced by a younger generation who took over with an eye toward making money from the earlier tradition of good hosting. They put less in and took more out. But even that is not the whole of it. River Park's loss of its 3.2 joints, the demolition of its grandstand and ballpark, the removal of the band-stand, the demise of the Christmas community sing around the thirty-foot pine—these changes and more—suggest a significant decline in the capacity of the townsfolk, generally, to entertain one another and to entertain anyone else. None of this constitutes an indictment against the town and its people, for the pattern is general and tied to factors beyond their control.

A New Version of Main Street?

The memory and example of the prewar small town and its Main Street have become sufficiently dim, such that many now claim that it has been reborn in the form of the shopping mall. In 1973, *U.S. News and World Report* contended that the shopping mall is replacing Main Street as the core of community belonging in America.[8] Elsewhere, Richard Francaviglia argued that the virtues of Main Street never really existed. To him, the shopping malls are as good as Main Street ever was; yea better, for they are attractive places whereas the small town was ugly and the people were petty.[9] Ralph Keyes proclaimed the shopping mall to be "the most tranquil and pleasant environment I'd ever found within suburbia." He likened it to a "town square of old," which allows people to "promenade among the familiar faces of those living within."[10] In Eugene van Cleef's book, one reads that malls "have benches for relaxation," that they are places where a shopper can "wholly relax," and that these "new promenades" are a "monument to what a determined people can do in a community."[11] These writers, and a good many others, skate freely on the brink of total nonsense. Anyone having that dual familiarity with prewar small towns and modern shopping malls will recognize that fact and be repelled by the comparison. A preoccupation with physical facades coupled with a lack of sociological insight is common among the mall's many fans.

That many consider the mall attractive is hardly surprising since most of the world around it is so ugly in contrast. Along the typical urban thoroughfare, one is greeted by an overhead tangle of utility wires, oversized and artless signage designed for the eyes of fast-moving motorists, litter, and, everywhere, a view marred by the ugliness of masses of parked and moving cars. Merely by eliminating the urban uglies, the interior of any mall is certain to seem pleasant. But, facades aside, the shopping mall is a sterile place when compared to prewar small towns and their main streets.

The mall, first of all, is "corporation country." In the typical mall, a major chain dominates either end of a promenade flanked on both sides by lesser shops, which must be compatible with, and offer no real threat to, that pair of retailing giants. Rightfully claiming that they are the major "draw" to the mall, the big stores can dictate the nature of their competition. Merchandising, not socializing, marks the character of the mall and those benches upon which shoppers may "wholly relax" are but token in number. Indeed, against the usual public relations flavor infecting a good deal of architectural literature, it was refreshing to note the candor in Arnold Rogow's comments on mall seating. Within one large eastern mall Rogow noted that "the forty-plus acres provide exactly three wooden benches upon which tired shoppers may rest." The fact, he also noted, corresponded with what the head of the local Chamber of Commerce had to say about the mall—that it "welcomes shoppers, not loafers."[12] A place for profit is not a place for friends, and the overriding emphasis in the malls is on merchandising.

Totally unlike Main Street, the shopping mall is populated by *strangers*. As people circulate about in the constant, monotonous flow of mall pedestrian traffic, their eyes do not cast about for familiar faces, for the chance of seeing one is too small. That is not a part of what one expects there. The reason is simple. The mall is centrally located to serve the multitudes from a number of outlying developments within its region. There is little acquaintance between those developments and not much more within them. Most of them lack focal points or core settings and, as a result, people are not widely known to one another, even in their own neighborhoods, and their neighborhood is only a minority portion of the mall's clientele. Research informs us that the average individual spends but five hours per week at a mall and, thus, the chances of being at a mall when a friend also happens to be there is small. The chances of their bumping into one another are even smaller.

But one need not rely on the arithmetic and probabilities that render mall life sterile. It is evidenced in the comments of the wife who now and then reports to her husband the "high point" of her day—that of meeting someone she knows at a local mall or supermarket. One hears it from children who no longer have third places like the drugstore and who come home all excited having met someone they know at the mall. Such places are not a "core of community involvement" but they are a gauge of it, and one that renders rather pitiful readings.

I have yet to see anyone playing checkers, chess, poker, gin rummy, cribbage, etc., in a mall. Yet, its literary cheerleaders say it is a place where one can "wholly relax." Even bowling alleys, which do make money, are excluded from the malls because they don't make it fast enough per square foot of space that must be allocated for that activity. I have seen no old-timers pitching horseshoes on the stay-off greenery around the mall; I see no children wrestling on that turf or playing any games there.

The displaying hobbyists of my acquaintance tell me how difficult it is to "set up" in the malls. Most of the stores have their square footage allocated on a predetermined basis by a remote and centralized computer system. What's there is rigid and inflexible. It can't be moved around to accommodate anyone else's displays. In those stores, signs aplenty admonish against smoking, drinking, and eating within. "No Loitering" signs are not necessary, for loitering requires space and all that is available has been assigned to narrow aisles and the display of merchandise.

Unlike Main Street, the mall is locked up until midmorning and it closes early in the evening. Whatever life it has is geared to the day's commerce. It is thus unavailable more hours of the week than it is available and, unlike Main Street, it is not likely to have a nighttime population distinct from the shopping crowd.

Many of the malls have bars within them, and my observations in the Midwest and South confirm those of Rogow on the East and West coasts— ". . . the social life of the mall has little appeal to adults. The bars cater mainly to grim, solitary drinkers whose eyes stare fixedly at television screens that are never turned off."[13] Those restaurants incorporated into malls are usually of the cafeteria sort, which are designed for high volume and fast turnover. In some, excessive cooling by the air conditioning system keeps people from developing a leisurely eating habit. To eat a hot meal in such places is to eat it *fast*.

The malls have their fans and they no doubt have their virtues. Moreover, some of them rise above the average in the amenities they offer. They are not, however, to be compared with the small town's Main Street of earlier times. The same conditions that destroyed the intimate character of Main Street are those that gave rise to the mall. Few people are more familiar with the essential differences in these settings than the CBS roving correspondent Charles Kuralt. Recently, Kuralt was interviewed by David Halberstram, who wrote the following: "He had just come in from working on a modern new shopping center in Kansas City, and the experience had depressed him. It had been an aimless world of disconnected people, teenage Mall Rats hanging around arcades, middle-class wives going to fancy lunches, even the farmer who sold the land and now just hung around because he had little else to do. 'All those people who deal with each other but don't know anything about each other,' Kuralt said. 'It's a place without a sense of community.' "[14] There, in a nutshell, is the difference between Main Street and the mall. It is of such proportions as to make the contrast obvious and any comparison ridiculous.

What the small town had and the mall never will have was identified in a recent book by Orrin Klapp. Klapp's subject was boredom, and for examples of it he admonished his readers to think not of tribal people telling folktales around the fire but of modern ones "inundated with output of media, switching channels on their television."[15] Klapp warned of the misleading stereotype, of the city dweller's tendency to regard small towns as "dull backwaters where nothing much happens." That stereotype is contradicted by studies of small town life, which reveal its built-in resistance to boredom, that being the "intense interest that small towners take in each other and minor happenings."

It is this positive aspect of small town life that the third place fosters in the larger urban context. An interest in people and their infinite capacity to amuse and enlighten one another is nurtured where personalities are freed from purpose and allowed free play with one another.

Thus, Robert Traver was not entirely accurate in criticizing the city for not producing any of those "characters" that small towns do and that reflect its greater freedom of expression. Indeed, one would be hard-pressed to find a better description of third place regulars than that of a "cast of characters." The mall, in contrast, is a drifting amalgam of nonpersons; there are no "characters" there.

CHAPTER 7

The English Pub

UNLIKE THE AMERICAN tavern or cocktail lounge, the English pub enjoys a good press, an aura of respectability, and a high degree of integration in the life of the citizenry. Three-fourths of the drinking done in England still takes place in public settings and, in the face of many forces that discourage its use, the pub hangs on. The typical London drinking establishment, in the estimation of Robert Goldston, is the remaining claim to a civic spirit within a city that has all but lost its civicism.[1] The ordinary English citizen also defends the locals for, apart from their daily use, the pubs have great symbolic importance. Hilaire Belloc's words are often quoted: "When you have lost your inns, you may drown your empty selves, for you will have lost the last of England."

The land of the pub is also the land of the club. They are polar opposites. The former helped usher England into her modern democracy while the latter still epitomize the divisiveness of England's long-standing and notorious stratification system. The word *club* derives from the Anglo-Saxon *clifan* or *cleofian* (literally, our cleave)—the word cleave meaning both "to divide" and "to adhere."[2] Thus, *club* represents a unity achieved for the purpose of division. The English club has served both to symbolize and enforce England's long tradition of inequality. The club has been the citadel of her stratification system; it has been the most glorified and romanticized institution of exclusiveness and snobbery in modern times. Common people have never been allowed so much as an annual opportunity to tour these bastions of the privileged. Though the pub is facing adversity these days, some find consolation in the fact that the clubs are worse off. Right on Belloc! The snubs and the smugs have exclusive clubs, but the soul of England resides in her pubs.

The word *pub* is short for public house or an establishment licensed by proper authority for the purpose of serving the general public. And have they been licensed! Some seventy-four thousand pubs are scattered throughout the island's less than twenty thousand square miles. And do they serve! Britain is the world's third largest beer market, and three out of every four pints is drawn from the beer pump of a public house.

The proliferation of pubs, averaging four per square mile, means that for virtually every Englishman (and recently for every Englishwoman) a pub exists close by. Because of their neighborhood proximity, pubs are also known as "locals." Every pub-goer has his or her local and every pub is someone's local. The pub has resisted confinement to commercial strips and underzoned night-life centers. It has remained small in scale and easily available. These features, plus its familiar hominess, undoubtedly account for the pub's high level of integration into English life and for the sustained appeal of England's strong pub culture.

The dominance of the pub among places of affiliation was clearly shown in the Worktown study, the most intensive investigation of pub life ever undertaken. Within that industrial center in the north of England, it was found that "more people spend more time in public houses than they do in any other buildings except private houses and work places."[3] The pub had more buildings, held more people, and took more of their time and money than churches, dancehalls, and political organization put together.

Was the pub unusually popular in Worktown? To the contrary, Worktown's pubs had less general appeal than pubs elsewhere. Dancing and pool games were not included there, and Worktown's population contained a disproportionate number of lower-middle-class families, who are the most likely to attach shame to drinking.

Clearly, the pub is the average Englishman's third place. What does it offer its patrons? Why does it enjoy such popularity and devotion?

The answer is far less complicated or mysterious than English writers usually suggest. The pub's favorable press is often romanticized. Writers are quick to proclaim its mystique, especially in comparison to "imitation" pubs on the Continent. A barrage of platitudes are leveled at attempts to create the pub elsewhere: "Real pubs are found only in England!" "Only an Englishman knows what a pub is!" "An outsider couldn't possibly create a pub!" There is some truth to these prideful claims, if only because the pub is part of the larger culture that nurtures it. But there is no magic in porcelain beer pulls, smoke-tainted pictures of Teddy, or momentoes of the local cricket team. Nor do the quaint signs, etched glass, and idiosyncrasies of pub behavior lend the English public house its essential warmth and verve.

If the pub is superior to the drinking establishments in most other cultures (and who would argue it?), the reasons are fairly simple and have to do with scale and warmth. Most pubs are built to the human scale. They are intimate, even cozy settings, designed more for an immediate neighborhood than a horde of transients and sometime visitors. Who better than a Texan would realize that Americans are rarely content with success on so small a scale? During World War II, Frank Dobie developed an abiding fondness for the clean little Anchor Pub in Cambridge. Reflecting upon the probable fate of such a place at home, he wrote: "If they operated such an establishment in America, they'd make a barrel of money. They'd enlarge it to take care of more and more customers and keep on enlarging it until it grew as big as Madison Square Garden, or else became a standardized unit in a chain. Long before either stage, however, it would have lost the character that makes the snug little public houses and inns of England veritable 'islands of the blest.' "[4]

Ben Davis, as knowledgeable a student of the pub as can be found and himself an Englishman, insists that the pub is really no more than a good place to engage in social drinking.[5] People go to pubs because they want to feel welcome. They appreciate a welcome more warm and personal than that extended by the grocer or bank manager. In the better and more serviceable pubs, the licensee is as much friend as tradesperson. People like to feel at home and in no way must the customer be made to feel out of place. The social drinker likes to give and enjoy friendliness. Above all, fellowship must prevail and it depends most upon informality. Snugness, not smugness, is the key if one is to feel the nearness of human company. The social drinker wishes to enjoy a good-hearted atmosphere in which honest expression triumphs over sophistication. As is the case almost everywhere, English publicans are given to experimenting with new ways to lure customers, but the sustaining tradition of the pub is just what Davis suggests. It is the kind of place the social drinker longs for.

Though the typical patron has his or her local, the Englishman does not confine his pub visits to a single or even just a few establishments. Pub-crawling is probably more popular in England than bar-hopping is in the United States. Further, the generous scattering of London pubs has encouraged many of her natives to keep a mental list of available "bolt holes."[6] The warmth of the little pubs and their no-delay service stand in pleasant contrast to the waiting, formality, boredom, and frustration evoked by city offices, museums, churches, concert halls, airline terminals, and retail stores. Not far from the likes of these may usually be found a pub into which one, given the least interlude of freedom, may "bolt" and therein soothe the irritations of urban chafing with an interval of pure felicity.

Singular Place, Plural Rooms

If more to promote trade than fraternity, publicans have nonetheless been consistent champions of inclusiveness. Under their roofs, if not in the same room, they have always sought to broaden the base of their patronage.

The earliest version of the pub was but a rural residence located along the coach routes in which the traveler could purchase a tankard of the owner's ale and enjoy the comfort of the kitchen while drinking it. Customers of "quality" were invited to share a portion of the parlor that they might avoid the "meaner" sorts in the kitchen. From its inception, the pub has catered to different classes of people by providing separate accommodations.

But for the most part, the pub has been a lower-class and working-class institution, and the publican's "recruiting" efforts have been aimed at the middle strata. The pub's meaner image was enforced by industrialization and the huge influx of workers into the cities in the early half of the nineteenth century. First to meet the new demand was the gin palace, which offered a glittering, elegant oasis amid the drab and dirty squalor of the cities generally and the worker's living quarters in particular. The gin palace responded to the needs of the crowded multitudes by means of a long bar, a large staff, and the introduction of "perpendicular drinking" in a society where tradition called for taking a seat by the kitchen hearth or in the parlor. Competing with the gin palaces were the beer houses, which sprang up in incredible numbers. Reacting to overwhelming urban growth, the government, by the Beer Act of 1830, allowed anyone to open a beershop free of control by the Justices. Some forty-five thousand of them opened within a period of eight years.[7]

The pub succeeded the gin palace in the Victorian half of the nineteenth century. Society became more respectable and government insisted upon a tighter reign over the nation's drinking establishments. The middle class, newly sprouted and burgeoning in the early half of the century, now came to full flower. These folks were keenly sensitive to the new class distinctions they had created and insisted upon drinking only with their own kind and, when drinking in public houses, demanded their own little niches in which to do it.

The architectural response to these new conditions was the creation of a large room with an oval or horseshoe-shaped bar-counter "chopped" into sections by means of highly ornate partitions. In these as in other fixtures, the new version of the pub incorporated many of the materials and motifs of gin palace elegance. One room might have contained as many as a dozen sections—separate bars, each appropriate to its social class of tipplers. Many of these were small, yet, due to an abundance of mirrors, claustrophobia or a feeling of isolation was avoided. Each bar looked onto an elegant bar-counter; partitions were abbreviated in height so that everyone could see almost all of the ornate and high-relief ceiling; and each bar allowed some glimpse of activities in the others. From behind the continuous counter, supervision of the patrons was facilitated by the abundance of mirrors on the back wall. Of all this, the licensing authority approved. The Victorian pub was an architectural invention that thrived with the growth of the middle class, which, as it in turn grew, continually subdivided itself into multiple social strata.

The pub of the mid-twentieth century combined the tradition of the original wayside inn, the gin palace, and the Victorian public house. Variation is continual and is accentuated as one moves from the south of England to the north, from rural area to urban center, and from the main routes of the cities to the off streets. The literature that purports to educate the reader as to the types of bars contained within the English pub is perplexing. Delving into it with any hope of clarification requires close attention to the date of the specific locale and description.

The continuities of the English pub, however, are not overcome by these variations. The changing configuration and altered use of the pub's rooms have been necessary to sustain the tradition of informal public drinking in England. Tradition survives only to the extent that the best of an earlier period can be adapted to pressures for change. Of particular interest, in the survival of the pub, is the changing use of its multiple rooms. "Institutions persist," as a mentor of mine was fond of saying, "for reasons other than those which brought time into being." So it has been with the pub's multiple-room arrangement. The evolving character and sustained appeal of most of these rooms is a subject of considerable fascination.

The Public Bar

The public bar is simultaneously the least and most of the pub's multiple rooms. It is the cheap side of the house. Its prices are the lowest because nothing is spent on upgrading it. The floor may consist of a mere continuation of the cobblestones used in the sidewalk outside. The tradition of sawdust on the floor has led to euphemistic references such as "sawdust parlour" or the "Spit and Sawdust." In some quarters, the public bar is also referred to as the "four-ale," in remembrance of the days when ale was sold there for only fourpence a quart. In the north of England, it is commonly referred to as the "vault."

The public bar is the most accessible from the street, and its patrons are the most visible to passersby. Its customers have no desire to be secluded from inquisitive eyes and disapproving judgment; the same is true of their wives, who often accompany them. There are no waiters here, and in the usual instance a single bartender serves the customers. If the public bar is operated by a barmaid, she is typically an older woman who may have spent her younger days in one of the classier rooms and possibly kept company with its patrons. Her age and disposition are such as to keep the place in order—even during Saturday night reveling.

There are no pictures on the walls save for the beer posters of the company that owns the pub. There are no cushioned seats, and the available chairs often have no backs. Totally devoid of refinement, the public bar is not colorful, as are the other rooms in the pub. Its colors, surfaces, and textures have a pale hue. The ambience is one of restrained masculinity. There is an honest simplicity, a down-to-earth character that may appeal to many who are socially superior to the usual patrons of the public bar.[8]

The public bar is the basic unit within most pubs not only because its meager appointments have been reduced to the basics but also because it represents the oldest tradition among pub rooms. Its lack of formality and pretension dates from that of the kitchen in the early wayside inn, the first version of the English pub. The public captures more of the third place character than do the other rooms. Here, the customers tend to form a single group and retain the habit of calling out to each other across the breadth or length of the barroom.[9] Elsewhere, the tendency of the patrons within the bar is to segregate themselves into small enclaves.

In the public bar, conversation is also the best. As one observer put it: "In the private bars there will hardly be a word of conversation, but the rest of the pub hums with talk of racing, cricket, football, dogs, and the weather and food."[10] And the brand of humor, a sure indication of conversation's quality, is also superior in the public bar: "In the saloon, they retell each other clean, unfunny stories if women are near, and dirty, unfunny stories if they are not. In the four-ale bar, where the real cockney wits drink, they don't need to rely on secondhand jokes. Their acid observations and also their lightning comebacks are spontaneous." The public simply offers more of what the pub as a whole affords the average citizen.

The public is the setting where English individualism manifests most joyously because it is exhibited among friends of suitable numbers to make the individual feel part of a larger unity. It is here, also, where restrictions on one's public behavior are least stringent. Patrons may even bring their own lunches without earning the disapproval of the management. One may burn the bar with a cigarette or spit on the floor and nobody cares. "You can do almost anything you bloody well like in the vault, short of shitting on the place," according to those who've observed the northern version of the public bar.[11] Where the public bar is thus most fully enjoyed, it is no surprise that owners spend most of their time in it. In such a setting, the English are, to quote Ernest Barker, "as free and unbound in spirit as the gulls on the cliffs of Dover."[12]

The public bar is also the basic bar in that its common-denominator appeal has remained constant while the other rooms in the pub have undergone modification to accommodate changing vogues in pretension and sophistication. It is, however, subject to invasion. When the other rooms are crowded, or where the other rooms don't serve the popular "mild," middle-class patrons exercise their license to invade the public. Those in working clothes cannot retaliate and invade the elegant bars, nor would they care to do so. Yet, only rarely are invasions of the public bar disruptive of the character of the place.

In one instance, at least, invasion proved fatal. Many fine pubs in London's West End were ruined in the late 1930s and early 1940s. The "Bright Young People," or the "flash trade," typified by the "trousered women of Chelsea and Bloomsbury" discovered the public bars and pursued within them their craze for the game of darts.[13] Only the lowly public bars then had dart boards, and the owners were not quick enough in placing fancier versions in the saloon bars and lounges. The invaders literally took over; the regulars gallantly made way for them, but, after a time, gave up and did their drinking elsewhere. The flash crowd was fickle, of course, and when it moved on to other "discoveries," all that remained was the wreckage of what had once been good bars.

In the United States, the college crowd has similarly ruined many a good place and threatened a great many more. McSorley's Old Ale House in New York City, *perhaps* the oldest bar in America, has survived urban renewal and the blood lust of feminists seeking to integrate or destroy it. But it faces its greatest threat in the form of college students who make meals of its cheese platters and take over the place at night.[14] Those invaders contribute nothing to the charm or the amenities that have attracted them; once those features are ruined, they move on to other victims. In a northern Wisconsin city, there is a tavern that has held to the twenty-five-cent draught as a treat to the customers who support its thriving package trade. In recent years, however, the college crowds began to pour in late at night in order to get the most from their dwindling financial resources. Their contributions to the old bar's tradition consisted of breaking beer glasses just outside the back door as they left the place or sought an open-air substitute for its lavatory facilities. The owner found it necessary to respond by closing early, thus leaving the older regulars to find another place in which to cap off a night out.

Back in the days when this writer was one of that infidel horde, our gang discovered a marvelous place at the edge of our college town and presumed to take it over in great numbers. The owner of the establishment was ready for us, however. He had tiled the basement floor, put in a bar and a separate lavatory, and welcomed us to that nether region where we were even "allowed" to tend bar for ourselves. Our kind were no more loyal than we were respectful of the man's regular customers, as he had evidently discovered long before, but he more than paid for his improvements in the basement and protected his civilized customers as well. There are many advantages to multiple rooms in the third place setting.

The Saloon Bar

Within the Victorian pub, the saloon bar was the height of elegance as achieved in public drinking establishments and it remained so until the advent of the saloon lounge. Here, subtle alterations of bright and dim lighting maximized the aesthetic effects of rich flock wallpaper, acid-etched glass, carved mahogany and rosewood, brass foot rails, Grecian caryatids, elaborate snob-screens, and rich red carpeting. The saloon bar bespeaks comfort, superiority, and elegance. It invokes a feeling, as one observer remarked, of "doing yourself well, and very pleasant that feeling can be." For the lower middle class, who were its original patrons and whose homes could not compete in elegance, the appeal must have been strong indeed.

By the end of World War II, many of England's pubs had become two-sided establishments. The public bar and the saloon bar had shown far more durability than the ladies' bar, the private bar, and the saloon lounge. "Not this side, please," was the cold greeting given to those who mistakenly entered the saloon bar lacking collars and with shoes unpolished. The best side of the pub offered its customers the best of everything there was to offer; the public bar remained short on comfort and devoid of decoration. In the saloon bar, patrons could expect to be served at tables, to relax in armchairs, to sit by a fireplace, and to flirt with the barmaids, if they so desired. No such amenities were available on the other side. The ambience of the public bar remained crude, while that of the saloon bar continued to be cozy and clublike.

In the saloon bar of the Victorian era, everything possible was done to conceal from the patron the fact that social inferiors were drinking under the same roof. Its worthies gained entrance to the pub via a side door. Once inside, they ordered drinks by opening an opaque window with pivot pins on one side and then closing it to retain privacy. Here an indefinite lower middle class of men could enjoy themselves "beyond the reach of their wives" and in the company of handsome, buxom blonde barmaids. All this is now a memory. By the early 1960s, the barmaids had declined in physical aspect, but there was still a degree of isolation in the saloon bar in which men drink with their wives "or with the wives of others."[15]

From the Victorian era to the present, class distinctions were changing in English society and these were reflected in pub life. In the twenties, "a man privileged to enter the Saloon Bar would *never* enter the Public Bar" and, of course, the invasion of the better side by such as a charwoman or a chimney sweep was even less likely.[16] The Saloon Bar then catered only to the lower middle class since both the middle and upper classes were "above" pubs and did their drinking at home or in their clubs. Thus, the saloon bar clientele of the time consisted of artisans, salespeople, clerks, and others of the lesser white-collar segment. By the 1960s, however, reporters could inform their public that the saloon bar was for the "rich and shameless" among social drinkers, suggesting both that higher social strata were discovering the pubs and that the desire for seclusion was waning.[17] Now, employers and officials, the "managing class," will grace the saloon bar unless the pub contains an even fancier saloon lounge to accommodate them.[18]

The once-sharp distinctions that had segregated the classes in the English pub have been greatly relaxed. Where the observation of difference remains, it is mostly a superficial one based on little more than appearance. Where one goes often depends on no more stringent criterion than how one happens to be dressed. And, for those suitably dressed for the saloon bar, nothing more than one's personal choice of which company to keep may dictate which side of the house to enter.

The Saloon Lounge

The saloon lounge was the last of the distinct pub rooms to emerge and, by the 1940s, was on its way out, having served its intended purposes. Its spacious elegance attracted a loftier clientele than had ever before frequented the pubs. The establishment of the saloon lounge had a decided effect in improving the image of the pub; it also gave the management justification to raise prices on that side of the house. The usual lounge, however, was more suited to the sipping of afternoon tea than the quaffing of bitters. Undoubtedly inspired by the lounging rooms of the early first-class trains and those of ocean-going liners whose patrons were now being lured to the pub, these rooms suffered all the disadvantages of such settings when used as drinking parlors. There was too much open space and the rectangular bar off to one side of the room was a sterile servery compared to the mahogany oval that often graced the saloon bar. The most basic feature of the lounge was its carpeting and, when the carpeting extended into the saloon bar, so did higher prices of drinks. Though prices were usually the same in both the saloon lounge and the saloon bar, the cost of drinking was higher in the former since tipping was expected. The lounge was introduced as an appeal to those who wanted something better than the saloon bar, and "better" often meant not that the furnishings were superior but that there was less resemblance to a barroom. By the 1930s, the typical pub could be expected to include a saloon bar, a private bar, a "jug and bottle," and, if large enough, a saloon lounge as well. The last was also called a "super-bar" at that time, and its inclusion within the confines of a public house was certain indication that the establishment had aspirations.

The northern version of the saloon lounge was commonly called the "best room" or, sometimes, the "music room," since it often contained a piano, which was never part of the tradition of the other rooms of the pub. Within the best room everything was different. Here was the place for women whom convention excluded from other areas of the pub. Here was the place that imposed a different kind of drinking behavior from that which men were used to in the public bar. Here they dressed up, sat down, and paid more.

Wherever the saloon lounge appeared under the roof of a public house, it was generally recognized that one did not enter it alone. The lounge afforded privacy within an otherwise public setting. Patrons expected not to be approached or engaged in conversation by those they encountered. Customers visited the saloon lounge in small groups and confined themselves to their intimate circles. The lounge bar or saloon lounge thus represented a polar opposite of the public bar, which the patron typically entered alone and was "fair game" for anyone wishing to approach him. The saloon lounge made it easy for status-conscious newcomers to feel comfortable. Its new trade appeared in the company of familiar friends and acquaintances and was not obliged to be sociable with strangers or those of different social position. The new and loftier clientele could discover the pub without need of those conversational skills required for active participation in the one-group informality taking place elsewhere under the pub's roof. They might listen to a gramophone as, in their own parlors, rather than contribute lively conversation, which is the real music of the pub.

The Private Bar

The usual essay on the English pub is a labor of love in which the private bar may be mentioned but not dwelt upon. The declining popularity of this lesser compartment does not alone account for the scant attention given it. Many aspects of the pub scene are fondly examined even though they, too, are fading away or now exist only in memory. The private bar, one suspects, is purposely slighted. It is a blot upon that healthier image that the pub enjoys.

The private is sometimes identified as a small bar catering to a social class between those who frequented the public bar and those who occupied the saloon bar. One account suggests that the private bar was the haunt of skilled laborers and the more "hard-boiled" white collar men.[19] But in many establishments it served as the "nuggy hole," a special compartment, usually quite small, for women. Before women of higher rank came to be as comfortable on the saloon side of the house as working-class women have always been in the public bar, the private served those among them who favored the pub.

Since World War II, however, a more apt description of the habitués of private bars would recognize them as secret drinkers. In these more recent times, the private has been the secluded lair of those who have come down in the world and are no longer comfortable amid the more gregarious and contented souls in the other areas. It is also the room apart for those who attach shame to drinking, who ask for their drinks in whispers, and who may not talk to one another.

Appropriately, the private bar has often been merged with the jug and bottle department. Jugs and bottles are filled with beer for customers who often wish to give the impression that they are buying for someone else. Their containers are wrapped in plain paper by a bartender who does not have to be asked to perform that desired service. While an atmosphere of camaraderie is likely to prevail in the pub's other rooms, here furtiveness and shame depress the atmosphere. The same liquors that serve as "conversational juice" in the other rooms fail to fulfill that function in this gloomy compartment.

The private bar, always more popular in the southern cities, should not be confused with the taprooms of the North. The latter are private in the sense that local convention usually reserves them for the pub's regulars—strangers wandering into them would be guilty of bad form. The taproom caters to the same class of drinkers as does the vault. Its prices are the same and its decor is just as austere, but the taproom is more of a sit-down place, a poor man's club in which games are played.

This brief review of the pub's different rooms may arouse the purist to protest such general descriptions, but it does serve to outline the origins and character of the different areas within the walls of the same building. The English pub still carries forward a tradition of multiple bars within one, even as the class distinctions that gave rise to them are being abandoned. Multiple rooms still serve to advantage in a variety of other ways, adding to the richness and resilience of this most venerable among the world's third places.

The variety of appeals offered in the same house maximizes accommodation. In the United States, by way of contrast, a tavern taken over by truckdrivers or millworkers seldom entices anyone else no matter how handy the location. The English pub, however, has always been able to cater to those of many walks of life residing within or passing through its locality. The inclusiveness of the pub is maximized by its several rooms; its flavor is not contaminated by the excessive rowdiness or sedateness, coarseness or gentility, of any particular clientele. In comparison with the American bar, the English pub is far more likely to belong to everyone. The breadth of its appeal also explains how the pub could be so prolific, though not so much now as in the past.

Publicans did not have to decide what kind of place they wished to operate based upon a singular appeal to one or another class of drinkers. The typical house appealed to all comers. It could thrive wherever there were people, irrespective of how those people differed in their preferred mode of social drinking.

In those regions and in those times when English men and women lived in two different social worlds, the multiple rooms of the pub accommodated this reality without excluding women. Where custom barred women from one or another of a pub's rooms, they were well-received across the hall. From the days of the alehouse on, women have not been denied in England as they have been, for example, in Australia. In the land down under, women have been excluded from bars and have taken their revenge in the polling booths with the result that "Aussie" pubs have closed their doors at the unthinkable hour of six o'clock in the evening. English women, in contrast, enjoy full access to the pubs and today account for about half of the entire pub trade in the United Kingdom. Clearly, multiple rooms have paved the way for English women, allowing them as much entrée to the pub as they have wanted.

Multiple rooms have encouraged experimentation within pubs and helped the pub adapt to a changing world. The saloon lounge lingered after its intended function (that of upgrading the establishment and thereby attracting both male and female middle-class patronage) had been served. As Davis observed, it remains as the ideal place in which to try new features and cater to new fads.[20] In the lounge, management may install video games, pinball machines, and various other diversions for which demand may run high for a time. In a one-room drinking establishment, such enemies of conversation and sociability might well drive away the regulars and cause the downfall of an otherwise good pub. Using the lounge as an experimental room preserves the tried and true appeal of the public and saloon bars during the course of the experiment. The modern pub, as Davis is well aware, is subject to pressures for change from many quarters—from authorities, from minority groups, from the bright ideas of the brewers who own most of them, and from the ever-present social reformers. The third room serves as a buffer against many of the shocks emanating from a variety of idealists who would put the pub under if given full reign.

The persistence of the basic types of rooms, each with its own flavor and decorum, continues to please patrons no longer concerned with either the social pretense or the price differences that earlier served to separate them. New generations of pub-goers find that the different rooms suit different moods. Ther: are times when one desires the informality of the public and wishes to banter with one and all. There are other times when one prefers a more intimate withdrawal and greater physical comfort. There are occasions when one is geared to the exercise of wit, and other occasions when wit is exhausted. A certain happy irony is evident: the circumstances that once broke the pub into separate compartments to keep the classes apart ultimately resulted in a variety of environments that all may enjoy.

Double Trouble

The benches and the brewers represent twin threats to the life of the English pub. Licensing magistrates combine excessive regulation with a misguided sense of public good, while the beer companies combine greed with mismanagement of their "tied houses." For the past seventy-five years, pubs have struggled against these forces and are losing that struggle.

Government's most obvious intrusion is the law that keeps the pubs closed two-thirds of the day and that has long since ceased to be necessary. England is no longer that "tight little island" it was a century ago. It is a sober nation in which the "beverage of moderation" is the most favored and most of it has a lower alcoholic content than America's Budweiser.

England's unpopular law was enacted in August 1914. Disturbed by impaired worker productivity in the war product factories, and using the broad powers of the Defense Act of the Realm, the Home Secretary severely restricted the pub's hours of operation. Prior to that time, the Edwardian pattern of pub use prevailed with a 5:00 A.M. opening and continuous operation until 12:30 A.M. closing time. Under the new restrictions, pubs cannot begin serving until eleven in the morning, after which they must close from 3:00 to 5:30 in the afternoon, with final closing at 10:30 P.M. The people deplore this policy. Like the income tax, it was meant to be a temporary measure but, like the income tax, it turned out not to be. The war ended and life returned to normal—except that enjoyable part that centered around pub gathering. Many prefer to believe that the policy persists out of fear that the nation's employees might drink as much as their employers if given the chance.

The severe restrictions laid on the pub's hours of operation are compounded by other capricious regulations. In the various districts, the law allows a given pub to open at 10:00 or 11:30, instead of the usual 11 o'clock in the morning. Also, an open door is not necessarily an invitation to come in and be served, for the law states only that the serving of beverages must cease during the prohibited hours. Thus, many pubs remain open in the off-time in order to air out or, as it often seems, to tantalize the citizenry. Finally, the law does not state that pubs must serve the public during the approved hours and, within them, publicans may open the doors or remain closed as they please. One can thus appreciate the bittersweet appeal of the old cartoon postcards that depicted two red-nosed regulars leaning against the mahogany bar with glasses filled and the caption reading: "What are the vilest words in the dictionary, Bert?" "Dunno." "TIME, GEN-TLEMEN, PLEASE!"

In Maurice Gorham's little volume entitled *Back to the Local*, there is a drawing by Edward Ardizzone that depicts one of those "sad little groups" of people who gather on the streets beside the pubs after the premature closing time. These groups, writes Gorham, are not the alcohol addicts or toughs spoiling for a fight. Rather, "these are the people who use the pubs; who meet their friends there, talk there, exchange the news there, and prefer the cheerful company of the bar to the strait confines of their home. They cannot bear to say goodbye to all that. They linger on the pavement, carrying on conversations they have begun in the warm, bright bar, whilst the lights go out behind them, the bolts are shot noisily home, and the iron gates close with a clang."[21]

Pub hours were inflexibly limited for seventy-five years in spite of the changing habits of the people. Work weeks became shorter and the work ethic weaker. People rise later and few avail themselves of the pub's first hour. Better it be added to closing time on Saturday night when the "sad little groups" linger longest. In the summer of 1988, afternoon closing was finally set aside, not in recognition of reasonable rights and freedoms of the citizens but in hopes that increased tourist spending would help a faltering economy.

Overregulation of existing pubs and reluctance to grant licenses for new ones have contributed to the declining number of public houses in England. So too, has the policy regarding the size and location of pubs, which is endorsed by the magistrates and brewers. The older tradition of small and numerous pubs is falling to the idea of fewer and larger ones. Government favors fewer pubs because it is easier to monitor them; the brewers because fewer and larger pubs mean more efficient (profitable) operation.

The older tradition maximized the proximity of these establishments to the people who used them. Forty-some years ago, a survey revealed that "90 percent of pub regulars don't walk more than 300 yards to get to their usual pubs."[22] It was that generous distribution of little pubs that led to calling them locals, and it was their neighborhood flavor that found them filled with familiar faces rather than those of strangers. The pubs built in recent years are larger, fewer, and farther between, with the result that people have to use their cars to get to them. Pubs are becoming "houses of call," where most of the customers don't know one another.

The benches and brewers are managing a double discouragement of the people's more sociable habits. They are discouraging the consumption of beer as well as the operation of pubs. Home consumption of beer is now around 25 percent and has more than doubled in recent years. More strikingly, beer consumption overall dropped by about 10 percent in the brief period from 1979 to 1981.[23] People are going to the pubs less and drinking less while in them. It's not a matter of "beer in front of the telly" at home now, for consumption is down overall. Beer has simply gotten too expensive and many people have given up the drinking habit and, alas, the social one as well. In the industrial North, especially, beer-drinking and pub-going traditions are fading fast.

The brewers are asking about fifty pence a pint as of this writing (about ninety cents American), and resentment against them is strong. Almost half the amount finds its way to the Chancellor of the Exchequer, however, as Parliament holds dearly to the sin tax proportions of duty on beer ushered in by Cromwell's people. When a nation of beer-lovers begins giving up its beverage, when beer can no longer be enjoyed because disgust over its cost sours its taste, tyranny has surely set it. Tyranny it is that would strip the few and simple pleasures from the working classes of any society. It was this same nation that once taxed tea so severely as to deny the poor their one means of entertaining and serving guests in their humble homes.

Americans disturbed at the extent to which our two major soft drink corporations are managing to force competitors' products off the retailers' shelves have only a small taste of what the English endure because of the tied house arrangement. The English brewing industry has long since become the major owner of the nation's pubs. As owner of a pub, the brewer not only controls the way in which draught is kept and served, but is also able to exclude the products of competitors from the establishment. Behind the little pub there is big money, and the fate of the place is subject to the usual dangers of absentee ownership and remote control committed to the single objective of profit.

Like the American auto manufacturer, the English brewer is reluctant to give the dealer or retailer a fair share of the profits. In each instance, relationships with customers are strained because of corporate greed. Both the auto dealer and the publican feel pressure to short the customer in order to survive. The Mass Observation team reported that the brewers often had the landlord's ill will since the majority of them did not give allowance for waste or spillage (an inevitable cost in serving draught beer). From the brewer's point of view, reported one landlord, only publicans who aren't really honest with their customers can be successful.[24] "You take a pub like mine, I wouldn't do anything wrong with the beer . . . 'e never told me directly what to do. The idea was that I should put water in it." And, as for the "smart" landlord, ". . . 'e gets in his cellar and gets his doctoring done, some of them use isinglass, some stoop to the method of having special glasses—the genuine landlord would fall to that before he'd fall to watering the beer." Isinglass was used to bring the specific gravity of watered beer back to normal.

The brewers have also been guilty of negligence in their stewardship of the English public house. The record of their husbandry is blotted—they have allowed physical deterioration to the point of repelling the customer, and they have introduced elements noxious to a sociable pub culture. As to its upkeep, a drinking establishment need not be elegant, but it must not be shoddy nor must it be allowed to deteriorate during the tenure of a loyal patronage. But shoddy many of the tied houses became owing to the greed and short vision of the owners. Maurice Gorham summarized this aspect of profit-oriented remote control:

> The rot sets in when remote accountants, noses glued to their printouts, initiate a nationwide cut in allocations of funds for both repairs and for furnishing replacements. Shabbiness sets in, the customers feel affronted, and the trade falls off. Area managers, looking at their books instead of their bars, decree that the wage bill must be cut in its turn. More often than not this means that time spent on cleaning is greatly reduced. The place begins to look still more unkempt, trade falls further, and again the wage bill must be cut. A downward spiral is in progress.[25]

Using profits to buy up old pubs and build new ones, the brewers often proceeded to lease their places to tenants whose application for license they had backed. The managers, in turn, would take only their beer in return for the favor. Inherent in this arrangement was a decline in hosting. Lewis Melville, a lifelong devotee of the English pub, was sensitive to the change in the host's attitudes that had become pervasive by the 1920s. His complaint was widely echoed: "Mine host no longer greets you with friendly comment about the weather: what are you to him? He is not the proprietor: he is merely one manager of a company that owns scores of public-houses—and he doesn't give a damn for *you*."[26]

In their desire to garner new trade and keep up with fads, the brewers have brought all manner of noisemakers and distractions into their pubs. In a report dating from the 1940s, Gorham spoke of the horror of the jukebox, which had "closed" several pubs to him. In another pub, one sat threateningly in the corner and "the regulars have sense to leave it alone, but any day a Frankenstein may walk in."[27] The friendly atmosphere of the public house, now as always, is based upon conversation and nothing should be allowed to destroy it. The brewers, however, have impaired conversation on a massive scale. Writing in 1981, Ben Davis did not confine his comments to jukeboxes: "What can one say of the miscellaneous, intercutaneous infestation of the juke boxes, one-armed bandits, pin tables, and the amusement machines which now buzz, click, bleep, chatter, and caterwaul in almost every bar in the land?"[28]

Success in running a pub, as in any place of business, means sharpening the eye as to who is *not* present among the customers as well as to who is. In their desire to broaden their trade, the brewers lose many once-loyal customers to the lesser breed who are more comfortable interacting with machines than with fellow human beings. But even they, Davis allows, deserve places of their own: "Let there be pinball parlours, halls of amusement, discotoria by all means. Let them even be licensed. But please don't bring this nonsense into other people's pubs. What is the sense of destroying one to gain the others?"

As the government's abuse of authority over the pubs is reflected in the sharply rising number of private clubs, so the brewers are paying for their faulty stewardship of the pubs in the growing popularity of wine bars in England. The wine bar is no longer the discounted haunt of elderly widows that it was forty years ago. It has become a source of genuine concern to the brewing industry, for the consumption of wine continues to climb while that of beer continues to fall. In part, the trend can be attributed to the quality of the beverages. The kind and grade of ingredients in beer as well as its alcoholic content have been declining despite rising costs to customers. A glass of wine is roughly equivalent in cost to a glass of beer but the former now has an appreciably greater alcoholic content.

Wine bars also press their advantage in food, providing a substantial lunch for far less money than it takes to eat in an English restaurant. The wine bars are comfortable, cosmopolitan, and favored among working women and the softer male that one finds everywhere throughout the modern world these days. A clublike atmosphere, fast service, and reasonable prices compete favorably against the new kind of pub designed by the brewer's architects and favored by the licensing magistrates. The threat to the brewing industry posed by the wine bars is not likely to pass soon, if ever. The regret is that the traditional atmosphere and unity of the public bar is found neither in the wine bars nor in those cushier pubs now springing up in the suburbs.

A Plus for the Neighborhood

"Well, I sure wouldn't want a damned bar in my neighborhood!" asserts the fellow American with whom I've been discussing our mutual lack of a convenient place to get together. He's got me at a disadvantage. I'm arguing about what might be, while he holds to a mental picture of the real licensed establishments as one finds them elsewhere in our part of the country. I must admit that if it became a question of moving a place like Big Al's joint, cement block by cement block from its present location into our development, my protest would probably ring louder than his. The stereotype of the American bar as a cheap-looking, ugly place does justice to all too many of them. By dint of appearance alone, such places don't deserve to exist within the residential habitat of self-respecting people at any socioeconomic level.

In contrast, the typical English local lends charm and color to the area in which it is located. Far from being an eyesore and environmental depressant, the pub often preserves a living example of a distinct architectural form and the best construction with local materials as well (hence the sadness when the brewers allow such roses to fade). Never a cheap block rectangle with an artless sign out front, the English pub is typically a solid and civilized-looking structure. Viewed from a distance it may resemble a small library, bank, supper club, small church, retail store, country cottage, or an inn. That aesthetically disastrous aggregation of parked cars beside the typical American tavern is absent from most British pubs. Outside and in, the settings in which the English take a drink or two in public are models to be imitated.

And what's in a name? May not the individual expect something better at the Dog and Badger than at Big Al's? Is not the English Sow and Pigs less likely to resemble a sty than the place that Jack calls his Lounge? Does not a weathered oil painting of a sign proclaiming The Farmer's Boy issue a more dignified call to cups than that shouted by the neon's red glare? We do have, it is true, places that are called the Steak and Ale, but it's hard to pretend that they have tradition; it is harder still to pretend that they are not cloned at other locations across town.

My characterization of the English pub has, alas, been more backward-looking than current. I've examined the traditional pub as inherited from Victorian times and extolled the English public house in its finest development. It is an inescapable fact that the character of the pubs is declining, as is their number and role in English life. Gorham's obituary on them begins with a brief and sobering statement, which pretty much tells the story: "For those of us who feel sad whenever a pub vanishes, this is a sad life. Progress, reconstructions, town-planning, war, all have one thing in common: The pubs go down before them like poppies under the scythe."[29]

And yet, as Gorham added, there are always signs of renewed life for the pub. May the English gain that measure of wisdom wished for them by Gwyn Thomas at the close of her article on the old inns of Cotswold. In the Fosse Bridge Hotel was a splendid bar about to go under when:

> Came the revival. The sun was let in. Parts of the fabric that had gone to tatters were repaired with material taken from a 15th century Cotswold cottage. The rooms are ample and serene. Lumps of wood like whole trees burn fragrantly in the marginal sort of way wood seems to have. The bar, as night comes in, gets crowded, and strong upon the air is the lulling burr of the Cotswold voices, as soft and assuring and convoluted as the wood smoke. Altogether, a happy symptom of survival. I wish the whole world would look at it, stop playing the fool, and follow suit.[30]

In England, the joys Gwyn Thomas describes as attending inclusive pub association now extend well into their upper-middle strata whereas, in America, they are largely confined to the working-class tavern. If the well-to-do of our nation favored the inclusivity of England's pubs half as much as the exclusivity they've built around the adoption of her church, they and the nation would be much better for it. Late in his life, Robert Frost consented to an interview by Edward R. Murrow and, when asked to name the worst word in our language, the poet and biographer unhesitatingly responded, *exclusive!* It was not, of course, those nine letters *per se* that appalled him; it was the inclinations of so many of his fellow Americans, particularly those of means.

CHAPTER 8

The French Café

IN HIS SALUTE to London, Paul Cohen-Portheim lamented the lack of cafés of the continental type in that city. It seems ordained, he wrote, "that you can have either cafés or clubs, but that both do not flourish under the same sky."[1] Like many before and after him, Cohen-Portheim had come to appreciate the differences between the English pub and the French bistro. Pubs, he found, are "only pleasant for a short time," whereas the continental cafés are "places to dwell in." Joseph Wechsberg, who has described the typical third places of many cultures, was similarly impressed by the sidewalk cafés of the French. The bistro's encouragement of the lengthy visit dictated the title of a feature he once wrote on the subject: "The long, sweet day of the Sidewalk Café."[2] Sanche de Gramont's portrait of the French people identifies the bistro as the natural habitat of many admirable types of people and he, too, sees it as "the kind of place you can spend your day in."[3]

The score of miles that separates French and English cultures thus belies the extent of the differences between them, and though the pub and the bistro are both third places, they are not alike. It is not a matter of which is better but of how each assumes its role in the lives of ordinary people in these two remarkable cultures.

The English date their pubs from the inns and taverns founded after the Roman and Norman occupations; the antecedents of the French bistro or sidewalk café emerged about five hundred years ago with the world's first coffeehouses in Saudi Arabia. From Mecca, they may be traced to Constantinople and eventually to Vienna, where the coffeehouse was introduced with remarkable success and was refined to an

elegance matched nowhere else. From Vienna, this "pleasant institution," as Wechsberg calls it, spread to France. Once established in this
cultural center of the Western world, the sidewalk café diffused outward to become the mainstay of informal public life throughout Latin
and Mediterranean cultures. It proved remarkably adaptable to urban
and village life, to Paris and the provinces, and to the rural and metropolitan regions in adjoining nations for which France offered a model to
be emulated.

Le bistro (as the French usually call it) encourages visits of longer
duration than the pub and is an even more available institution. Against
London's hundreds of pubs, Paris has thousands of sidewalk cafés—
Gunther put the number at 13,977 in 1967.[4] In the mid-1930s, Lebert
Weir reported some eight hundred thousand cafés throughout France,
or an incredible "one café to about every fifty people."[5] If that estimate
was accurate, there were tenfold more cafés on a *per capita* basis to serve
the French than pubs and private clubs combined to serve the English.
At four per square mile, there is hardly a shortage of pubs in England,
and the far-greater proliferation of bistros simply suggests that the
latter play a broader role. In his text on urban sociology, the Frenchman
Paul Henry Chombart de Lauwe assigned the bistros major importance, not because of the usual sentimental appeal in which the café is a
"club" for poor people, "but because it is situated at all levels of
residential life and because it touches all its problems."[6]

Any reference to the bistro as the "club of the poor" is inaccurate.
"Poor man's club" is a common euphemism for third places in some
cultures, but it does not apply to the French. Le bistro is a democratic
and encompassing institution to which all are welcome, and there are
no compartments into which the various grades of humanity are segregated, as in the pubs across the Channel. It is true that the café has
had a male tradition, but not of an extent to have caused resentment
between the sexes. The typical bistro is a third place belonging to
everyone.

Physical Description

As may be inferred from their phenomenal number, sidewalk cafés
are often modest physical structures, and the typical neighborhood
version survives by serving the needs of only a small number of nearby

families. The genius of these places is manifest in the fact that so little serves so well. Le bistro consists of an outdoor and one or two indoor areas, the most important being the *terrasse*, or the outdoor tables, chairs, and that portion of the sidewalk upon which this furniture is placed. Where the sidewalks are spacious, the *terrasse* area is expanded or retracted to meet customer need. In some of the more popular resort areas, *terrasse* seating may extend as much as fifty feet from the entrance proper.

The dominance of the sidewalk area is evident in several ways. Cafés or bistros are often referred to as *terrasses*, and it is the unusual place that can succeed without providing outdoor seating. In frequent visits to the cafés, one soon notes that customers are not evenly distributed throughout the premises. Most prefer the sidewalk section, and the preference is so strong that not even the cold days of winter discourage it. Knowing better than to expect their customers to come in from the cold, the *patrons* set out small stoves or braziers near the sidewalk tables or erect glass enclosures to surround them.

Immediately inside the structure is a room containing a *zinc* or bar-counter and a desk for the cashier (usually the *patron*'s wife) at which change is made and such items as cigarettes, lighters, postage stamps, and lottery tickets are sold. The inner tables are larger than those outside and there may be booths along one wall. Those who play cards or chess usually do so here and toward the back. Behind the desk or the *zinc* may be found a number of pigeonholes into which are sorted letters and other messages for customers who use the bistro to conduct business and arrange their social affairs. A vintage-era telephone is available to serve nearby residents who do not have one, and there is often a small line of people waiting to use it.

There may be a back room created by modest partitions extending from both side walls. Atop the partitions, which are usually low enough to see over if one is standing, there runs a diminutive and purely decorative brass railing. This area is for lovers who wish to be apart from the crowd. The arrangement works out well. No one else would normally wish to be in the back, removed from the congeniality and superior view of neighborhood life out front. In a favorite place of mine, albeit one of unorthodox layout, nothing but an open railing and one step in elevation off the main floor separate lovers from the main crowd. They may as well be shielded behind a solid wall, for no one pays any attention to the occasional couple or couples who use the area for intimate talk and necking. The French are demonstrative and take little note of open displays of affection. As Fernando Diaz-Plaja reports, the spectacle of lovers entwined commands no one's attention; but "foreigners, particularly Spaniards or Italians, stop and watch in amazement, but this reaction is so unusual that the French stop to look at *them*."[7]

It would be hard to imagine a more recognizable third place than a French bistro. Traditional third places tend to have physical features that unmistakably indicate what they are—these are sometimes called signal fittings. Thus, the American saloon had its swinging doors and brass spittoons, the English pub its beer pump handles and dart boards, and so on. The equipment that makes le bistro unmistakable consists of its outdoor wicker chairs, its small, marble-topped tables (about eighteen inches in diameter and pedestal based), and an overhead awning rolled up or down according to the angle and intensity of the sun's rays. As these key visual elements protrude into the street, they as clearly bid the passerby welcome as they proclaim the place's identity. Most of its customers do not really enter a bistro. By taking the preferred seating on the sidewalk, one remains as much out as in.

Bistros normally have no signs outside indicating their names, and for the best of reasons—most have no names. Naming something is the first step toward advertising it, and the French have always been admirably suspicious of advertising—only in recent years have they permitted it on television. But the major reason for not naming a bistro is simply that the neighborhood café doesn't need a name. Its *patron* has filled a local niche and is content with his small, steady business. He has little interest in making his place a port of call to outsiders. The bistro belongs to everyone who lives in or happens by the neighborhood. It is as familiar to its regulars as one of the rooms of their apartments; its unmistakable and protruding presence into the street provides all the advertising that another enterprise might need. The noname bistro also attests to the intense loyalty of its regular customers. The French are not pub crawlers or bar-hoppers, as are their English and American counterparts. A Frenchman has his place, and he confines himself almost exclusively to it. His place is referred to merely as le bistro, and when he tells his wife that he's going to the café, she knows exactly where he may be found.

Joseph Wechsberg is unerring in his summary of the bistro's structural essence when he remarks that such places cannot possibly be mistaken for anything else; that they represent more an emotional than an architectural edifice; and that they consist of "two-thirds atmosphere and one-third matter."[8] That the typical one has inadequate plumbing makes no difference. How many Americans have undergone the shock of opening a water closet door only to find two concrete foot pedestals rising an inch or two from ten square feet of murky water? Yet, the shock passes quickly, and the charm of the sidewalk café is not tainted.

The bistro benefits mightily from not being separated from the view and life of the street along which it is located. These establishments are a far cry from the dimly-lit escapes from life found in other nations. The openness of the bistro lends a legitimacy born of visibility. Whereas the citizenry of another nation may wonder what manner of unsavory conduct might be taking place in the seclusion of its bars or lounges, the French bistro hides nothing. What one sees is what there is, and it is pleasant. Just as the Japanese haiku poet observes that it is a neighbor's burning leaves that make his autumn, so it is the familiar presence of neighbors seated at the outdoor tables of the nearby bistro that makes the Frenchman's community.

Those who have sought to account for the durable appeal of the sidewalk café are convinced that its secret lies in the unique blending of the public and private that is promoted most of all within its terrace region. "It combines the right degree of familiarity and impersonality," says Sanche de Gramont, noting that in such an environment one is content to remain inuefinitely.[9] Privacy is a recognized right of those who visit le bistro, and that right is honored in the characteristic demeanor of the French people. The American Francophile Florence Gilliam wrote: "I know of no look in the world—unless it be the sightless gaze turned upon one another by riders in the subway—that is so impersonal as the one on the face of a person in a café not in immediate contact with the other occupants."[10] Wechsberg's assessment is the same: "Sidewalk café regulars may practically sit in each other's laps, but they never overhear one another's conversations."[11] The people-watching (and listening) that Americans so often consider entertaining or edifying (but in any case acceptable) is not found here. If one does wish to engage a stranger in conversation while at a bistro, he or she may make those overtures that would be out of place in the streets. Those approached may encourage a long chat or a brief one. In the bistro, conversations are begun and ended as easily and frequently as one wishes. The visitor may join a table of friends, circulate among tables, or be left alone to write a letter or read a newspaper, if he or she so desires. There is no pressure to interact with others. The bistro thus offers privacy or sociability to individuals and groups. Its capacity to accommodate people according to their varying moods and numbers contributes greatly to the broad appeal of this neighborhood institution.

A Sublime Habitat

One can drain only so much explication from an analysis of the bistro itself. The larger setting, the environs, are also of major importance. As may be inferred from the bistro's terrace feature and its popularity, there is a reluctance to be cut off from the world immediately beyond the café. That world is pleasant and the habitat in which the French café exists is beneficial to its health; the milieu encourages the place's vitality.

For an illuminating contrast, one need only look to New York City. In the mid-1950s, New York had but one sidewalk café for each three million of its inhabitants or, to be more precise, exactly three. By the late sixties, after their appearance was encouraged to help cut down on street crime, there were but a hundred. For the most part, establishing sidewalk cafés in the Big Apple is akin to transplanting palm trees to Pittsburgh. The environment is not conducive. In a marvelous and richly-illustrated book, which should be a required text for every American who lives in a city, Bernard Rudofsky has included a photo of one of these "so-called sidewalk cafés" on one of New York's avenues.[12] It is nothing like that which the French enjoy. It is not open; it is a shack with windows allowing only a view of the avenue directly in front. Its walls hide from sight an exterior fire escape (the hallmark feature of American architecture, according to Rudofsky), a vacant lot filled with automobiles, and other corrosive elements of the American urban landscape. The appendage does not resemble a sidewalk café, as Rudofsky observes, as much as a street lean-to of the type that the city fathers of New York felt compelled to abolish centuries ago. Few visual comparisons more dramatically reveal the dependency of third places upon their habitats as does the New York sham imitation of the venerable French sidewalk café.

Recently, a youthful friend of our daughter spent a summer in France. Upon her return, she struggled for words to communicate those pleasant and inspiring surroundings that greeted her in village, countryside, and city alike. "Was it as though," we suggested, "one could set up an easel and paint a beautiful scene almost anywhere?" "Yes," she said, "that's it." "Was it," we continued, "that there were no weeds, no junkyards, no profusion of overhead wires, no litter, no gaudy billboards. . . ." "Yes," she said, "everything was beautiful."

France has been blest with a pleasant and natural habitat, and her people have been admirable stewards of it. When Wechsberg suggests that Florida's climate is every bit as conducive to the sidewalk café as that of southern France, he invites disagreement.[13] Florida's humidity is oppressive by comparison and, in Florida, the natives wage a relentless battle against insects. Window screens are not even necessary in the south of France. The French climate is a spoiler for Americans who spend time there, the deprivation of which is not even compensated for by sunny California.

It is the man-made features of the environment, however, that deserve the most comment. For a variety of reasons, some conscious and others not, French culture has preserved a man-made environment that is both aesthetically pleasant and built to human scale. Throughout modern times, the desire to retain the life of the street has prevailed. Even in Paris where the automobile represents a real and ultimate threat, the life of the street and that of the bistro persist side by side.

The French confronted the threat of the automobile as soon as it came into use and developed a preference for small cars. The average-sized woman literally towers over the French version of a station wagon. Interior crowding does not distress the French, who become accustomed to it in their living quarters early in life. Visiting Americans may explain the diminutive French cars in terms of relative cost (the presumption being that *if* the French could afford them, they'd all be driving big Detroit models). The anthropologist Edward Hall sees it quite differently. Hall insists that the French are aware of the consequences of the size of the cars they drive. "If the French drove American cars," he writes, "they would be forced to give up many ways of dealing with space which they hold quite dear."[14] Changes in the size of automobiles, they understand, would have repercussions throughout the entire culture.

Because their cars are small, the French can preserve a seventy-foot-wide sidewalk along the Champs-Elysees. With large American cars, that noble avenue would become the scene of mass suicide. The French are amply rewarded for squeezing themselves into small automobiles. As a consequence, the life of the street is preserved for the pedestrian, for le bistro, and for the eyes and ears. When the automobile is sub-dued, the street remains inviting to those who shop afoot, to those for whom the daily promenade is a cherished form of relaxation, and to those whose social life depends heavily upon the neutral ground of the sidewalk café. And, when these marvelous benefits are available with-out the need to drive somewhere, the car remains smaller not only in size but in importance as well.

On my office wall I keep a photograph of a small bistro located in one of the southern provinces. At one of two tables out front a regular is snoozing as he waits for his pals to arrive. In contradiction to the usual namelessness of these out-of-the-way places, this establishment has a bold and brightly-lettered front awning flap, which proclaims in larger characters: BAR du XX.e SIECLE. XVIIe siecle would be more like it! The structure is centuries old and everything about it, save for that claim on the awning, indicates its age. I suspect the old *patron* hoped such advertising might lure American military personnel who mean-dered his way. His establishment and every building around it was ancient (Calvin's house, intact, was nearby), and there were few indica-tions of any modern face-lifting within the entire quarter. If small cars are typical of the French scene, old buildings are even more so, and while their age and architecture may disturb the progressive, these structures have preserved French villages and most sections of French cities at the human scale.

Several factors have combined to preserve the old and traditional, housing included, in France. The majority of the French are comfort-able and have been so for many years. A style of life enriched in the informal public sector has minimized the importance of the home as a living and entertaining center. The French entertain and are enter-tained in public places. In trying to encourage the people of his country to adopt the ways of the Americans, Jean Fourastie wrote disparagingly of the typical French residence: "The traditional house is fundamentally a fort. It is not active but passive. It protects, it does not serve."[15] To compound what he considered the inadequacies of the French house, Fourastie discovered that, rather than building new homes, the French kept repairing the old ones. Examining comparative data for 1948, Fourastie found that "our [French] construction workers build only three new homes while the same number of American workers are building twenty and the English workers are building thirteen."[16] Time, however, would not favor Fourastie's vision. While Americans were hastily erecting their Levittowns, only to see many of them fail dismally in the short span of twenty years, the French were staying with arrangements that had stood the test of centuries.

Fourastie could not have foreseen the disasters of urban renewal that would taint his American model and would fail to such an extent as to engender a grass-roots reaction in favor of historic preservation and urban restoration in its place. In retrospect, the following passage from Fourastie's book is not the damning argument he intended it to be:

> The problem of the general organization of the economy is the principal one here. It may be summarized in a very simple phrase—France repairs instead of building. Our construction labor is engaged in making repairs. They patch up old houses. They remodel the interior of bars and cafés in Paris and in the provincial cities. They dig and fill in, pave and tear up. They install bathrooms in old houses as best they can. They prop up crumbling walls and replace the roof over rotted rafters. This is what two-thirds or three-quarters of our 700,000 building workers do. Only a small number of them actually build new houses. Thus, it is not surprising that the total number of new houses is laughably small.[17]

Fourastie's prose makes French workmanship appear shoddy but, that bit of self-serving rhetoric aside, he had unwittingly described the approach to housing that now excites many Americans far more than does new construction. Invoking a fallacious equation between automobiles and housing, Fourastie then proceeded to leap to a conclusion certain to delight developers the world over: "Only expenditures for new products [houses included] lead to real improvement in the style of life."[18] To the contrary, it is the emerging wisdom of our time that housing built within an environment that denies a sense of community represents a deterioration, not a real improvement, in the style of life.

The rent freezes, which prevailed in France up until 1964, also functioned to preserve traditional life-styles against the changes inherent in industrialism. Once a family found a place to live, it secured a long-term lease at low cost and refused to move. People would remain in areas of unemployment while, elsewhere, jobs went unfilled. Mobility remained low in France because people refused to move to where the jobs were and refused to move in order to secure better jobs. "The French workingman," wrote Sanche de Gramont, "will not migrate . . . he is in a cocoon made up of family, cronies, and habits, and the prospects of a better salary will not induce him to leave it."[19]

Conservatism grows with the investment in a locality. The longer individuals remain in a given area, the more they resist both change and the idea of moving. Once the French worker finds a tolerable work situation, a suitable dwelling for his family, and a bistro at which to enjoy the companionship of his pals, he becomes an immovable object. Why should he move? The concept to which Sanche de Gramont applies the cocoon metaphor is nothing less than the tripodal base of the good life. Having established his first, second, and third place, the Frenchman wisely proceeds to enjoy them. They are satisfied individuals, neither lonely nor dependent upon tomorrow to bring life's rewards.

The American, having achieved an outwardly similar situation, is far more easily dislodged from it, for the American is conditioned not to be satisfied. As professors Wright and Snow point out, some $50 billion each year is spent on advertising in the United States to promote a consumption ideology as strong and pervasive as the propaganda of any totalitarian nation. The result is that Americans

> believe that progress and individual completion—long the twin goals of Western civilization—are achieved through the consumption of goods and services. Many of us would deny that we, personally, hold such a belief, but most of us behave as if we do. We labor to consume, and we consume in excess of need in order to feel successful, powerful, sexual, or just adequate. Our culture requires that we feel and act this way.[20]

Individuals who can remain content, satisfied, and impervious to the pressure to advance by moving or to the exhortations to consume are rare. They are an anomaly within our culture, not its product. Only recently have the French allowed advertising on television, and they are likely to regret lifting the ban. The bottom line in advertising is: you are incomplete until you purchase these products. Once that message really gets across, no job, no family, and no bistro will ever really satisfy the French as they once did.

In addition to the other aspects of the bistro's surrounding environment that make it pleasant, the walkways, roads, and buildings have been built to human scale. The street scenes around the typical bistro have a familiar pattern yet are never the same. The buildings do not dwarf the people and the streets do not stretch into endless monotony. The structures have varied facades but are harmonious with one another. It is not possible to communicate a wholly visual impression using just words, but visitors to the French Quarter in New Orleans can grasp the imagery by making a few adjustments. Imagine, then, Vieux Carre without its boring grid pattern but with streets veering off at different angles. Replace the delta flat with rolling countryside. Imagine the streets to be of differing widths, with sidewalks wide enough to afford terrace seating. Remove the signs that hang over the street. Put in an open square or two for weekday volleyball and Saturday flea markets. Remove, also, the crowds of tourists and all vehicles over two horsepower. There! You just about have it: here is a quarter built to human scale, ideal for human contact, and capable of housing as many residents as any sterile, high-rise project using the same square footage.

More Than a Bar

Americans have been overtaken by the car culture in which we live. We drive to everything and everything is scattered. Few of us have a nearby place where an assortment of essential goods and services is available. Sometimes, perhaps on a vacation, we get the flavor of some out-of-the-way center. It may be a little general store at a crossroads where one can buy groceries, have coffee or a sandwich, buy gasoline and outboard motor oil, use the restroom, obtain a fishing license or a burning permit, leave a message, or arrange to meet a stranger to the area. The neighborhood bistros of France are much like these outposts but, of course, they are close at hand.

Wine is the French national beverage and daily staple. Those families who do not make their own need only send a child with an empty bottle or two to the local bistro. Where *tabac* shops are not close by, it is the neighborhood bistro that is licensed to sell cigarettes. Lottery tickets, as pervasive a part of French culture as the bolster and bidet, are sold in the cafés. Those permitted to make their own brandy obtain the necessary declaration forms at the café, which also sells the little stamps that must be affixed to every legal document. Many cafés are also convenience stores at which local residents buy groceries and bags of coal. But most likely to impress the American visitor are the services that the *patron* and the help perform for their customers. The waitress at a bistro, or the owner if there is no waitress, counts it a part of the job to transmit telephone messages, look after customers' packages, and run errands for the regular clientele. In the neighborhoods, the ties among the *patron* and local family heads are strong.

The bistro also provides convenient and congenial neutral ground upon which much business is conducted. In this, it bears a resemblance to the English club and the early English coffeehouse, which was its precursor. Soliciting of all kinds is conducted with greater ease when neither home nor office imposes obligation or disadvantage upon one party. Nor is the Frenchman's home anywhere near as open to outsiders as is the American's. People involved in local politics, for example, do not meet in their living rooms but in local bistros. For every French citizen, the bistro provides an immediate political forum. When Laurence Wylie conducted his study of the villagers of Peyrane, he found that custom precluded entering the homes of his subjects. Instead, he administered his Rorschach tests at a back table of the local café, an area that quickly became known as his office.[21] When the typical French family wishes to entertain, it does not do so at home. Dinner guests are taken to restaurants, whereas most casual entertaining is done at the bistro.

Le bistro is a favorite place for writing letters and, for a surprising number, it is a place to write books as well. The capacity of these environments to inspire author and artist has become legendary. University students invade the cafés to study, compose, and discuss. In Toulouse, where the cafés are exceptionally large and the students numerous, it is an evening's delight to stop in and lay oneself open to pleasurable interrogation by youths from the university.

In the small villages, the café is less a *terrasse* from which to view the passing parade. It is more apt to play an expanded role as a community recreation center. This function of the bistro in the smaller settings has been well-documented in Wylie's description of a little "Village in the Vaucluse," a chapter of which is devoted to the town's café life.[22] The village is Peyrane, one of seven neighboring villages in which motion pictures are shown one night each week at the local café. Tuesday night is Peyrane's turn in this circuit, and the man who shows the movies signals his arrival with an automobile horn blast that begins a mile from town and doesn't cease until he pulls up in front of the café. The owner of the café helps him carry and set up the equipment and about three dozen people show up for the film. The adults pay fifteen cents and the children are admitted free. When the show is over, nearly everyone leaves without comment, the sleeping children getting a ride home in their parents' arms. The Tuesday night movie ritual, reports Wylie, never varied throughout his year's stay in the village.

The *place* directly in front of the Peyrane's single café is the setting for the town's *boules* contests. Next to hunting, this is surely the men's favorite pastime. In fair weather, it is played every evening. The café owner, himself a fan of the game, has lights strung up outside. Each Saturday night during the *boules* season, he sponsors a tournament and awards prizes to the winners. The games go on until the wee hours of the morning and are accompanied with such spirited arguing as to have reduced property values in nearby residences. The Spaniard, Diaz-Plaja, insists that this game is perfect for the French since the tongue seems to get a thousand times more exercise than any of the body's muscles.[23] It is not uncommon for discussions of strategy and tactics to occupy a quarter of an hour between tosses of the heavy black balls, and the lapse is far from a quiet one.

In cold weather, *boules* gives way to *belote*, a card game much like pinochle, which every villager knows how to play. The café owner also organizes Saturday night tournaments around *belote*, and these are more lucrative than the *boules* contests are to his business. Cardplaying invites more drinking than *boules* and, again, the sessions are lengthy. This game beckons the women as well, and fifty or sixty contestants must be narrowed down to a pair of winning partners every Saturday night.

The daily rhythms of Peyrane's café are resonant with those of bistros throughout rural and metropolitan France. The two aperitif hours, noon to one P.M. and six to seven P.M. are observed on all working days. The noontime group consists strictly of city men who consume a vermouth-type aperitif and buy one round (or *tournee*) for each man present; the larger the group, the more is consumed. The evening aperitif hour is observed by a larger, less intimate, less formal, and more animated group of men. The preferred drink at this time of day is neither red wine nor vermouth but *pastis*. This milky-looking, sweet, anis-flavored concoction is the most popular aperitif throughout the south of France. Those gathered at the café prior to a late dinner at home drink more than the noontime assembly. Voices are raised and tempers flare when politics are discussed, but the drinking usually stops short of drunkenness.

The café is thus a men's club. It also serves as a home for those whom Wylie identifies as the "Lonely Ones." They too, are males, five or six in number, who are bachelors, widowers, or divorcés, and who live alone. They are the poorest adult males in the community. The café is the center of their existence, and they drink only small glasses (*canons*) of red wine (the "poor man's aperitif") and can afford no more than a couple of these a day. They are the bane of the café owner's life. When not at work or sleeping they will be at the café, where they read newspapers, play cards, trap the owner's wife into conversation, or sit doing nothing. At mealtime, they are wont to bring their own bread and cheese and intrude upon the owner's family.

In larger villages where there are numerous cafés with each serving a distinct neighborhood, bistro life is more apt to reflect a class structure no longer recognized in France's formal institutions. Thus, for example, though anyone may enter any of the fifteen drinking establishments of Wissous, a village of some two thousand inhabitants located near Paris, the people segregate themselves according to their family's standing in the community.[24] Yet, hierarchy continues to fade in the face of the new dimensions of social life. A civil servant ranks with a well-to-do farmer, but they are seldom interested in associating with one another. The various cafés are more apt to host special-interest groups now, which cannot be ranked, than the older class memberships. The informal public gathering places are in flux, but they continue, as always, to represent the basic, grass-roots fora of political life.

That *le bistro* is more than a bar or a drinking establishment is confirmed by the most casual observations. Yet, the bistro is very much a place for drinking. France holds dubious records in the area of alcohol consumption. It is the world leader in producing cirrhosis of the liver and cretinism. Francois Nourissier reported in 1971 that "We won— and kept—the title for being the world's biggest drinkers, with some twenty-seven litres of alcohol per head of population per annum. This is well above three times the American consumption and four times what the English put down. Only the Italians offer any serious competition for this grim distinction."[25]

The question, though, is whether one must accept the conventional liberal view of the problem. Nourissier is obviously of that camp, for he also insists that "what is needful is to remove the reasons and the opportunities for over-indulgence. The first scandal consists in the appalling number of cafés, bistros, taverns, bars, brasseries, and drinking places of all kinds, from the plushiest to the most squalid."[26]

While it is no doubt tempting to blame public drinking places within a nation of people who drink too much, it is often a mistake to do so. We have already observed the negative correlation between drunkenness and the number of pubs in various regions of England. Public drinking is usually a far more controlled and civilized form of alcohol consumption than that which takes place in the home or in other settings. Public drinking establishments have reputations to maintain. It may well be that French drinking is most abused apart from the bistro scene and that the bistro, like the English pub, is guilty only of encouraging a moderate and social form of consumption. This, indeed, may explain why de Gaulle's move against the proliferation of bistros produced no positive results. In the mid-fifties, de Gaulle's government prohibited bistros in the proximity of factories, schools, and sports arenas, but the passage of time brought no reduction in alcohol consumption.

Well do I remember the French worker speeding past the bus stop on his Vespa in the half-light of early morning with six bottles of *vin rouge* in his saddlebags and reaching back to grasp, uncork, and drink in one practiced motion. I also recall the varied troop who came daily to the corner grocery with empty bottles to be filled at eight cents per litre. And who could forget the *water*—that sometimes greyish, sometimes yellowish liquid with all manner of little things suspended in it there for all to see who held it up to the light? To some the bistro may be emblematic of French alcohol consumption but there is every reason to doubt that it is the cause of it.

It should be noted in this context that European bars do not encourage compulsive drinking, as do those in the United States. This is especially true in France. Though the custom is fading somewhat, it has long been a bistro tradition to serve each drink on a saucer and to remove only the glasses from the table as they are emptied. The saucers accumulate, with the result that all may see exactly how many drinks each person has had. The bistro, obviously, is not the place for heavy drinkers. It exposes them. The effect may be seen vividly in Brassai's pictorial study of underground Paris.[27] Against the dark colors all around, the thick white saucers glaringly stand out in Halasz's café scenes. A mere glance around the place would be sufficient to identify anyone within a bistro who might have been drinking excessively. In other countries, care may be taken to make each drink appear to be the first served.

European bars—and particularly the French—temper alcohol consumption in yet another way. They offer a broad range of nonalcoholic beverages along with beer, wines, and spirits. The English pub sells a good bit of ginger beer, bitter orange and bitter lemon Schwepps, Orange Squash, and Ribena (black currant juice). In the summer and autumn, many of them sell formidable quantities of locally-produced cider, a highly-regarded beverage. It is France, however, that offers nonalcoholic equivalents for almost all drinks, including beer. All common fruits are pressed into service so that one may have a *jus de poire*, a *jus de peche*, a *citron pressé* (lemonade), etc.[28] I recall, particularly, a bottled product that came in three flavors: orange, lemon, and lime. The orange was reminiscent of Orange Crush, a drink that came in thin, ribbed, brown glass bottles and that has since almost disappeared from the American market. The French version has a bit more body and tang. Unfortunately, the popular label was *Pschitt*, pronounced exactly as one might fear and embarrassing to order in the presence of other English-speaking customers. What a marvelous disregard for the commercial possibilities within English-speaking markets was manifest in that label.

Café, of course, is the French word for coffee, and the black elixir remains a popular bistro beverage. In the Mediterranean area, custom usually favors espresso. The machines that produce it are large and expensive, so not all bistros have them. Espresso coffee is sipped sparingly and small amounts are sufficient. It bears little resemblance to the

Let us learn from cities where sidewalks are, among other things, a good place to put chairs.

Many Americans learned to enjoy Europe's sidewalk cafés and the relaxation they offer, as did these GI's in their "civvies."

A typical Greek *taverna* suggests that good company and good conversation do not require a lavish setting.

The austere plainness of this Nicosian setting accenuates the essence of the third place—people enjoying one another's company.

The library atmosphere of the Austrian café promotes both literacy and sociability.

An Istanbul café—hangout for cronies or lovers.

Some elderly gentlemen on one of the Kyklades Islands demonstrating that a third place is better than an old folks home.

Entrepreneurs around the country are being inspired by *The Great Good Place* to revive existing and to open new "third place" enterprises and businesses. On the pages following are just a few examples of how they're helping to change the landscape of our cities and towns and the lives of their inhabitants.

Patrons enjoy a Saturday morning on the patio…

At the Third Place Coffeehouse in Raleigh, North Carolina, owners Rich Futrell and Ty Beddingfield set out to create, in their words, "not only a successful business, but also a successful community gathering place where neighbors, friends, and individuals can meet, relax, and enjoy themselves over a selection of light meals, exquisite desserts, and the finest locally roasted coffee available."

…and some quiet time inside at a window-side table.

Opened in November 1998 in Lake Forest Park, Washington, 12 miles north of downtown Seattle, Third Place Books was founded by Ron Sher, who named his store in homage to this book, a major inspiration. "Third Place Company was founded to re-introduce a real third place into communities," Sher says. Its cornerstone, Third Place Books, combines, as Sher puts it, "the best of the eclectic antiquarian used bookstore, the modern book superstore, and the neighborhood library, all in an environment of a communal living room."

Half of Third Place's 45,000 square-foot space is occupied by The Commons, which contains seating for 500 and is bordered by a professionally equipped stage, a demonstration kitchen, five restaurants, and this giant 8 foot x 8 foot chess set with 2 foot high chess pieces.

Friday morning storytelling with Debbie Deutsch of the Seattle Storytellers' Guild inspires young eyes, ears, and imaginations and provides a popular gathering opportunity for neighborhood moms and dads. Afterward, parents and kids can usually be found in the Commons, chatting and lingering over coffee, tea, and baked goods.

Housed in a former Roman Catholic church and Franciscan monastery, Old St. George in Cincinnati, Ohio, calls itself a "great good place for community and spiritual renewal."
Its facilities include a great hall, library, dining room, bookstore, coffee house, and offices for not-for-profit agencies; it celebrated its fifth anniversary in July 1999.

Photos of Old St. George © Old St. George

The Cincinnati Film Commission, one of many community groups that utilizes Old St. George, holds a "Hollywood Does Halloween" party in the center's Library.

Annie Cheatham has spent a lifetime founding great good places. Her most recent venture, which she founded at about the same time she read *The Great Good Place*, is Annie's Garden Store and Gift Shop in Amherst, Massachusetts.

Photo of Annie's Garden Center © Annie Cheatham

Elders offer much-needed help at the height of transplanting season, when thousands of shoots need to be moved from one container to another and there can't be too many hands pitching in.

At Tunnicliff's Tavern on Capitol Hill in Washington, D.C., proprietor Lynne Breaux carries on a tradition of hospitality begun in 1796, when William Tunnicliff opened the Eastern Branch Hotel. "Tunnicliff's is a great, good place," Breaux says. "It is where politicians, poets, and people of all ages, occupations and cultures converse and celebrate." Pictured here is a recent weekend celebration.

Author Ray Oldenburg (center) at his own local great good place. In 1996, Tracy and Steve Spracklen opened their Good Neighbor Coffee Shop in Pensacola, Florida, not knowing that the author of *The Great Good Place*, a book that had inspired them, lived in town. Here is the author at the Good Neighbor Coffee Shop having his weekly "Coffee with the Cops."

weakly-made blends that Americans drink. Espresso is served in a delicate three-ounce demitasse along with a small spoon of proportionate size. The taste for espresso, once cultivated, stands on its own; the manner of drinking it undoubtedly appeals to the French fondness for ritual and ceremony and early inclines them toward it. My image of the French café remains fixed upon one man who appeared daily at a bistro we also favored. He was a sedate businessman of greying middle age who wore dark suits, dark neckties, and, always, a dark waistcoat or sweater. He preferred a booth in the middle region of the café. Black espresso with sugar was his unvarying order and he followed an elaborate ritual in dissolving two miniature sugar cubes at its surface. He was never seen to slouch in his seat but sat in upright dignity as he sipped small amounts of coffee with a grace worthy of royalty. Whether the beverage or the ceremony sustained him most remained a mystery, as did the question of why he frequented a place fairly thick with Americans. Perhaps he had taken it upon himself to impart a few lessons to those of less civilized ways.

A Style of Life

The gentleman just described would never succumb to the convenience of a modern vending machine with its coffee-flavored hot water and plastic cups through which its sorry beverage burns customers' fingers. In his allegiance to tradition and in maintaining the art of *delassment* within an industrial world, he represented the posture of his nation as it has confronted the technological revolution. The nations of the industrial world differ in the extent to which they have availed themselves of technological advances in order to increase productivity and gain consequent increases in the standard of living of the people. France, which has been in a position of leadership among the nations of the world, fell far short of maximizing its potential for increasing both its gross national product and the material well-being of its people. It is no easier to judge this fact than it is to explain it. There is as much to admire as to lament in the French stance vis-à-vis industrial productivity. My purpose is to show the relevance of the third place to the French case.

Fourastie, in his book-length attempt to persuade his countrymen to adopt the ways of the Americans, distinguished between level of living and style of life.[29] Both refer to modes of consumption, with level of living being "a measure of the consumption of all goods and services that can be valued in money, that is to say, those obtained with salaries and other money, which constitutes purchasing power."[30] Style of life, on the other hand, refers to "areas of consumption where a monetary evaluation is difficult and rather futile" and includes climate, neighborhood, urban facilities, leisure preferences, the length of the working day, and the like.[31] Once the basic needs of life are met (and there is relatively little poverty in France, where the great majority of the population is comfortable), a society may choose between maximizing the productive potential of its technology or preserving a valued way of life.

Without question, France was a nation to be emulated long before industrialization put the nations of the West on new terms. Indeed, Thomas Jefferson remarked that every man had two countries—his own and France. It should not be surprising, therefore, that France was not predisposed to sacrifice all to what she perceived as the dubious benefits and costs of all-out production. And she did not. The collective decision of the French to preserve style of life over level of living has, in some ways, been costly. Fourastie is convinced, for example, that if the French had adopted the same length of the work week as the United States from 1920 to 1939, her industrial might would have been sufficient to discourage the Nazis.[32]

In Fourastie's analysis, France's problem stems from the fact that she reduced productivity prematurely, and he documents his argument thoroughly.[33] The question he never answers is *why* she did so. His data, to the contrary, suggest that she should not have done so. Domestic conditions seem to have been such as to urge an increased level of living. Homes were typically without bathtubs or showers. Domestic technology was inefficient; housework took three times as long for the French woman as for the American. By the end of World War II, sewer connections for residential buildings were almost nonexistent in many cities.[34] Running water was slow to catch on and homes and other buildings had from 5 to 10 percent less heat than their American counterparts. Why didn't personal situations, multiplied millions of times over, spur a drive for an improved level of living? Clearly, it was not laziness on the part of the French people. The French may rank high in avarice but not sloth; they rise early, work hard when they work, and retire early. Nor was it a matter of technological backwardness, for the French have made outstanding contributions in all areas of science.

The weight of French social institutions no doubt accounts for some of the differences between the French and American record of industrial productivity. The United States, whose people are highly mobile and whose institutions were not as firmly entrenched, gave itself more eagerly to the quest for an increased level of living. Among Americans, style of life has largely become a matter of what money can buy; that is to say, the level of living dictates style of life more in America than in France. Even one's access to public entertainment depends upon how much money one makes in America.

Everyday French life was preserved as much because of the *balance* among its institutions, perhaps, as because of the weight of their tradition. The French expect more from their institutions than do Americans, and theirs had provided the tripodal base of the good life. The fulfillments of home and work coexist with a full, informal public life available to all French people. The limitations of the French dwelling have been compensated for by the fact that the French do much of their living in the informal public sector. The French home, unlike the American one, has not become a showplace of personal acquisition. To the contrary, many a French villager put off acquiring a television set because the necessary antenna suggested social pretention. With respect to work and work conditions, the French have been keenly aware of the "automatic and coercive character of modern labor"; of the fact that the rhythm of industrial work does not fit human nature as does that of agriculture, which is based on the seasons.[35] For legions of French, the time spent in *le bureau* is justified mainly in that it purchases time at *le bistro*. As Wechsberg puts it, the sidewalk café is an institution that "flourishes best where the pleasures of companionship are more appreciated than the rewards of industriousness."[36]

Companionship for the French is not left to individual inclination, to spare time, and to chance, as it so often is for Americans. The French creed of liberty, equality, and fraternity is institutionally implemented. Companionship or fraternity is firmly established in time and place. The lunch hour is two hours long, one hour for fraternity. The dinner hour is late because the hour preceding it is dedicated to fraternity. In each case, the bistro is the usual setting in which fraternity is pursued. Where level of living obscures style of life, the brown bag lunch may be wolfed down in 15 minutes or less and in private, but this injury to the style of life never caught on in France. Despite the increased difficulty in obtaining a license to operate a café in France since de Gaulle, there is still one café for every thirty-two adult French citizens.[37] Those who explain cultures in terms of the inner character of a people sometimes suggest that the French regard for fraternity is exaggerated. We are not as impressed with such psychic interpretations as we are by the fact that fraternity or companionship is amply provided for in French society and that the times and places provided enjoy a remarkable vitality.

Earlier I argued that escalating human stress is not an unavoidable condition of life in the technological age, that it is possible to install certain features of urban life that soothe and allay stress, just as it is possible to create systems that make stress endemic. The French bistro provides living proof of these contentions.

CHAPTER 9

The American Tavern

A RECENT BUSINESS REPORT on bars and cocktail lounges begins with the warning that anyone going into the bar business these days will face numerous difficulties.[1] The report describes today's customers as a fickle clientele who crave new surroundings and excitement; who are susceptible to gimmicks; and who are quick to abandon old watering holes without so much as a backward glance or a twinge of regret. In order to make a go of it, would-be publicans are informed, they must be able to keep up with trends, cater to an increasing demand for sophistication, be flexible, and be prepared to offer an ever-changing folio of amusements to capture their share of the customers. Though the report focuses on the California bar trade, it signals nation-wide trends in the relationship between American drinking establishments and their customers.

Neither the clientele described in that report nor the management policies deemed necessary to attract them are the stuff of third places. It is well to recognize this at the outset of our discussion of taverns, for those to whom I've described the idea of the third place often respond, "Oh, you mean like a tavern!" The problem with equating the third place with the tavern is that, in the majority of cases, the equation is wrong. Though the public drinking establishment in any culture has obvious potential for becoming a third place, that potential is less often realized now than in the past. The third place tavern is on the decline in American society.

During our colonial era, the tavern was the focal point of community. Combined with lodging facilities as an inn or ordinary, it was "a forum and a community center, a place for genial self-expression, and, for the

165

traveller, a home away from home."[2] In the new communities that sprang up on the frontier, the tavern or saloon was usually the first structure erected. When many of these towns gave their last flicker of life, it emanated from the windows of a saloon—the last place to close down. In the growth of our cities, it was the saloons (German and Irish, mainly) that afforded the melting pots for an ethnically diverse population. For the working people, the tavern has been a social club and a warm complement to the cold life of the factory and, in earlier times, good drink and good fellowship were all that were required to endear an establishment to a loyal clientele and assure a steady replacement of its numbers.

That magnet, however, has lost much of its attraction power. Few trends in American life are as pronounced as the rejection of the public drinking establishment. Despite the greater comfort offered, despite the flocked wallpaper, giant television screens, topless waitresses, wet T-shirts, two-for-the-price-of-one drinks, a lowered drinking age, appeals to women who appeal to men, rock musicians, and a host of other lures, American drinking establishments are losing ground to the private consumption of alcoholic beverages. While per capita consumption rates for alcoholic beverages in the United States changed little since the end of World War II, the proportion consumed in public places declined sharply. One report describes a drop from about 90 percent to about 30 percent from the late 1940s to the present.[3] Another source insists that the decline has been even more severe, claiming that in the East and Midwest (where public drinking is most popular), only 9 percent of alcoholic beverages are now consumed in taverns and restaurants combined.[4]

The tavern is a failing institution, perhaps even an endangered species. The number of licensed drinking establishments in the United States has declined about 40 percent since the end of World War II, and the trend continues. Some count the decline of the tavern as progress, a step in the right direction. Yet, Americans drink as much as when the taverns thrived, and the decline of public drinking may be more lamentable than encouraging. While avoiding few, if any, of the problems surrounding the use of alcoholic beverages, the nation is losing the socially solidifying rituals of public drinking within inclusive and democratic settings. It should also be noted that America experienced the bulk of its current drug problem only after the private consumption of alcohol became the vogue. America comprises but 8 percent of the world's population but consumes 70 percent of the world's drugs. The privatization of drinking, the habit of "getting high" away from the public light, I'm suggesting, may well have been a contributing factor to one of our major social problems.

The licensed drinking establishment is a useful indicator of the quality of informal public life within a society. Both the character and relative popularity of such places tell us much about the ability of the people to achieve and celebrate community, to enjoy their cities, and to reserve time and place during which to enjoy the company of their fellows amid strivings to survive or succeed. Though other kinds of public gathering places also give these indications, those that serve alcoholic beverages have a unique potential to do so.

The Basic Synergism

The unique potential of the public drinking establishment to become a third place or core setting of informal public life derives from a fundamental synergism that comes into play wherever alcoholic beverages are part of a culture. *Synergism* (from the Greek *synergos*) refers to the cooperative action of different agencies such that their combination yields a greater effect than the sum of their effects achieved independently. The talking/drinking synergism is unquestionably at the foundation of the third place tavern and beyond that, I suspect, it is the synergism that has sustained tavern life throughout history.

To be sure, public drinking establishments may combine drinking with other activities, and the industry's current scramble to discover those that will draw customers is nothing new. Gambling, sexual foraging, staged entertainment, drawings, and the like have been around since the competition first opened its doors across the street.

All such adventures in marketing aside, the third place tavern combines drinking with conversation such that each improves the other. The talking/drinking synergism is basic to the pub, tavern, *taverna*, bistro, saloon, *estaminet, osteria*—whatever it is called and wherever it is found. The art of drinking is not acquired with the purchase of Old Mr. Boston's guide to mixing drinks. It is learned in the company of those who combine moderate intake with scintillating conversation, for just as conversation is enhanced by the temperate use of alcohol, the artful and witty game of conversation moderates consumption of liquor. As Tibor Scitovsky remarked with respect to those who know how to use a public drinking facility, "a half-pint of beer is to talk as a bed is to making love—one can do without but does better with."[5]

Tempered drinking "scatters devouring cares" as Horace observed and dispels "all unkindness" as Shakespeare knew. In a relaxed and socially conducive setting, drinking becomes the servant of those assembled by easing tensions, dissolving inhibitions, and inclining people toward their latent sense of humanity. The art of drinking subordinates that activity to its senior partner in the synergism, that of talking. It is a telling truth that the abuse of the synergism, excessive drinking, is first signaled by impairment of the power of speech.

That drinking is maintained in balance with talking in third place taverns is well documented. Studies that focus on drinking patterns make it clear that the tavern's regular patrons do not go there primarily to drink. Drinking for its own sake, as many authors point out, can be done far more cheaply at home. A survey conducted in 1974 revealed that the average tavern customer consumed 2.41 drinks during an average stay of approximately one hour; that 45 percent of the patrons consumed only one drink; and that beer was by far the most popular beverage. The authors registered surprise at finding that "so many men had so few drinks."[6] Another study encompassing some 170 taverns in New York State reported that many taverns attract nondrinkers who nevertheless had the tavern habit.[7] "Where the hell else can a guy meet his friends?" one subject was quoted as saying, thus revealing the primary motivation behind tavern-going. A 1978 study focused on the "style of drinking" as it was observed along many a lengthy tavern bar-counter.[8] The usual style involves being served a beer, drinking a third, half, or all of it soon after, and then setting the bottle or glass aside for a period of from ten to forty minutes. The author commented that "this style of drinking produces a general appearance along the bar of the drinks being relatively unimportant. Hands move frequently to cigarettes and matches, but the long row of beers looks neglected."

These studies are also in accord on the subject of drunks and drunkenness within the taverns. The phenomenon is rare and considered deviant and undesirable among tavern regulars. In my own survey of seventy-eight Midwestern taverns, I encountered but four unmistakably intoxicated customers. Two were young women just recently of drinking age, in a place of low repute. The other two appeared to be chronic alcoholics and homeless men of the street who were soon sent back to it. I encountered no drunkenness among regular tavern patrons.

Though drinking is the junior partner in the talking/drinking synergism, it is drinking that secures the setting. We are almost always and everywhere equipped to talk, but drinking requires a staged setting. There must be beverages and Ganymedes to serve them. There must be equipment for their preparation and service. There should be seating for everyone, and all of this in a place apart. Arrangements should encourage a regularity of gatherings, for synergisms must occur in regular patterns if they are to serve their functions. In social terms, they must be ritualized.

The most important aspect of the drinking ritual is that it takes place among friends. The average American, like his or her counterpart elsewhere, is more likely to drink with friends than with relatives, neighbors, or strangers.[9] A third place tavern must regularly attract a goodly number of people who are already friends, or it must successfully encourage friendship among those who first encounter one another on its premises. Many places fail on both counts.

When one uses the ear rather than the palate to judge a drinking place, taverns sort themselves into three types and the measure of friendship's breadth underlies them all. I refer to them as deadly, B.Y.O.F., and third place taverns.

The deadly place is often encountered where the tavern's location attracts a transient crowd, such as in shopping malls, hub areas, or along commercial strips. Typically, upon entering these synergistic failures, one finds that all eyes turn toward the open door. It is as if the mute assembly expected a minor celebrity to enter. Disappointed, the patrons turn their heads away. There is to be no relief from the strained silence that hangs heavy in the air.

Customers in these places wear unhappy looks. In what should be the "friendly tavern," the customers remain as aloof from one another as strangers riding an elevator. What the new arrival confronts is as much like a wax museum as an assembly of living creatures. Rather than satisfying the sociable urge, this kind of establishment and its dour inhabitants frustrate it all the more. There is an atmosphere of lethargy that edges toward despair.

Such a place embodies a sad irony. Having entered it to gain a respite from loneliness or boredom, its patrons manage no more than to remind one another of those sorry states. Numbers don't seem to help. Silence reinforces itself and the longer it persists, the more unlikely it will be broken.

This unfortunate condition is common where Americans share space with strangers. Our world-renowned gregariousness often seems to be a bottled-up quality lacking outward conventions for "breaking the ice." We don't go in for perfunctory introductions to or handshakes with strangers who share public rooms with us. The norms that now govern strangers in taverns are those that preserve the individual's space and privacy.

Some time ago, curiosity led me to visit an establishment reputed to have a pleasant atmosphere and an enticing bill of fare. It had a handsome long bar in gleaming light oak along which were placed fourteen large bar stools. The first, third, fifth, seventh, ninth, eleventh, and fourteenth stools were occupied. Nobody was talking. Momentarily I wished I had my wide-angle lens, for here was a classic visual example of how Americans remain lonely when together. "Anybody got a good story for me?" was my brazen challenge to this deadly company. Fortunately, number five had several. Unfortunately, they were not good, but I repaid him in kind. The two of us, at least, triumphed over the demon of alienation that held the others in its grip.

The bartender there, like so many these days, was a young fellow with little inclination to socialize and not much to offer when he did consent to speak. He was not that font of local information, that symbol of authority, that arbiter of disputes, or that "character," which bartenders ought to be. The women customers, I suspected, probably saw more in him. He was not the catalyst necessary to get timid patrons talking to one another. Most deadly bars do not have hosts or hostesses who promote conversation in the place. Good bartenders have the knack of getting their customers together and of making sure that the return patron will have at least one personal greeting each time he or she stops in.

In a region of the country where the tavern tradition is noticeably underdeveloped despite a generous number of licensed establishments, two enterprising gentlemen have capitalized on the prevailing ignorance about tavern hosting. They buy a place with that deadly atmosphere I've described. Business is poor and the price is accordingly low.

They take it over and "do their thing," which is good hosting. They learn patrons' names quickly, greet them enthusiastically, introduce them to one another, and, soon, the place is crowded. Even in those off-hours when other places may be empty, theirs has both bodies and life. The location may not be all that advantageous, but the place becomes a "gold mine." Then they sell it, find another disaster of a bar, and work their magic all over again. Hosting is not the only consideration in the evolution of a third place, but few factors are more important. A tavern always reflects the personalities behind its bar.

The B.Y.O.F. (Bring Your Own Friends) tavern may initially offer a convincing illusion of a third place, particularly when it is crowded. Conversation is the main activity, and everyone is talking. The illusion is one of unity, of everybody enjoying themselves together. Upon closer examination, however, one finds that there is no unity. People enter such places in pairs or larger clusters, stake out their territory at bar, booth, or table, and remain rooted there. They talk only loudly enough to be heard within their own small group. Should any patron speak or laugh boisterously, he or she will be ignored or acknowledged with frowns and disapproving glances. Laughter is infrequent. The individual entering alone is almost certainly doomed to remain that way. The patrons, by their choice of seating, the positioning of their bodies, the contained volume of their voices, and their eye movements indicate that invasion of their group by others is neither expected nor welcome. Nobody meanders from one group to the next. No one calls out to friends across the room.

B.Y.O.F. places tend to be cushier ones, with parlor ambience, carpeting, and comfortable seating. Their happy hour includes free snacks and exotic cocktails for the ladies. The volume of business picks up toward the end of the week and after four o'clock in the afternoon when groups of teachers, office workers, nurses, and secretaries let their hair down and thank God for Thursday and Friday. At other times, these places have prolonged slack periods, often with no customers.

The settings afforded in most B.Y.O.F. bars are subdued and relaxing, as a rule. They are conducive to conversation, which flourishes when the crowd is in, but only among those who enter together. Since those who wish to talk with others must bring those others with them, the setting becomes incidental and not likely to engender a loyal patronage. When a cushier place opens somewhere else in the area or when another bar or lounge improves on the happy hour price reductions, patrons are quickly lost.

In the third place tavern there is a degree of unity among the patrons that far exceeds their mere sharing of the same room at the same time. The sense of oneness manifests itself in a variety of observable ways. One sees it in the manner with which patrons enter and ultimately take their positions in the barroom. Most of the clientele of a third place tavern enter alone and are warmly received by those already there, but alone or with others, they act differently from those entering a B.Y.O.F. bar. In the latter, newcomers tend either to stand dumbly while pondering where to sit or make a beeline to some preferred spot as if to get there before others beat them to it. In the third place tavern, there is no urgency to capture a seat. To the contrary, the entry is often like a processional during which the newly-arrived survey the company while it notices them (lest one be chided with "Hey, Joe, I didn't see you sneak in!"). Greetings are extended along the way as the latest arrivals take their measure of the place before sitting down or sidling up to the bar and ordering a drink.

Once served, the denizens of third place taverns are not constrained to stay rooted, as are those in the B.Y.O.F. taverns. They typically avail themselves of the freedom of movement that most American taverns allow. Familiar patrons may stand awhile, sit awhile, and meander about sampling the flavor of other groups and conversations. They may even accost strangers who seem to be enjoying themselves. Out of their loyalty to the place and consequent familiarity with it, third place regulars come to view the tavern as theirs and feel at ease roaming its length and breadth.

In their manner of talking, third place patrons differ from those of other bars. The contrast was evident in two bars I happened to have observed in the same afternoon. After having spent some time in a jolly place nearby, I entered what was reputed to be the "in place" for the youthful "pretty people" of a small Midwestern city. It was the haunt of young professionals, junior executives, and the spawn of local well-to-do families. The style of dress was fledgling attorney and career-woman-after-hours. The patrons were nice-looking people almost without exception and well-behaved except for a bit of bad sportsmanship at the billiards table. Yet, the atmosphere seemed unfriendly, almost conspiratorial.

Why, I wondered, should I have gotten that feeling? I looked about for clues. In surveying the seventeen occupants, I noted a foursome in the billiard nook, one loner, and six conversational pairs seated about the centrally-located rectangular bar. Each of the six pairs of talkers hunched toward each other, heads close and slightly lowered, and spoke in low voices. Now and then one of them would glance outward, not to catch the eye or attention of others but in what appeared to be cold appraisal. Beyond the foursome at pool (who played a more quiet and undramatized game than one usually sees in bars), the conversational groupings remained small. The talk was intimate and secretive, as much when the conversation was between two males as when it was between a male and a female. The scene may have been typical or atypical for that place and for those people. In any case, it served to illuminate the different character of third place conversation.

What one usually hears in the third place tavern is a hybrid between casual chatter and a public address. The patrons have a habit of speaking more loudly than is necessary for them to be heard within their immediate circles. How conscious or intentional this is I cannot say, but the effects are clear. The boldness of the talk reflects and establishes the self-assurance of the speakers. Projecting voices signal a disdain for intimacy and privacy and a posture of openness to the larger group. The extra three to five decibels allow comprehension among those not in the immediate circle and invite response and participation from them. The employment of extra volume operates as a mechanism encouraging inclusion, wider participation, and unity within the third place tavern.

To be sure, voice levels will drop as discretion now and then dictates, but they will also rise above the usual din of unorchestrated orations and pontifications. Now and then a voice is raised in directing a question or an observation at someone far across the room. This is frequently done when the message is intended to gain a laugh at someone's expense, for the wider the audience, the greater the effect. Others know the characters thus engaged in verbal dueling and appreciate their exchanges. Additionally, loud hoots, hollers, screams, and wails of lament may pierce the air. During the course of my observations, such outbursts were anticipated, and when they occurred I jerked my attention, not to the communicating parties, but to the faces of those not directly involved. In third place settings, those others typically register amusement at the long-range vocal missiles or, if they become too frequent, ignore them. But rarely would anyone register a frown or otherwise express irritation as one may expect in B.Y.O.F. bars where people resent intrusions on their attention and privacy.

Topics of conversation do not appear to differ greatly between third place taverns and the other kinds of drinking establishments. Sports, recreational pursuits, news events, and politics are on the agenda. It is my impression that local matters are more likely to be discussed in third place taverns, probably because they appeal to the interest of everyone. The most striking difference in the content of barroom talk is that in the third place taverns, as opposed to the others, there is an almost continual interweaving of the topic at hand with comments about the discussants' personalities. Third place discussion may begin with all due attention to some subject, but a minor epidemic of *ad hominem* remarks is almost certain to break out somewhere along the way. At times, the subject of conversation is totally subverted to the fun the speakers poke at one another; topics introduced in all seriousness become but trapezes for the display of wit and personality. Those times are frequent in the third place tavern and it is for that reason, I suspect, that talk there is so enjoyable to the patrons.

A Hard Core of Regulars

The single essential element of a third place tavern from which all other characteristics derive is a hard core of regular patrons. A tavern that has its loyal regulars is truly a gathering place; one without is but a port of call. In some third place taverns the regulars constitute a small minority, in others they are in the majority, and in some places, they constitute the totality of the patrons.

What are tavern regulars like? How do they differ from other people? The anthropologist Cara Richards gives us a good deal of descriptive information about them and, beyond that, interesting clues as to their inner character. Due to a most fortunate bias, over 90 percent of the taverns in her survey were the homes-away-from-home of a steadfast corps of regular patrons.[10] What follows is drawn from her report.

The majority of tavern regulars are male and married. A wide variety of blue-collar and white-collar occupations are represented among them. Notably absent were teachers, doctors, lawyers, and clergy. Richards found, as have others, that tavern regulars have a low level of involvement in formal voluntary associations and that tavern life and tavern friendships provide what others find in Rotary, Optimists, and other such organizations. This is not to suggest that the tavern is a second choice or a haven for those not so welcome elsewhere. Rather, the tavern is *preferred* over formal voluntary associations by a good many people. Often downgraded as the "poor man's social club," the tavern can often be everyman's perfect club. There are no dues, no command performances, no official duties, no unavoidable stuffed shirts, no pressures to assume responsibility, etc. There is far less in both the membership and the protocol of a tavern group to remind one of the work bureaucracy than is found in voluntary associations. There is also less reflection of the social hierarchy in tavern life than in Rotary, Kiwanis, church life, or other forms of voluntary organization. In social structural terms, tavern life represents the polar opposite of the bureaucratized workplace and for many, if not most tavern regulars, this adds much to its appeal. The tavern offers as clean a break from structure and pretention as any establishment can offer. It is casual, relaxed, and ultimately democratic.

The apartness of a regular's tavern involvement from other ties corresponds with the manner in which typical tavern regulars come to discover a place and establish themselves within its company. One of Richards' most intriguing findings was that *none* of the tavern regulars she encountered had been brought to their (eventual) third places by friends. Rather, they found the tavern on their own and won acceptance there on their own. They relied on no formal or informal networks to find a place or to keep them company within it. Friends, Richards goes on to report, are important to tavern regulars, not in the discovery of good places but in bringing the regulars back to them. The friendships that account for regular patronage are not those made previously but those made in the course of repeated visits to the tavern and among the other regulars.

Just as typical French citizens or typical Londoners find a place on their own, so might Americans be expected to do the same. We are a land of *individuals*, are we not? And yet many Americans enter taverns only in the safety of numbers; many would not consider going into one unescorted by friends—friends very much like themselves. I suspect that it is not so much a matter of class consciousness as occupational cloistering. I frequently encounter successful business people out rubbing and bending elbows with both white- and blue-collar wage slaves, but can count on one hand the number of professional colleagues who find and frequent bars on their own. The cloistering is even more obvious among public school teachers, for whom tavern drinking is now permitted. Not only do they go to taverns together, they often do so in such numbers as literally to take over the places they select. Teachers' bars have become a separate area of field investigation.[11] Similarly, lawyers have their places, which they tend to visit en masse. Richards, it will be recalled, found no teachers or lawyers scattered among the diverse groups of regulars in her taverns.

The font of the professions is the university, and it is worth asking whether the student's university experience is such as to discourage individualism in the discovery and incorporation of third places into adult life-styles. There is no question but that the university experience promotes drinking, and that much of it is tavern drinking. College students do more drinking than any other category of people of comparable size in the nation. The pattern, however, does not condition young drinkers to show loyalty to one place.

Friends and frequenters of the tavern may generally be divided into two sorts: those who show loyalty to a place and its regulars, and those who show loyalty to a drinking group but to no specific place. The subculture of university life seems to encourage the latter. Within that culture, the traditions of crashing, slumming, bar-hopping, and nocturnal prowling are strong. But those who frequent taverns as members of a roving band do so over a relatively brief span within the life-cycle. A significant dropout occurs upon graduation, an event that disbands many drinking groups. Many go on to find kindred spirits in the workplace, usually among college grads who had the same sort of training in social drinking elsewhere. Within this pattern of social drinking, any given tavern need not be particularly friendly or otherwise special. It is the cruising group that is special and provides all the friendship required. For the merry band, any tavern to which one brings his or her own friends will usually suffice.

But this pattern is not suited to life's long haul. As the merry band gets older, as its members marry and have children, as the once boundless energy discovers limits and as hangovers become more discouraging, the bar-hopping forays become less frequent and more difficult to organize. A few balding and paunchy stalwarts attempt to relive their college outings, but middle and old age call for a different relationship with public drinking places.

When the gang slows down, suffers attrition, and the majority outgrow their carousing habits, loyalty to a place comes to offer the more promising alternative for a continued pattern of friendly social drinking. But that pattern is different. It involves making friends as an individual with a more diverse group of people. The insular "groupiness" of much youthful tavern drinking may not be conducive to this.

How regular are the regulars of third place taverns? Richards found them to be *very* regular. The majority stop in at least once a day and none appear less than twice a week. Those who work nearby may stop in "several times a day." The average stay varies in duration from one to three hours. Frequency of visit, as well, depends upon proximity. The closer the tavern to where the regular patron lives or works, the more often he or she will visit it.

One final and important finding from Richards' investigation into the nature of tavern regulars deserves special mention in a society in which the planning and reshaping of cities is based on prior surveys. In response to these surveys and to the inquiries of the social scientist generally, tavern regulars are typically their own worst enemies. When asked how often they "go out with" or "get together with" their friends, tavern regulars usually reply "seldom," "rarely," or "only on special occasions." In fact, they go out almost every day and get together with their friends just as often, but they do not *count that*. As Richards notes, a quiet evening at the tavern is counted much as a quiet evening at home. The result is inaccurate surveys.

Typical tavern regulars have established the tripodal base of their contentment. They have incorporated home, work, and sociability into a daily pattern of activity and attendance. But, to the social scientist who measures involvement in terms of formal memberships, tavern regulars appear to have impoverished social lives, with too few relationships for normal human development. Survey results inaccurately show them as people for whom any kind of housing and neighborhood would do as well as their present situation.

The Decline of Third Place Taverns

We have already taken note of the sharp decline in the proportion of drinks consumed in public settings. Closer examination of the nation's drinking habits reveals, however, that not all types of drinking establishments are suffering the effects of that larger trend. A recent and lengthy analysis of the bar business identifies four basic types of public drinking establishments existing in the nation's cities today. These are the neighborhood bar, the pub or tavern that caters to the "singles" crowd (success here depends upon attracting a balanced number of males and females and providing an atmosphere conducive to their meeting and mingling), the nightclub or cabaret that provides live entertainment on a regular basis, and the disco, which has come to mean a place for dancing.[12] Of the four, the neighborhood bar is experiencing the sharpest decline by far and, of the four, it is the only one likely to be a third place.

Recently, an official of the Illinois Licensed Beverage Association estimated that, in the period since the end of World War II, the number of local taverns in Chicago dropped from ten thousand to four thousand.[13] Milwaukee lost about nine hundred taverns during the same period, and urban renewal in Baltimore and Cincinnati has purged those cities of a great number of neighborhood bars.[14] An official of New York's Licensed Beverage Association reports that of all the bars that lined Third Avenue at the time the el was torn down, only a third now remain.[15] In Los Angeles, where neighborhood after neighborhood is maimed by the construction of more freeways, local taverns are disappearing at a rapid rate.[16]

Taverns are being demolished in old neighborhoods and prohibited in new ones. The sterilized and purified suburbs broadly developed since the end of the war are hostile to virtually all kinds of establishments that might serve as informal gathering places, especially taverns. Members of older neighborhoods who moved to the newer suburbs, as Paul Kluge observes, can get together with others at the country club or golf course now and then, but back in the city "the poor stiff just takes a bottle home."[17] The third place tavern relies on a hard core of regular patrons and those patrons must find the tavern convenient in order to incorporate it into daily life as a third place. The steady trend is for taverns to be divorced from residential areas, and that trend affects their character, their popularity, and the makeup of their clientele.

During the same period following World War II, when the proportion of drinks consumed in public places plummeted from 90 percent to 30 percent, two large new categories of drinkers were welcomed into the public establishments. A lowered age of majority brought in multitudes of drinkers previously excluded, and the new freedoms of the single female brought in many women drinkers. Even with these massive injections of new bar patrons, the trend continued in the direction of doing more drinking away from the tavern than in it. The rejection of the tavern by its traditional mainstay trade—married males at or nearing middle age—is even greater than most statistics suggest.

The simple neighborhood bar gives testimony that a good third place is often as plain as dirt and need not be otherwise. Kluge summarizes such a place nicely, describing it as "a plain, unvarnished pouring place, where the drinks and the drinkers, the faces and the conversation, are as slow to change as the records in the jukebox or the plumbing in the men's room."[18] But plain will no longer suffice. Nowadays small business advisors stress a lively ambience, decor based on a clever theme, lots of entertainment, "island" bars to encourage mingling and meeting, and a careful choice of colors and accessories. The third place setting has one fundamental interior requirement that puts all others far in the background, and it is *who* one can count on meeting there. As a place fails that criteria, it must turn increasingly to gimmicks and competitive decorating, as is currently the case.

I've weighed the content of a good deal of recent literature concerning the tavern business as issued by the brewing companies, beverage associations, and general business periodicals. Much of it is rampant with hype and promotion, and the use of statistics is pronounced. Those statistics, however, tend to focus on profit and how to maximize it, and not on the dwindling portion of the population remaining friends of the tavern and how to keep them. One is led to wonder about the ultimate effects of the image of the trade as it is being presented to the tradespeople themselves. The main thrust of the advice concerns maximization of profit at the customer's expense.

The drinking public is not unaware of these practices or of the escalating cost of a barroom visit. I've asked many a middle-aged man why he has given up the tavern. The usual response is: "I can make a better drink at home, a helluva lot cheaper, and drink it in quieter surroundings." Neighborhood tavern operators struggling to hold onto their regular customers are even more aware of these discouraging trends. In the survey of Midwestern bars conducted in 1981, I learned that many neighborhood tavern owners absorbed as many as four price hikes before passing some of the increased cost on to their customers. One owner posted a bittersweet notice on her back bar: "Due to rising costs everything is now a nickel more." In response to my compliment on the attractive price of the house's basic highball, a lovable old dame behind the bar of a southern lounge said, "Hell, if I raised the price my regulars would crucify me!"

The experts also urge bar owners, present and prospective, to gear their advertising to the needs of the customers. Owners are told that customers are lonely, looking for a good time, looking to meet someone, ready for some fun and excitement, ready to get away from the rat race, tired, and frustrated. The list goes on, but you get the point. "Customers come to a bar seeking pleasure and companionship. So hit that hard in all your advertising."[19] As never before, the tavern industry is aware of the alienation bred by our modern social structure and, with all the sophistication of modern marketing techniques, it is capitalizing upon it. But the abuses of *caveat emptor* are not immune from the risks of *caveat venditor*, and the seller must eventually beware.

It was predictable, to take a recent example, that the industry's cultivation of the female customer in "singles" bars would eventually incur its costs. By the early 1980s, the message in many letters to the advice columnists was clear: "Women of America, get smart! You don't want the kind of men you'll find hanging out in bars." Thousands of bars were making healthy profits out of the unhealthy business of bringing young women into contact with just those unsavory men. In the long run, the reputation of the American tavern suffered a setback—no matter that "the kind of men" women find in taverns are the ones their presence attracts.

The quality and reputation of the tavern in society depend upon the nature of its synergy—on the activities that the tavern combines with drinking. Taverns lose status where they encourage gambling. They gain status where they serve as informal community centers. They lose status when they play host to those at or beyond the margins of lawful behavior. They gain status when they are suitable places for the whole family. They lose status (as we are now seeing) when they assume a role in the mate-selection process. They gain status where they offer a good lunch. They lose status when they harbor prostitutes. They gain status when they sponsor athletic teams. They lose status when they sell to minors. They gain status when they serve as the informal social clubs of decent citizens.

There are no surprises among these examples of what helps or hurts the reputation of the tavern. Why, then, has the reputation of the tavern not improved? Why has the tavern industry lost the bulk of its traditional trade? If there is so little mystery surrounding the idea of a good tavern, why has a nation of drinkers largely turned away from these establishments?

The major factor, and the one that lies behind most of the others, is *proximity*. A place that is close to the homes of its regular customers, which encourages people to come as they are, need not offer much more than the company it easily attracts. It is what the English call a local, and it is always as good as the neighborhood in which it is located—no better and no worse, except that it makes a real neighborhood out of what might otherwise be nothing more than strangers who happen to live near one another. Homes surrounding country clubs have a local, and the homes of the low-income families (if not yet assaulted by urban renewal) have them on many corners, but the local is no longer available to the middle class.

Many middle-class Americans escape the boredom of their neighborhoods in various kinds of drinking establishments that must be reached by automobile. In perusing a local zoning code, I found that every tavern must have one parking place for each two employees and one parking place for every three customers' seats. This formula for tragedy produces a high yield. Up until the 1950s, the drunken night owl staggering home from the tavern and hanging onto the lamppost to stay upright was the basis of many cartoons and dime-store mementoes. The staggering is now done behind the wheel of a car, and one can find no humor in it. The homeward-bound-sot cartoons have been replaced by public service announcements aimed at the drunk driver, and the viewer is made aware of the high proportion of accidents in which alcohol is involved. More impressive to me is the great number of accidents that are caused by *sober* drivers. Driving is a hazardous, complicated, and attention-demanding activity. At night, when most drinking occurs, it is even more fraught with danger. Why should a nation of drinkers arrange their municipalities such that drinking and driving are frequently and almost necessarily combined? "Gasoline and alcohol don't mix," says the American slogan. Of course they do. Our urban planners mix them all the time and in great doses. See the zoning codes for confirmation.

Perhaps one day Americans will manage a place for relaxed social drinking of suitable character so as not to destroy the market value of any home within walking distance. Maybe it will happen in one of those tract housing developments in which impending deterioration encourages people to take a chance. One of the existing houses might be converted—no parking lot, no neon signs to attract outsiders—just a local for the locals. Perhaps the irresistible convenience of such a place would allow it to survive as a small, steady-state business without need of an outrageously expensive hard liquor license. The owner might live overhead; the family might help run the place. Maybe morning coffee will be available. Ah, but I'm drifting into fantasies of neighborhoods of, by, and for the people, and that belongs to some future generation, not mine.

CHAPTER 10

Classic Coffeehouses

HISTORICAL ACCOUNTS INDICATE that those loungers who invaded the old country store helped themselves to a considerable variety of consumables stocked in bulk. In the days before the Smith Brothers introduced individual packaging to protect their cough drop enterprise (proprietors were putting cheaper substitutes in the Smith Brothers jars!), the hangers-on at the general store dipped into barrels, buckets, crates, tubs, and jars for such items as Herkimer cheese, dried prunes, licorice, dried herring, pickled herring, crackers, and tobacco.[1] Notably absent from the inventory of consumables are *liquids*: There is no evidence that cider, tea, coffee, sarsaparilla, or even water were regularly drunk around the pot-bellied stoves. Similarly, the gatherings at River Park's express office were occasions at which much tobacco was smoked and much was chewed, but there was no coffee.[2]

The absence of lavatories in those places and a social milieu devoid of coffee break rituals, omnipresent vending machines, and massive soft drink promotions no doubt helped to condition the cracker-barrel set to do without beverages during the periods of their assembly. Dry oases such as those, however, are an anomaly among the third places of the world. The general rule is that beverages are of such importance as to become veritable social sacraments. "Every social lubricant," observed Kenneth Davids, "has its home away from home, its church, as it were, where its effects are celebrated in public ceremonies and ritual conviviality."[3] Indeed, the majority of the world's third places have drawn their identity from the beverages they have served. There are or have been ale houses, beer gardens, tea houses, gin palaces, 3.2 joints, soda fountains, wine bars, milk bars, etc. The Czech *Kavarna*, the German *Kaffeeklatsch*, the French *café*—all derive from the respective words for coffee. Typically, the third place is a watering hole of one sort or another.

Social sacramental beverages or "lubricants" are almost always either stimulants containing caffeine (coffee, tea, and the various colas) or narcotics (beer, wine, or spirits), which contain alcohol. Milk bars have rarely gained much popularity. During prohibition, many attempts were made to provide saloons that did not serve alcoholic beverages so that the common people might not lose their social centers along with their beer and whiskey, but they failed.[4] The relationship between the social system and the nervous system is a close one. Whatever mental and emotional states the daily struggle induces, the third place and its social lubricants are the correctives.

Caffeine beverages encourage behavior different from that associated with alcoholic drinks. How much of the difference may be attributed to the chemicals themselves is difficult to ascertain; in either instance, behavior is largely the product of cultural learning and may vary widely from one society to the next. Yet there are definite patterns that cut across the world's cultures. In the Moslem world, where coffee drinking began, that beverage is the "wine of Apollo, the beverage of thought, dream, and dialectic."[5] Similar effects are noted in the Christian world. Coffee spurs the intellect; alcohol the emotions and the soma. Those drinking coffee are content to listen contemplatively to music, while those drinking alcohol are inclined to make music of their own. Dancing is commonly associated with the consumption of alcoholic beverages but not at all with coffee sipping. Reading material is widely digested in the world's coffeehouses but not in bars. The dart player drinks ale inasmuch as deep thought is not the essence of his game, but the chess player's drink is coffee.

The present concern, however, is not with the general physiological effects of alcohol or caffeine per se, but with the social consequences of the settings in which they are made available to a consuming public. Earlier, I described third places that have emerged on licensed premises. Here attention is directed to those centers of civility whose identity is derived from the coffee bean.

The Penny University

Vienna boasts of having the first coffeehouses in Europe, but by a third of a century, England lays claim to the first in Christendom. In

1650, an enterprising Jew remembered only as Jacob opened the first coffeehouse in Oxford. Shortly thereafter, others were opened in Cambridge and London. The coffeehouse and its "bitter, black beverage" were initially regarded as a novelty—but not for long. The democratic atmosphere of the coffeehouse, its equally democratic prices, and the pleasant contrast it offered to the drunkenness that plagued the inns and taverns of the seventeenth century brought it quick popularity. By the end of that century, any man in London could easily find a coffeehouse. He needed only to follow his nose down the nearest street.

Within twenty-five years, the coffeehouses' popularity had precipitated a small crisis in the government's monetary policy. The shortage of legally minted small change prompted the coffeehouses to issue their own coins or tokens, which were generally honored by all the shops in the immediate area. The tokens were variously stamped from brass, copper, pewter, and even gilded leather. Those remaining in various numismatic collections are often the only proof of the existence of a coffeehouse that has long since passed into oblivion.

In the era of its reign, which some set at two hundred years, or from 1650 to 1850,[6] the coffeehouse was often referred to as the Penny University. A penny was the price of admission to its store of literary and intellectual flavors. Twopence was the price of a cup of coffee; a pipe cost a penny; a newspaper was free. The coffeehouse of the seventeenth century was the precursor of the daily newspaper and home delivery of mail; it was the prototypical club at which many Englishmen conducted business affairs. Indeed, many customers kept regular hours in order that friends and clients would find it easy to contact them. Whether on a regular schedule or not, many Londoners dropped into the coffeehouse several times a day in order to keep abreast of the news. Customarily, the literate would read aloud from the house's newspapers, tracts, and broadsides so that the illiterate could digest the contents and discuss the issues of the day. One of those broadsides, dated 1677, proclaimed in simple verse:[7]

> So great a Universitie
> I think there ne'er was any
> In which you may a scholar be
> For spending of a Penny.

The breadth of its invitation, the inclusiveness of its ranks, and its unequivocal acceptance of all men, lent an aura of excitement to the early coffeehouses. The joy of discovering people whom tradition had suspended in their respective places was endemic to the new coffee establishments and soon became epidemic within them. The coffeehouse was democracy at birth, equality incarnate; it was a heady and hearty involvement that prompted one observer to liken it to Noah's Ark in which "every kind of creature" may be found.[8] Another proclaimed that from his vantage point in the coffeehouse it was like being atop St. Paul's steeple from which "I can look down and see all of London."[9] Many observers of the new scene saw the coffeehouse as a necessary development in which the "friction" of free association provided just what was needed to grind off the rust of an outmoded social order.

A common code of behavior governed London's coffeehouses and a set of Rules and Orders was posted in each. Of its thirty lines of substance, the first six enforced the *leveling* of coffeehouse visitors. It said in effect, that all were welcome and could sit down together; that there were no privileged seats and no requirement that anyone should give up his place to those "Finer Persons" who might chance to enter. It is remarkable that those of all backgrounds complied readily and observed the spirit as well as the letter of rules and orders of the coffeehouse. Not only was one in a ragged coat free to sit betwixt the belted earl and the gartered bishop, here he was assured that these worthies would answer him in civil terms.[10]

The ensuing rules of the coffeehouse served to encourage observance of the primary imperative: All were to be equal under its roof. The prohibitions against dice and card games not only made the house more quiet and "free from blame," as was stated, they also prevented displays of greater (or less) wealth. In like fashion, betting was limited to five shillings and the winners were encouraged to treat the others. Those guilty of swearing paid the house a twelve-pence fine and those guilty of starting a quarrel were obliged to treat those whom they had offended. Humor was kept innocent, political matters were addressed with due reverence, and the Scriptures were not to be profaned. In sum, the rules and orders ensured a suitable degree of gentlemanly behavior, which unquestionably made easier those unprecedented associations among men from different walks of life.

One of the most important of coffeehouse rules was *not* posted. Women were excluded from the premises. The Noah's Ark metaphor was thus a limited one, for no mates accompanied the visitors to the coffeehouse. The absence of women no doubt made it easier for men to ignore the status distinctions that heretofore had divided them, but the new relationships strained older ones. As husbands delighted in the richly diverse and colorful company with whom they took their coffee, their wives were anything but delighted. "For the first time in history," declared Aytoun Ellis, "the sexes had divided!"[11] Scarcely two decades after it first appeared and emerged as exclusively male, the coffeehouse became the target of *The Women's Petition Against Coffee*—a remarkable manifesto, observed Ellis, and indeed it was.[12]

Until recently the language of the Women's Petition was considered to be so obscene and vulgar as to preclude its printing. The first definitive history of the English coffeehouse appeared in 1956, and it must have pained its author to omit the ten paragraphs of that brief but colorful document. Five of those ten paragraphs (including the first four) made the claim that the "base, black, thick, nasty bitter stinking, nauseous Puddle water" causes impotence in the male. Contending that Englishmen were once justly esteemed the "Ablest Performers" in Christendom, the document proclaimed a new and deplorable state of affairs as brought about by coffee:

> But to our unspeakable Grief, we find of late a very sensible *Decay* of that true *Old English Viguor;* our Gallants being every way so *Frenchified*, that they are become meer Cock-sparrows, fluttering things that come *Sa fa*, with a world of Fury, but are not able to *stand* to it, and in the very first Charge fall down *flat* before us. Never did Men wear greater Breeches, or carry less in them of any Mettle whatsoever.[13]

From the coffeehouses, charged the petitioners, the men came home "with nothing *moist* but their snotty Noses, nothing *stiffe* but their Joints, nor *standing* but their Ears."

In addition to the allegation of impotence, the petitioners claimed that coffee was turning men into gossips and tattletales, that the pennies spent for coffee took bread out of the mouths of children, that Englishmen had become better talkers than fighters, and that the coffeehouse was "only a Pimp to the Tavern" in that men were alleged frequently to migrate between the two.

The women's sentiment was as strong as their public charges were silly, but the division caused by the coffeehouse was real and the women were all too aware of it. The petition contains an interesting reference to the inns and taverns of that era against which many criticisms might also have been leveled. But here there was allusion to the "good old primitive way of ale-drinking." What was good about it, apparently, is that the inns and taverns admitted women. The consumption of ale might not, in fact, have made Englishmen the "ablest performers" but at least it tended to aim their thoughts in the "right direction." Also, the women's objection was prophetic. Ultimately the coffeehouse would give rise to the men's club, and these would exclude women to an even greater degree. In the club, men would take up residence in the upper rooms, where it was often possible to live better, cheaper, and with less burden of responsibilities than in a family setting. In the clubs, men would be able to put themselves out of feminine reach altogether; there, many an Englishman would find a permanent alternative to marriage and family life, substituting instead his business, his club life, and his cronies. *Tea*, not coffee, has emerged as the ritual beverage of English family life, and the divisive tradition of the coffeehouse may have been the cause of it.

Wives-left-home were not the only parties critical of the coffeehouses. A year after the Women's Petition appeared, a far more inflammatory document was issued by King Charles II bearing the title *A Proclamation for the Suppression of Coffeehouses*. Fortified, perhaps, by the appearance of the Women's Petition, the king was moved officially to charge that coffeehouses fostered idleness, detracting tradesmen and others from their lawful calling and affairs. Those allegations, however, were so much smoke-screen; the real objection was that the coffeehouses give rise to "False, Malicious, and Scandalous Reports," which spread widely and contributed to the "Defamation of His Majestie's Government." Charles thus joined the long ranks of despots who feared the coffeehouse from its inception.

Charles' intention to eliminate those public forums in which men think clearly and speak boldly had an unflattering irony about it. Cromwell had endured the presence of the coffeehouse and it had cost him; Charles' friends had made abundant use of the free atmosphere of the coffeehouses to achieve his restoration. The king's attempt at suppression of the coffeehouses was met with a mighty public outcry, one that joined all political parties in a harmony of political dissent. The king was assured that his edict would not be obeyed and that his poorly-veiled display of tyranny might well cost him his position. Within ten days of the issuance of the suppression edict, a second proclamation retracted it.

The king and his court would have preferred to answer to no one about the setting of the agenda of political issues or their preferred manner of disposing with those issues. The preservation of the coffeehouse was tantamount to the preservation of free speech and the will of the people in directing their own destiny.

The seventeenth-century English coffeehouse played its major role in the establishment of individual liberty because of a unique combination of circumstances. The place had appeared as a new forum, free of the encrustations of the past. In the coffeehouse, men from all parties and stations could mingle in innocence of the old traditions. In the absence of an established press, face-to-face discussion in the permissive atmosphere of these second-story halls represented a single and vital mode of democratic participation. In the process of this unprecedented mingling, people became sensitive to one anothers' situations and found common interests and sympathies. They soon discovered, as well, the strength of their numbers and their mutual stake in individual freedom. Those optimal conditions changed, however, and never again would the coffeehouse be as important in the Western world as it had been in seventeenth-century England.

During its reign, the coffeehouse was the center of business and cultural life as well as a political arena. Many of the nation's largest trading companies were headquartered in the coffeehouses, and London's stockbrokers operated within them for over a hundred years. Only when those establishments fell into decline did the brokers finally acquire their own quarters and establish an Exchange. For many years, Lloyd's of London operated out of a coffeehouse, which provided a place where the city's unorganized marine underwriters could mingle with knowledgeable men of the sea and benefit from their gossip. Not long after, Lloyd's also became the setting for the auctioning of ships. [14]

The era of the coffeehouse coincided with one of English literary attainment unmatched before or since. At the coffeehouses, literary men found their inspiration, themes, and audiences. John Dryden held forth at William Urwin's establishment on Russell Street for many years and from that public base provided commentary on the latest poems and plays. From the forum that Will's offered, Dryden broadened the literary audience and set standards that would elevate the quality of English letters for the next one hundred years.

Across Russell Street from William Urwin's establishment and about a dozen years after the death of the man who made it famous, Joseph Addison installed Daniel Button as master of Button's coffeehouse. From that headquarters, Addison played a leading role in encouraging literacy, reforming English manners, interesting the common man in art, life, and thought, and establishing the prototype of the modern newspaper. Addison is reported to have spent his mornings in study but, in the afternoon, he took himself to Button's for at least five or six hours, often staying far into the night. In that milieu, he created *The Spectator, The Guardian,* and contributed to his friend Steele's *Tatler.*

Addison was possessed of a clear and unwavering sense of purpose, and he knew how to employ the features of the coffeehouse in service of his worthy goals. Harboring as much disdain for the moral tyranny of the Puritan as for the cynical immorality of the Cavalier, he sought to elevate the thoughts and ideals of his countrymen above them both.[15] Whereas previous publications were largely limited to political content, Addison included essays on the arts and proper behavior. As he had calculated, the coffeehouse was not only the place to take the pulse of the people and to formulate ideas, it was also a circulation department. Much of the content of his papers was addressed to women and was included on the astute assumption that the men would carry their copies home to their wives.

His manner of soliciting articles and literary contributions for his paper also gave indication of Addison's ability to exploit the coffeehouse. His workers took great pains to create a large, wooden lion's head with mouth open and appearing as "ravenous as possible." The open mouth led to a wide "throat" and a box placed immediately below. With tantalizing fanfare, Addison announced that the lion would remain against the west wall of Button's, there to receive the essays and other contributions of those having something to submit for publication. Addison, of course, was the "stomach" who digested the ensuing contributions, and he made sure that everyone understood that he held the sole key to the box beneath that lion whose mouth and feet symbolized thought and action. Following Joseph Addison's death and the closing of Button's, the lion's head was transported to a nearby coffee-house and later to the Shakespeare Tavern. It was eventually acquired by the Duke of Bedford and remains to this day in its niche at Woburn Abbey.

The success of Addison's journalism is most easily seen in the number of its imitators. Between the first appearance of *The Tatler* in 1709 and the publication of Dr. Johnson's *Rambler* in 1750, over one hundred "essay papers" were published. Prior to Addison there were no provincial papers, but within a dozen years of *The Spectator*'s appearance, there were seventeen of them. More gratifying to Addison than this legion of imitators, one suspects, would have been the observation of a Swiss visitor to England some eight years after the essayist's death. "All Englishmen are great newsmongers," wrote that visitor. "Workmen habitually begin the day by going to coffee rooms in order to read the daily news."[16] No one had done more than Addison to stir his countrymen from their seeming contentment with a life of illiteracy.

Addison's accomplishment was all the more remarkable for, in effect, he lectured his readership and held up an unflattering mirror to his fellow London townsmen. He jerked up short those lampooners who mocked virtue. He chided the fops and steadfastly resisted every temptation to win the average reader by encouraging his slovenly habits. It may well be that English times and temper were ready for self-improvement. But it is doubtful that Addison, Steele, Garth, Defoe, Berkely, Atterbury, or any of the other leading journalists of the day would have been as successful in the absence of the coffeehouse. There could be no substitute for that regular, immediate, and face-to-face contact with those London townsmen who—in the language of today's journalists and sociologists—were society's "opinion leaders."

After an illustrious reign of almost two hundred years as the center of political, social, and cultural life, the English coffeehouse slipped from the scene. By the middle of the nineteenth century, it no longer had any impact on English life. Its demise is often attributed to the advent of home mail delivery, the daily newspaper, the greed of the coffee-sellers who wanted to monopolize England's emerging fourth estate, and other changing conditions. The coffeehouse, however, was fundamentally a form of human association, a gratifying one, and the need for such a society can hardly be said to have disappeared. It is entirely plausible that the coffeehouse failed in its own right; there is abundant evidence that it began fraying at its edges early on and that insufficient care was taken to preserve it. The mindless lampooning of every sacred institution and belief became rampant within them; the sale of intoxicants came to be tolerated. The openness and equality of the original establishments gave way to partitioned seating and single, large tables were replaced by strategically placed smaller ones. Even in Dryden's latter days, those not privileged to a pinch of the master's snuff were regarded as of lower caste. In many of the literary houses, the customers set aside the printed essays in favor of a hand of cards at a gaming table. The coffeehouse crowd began to sort itself by occupation and trade; it lost interest in the democratic ethos of the original establishment.

In sum, the original principles upon which the success of the coffeehouses were based were too often ignored, with the consequence that the number of undesirables multiplied. It was that fact, more than any other, that gave rise to the exclusive club and a control over membership that offered protection from the drunk, the artless lampooner, the hawker of patent medicines, the gambler, the thief, and the bad-mannered generally. As it turned out, the clubs were not the solution they must have seemed. White's, to take an example (and perhaps the most famous of them) was variously controlled by gamblers, dandys, or political ideologues. And, in their latter days, the most prestigious among the clubs became notorious for their anticonversation atmosphere. It is not fitting that the English coffeehouses, once third places without parallel, should ultimately evolve into elegant wax museums for the living dead. Where there is no talk, there is no life.

The Viennese Coffeehouse

It is part of Viennese legend that the world's first coffeehouse was hers; the myth is all the more cherished because of its association with Vienna's finest hour, the Austrians' victory in the Second Turkish Siege. One myth regarding the origin of the coffeehouse, I have found, is likely to be followed by another. A seasoned and cosmopolitan writer recently admitted to having believed and promulgated the Viennese version. Once enlightened, he meant to set the record straight. The world's first coffeehouse, he explained, did not appear in Vienna in 1684, but in Constantinople in 1540. From there, he went on to clarify, the institution spread to Europe, *then* to England.

Alas, the embarrassment continues, for by the time the "first" coffee-house appeared in Constantinople, in 1540, a Saudi Arabian viceroy had already closed down several of them in the city of Mecca. Nor did coffeehouses spread from Europe to England. By the time the first such establishments were seen on the Continent, Charles II had already issued a proclamation intended to reduce the formidable number of them, which had gained wide popularity in London over the previous two decades. It would appear upon more careful investigation that the first coffeehouses were Arabian and that both the brewing of the coffee bean and its availability in public establishments have been around for about five hundred years.

The Viennese coffeehouse, however, has several distinctions that do it far more credit than merely being first. It has changed least, endured longest, and been the most imitated among all its counterparts in Christendom. Well before World War I, in one foreign city after an-other, there appeared establishments calling themselves Vienna Cafés. Typically those pretenders sought to employ waiters with accents, served coffee in tall glasses, and called any brew with milk in it *melange.*[17]

Though Vienna has many coffeehouses that have not kept up the glittering appearances of their youth, she still lays just claim to being the city with the gilded cafés. There is more sheer elegance about the Viennese coffeehouse than will be found in most third places of other cultures. It could hardly be otherwise, perhaps, for, as the tourist brochure puts it, Vienna "has had twenty centuries to perfect the art of living." Whereas other European capitols have sacrificed their splen-did, aging structures to the artless rectangles of modern glass-skinned skyscrapers, Vienna looks much as it did under Franz Joseph. Amid the splendor of baroque architecture and the city's extensive parks, the gilded cafés seem hardly threatened by the sweep of progress, which is changing so much of the face of Europe. Vienna has had an illustrious history and remains the epitome of urban living. Its coffeehouses are its most cherished living reminders of the glory that was, and they con-tinue to serve as the major social centers of Viennese life.

Unlike the second-story establishments that rose above the squalor of the London streets, the Viennese café offers its greatest charm at ground level. Like the French bistro, the Vienna café typically extends into the street. Whereas the former boasts a terrace, the latter offers a

garden. The major difference between them is one of physical demar-
cation. At the bistro, it is usually impossible to say just where the
terrace ends and the sidewalk begins, but the Austrians, more inclined
to privacy, enclose the sidewalk area of the café with a barrier of potted
plants or an ornate iron fence. In Vienna, unlike France, the indoor
area holds more appeal and many more of the customers than the
sidewalk area. The Viennese coffeehouse has always had more of a
physical presence than its London counterpart; it remains an integral
part of the cityscape, an elegant institution that, more than any other
kind of establishment, symbolizes city life.

Elegance alone, however, does not account for the superiority of the
Vienna café. Like the whipped cream that so many Austrians take on
their coffee, it is preferred but not essential; more important factors
account for the abiding appeal of the Viennese coffeehouse.

The quality of domestic life among the Viennese promotes the city's
cafés. Few people own houses, and the great majority of the residents
have always been apartment dwellers. Thus, the pervasive mode of
housing requires less time at home in housekeeping and domestic
maintenance and allows more free time in the off-hours of the working
population. Also, the reduced space and facilities of apartment living
create a greater demand for public places offering informal relaxation
and social contact than is found in other cities. The Viennese expect to
do much of their living and to find daily satisfaction within public
settings.

Unlike their English counterparts, the coffeehouses of the Austrians
have never barred women. To the contrary, the café represents an
integral, fondly-anticipated part of many an Austrian housewife's day.
At about four o'clock each afternoon, when their English counterparts
are taking tea in their flats, the Viennese coffeehouse is invaded by a
lively collation of local ladies. It is the time of their *Jause*, an interlude
devoted to gossip and the consumption of rich chocolate or sponge
cakes heaped with *Schag* (whipped cream) and downed with several
cups of dark-roasted coffee. Many women forego lunch in order to
indulge themselves in this Viennese version of afternoon tea. The hour
given to men's gossiping is that directly following lunch, so these
similar functions are not mixed. Male customers are abundantly present during the ladies' *Jause*, but there is no competition for seating. By

some quirk of Providence, perhaps, the women prefer those larger tables in the center of the room that the men have never favored.

Credit for the enduring quality of the Vienna café must also be given to its waiters and their exemplary tradition of service. The men in black create an atmosphere of personalized accommodation while maintaining careful control over the life of the café. Customers are greeted by two, even three, waiters upon their appearance. After a few visits their names are known, as are their preferences in reading material and the way they take their coffee. In the lead among the waiters who greet the customer (in a manner likened to a reunion of old friends)[18] is the head waiter, usually dressed in a tuxedo and universally addressed as "Herr Ober." At his side is the waiter to whom the customer's order is relayed and who will serve it. Often, there will also be an apprentice whose duty it is to bring customers this institution's symbol of hospitality—a fresh glass of water.

It is the experienced, seldom-deceived eye of Herr Ober that correctly assesses the rank and occupation of each new customer, whom he then greets by title. From a stack of fresh newspapers, Herr Ober selects a half-dozen from among many more, having judged the newcomer's reading tastes and station in life. The customer is steered to the location that the head waiter deems appropriate, and neither loyalty to the establishment nor generosity in tipping its staff will affect Herr Ober's judgment. Customers are put where they "belong" and, at the Viennese café, some belong more than others.

In this as in the German culture, the habitués of many public places claim their own table, which is "permanently reserved" but not usually marked as such. The loyal regular is a *Stammgast*, and both the table and the group of cronies who daily congregate at it are known as *Stammtisch*. Unlike the English coffeehouse, in which anyone could approach anyone else, individual or group, and be accepted, the Viennese coffeehouse is constituted of small private worlds. The members of a *Stammtisch* make no bones about letting outsiders know they are not welcome to join the group. Though Herr Ober's actions in directing the customer to a given location may seem dictatorial and capricious, he is often doing no more than protecting the territory of the regulars.

The foreign visitor may not appreciate the nuances of decorum that mark the character of these legendary and romantic cafés: The initial confusion over what to order (even the lesser places offer about two dozen variations of brewed beverage and only an ignoramus would simply ask for coffee), the formal attire of the staff, the control of seating arrangements, and the obsession with titles, contribute to an overall effect that some find pompous or stuffy. Those who make a habit of the cafés, however, soon find them otherwise. After a few return visits, one is made to feel special. The personalized service for which these establishments are renowned takes effect. The customer's coffee, reading, and socializing preferences are remembered and catered to. Those who avail themselves of the Vienna café find an elegance of service and surroundings at prices far more modest than would be required to match them anywhere in London, Paris, or Rome.

The obsession with titles soon reveals its humorous side as it becomes clear that Herr Ober bestows an instant promotion upon almost everyone who enters his establishment. The military officer whom the head waiter correctly identifies as a major in civilian clothing is addressed as "Herr Colonel." A director (of anything) becomes "Generaldirecktor," and so on. Such impish appeals to the customers' egos are at their most devious when a "nobody" walks in and is greeted as "Herr Doktor." There are many who congratulate themselves on their manner and appearance for the rare one who may suspect that the staff is enjoying a laugh at his expense.[19]

In Austria, as in Czechoslovakia and other central European nations, the modern daily newspaper has lent much to the popularity of the coffeehouse. This aspect of the Vienna café is all the more interesting when one considers that it was the advent of the daily newspaper that greatly contributed to the *decline* of the English coffeehouses. No longer needing to visit the coffeehouse in order to keep abreast of happenings, the Londoner eventually found little reason to visit them at all. But for the Viennese, there could not be a more ideal place in which to read the newspapers. There in the coziest of surroundings, one can read as many of them as one pleases and all for free should one prefer not to order from the menu. This tradition of public service is reported to have produced, in certain people, a phobia of sorts. Those afflicted are known as "professional readers," and they harbor an abiding fear that something important might be missed if all the papers are not scanned every day.

The advent of the dailies transformed the Viennese coffeehouse into a reading room, and many observers have aptly employed the word library in describing both the ambience and the arrangement of tables within these cafés. Originally, the Viennese coffeehouse offered just coffee, but within a century of its beginnings, this institution was imposed upon to offer a succession of new features, of which the newspaper was but one of the more compatible. There was an early objection to smoking but it was permitted at about the same time billiard and card rooms were added in the rear. An even greater resistance was offered to the preparation and serving of food in the coffeehouses of this city. Eventually, however, meals were served, and those who know Vienna have long understood that the best place to get breakfast is the coffeehouse. Lunches and dinners are served also, but coffeehouse purists are disdainful of allowing food odors to contaminate the scent of freshly-brewed coffee. For the purists, it is only after the despised white tablecloths are removed that the coffeehouse is restored to its proper state. As in the English club, there are writing desks and telephones available for customer use. Many people keep regular hours at the coffeehouse and conduct a variety of business transactions on its premises. Its features contribute to the many facets of its character, and the Vienna café clearly belongs to that Mediterranean-based league of third places which invite frequent visits and lengthy stays.

Descriptions of the patronage of the *Weiner Kaffeehaus* over several decades are consistent in reporting that distinctively different crowds use the coffeehouses in different ways and at various times during the day. In recent times, breakfast is served earlier than it used to be and the game-players make their invasions later in the day—two possible indications that people may live less leisurely than they once did. After the breakfast tables are cleared, the remainder of the morning finds the coffeehouse used as a message center, private office, and library. Just before noon, the white tablecloths are spread and the lunch crowd soon arrives. At 2:30 P.M. (formerly earlier) the tables are cleared and patrons renew their friendships with a lot of black coffee and gossip. At 4:00 P.M. the women's *Jause* begins and lasts until 6:00, when the participants must go home and cook for their families. Next come the chess, card, and billiards players, who are in the majority until the theater crowd begins to arrive.

These major tides of regular patronage, however, merely suggest the diverse uses to which the Vienna café is put. During its eighteen or so hours of daily operation, the Viennese coffeehouse is many things to many people. Its breadth of accommodation remains as great as Mac-Callum described in the late 1920s:

> Between eight in the morning and two at night, the café sees quite a large portion of the life of Vienna. Hither come people in every humour, and for every reason, people in the best of spirits and people in the blues, those that want to kill time because they have cash to spend, and those that need to pass as much time as they possibly can on a minimum expenditure, those that are hungry and those that are more than satisfied. The Vienna coffeehouse is the place for them all, a meeting place for lovers, a club for people of common tastes or interests, an office for the occasional businessman, a resting place for the dreamer, and a home for many a lonely soul."[20]

The Viennese frequent their coffeehouses for a variety of reasons and at a variety of times; these venerable establishments take guests as they come. Whatever the mood, occasion, or social position, the institution is adequate to it. There can be few better examples of the extent to which informal public gathering places can virtually become a way of life.

I doubt there exists a body of reports more plagued by the myth of "the good old days" than that growing out of third place experiences. Indeed, the worth of a third place tradition often seems to depend upon how much of it has been lost to the less desirable consequences of social change. Even here, however, the Vienna cafés reveal a superiority. Save for the dark period under the Nazis (who favored beer halls but feared coffeehouses) from which they fully recovered, the cafés of Vienna have never really waned in vitality or popularity.

In the eyes of the purist, the coffeehouse has suffered from the inclusion of the restaurant function and has lost its superior ambience to the Americanization of the premises. Bright colors, chrome fixtures, the substitution of mirrors for the smoke-stained dark paneling, and a noisier crowd have given the conservatives cause for lament. The younger generations are accused of having a less "clubable" inclination. "Envy and private interests have taken the place of revolutionary enthusiasm and solidarity," complained an observer in the late 1920s.[21] Careerism, materialism, and marriages that require more accountable husbands tend to devalue the "wasting" of time with friends and have doubtless wrought changes in Vienna, as they have elsewhere in the modern world. If the coffeehouse looks less like the clubs of "independent husbands" than it once did, it is in part because there are fewer such creatures around these days.[22]

But the health and vitality of an institution should not be judged only by the fading standards of what may have been its better days. The survival of the coffeehouse depends upon its ability to meet present day needs and not those of a romanticized past. The Vienna café has kept apace of the times. In essence it is still what it was. Once within its walls, many a visitor still succumbs to the illusion that time has turned backward, that Franz Joseph is still in power, and that there could be no better place to be. More than this can hardly be expected.

PART III

CHAPTER 11

A Hostile Habitat

LIKE ALL LIVING things, the third place is vulnerable to its environment. Far more important than the architecture and appointment of these establishments is the habitat in which they may or may not be able to blossom and thrive. There is much in their favor. Unlike hospitals or libraries, which have exacting, complicated, and expensive internal requirements, third places are typically modest, inexpensive, and small by comparison. Further, places not even built for the purpose can be taken over by a local citizenry and pressed into service as informal social centers. The simplicity of its requirements has made the third place a hardy perennial, capable of sprouting in a variety of forms in most urban cultures.

It does not thrive universally, however. The third place is seldom found in America's newer urban environments. Whether one looks where urban renewal has changed the older city or in the wake of the new urban sprawl, the Great Good Gathering Places are not to be found. That the third place so rarely and feebly takes root in the new "built environment" gives cause to wonder about the suitability of this habitat for healthful human habitation. We are, after all, social animals. We are an associating species whose nature is to share space just as we share experiences; few hermits are produced in any human culture. A habitat that discourages association, one in which people withdraw to privacy as turtles into their shells, denies community and leaves people lonely in the midst of many.

In the Debris of a Previous Order

Third places are most likely to be old structures. They are frequently located along the older streets of American cities, in the neighborhoods or quarters not yet invaded by urban renewers. Within those older sections exists the fading image of the city itself and the kind of human interaction, the easy and interesting mixing of strangers that made the city what it was. The new "built environment" affords so little of that kind of interaction that it no longer deserves to be called a city.[1] And, on a larger scale, the new, corporately-controlled technological order has so atomized the citizenry that the term "society" may no longer be appropriate.[2]

In the past, American gregariousness found its expression and established its numerous outposts without plan or even a conscious sense of purpose. The people simply invaded, took over, commandeered, or otherwise appropriated a wide variety of establishments never intended to serve as social centers. The cracker-barrel circle of the old country store never counted it *their* responsibility to build or fund a public lounging area. Those crusty stalwarts simply inveigled their way into space designed for quite another purpose. Small-town druggists did not assume it their duty to provide the main hangout for the local adolescent population. It just worked out that way. The waiting seats a barber had to offer were not intended for the use of noncustomers, but that was often their major use. The local post office was not kept open twenty-four hours a day to allow the locals a place to chat and exchange news, but it was appropriated for that purpose as much as for any other. Hotel coffee shops were there for guests, but were often most used and relied upon, if not most appreciated, by locals.

Sociable Americans and their cronies could formerly insinuate themselves into one such place or another and act quite at home while doing it. *No longer!* The planners, builders, and owners have learned how to discourage the social use of their establishments. The modern retail establishment and public office building are now hostile to the loitering, lounging, and hanging-on that are part and parcel of an informal public life. The aisles, counters, and shelves—the layout—of the new establishments precludes sitting around and even just standing around in conversational groupings.

Part of the problem, then, is that Americans have been able to assume that places for connecting and associating would somehow naturally be there . . . unlike cultures that took care to space enough *bier gartens* or bistros to gel their urban localities into a collective life. In contemporary urban America, congenial public gathering places are rare. Here and there a handful of urban dwellers may find camaraderie, often to their surprise, in a laundromat. And sometimes a writer will encounter one of these settings and write about this tiny but glowing ember of humanity among the cold ashes of our public domain, and do so as though it represented an American triumph. Our expectations seem as small as the amount of space we've preserved for an informal public life.

Where once there were places, we now find *nonplaces*. In real places the human being is a person. He or she is an individual, unique and possessing a character. In nonplaces, individuality disappears. In nonplaces, character is irrelevant and one is only the customer or shopper, client or patient, a body to be seated, an address to be billed, a car to be parked. In nonplaces one cannot be an individual or become one, for one's individuality is not only irrelevant, it also gets in the way. Toby's Diner was a place. The Wonder Whopper, which stands there now, is a nonplace.

Corporations take immediate hold of new areas, from the development of the residential sites to the malls that serve them and the fast-food outlets that command all the choice locations. In areas developed long ago it takes them longer, but the corporations also infect that environment. The locally-owned lunch counter soon enough finds itself competing with a newly-built, fast-food nonplace. In its decline, the old diner continues to enjoy the trade from its loyal customers, an assortment of regulars for whom it represents much more than just a place to eat. But the real place fails to attract the others. The transients and other occasional diners flock to the familiar logo, to the plastic place where the help is almost as transient as the customers, where high school students first learn to be a cog in the system, and where management warns every employee not to call the grease "grease" upon pain of termination. Before long, another third place disappears. The nonplace that takes over makes life a little less confusing, a little easier, for people new to the area. A familiar logo beckons. It offers the predictable and the familiar to the nation's nomads, but it offers a real place to nobody.

A few people (too few!) see these nonplaces for what they are and resist them. One such individual, a mother of two young children, used a place called Jerry's to wean her children from the sterility of the hamburger chains. About Jerry's, she said, "People seem to 'belong' there. The atmosphere is relaxed and friendly, everyone is spoken to and many people see friends there. Their style is entirely reliant on the personality of the people. It's old and a bit rundown but it's an excellent place to go when one wants to feel better, have a sense of belonging, or relax. If you haven't been, try it!"

That mother's description of Jerry's reminded me of a place located in one of our northern cities that serves an almost ridiculously oversized roast beef sandwich. Surely, there is no other place like it. The building seems as old as the street on which it is located. The operation of it violates all the principles of efficient franchise management. One has to wait in a long and *very* slow-moving line, but here that curse of group life has been transformed into a pleasant experience. It's a "talking line" within which people are "pointed" in all directions as they shuffle and sip beer and gab their way toward the host. One comes, eventually, to a giant of a man, a retired wrestler who demonstrates to new customers just how to get a secure grip on an inadequate paper plate as he heaps the sandwich to overflowing. He doesn't stop until the roast beef begins to spill onto the floor. For each customer he has a comment, a quip, an observation, a *bon mot*, just one per—but one as choice as the meat.

Three or four steam tables would obviously accommodate the customers faster. Opening a similar place across town might seem like a good and profitable idea. Taking care not to let little pieces of beef fall to the floor would doubtlessly increase the profit margin. But now we're talking like the chains think. Our friend offers a unique experience and reducing it to a common one would destroy it. He knows that, and most of his customers realize it as well. His place is modest in decor. It has none of the brightness of the franchise places. It does well, however, and it does so not by intruding golden arches above the skyline but by word of mouth among regulars, who get a lot more there than a fine roast beef sandwich.

Such places are rarely appreciated as much as they should be while they are still operating. When a place such as this burns down, however, it is much like the death of a beloved first citizen. The community no longer seems the same; much of its character and charm seems to have depended on that place. I made this point a couple of years ago in a lecture and not long afterward just such a place was temporarily closed due to a fire. A woman who had heard the talk made a point of contacting me about the incident. "God, it *is* like a death," she said. "I didn't realize how much we counted on going there and it being there."

Another local gathering place, a newcomer, a fledgling third place, neither as charming nor as entrenched in local habit, was lost. A supermarket chain had reserved six or seven percent of its floor space for tables and chairs near a little deli counter. It immediately attracted Sunday-morning regulars, swing-shift regulars, those who enjoyed a little relaxation, coffee and gossip between the efforts of filling a cart and paying for its contents, and others. Subsequently, the facility was torn out. We quizzed the help and learned that many customers were disappointed to the point of anger and that the decision was made in a main office hundreds of miles away. One may surmise that a "bean counter" kept tabs on the profit yield of that square footage, found it less than that generated elsewhere in the store, and made his or her recommendations. Thus was a vestige of the better cities of the past removed from the store, bringing it more in line with the modern urban environment.

The modern urban environment accommodates people as players of unifunctional roles. It reduces people to clients, customers, workers, and commuters, allowing them little opportunity to be human beings. It constricts and constrains. One place allows for one kind of activity and in the name of efficiency (for whom?) it discourages other kinds of activities. Taken together, the urban environment attends to far fewer human needs than it did in the past. Few understand this better than the architectural critic Wolf Von Eckardt, who makes the case as follows:

> We have more to gain [by consulting] our planners than our psychia-trists. We can achieve more to improve our relationships with others by participating in community planning, rather than group therapy en-counters. What ails us—most of us, anyway—is not that we are incapa-ble of living a satisfactory and creative life in harmony with ourselves, but that our habitat does not offer sufficient opportunities. It hems us in. It isolates us. It irritates and disrupts.[3]

The speed with which the built environment is being transformed, the rate at which a new and wanting order is being created, is remarkable. Two factors seem to account for this overnight transformation of the environment. First, it is all done without involving the people who must *use* the facilities that are being constructed. As the socioeconomist Robert Theobald has noted, planners are averse to involving people because "people foul up systems, they get in the way. They make things untidy, they have whims, ideas, loves, hates, emotions; master plans don't have any room for the freedom of people."[4] The second factor is a technical one; in the words of Lionel Brett, himself an architect and planner:

> The cause is simply that people learn from one another. The process was held back for centuries by poor communications, primitive technology, and the need to make do with local resources. Even so it steadily persisted. Now all these impediments are swept away and the difference between places becomes more precious as they become more precarious. Anything the designer can do, even to the point of affectation, to keep them alive will make the world a more interesting place to live in.[5]

In urban America, the demonstrated inability to create a suitable human habitat is brought to horrifying proportions by the speed with which an *unsuitable* environment is being manufactured. Even as our corporations now realize that their futures are jeopardized by imposing systems upon employees without their input, we continue to impose equally-flawed urban planning upon citizen-users as though their involvement in the process were not crucial to success.

One might suppose that the intellectuals of the planning and architectural professions, the book-writers, would have a broader and better vision. I have found little to be encouraged about here. I've scanned scores of books and manuals on the subject never to find the barest mention of lounges, taverns, bars, or saloons. Of doughnut shops, coffee shops, pool halls, bingo halls, clubs, lodges, and youth recreation centers the same may be said. These places apparently don't belong *anywhere* in the thinking of the planners.

In what one might suppose to be a bible of the profession, the *Community Builders Handbook*, I found mention of bowling alleys only, among potential third places. These, however, were identified as "poor money makers" and should, the authors explain, be kept away from shopping centers. They should be built as free-standing, single-tenant structures, it was stated, but no mention is made as to *where*.[6]

More interesting was the title of the manual. It was a misnomer. The book was not about building communities. It was about building *shopping centers!* Only in a society where consumerism has overtaken any vision beyond it would such a confusion occur. The long-time citizens of Paducah would not be confused. Until recent times, their municipality was a lively and pleasant community. Life and social intercourse centered around Paducah's downtown area. Then the developers created the splendid Kentucky Oaks mall, locating it out by the interstate (presumably to gain both the local trade and a sizable amount from those in transit). The mall was constructed according to many of the principles and formulas stated in the *Community Builders Handbook*, but the result was not the creation of a community. Many of the residents insist that it *killed* a community—theirs! The mall may offer a pleasant diversion in the best sense that malls can, but it is not a community.

It is also a perfect example of what Ray Bradbury referred to as the "Juggernaut Shopping Malls," which smother and crush the real places in their way. "The pattern is familiar now," writes Bradbury. "We have seen it repeated and repeated by mall builders who think too much and City Fathers who think too little."[7] Rather than building high altars to consumership, Bradbury would rather we "invent" a "People Machine":

> What are we talking about? Not just a shopping center where people come to buy one sheet, one shirt, or one shoe, but a place where lingering, staying, dawdling, socializing are a way of life. A refuge from the big city, or sometimes worse, your own parlor. A place so incredibly right that mobs will rush to it crying "Sanctuary!" and be allowed in forever. A place, in sum, where people can come to be people. The idea is as old as Athens at high noon, Rome soon after supper, Paris at dawn, Alexandria at dusk.[8]

I find it irritating when those to whom I talk on the subject relegate third places to the past. "Oh," they'll say, "you mean like the old neighborhood tavern or the soda fountain that used to be in the drugstore." They are, of course, more right than wrong. The third place does belong to the past in the sense that most of them are to be found "in the debris" of a previous order. My response is well rehearsed by now and it goes like this: We don't want the past. We can't have the past. We don't need the past. *We need the places!*

The End of Free-Ranging?

Third places thrive best in locales where community life is casual, where walking takes people to more destinations than does the automobile, and where the interesting diversity of the neighborhood reduces one's reliance on television. In these habitats, the street is an extension of the home. Attachment to the area and the sense of place that it imparts expand with the individual's walking familiarity with it. In such locales, parents and their children range freely. The streets are not only safe, they invite human connection.

Few of us range as casually, as freely, or as comfortably in our neighborhoods as our grandparents did in theirs. Indeed, many homes have no sidewalks out front. People are expected to come and go in the privacy of automobiles. Traveling in this manner, people cross an environment without ever becoming part of it. The resulting habitat discourages contact of any kind between those who have the potential for becoming, if not the best friends, at least the most *available* ones. The ancient Chinese wisdom suggesting that "a friend in one's own village is worth a hundred in the capitol" has little currency in urban planning. I called a city planner's office one day, curious as to what percent of area homes had no sidewalks to serve them. They didn't know. It was not considered important. We aren't expected to free-range as in the past but to make more "strategic" trips, none of them by walking.

In an intriguing social commentary entitled *The Broilerhouse Society*, Patrick Goldring traces the recent history of the chicken. That creature formerly had the liberty of ranging freely about the farmyard, pecking and scratching when and where it pleased. Chickens, moreover, were in contact with the natural world, with its days and nights, its seasons, its warm weather and its cold. One might say the birds enjoyed "chicken's rights," chief among which was the right to wander freely about their environment. No longer. Most chicks are now hatched and confined under highly controlled conditions. Night and day are artificially controlled and accelerated by colored light and a bare minimum of physical movement is allowed. Chickens survive on tasteless and flavorless formula food.[9]

Goldring's Britain, he charges, is becoming like that for human beings. "Broilerhouse man, living on what is often tasteless and flavorless food, lives a life which is increasingly better organized but is also becoming tasteless and flavorless as his food."[10] But most importantly, free-ranging is being curtailed. We are well on the way, Goldring contends, to a life-style in which we live in one small cell and are connected to another small cell, where we work, via commuting in yet another small cell. Of the domestic cell, Goldring suggests:

> The Englishman's home today is not his castle. It is his centrally-heated, bright, combined nesting-cage and exercise run. The family-sized television replaces the crowded cinema, the bottle of beer from the off-license, the visit to the pub, the telly discussion, the pub argument. Furnishing and decorating the home have become subjects of absorbing interest to the nation while public architecture has degenerated into a featureless bore.[11]

Goldring stresses television's heavy contribution to the broilerhouse society. It creates shut-ins of almost everyone; it makes confinement to the domestic cell tolerable. To do so, of course, it must provide more than mere entertainment. It is not only art, it is also advisor and instructor. Television brings the rest of life into the home. "Don't go out and live," say the television programme chiefs. "Just stay in the privacy and comfort of your own homes and we'll live it up for you."[12]

Human beings are not like chickens. Nobody in a white lab coat can turn the keys on peoples' domestic cells and lock them up. The broilerhouse society of humans, however, doesn't rely on locks and keys. It relies on *management*. It is management's role to convince people that a restriction of life is what they really want; that it is in their best interests and they have but to realize it. Many in the United States as well as in Britain already have.

If one takes Goldring seriously, and there's certainly enough evidence to warrant doing so, then such things as high crime rates and the filth and fragmentation of our cities begin to fit into the picture. Such conditions serve to convince people that the home is the place to spend most of one's time; that there's little out in that "jungle" that one might need or want. And when the police close down another park at night because some of the free-rangers aren't cooperating with the parks' custodians, it seems like the correct thing to do. If the home and the job take up all the slack, then, of course, there will be no need for third places and the absence of them will be another feature of the broiler-house society.

A Tradeoff

Victor Gruen writes of an acquaintance who had come to America from his native Naples: "In the old country the man's quarters were humble and his shower merely dribbled. Once he had showered and dressed though, he knew why he had done so. There were places to go and friends to visit. In America, he found, the home is more comfortable, and the shower works well—but where is there to go?"[13] The little anecdote illustrates the important distinction between the two kinds of environments that Gruen proceeds to describe. There is an "immediate environment," which surrounds each of us as individuals and there is a much larger one, the public one, which we all share. Though the average American enjoys a better immediate or individual environment than people in most other nations, our public environment is of "disturbingly low quality."[14]

Americans have done an about-face. From visions of municipalities that would be the spatial implementation of democracy, popular imagination has shifted to the private home. As the architect and urban planner Dolores Hayden has put it, "The dream house replaced the ideal city as the spatial representation of American hopes for the good life."[15] It has been a shift from the hope of a collective "good life" to an individual scrambling after it. The model city was to be a cure for social ills; the dream house is clearly an escape from them.

Hayden documents the shift. In the decades since 1950, our dream houses got bigger and bigger until Americans "enjoyed the largest amount of private housing space per person ever created in the history of urban civilization."[16] In over ninety percent of American homes, there is but one person per room or fewer. Usually fewer, for one recent reference book reports that:

> The typical American home has 2 rooms for every person. That gives us the most spacious accommodations in the world. The average Israeli home, for instance, is 3 times as crowded, with 1½ people for every room.[17]

As homes acquired master bedrooms, gourmet kitchens, tiled hot tubs, and patios with gas-fired barbecues, the public environment lost most of the facilities that had earlier provided amenities and entertainment for one and all. Only a few old-timers can now point out where the bandstands and their free concerts used to be; where the pavilions once stood along water's edge; where townspeople once gathered to sing carols around a shapely evergreen. We have traded off our interest in public space for a more restrictive and personal concern with our better homes and gardens.

The resulting neglect of the public environment is all too obvious. Peter Blake published a photographic essay of America's urban public space and gave it the appropriate title of *God's Own Junkyard*.[18] Ian McHarg, reflecting upon the course that the American experiment has run to date, says that "while Madison, Jefferson, Hamilton, and Washington might well take pride in many of our institutions, it is likely that they would recoil in horror from the face of the land of the free."[19] Our favorite pictorial views of our cities are those taken several thousands of feet away from them and usually at night. We prefer skylines on smogless days and the glitter of lights at night. Close up, we get the kinds of pictures that illustrate textbooks on urban social problems.

Unsavory visual images are but part of a deeply-ingrained and negative image of our cities. Around the core word *street*—the most public of all places—a discouraging vocabulary continues to grow. In America, "the street" refers to networks of people and their activities that operate broadly and illegally amid the unwholesome, corrupt, and poorly regulated conditions of public space. *Streetwise* refers to the ability to survive in the hostile and indecent inner-city environment. *Street value* is that in which life-destroying drugs are expensive while life itself is cheap. Wayward souls may not need rescuing from the clutches of Satan in our secular society, but they do need to be saved from the street. What program or diversion for youth in America does not find justification in "keeping kids off the street"?

The tradeoff of the public domain for the private retreat from it has been encouraged by the course that the nation's economy has taken. From the beginning of the twentieth century peacetime industry has been producing more than is being consumed. Government and industry sought to raise the level of consumption of the American people. Both the Hoover administration and a fully emerging advertising industry saw the long-range advantage in maximizing the number of young couples who would occupy single-family dwellings and equip them with the products of the nation's factories.

By mid-century, Americans were moving into communities without sidewalks, social centers, or corner stores. The overequipped home was mass-produced in underequipped neighborhoods. Diversions and facilities that had previously been available only in public space and for the shared use of the citizenry came to be the objects of private consumptions and use. These included swimming pools, pool tables, picnic grills, liquor bars, the movie screen and quality musical sound, and even tennis courts. Earlier, shared forms of entertainment and diversion brought people together. They were good for community but not good for the economy. The worst student of arithmetic could understand that more money would be spent in a nation where every household tries to own what a community once provided for all.

Currently, Americans spend about 90 percent of their leisure time in their homes.[20] Is the figure so high because home life is so attractive or is it because we have created a world beyond the home that no longer offers relaxed and inexpensive companionship with others, a commodity once as easily obtained as a stroll down the street? The trade-off continues as those who can afford it seek to remedy the discontents of the overequipped house through the purchase of even bigger and better-equipped ones. But the return on such investments is as limited as the extent to which a household can substitute for a community.

Managed Mislocations

The urban planners' major contribution to the boredom and to the intolerance of our times is unifunctional space utilization. People and activities are compartmentalized and protected from the incursions and intrusions of that which is different from the singular function or particular segment or population for which the space was designated. Each housing development is designed for its narrow band on the spectrums of income and social status. Each major urban activity has its own center or district. The places where we get educated, shop, find medical care, work for a living, conduct business, play, and retire are all kept remote from one another, and none of them are within walking distance of the average American's present address. Eventually questioning his contribution to this kind of planning, Victor Gruen came to the conclusion that it "creates a climate of conformity and intolerance and also, because each [unifunctional center] lacks the admixture of any other urban functions, of sterility and boredom."[21]

Confining the use of space to a single function is useful to many forms of productive activity, but the principle has been extended to realms where it doesn't belong and where it now serves to erode the fabric of society. Chief among these are residential areas where there is so little of interest outside peoples' homes that the privatization of life is no longer optional but spatially enforced. The triumph of the dream house over the model city is now preserved by law; specifically, by zoning regulations that prevent inclusions of the kinds of physical spaces, facilities, and their proximities as are essential to community. Beginning with a resolve "to promote the health, safety, morals, and general welfare of the inhabitants of ____," zoning ordinances do as much to promote loneliness, alienation, and the atomization of society.

When at dinner talks I wish to illustrate the point, I invite my listeners to place a coin in the center of their saucers. They thereby create a model for tracking the fate of the American neighborhood. The coin represents one's house and lot, the remaining expanse of the saucer contains that which is within walking distance of one's home, and beyond the saucer are all those things to which one must drive or take some other form of mechanized transportation.

In that space between the coin and the saucer's edge—within walking distance of the house—was once contained the stuff of which communities are made. Goods, services, diversions, and gathering places attracted a pedestrian population that formed relationships out of its shared use of the neighborhood's facilities. But in the new neighborhoods these things have been removed. Some of what was there is gone for good. Much of it has been transported into the home as private versions of that which people used to share and gain community from the sharing. The rest has been removed to faraway centers to which one must drive and at which one does not know many people.

While the planners in Chicago were busy sterilizing neighborhoods and thereby reducing that city's desirability as a place to live, Mike Royko suggested a "new" plan to them. In it, people would actually be able to walk to the stores, buy groceries, and walk back home. One could buy clothing and malted milks, guitar strings and postage stamps, get a tooth filled or a will drafted—all by way of a modest stroll. A nearby busline would take people downtown faster and less expensively than possible by private automobile, and families could get by with one car and even none at all.[22] The journalist's wisdom, however, goes unheeded. Perhaps the next generation of planners will find it easier to realize that the present one has made a negative contribution to the livable city.

The sterilization of the residential neighborhood has brought the curse of the office right to the family hearth. Home life is now beset with scheduling difficulties and those trying to raise children in the suburban tracts find that life can be more hectic at home than at the office. Children have to be enrolled in and driven to faraway programs if they are to have experiences outside the home and school. Local games of "work up" in vacant lots are replaced by organized youth baseball. Kids who used to build clubhouses in backyards are now driven to crafts programs. Grade-school kids yearn for summer vacation, only to have their parents enroll them in a variety of summer classes because the neighborhood offers too little to entertain and occupy children. Of course, these new neighborhoods often look nice. So does Forest Lawn.

Automobiles did not cause the unifunctional design, but they made it possible. If rarely stated, the facilitating principles are simple enough: 1) the car can connect all points no matter where they are located, and 2) everyone who counts has a car. Planning seemed easier for a while. The earlier "messiness" of mixed space use was avoided, and it looked like cities could be as neat and tidy as those little sandbox models for which designers give one another awards. But the unifunctional dream soon became a nightmare of auto congestion. The sterilized neighborhood contained nothing; people had to take to their cars for all those goods, services, and diversions once located within them.

Since each major urban center served but a single function, parking lots began to multiple rapidly. Culture center parking serves only its patrons and is not used most of the time. Mall lots are all but vacant after nine in the evening. Arena lots, school lots, medical center lots, etc., enjoy no shared use but must be there. We have arrived at that point where the addition of a family of four to the typical urban area necessitates an additional ten thousand square feet of parking space to accommodate members' vehicles at home and in the variety of separated centers at which they will have to park them. And now, we must use up a lot of land to secure houses and lots away from the congestion of auto traffic.

Nothing was harder hit by unifunctional planning than the typical third places of American society. The compartmentalized city is hostile to the third place for it denies the essential proximity between the establishment and its users. The tavern, diner, and corner store have not followed the middle-class family in its migration to the suburbs. And, in the inner city, urban renewal puts low-income families into sterilized housing projects and eliminates the tavern, diner, and corner store from their lives as well.

More recent versions of these old establishments appear now at commercial centers and along the "strips," but their third place character does not survive relocation in remote settings. At most one finds a mere handful of third places clung to by a minority of commuters whose paths cross at some designated hour and whose longing for sociable contact overcomes the overworked American virtues of individualism and privacy.

When the doctor leaves the neighborhood and relocates in a medical center four miles away, one may still receive the essential service. When the Mom-and-Pop grocery closes, one can still get the essential victuals at the supermarket a mile and a half down the avenue. But when the tavern is removed from the corner and put out on the strip, its essential character is lost. When gathering places are situated too far from home, the patron no longer knows the other faces. What should be a lively assembly easily becomes the haunt of the living dead. The bottled spirits of the remote lounge are more an embalming fluid than a lubricant to lively conversation.

The unifunctional approach to space is invariably accompanied by a similar approach to *time*. There is work time and a workplace, a family time and a family place, shopping time and a shopping place, etc. Thus do the planners account for our lives. In countries where people enjoy their cities far more than we, there is also social time and community time. A large and solid block of time is laid right in the middle of the day during which the stores, shops, and offices are closed and people devote themselves to the cultivation of things finer than their jobs. In some regions it's a two-hour shutdown, elsewhere it's three hours, or even four, as we found years ago in Madrid. In any case, the individual has time to retain the social amenities of the noonday meal, as opposed to the fast-food mode or "bagging it." He or she also has time to go home; but mainly, there's an extra hour or so for the cultivation of relationships with cronies, business associates, relatives, and others. Would American cities look better and more homelike if they were shut down for a prolonged midday period during which people tried to relax and enjoy them? If the champions of the work ethic need reminding, there are as many millionaires per capita in beautiful and relaxed Barcelona as in any of our urban pressure cookers.

Time and place are intimately related. Our culture disdains the use of time for "hanging out" even as the places for doing so are being systematically eliminated. In a world where people feel compelled to justify lying around on a beach in terms of "getting a tan" or sitting around in a park as "people watching," it should come as no surprise that, to satisfy the social urge, we find it necessary to invent a variety of clubs and fraternities and imbue them with some lofty purpose.

But the wider pursuit of sociability and "purposeless" contact essential to community is under a real and growing threat. That which finds no space designated for it on the planners' boards or on management's schedules is in danger of extinction. In the narrow view of human life and human needs envisioned by current planning, the city itself is likely to be lost. No one, perhaps, has seen this more clearly than Adolf Ciborowski, chief architect of the reconstruction of Warsaw, who put his finger on the major threat to urbanity and civicism in our time:

> Today man has come to a paradox. A third kind of destruction of cities has now been added to nature and men at war. The builders of cities are now simultaneously the destroyers of cities. Man does not require a war any longer to destroy the settlements of his fellow men. He virtually destroys the town's direction in the process of construction. That process, although creative and progressive in principle, is disastrous to the well-being of the people and to the reasonable function of the town.[23]

The Jane Addams Complaint

Few people have been in a position to observe and record the effects of the private exploitation of the public environment as was Jane Addams. The great numbers of hapless young women she came to know had migrated to Chicago from the rural countryside, and Miss Addams was intimately familiar with the contrast between those two worlds. The dance halls of Chicago, the gin mills of fictional jargon, bore little resemblance to the wholesome public dances of rural society. And, beyond those sordid establishments, the city provided little. Miss Addams wrote of the multitude of youthful women who had migrated to the city and who walked its streets night after night in search of some form of pleasure and diversion. "Apparently," she concluded, "the modern city sees in these girls only two possibilities, both of them commercial: First, a chance to utilize by day their new and tender labor power in its factories and shops, and then another in the evening to extract from their petty wages by pandering to their love of pleasure."[24]

The city denied and refused any responsibility for the wholesome play and recreation that must accompany work if people are to find contentment in life. Whenever anyone proposed that publicly sponsored facilities or programs be provided to meet the leisure and recreational needs of the city's youth or of its working classes, the fiscal conservatives won out. It was "wrong" to spend tax money for the object of permitting people to have fun. It was "wrong" to compete with recreational activities provided in the private domain; the municipality should not compete with businesses that offer diversions for profit. It was "wrong" to impose upon American individualism— leisure should be left to the individual. Finally, it was pointed out, there exist several sectarian and philanthropic organizations to look after such needs as may exist among the indigent.

Years ago, in the region of Europe known as Bavaria, there was a succession of monarchs who held to a common policy: Citizens, when their day's work is done, should be able to go out into the community to enjoy themselves amid their friends and fellow townspeople and, in so doing, should incur no more expense than they would by staying home. That policy made for happy villages and contented people and it exists at one end of a continuum of civic responsibility as vested in the leadership. That was one end of the continuum. The American industrial city stood at the other.

Miss Addam's complaint was twofold. Not only did city government refuse to provide space and facilities for the recreational needs of the citizenry, it also failed to exercise reasonable control over those who profited from the lack of wholesome public facilities. She saw in this the persistence of an old Anglo-Saxon tradition dating back to seventeenth-century England: "Since the soldiers of Cromwell shut up the people's playhouses and destroyed their pleasure fields, the Anglo-Saxon city has turned over the provision for public recreation to the most evil-minded and most unscrupulous members of the community."[25]

That tradition continues. All manner of experiments in profit go on in the nation's cities. I recently took note of a two-story bar and cabaret, which enjoyed a location adjacent to a modern shopping mall. Early in the evening women only were admitted to the upstairs barroom where they were given free drinks for a period of two hours, after which the "gates were opened" and men were allowed to rush upstairs to join them. Drinks on the house, once a courtesy commonly extended to loyal and well-behaved customers, are otherwise rare nowadays. They are most often used as a draw, to lure the female customer. That tactic achieves two purposes, both profitable. It encourages the female to acquire the drinking and cocktail lounge habits and it draws male customers away from competitors' places—this based on the sound assumption that men will go where the women are. No sign, outside or in, actually spells out the nature of the "draw." It is not necessary to specify the possibility that the male customer may make a sexual conquest of a woman the house has put in a party mood.

Through its long history, the same sun-belt city has failed to provide municipal swimming facilities for children even though the weather is oppressively hot five months of the year. The people in control have always been able to afford their own private swimming pools or transportation to the beaches.

In 1967, demolition took place on the Opera House at 39th and Broadway in New York City. The structure was destroyed despite a glaring need to retain a facility of its kind in that part of the city. The Metropolitan Opera Association, however, did not want any competition and it had a compulsory demolition clause written into its sales agreement. As Nathan Silver observed, "The Met, usually with capacity audiences, 'couldn't afford' competition, and New York 'couldn't afford' anything but free enterprise opera."[26]

In some of the nation's cities, unscrupulous businesspeople purchase retail stores that have failed in this era of outlying malls, acquire them at a low price, and then proceed to make porno shops of them. Usually, this is carried off right in the downtown or "showplace" areas of the city. Whatever profit realized at such shops is often incidental to the real "kill" the owner may anticipate when the area comes under an urban renewal program, at which time the lots on which such buildings are located command a premium price. The existence of the porno shops, of course, adds considerable impetus to the demand for urban renewal. Things work out rather nicely for entrepreneurs who understand the failings of our system and who have no qualms about taking advantage of them. They and their right to debase communities even as they profit from doing so are guaranteed by the Constitution, but their real benefactor is that Anglo-Saxon tradition alluded to by Jane Addams. The prominent downtown porno shop emerges where the municipality has failed to take an active responsibility for providing the places and atmosphere for wholesome play and social relaxation.

It is interesting to speculate as to the long-term effects of the refusal of American city governments to recognize and adequately provide for the social and recreational needs of all the people. That failure may be a major reason why the American pot never melted all that well. Had our municipalities been generous in the provision of "everyman's land" playtime facilities, had they provided wholesome and inclusive downtown settings where people could mingle freely and pleasurably at little or no cost, we might now have a healthier, more closely knit population.

Putting a different twist to the matter, how substantial have the recent gains against segregation in the United States really been? What does integration count for when little remains of a public and collective life? What does the right to associate mean in a land where people retreat to the privacy of their homes and where residential segregation remains solid?

When compared with the amenities, comforts, and leisure facilities that affluent Americans enjoy in the private domain, the condition of public facilities is now even worse than in Jane Addams' day. Writing in the guise of de Tocqueville revisiting America, Paul Gray laments the decline of the word *public* in the United States. Whereas the real de Tocqueville was impressed by the number of public works in a nation that had "no rich men" at the time, Gray finds that the emergence of "many rich men" corresponds with the debasing of public facilities. The American rich "prefer not to avail themselves of services that are provided to the multitude." They hold negative views toward the public schools, which their children do not attend, and toward public transportation, which they do not ride. Worse, the millions of middle-class Americans who hope to become rich adopt these views and hope one day to be able to "purchase the splendid isolation for themselves." The comfort of the average urbanite and the conditions under which "ordinary people" live concern fewer and fewer people.[27]

The trend described by Paul Gray seems to feed itself. The more that class of people who used to provide community leadership turn their back on community, the worse things "public" become, with people finding more and more cause to retreat from them if only they can afford to do so. The rejection of responsibility for facilities all are meant to share and, beyond that, the identification of the "good life" as an escape from common Americans, may well be the system flaw that can cause the collapse of the American experiment. What was it Lincoln said about a house divided against itself?

The Cost of "Going Out"

It might have been predicted that by the present stage of our techno-logical and economic development there would have emerged a great number of public places in which the multitudes could spend time at little or no expense, deriving both pleasure and satisfaction from fruits of an enlightened urban culture. Indeed, would this not be the mark of a truly civilized society? But such is not the case. Casting an eye upon America's urban environment, one may be struck by the *absence* of such places.

Recent years have been "boom" ones in the manufacture and sale of home entertainment products, and the major reason suggested by the experts is the prohibitive cost of entertainment in the public domain. People *like* to go out, but the high and ever-rising cost of doing so discourages the habit.

Alternatives to spending money in the area of leisure time activities have diminished greatly. The commercialization of more and more of what people want, need, or expect out of life has reached appalling proportions. Almost every form of escape from the competition and commercialism of the marketplace is coming under the control of the marketplace. The key to the whole interconnected system seems to be that of leaving the individual never really satisfied but always seeking, always hoping, and forever convinced that commercial establishments and commercialized forms of leisure can offer what is missing in the quest for contentment.

The "invisible hand of the market" which, Adam Smith claimed, would usher us toward greater social harmony irrespective of the intentions of businesspeople, has not done so. The "hidden hand," hardly even disguised anymore, never rests. It fidgets constantly in expectation of new prospects for commercial success. It is quick to meet each new form of human frustration and human longing with commercialized solutions.

Preparation of the individual for this pervasively accepted form of treason against community life begins early. At the exits from supermarkets and variety stores are found machines in which children deposit a quarter and receive for it a small plastic globe containing an item costing, on the average, but a few pennies to produce. It proceeds in the youngster's purchase at the cinema of a paper cup filled mainly with ice, to which an inexpensive cola solution is added for the cost of a dollar or more. It continues in school systems where excessively priced junk food is made available in vending machines. Meantime, police departments, road departments, and park boards are finding more areas from which to bar youngsters who might enjoy themselves cost-free. The adult world seems to be participating in a roundup that drives children toward commercial exploitation. We have almost convinced ourselves that children cannot play games without first purchasing an array of equipment with which to do so. Socialization to commercialization is highly effective. Early on, the young citizen comes to realize two things: 1) that entertainment and relaxation cost money and, 2) that one must not expect a dollar to buy very much.

A young couple attending a movie and having a soft drink and popcorn now pay about fifteen cents a minute for the enjoyment received. Were movie houses once the havens of escape and diversion for the multitudes of the poor during the Depression? It seems hard to believe.

The contemporary entrepreneur correctly senses the need and the willingness to pay for excitement, entertainment, and pleasurable relaxation among people for whom daily life offers too few of these things. "Ripping off" a public starved for these commodities has become so easy as to taint better judgment. The entertainer Norm Crosby sees this in the short-sighted, self-defeating greed that is taking over Las Vegas.[28] Crosby contrasts the men who made Las Vegas with the corporations and their computers and controllers who have taken over more recently. The local pioneers, Crosby says, "were not Rhodes scholars . . . but they were brilliant. They knew everything to do and they did it. The secret was to give customers as much as you could as cheaply as you could because whatever they had left, they spent in the casinos. Today, the corporations figure if a steak sandwich costs seven dollars, they'll charge fifteen dollars. In the old town, if it cost seven dollars, they'd settle for five dollars. The new group may be no more or less greedy than the old, but they're less wise. Of the earlier and seemingly generous businesspeople, Crosby says:

> They weren't crazy. Nor were they philanthropists. They knew if they gave you the best of everything, you'd be back. You could lose $100,000 and couldn't wait to get back. Nowadays, a guy who comes here and loses $100,000 goes bananas when he has to pay 75¢ for a Coke. That's what's driving them away.[29]

Whether the new group of businesspeople are not as wise as the old remains to be seen. The trend now is to give a cut rate on nothing, much less give away anything for which the house can charge. Within another generation or two, gamblers may no longer be upset by the high cost of Cokes and sandwiches.

The fate of the marvelous game of snooker illustrates many of the ills that have beset public forms of diversion and entertainment. To almost everyone familiar with snooker, it is the queen of pool games. Snooker is to ordinary pool as chess is to checkers. As one typical convert to the game remarked, "Shoot, after playing snooker, regulation pool bores me to tears."[30] In the better days of pool, if there was but one active table in a poolroom, it was a snooker table. Why has the better game disappeared in favor of the lesser one?

There are many reasons, all of which center on profit and an insistence that it be maximized. First, the snooker table takes up more space. The usual American snooker table is five-by-ten feet, whereas most public places offer but a seven-foot long version of the nine-foot table required for regulation pool. The smaller the table, the more will fit in a room, and the more tables the greater the income from them. More importantly, perhaps, snooker tables have a restricted appeal. As a retailer of amusement devices put it, "Wives and kids don't like it. You can't fram the balls around." Snooker is not a game for amateurs and pretenders. On the small table with the big pockets, one can slam into an aggregate of balls and greet totally accidental "makes" with the aloof hauteur of one who actually knows what he or she is doing. It doesn't work that way in snooker.

Nor does snooker lend to the "coin-op" conversion that frees the house from keeping time and issuing equipment. The house prefers to limit its efforts to the removal of money from the coin boxes. Snooker tables couldn't hold up under the neglect; they must be carefully maintained. The game would be all but impossible on tables in the condition one finds them in the average pool hall or tavern today.

The game of pool is deteriorating as the size, condition, and no-retrieval-of-balls features all represent the dominance of the profit motive over the finer possibilities of the game. For most, there is nothing left but versions of eight ball as dictated by the no-retrieval feature of the coin-op table. These tables do "give back" the cue ball, of course, and it is with mixed feelings that we hear of a recent poolroom problem. It seems customers are taking the cue balls along with them as souvenirs.

The more popular the diversion, the more the public is likely to be "ripped off." The accumulation and dissemination of techniques for maximizing the "take" from consumers out to enjoy themselves increases with the size of the market. Consider, in this regard, the matter of dining out. The wine consumed during a dinner out costs approximately 265 percent more than that purchased in a package store.[31] The profit is immense and the house is keenly aware of the fact. A recent periodical published for those in the trade gives the following advice:

> Many top restaurants don't put water glasses on the table—only a glass for wine. Patrons who want water must ask for it. Wine service makes "cents" also: The restaurant has to pay for both the water and its service. Only the wine pays its own way—makes "cents" to serve![32]

The water a patron might drink was once considered, like the overhead, a part of the service included with the meal and paid for in the increased cost of dining out rather than cooking for oneself. Now, however, the tendency is to look at every minute aspect of service and to subject it to a cost accounting of its own.

The same feature that encouraged the promotion of wine and the elimination of water also favored the suggestion of dessert wines instead of coffee. The reader can no doubt anticipate the argument:

> Increasingly, restauranteurs are evaluating the relative value of serving coffee versus a dessert wine to top off the meal. To sell a cup of coffee you have at least nine items of expense: coffee, sugar, cream, cup, spoon, heating equipment, fuel, and labor. Wine, poured directly from a bottle into a glass is comparatively simple—and more profitable. [33]

Elsewhere in the periodical, one finds a recommendation to tavern operators to install computerized bar service systems:

> To dispense a drink, the bartender presses a button on the keyboard console, of the size and price level of the drink. He picks up the bottle with the activator ring and dispenses the precise amount of liquor while the price of the drink is being recorded. Benefit? The customer sees his brand poured and the bar manager has total control and accountability for every drink poured. Possible disadvantage? Since all drinks are accounted for, it eliminates "drinks on the house," used by some bartenders to promote customer good will. [34]

Note carefully the reference to the "possible disadvantage" of eliminating the occasional free drink to promote customer goodwill. It is not a "serious" or even an "unfortunate" disadvantage. It is not even, simply, a "disadvantage" but only the "possibility" of one. The judgment is already made. Since the drink on the house for the loyal customer is already on the way out, let's give it that last little push.

The evolving attitude toward Americans out to find enjoyment in the public sector is becoming ever more clear. Give them nothing without charge (hold the water), discourage the low-profit items (coffee), and push the big-profit items (wine before, during, and after dinner). And, since it's a night out and they're in a festive mood, triple the cost of the wine! The new mentality traces the customer's every step and asks Where can we charge? and, How much can we get away with charging? At major events, parking will not only cost, but it will be an exorbitant cost. The three dollars we last paid just to park for a ballgame used to buy the ticket and a hot dog. Beer at events is about double the tavern price.

Avarice knows few bounds when there is a special aura of revelry or festivity surrounding an event. A few years ago, a small north-central city boasted the "Biggest Class Reunion Ever Held in the United States," to which everyone who had ever graduated from a large and very old high school was invited. By ten o'clock of the first evening of festivities, the local saloon-keepers had many of their waiters and waitresses out on the street (illegally) selling beer at two and three times the normal price. In this manner did those merchants "honor" the graduates whose families had kept them in business throughout the years. Some of the merchants said it was "a matter of supply and demand—just like OPEC" and they beamed with pride at their grasp of things. Big reunions have become the thing in that little city now. The merchants really get behind them.

That younger crowd, whose inner juices compel them to go out on the town with a force that only time will overcome, are vulnerable to many forms of exploitation. A college student of my acquaintance took his favorite girl to a new disco place back in the early seventies. He spent over fifty dollars for admission fees and what he called "really bad drinks." I inquired as to the exact nature of this expensive entertainment and learned that the management provided the space, taped music, and those terrible and overpriced drinks. The real entertainment consisted of young patrons dancing in tight-fitting and otherwise fetching outfits with more watching than dancing. The entertainment, for which the young crowd paid so much money, was provided largely by themselves.

Perhaps it is because America is the world champion in both the achievement and exportation of modernization that its people overlook one of modernization's major consequences. It is the transformation of traditionally free forms of public entertainment into that which is cost prohibitive—at least on a routine basis—for the majority of people. The bread and circuses that placated a Roman citizenry of old included, at least, *free* circuses. The American middle mass is mollified in much the same way, but entrance to our arenas is far from free. That salaries running to six and even seven figures are paid to Neanderthals named Bubba testifies both to the need for collective forms of diversion in the society and to the greedy profit-taking made possible when the society is otherwise unable to satisfy such needs.

In Iran, where this particular evil attaching to modernization is more critically compared with the ways of the past, the sense of loss is greater than in our experience. As the writer Motamed-Nejad put it:

> Before the craze of modernism and the advent of sophisticated means
> of transmission in Iran, people had a variety of places to go for . . .
> entertainment, which provided more genuine pleasure than their coun-
> terparts in modern life, i.e., movies, restaurants, cafeterias. Mosques,
> Tekiehs (religious playhouses), public squares, market places, and cof-
> feehouses were the popular centers of public attraction. People could,
> almost at any time and always free of charge, enter those places to
> entertain themselves by the amusing and instructing performances of
> storytellers, reciters, chanters, and preachers. In lieu of modern cafete-
> rias, there existed large teahouses in every corner of Tehran and all
> provincial towns.[35]

The fleecing of a public desperate for collective fun and frivolity and
lacking the older community contexts that rendered these easy and
natural, is on the increase but it is not universal. There are places that
remain customer-oriented, and not in that false sense that is a theme
among modern hucksters. There remain places where the hosts have
the guests' best interests at heart as well as their own; places where the
"itch," as Walter Kerr refers to it, is held in check. It is that itch to turn
everything that a place might offer to profit that must be checked if an
establishment means to court the long-term satisfaction of its customers. Insofar as most third places are business enterprises that must
show a profit, the matter bears some explanation. Short of essaying a
treatise on economic theory, I shall attempt to illustrate by focusing on
an ordinary tavern of the good third place variety.

To begin with, whatever price is demanded for a drink serves to
eliminate any question of benevolence on the part of the house and its
owner, who is *not* running a charity or doing social work. Because they
pay for what they consume, patrons retain their dignity and owe no
homage to the innkeeper. The exchange, furthermore, is made willingly and yields a surplus of value to both parties. Each is happier after
the exchange of coin for draught. The patron values "that drink in that
place at that time" more than his coins, and the owner values the coins
more than the drink served. The transaction, of course, goes on within
a climate in which both the owner and the patron are aware of the price
of drinks generally. Regulars at a third place typically understand that
the owner is doing about as well by them as possible.

Beyond that fundamental exchange, hosts who have their patrons'
interests at heart (and their own, over the long run) have several op-

tions. They can retain a few old one-quarter-per-game pool tables largely for the pleasure of their patrons, or they can install fifty-cents-per-game tables with the intent of making more money. Owners can offer popcorn or pretzels free of charge, or they can calculate per-serving profits on them. They can "push" drinks or learn the signals that their regulars give when and if they wish another round in their own good time. Owners can cater to their big-spending customers and ignore the others, or they can make them all feel equally welcome. In such decisions, hosts who can control the itch will do well in the long run, will have more business in the slow periods, and will have a more satisfied patronage overall.

Third places characteristically make profit on the sale of coffee, doughnuts, sandwiches, beer, wine, liquor, soft drinks, and a variety of snack foods. Costs of these commodities rise and must be passed along to the customers, at least in part. Having given up on the taverns where, as a young man he used to meet his friends, one middle-aged Wisconsinite told me, "I can make a drink at home and make it cheaper than they do in any bar in town." Certainly. Anyone can. But few would visit taverns if only drinking were involved. If there is any point at all to a third place, it is that it offers so much more than just a cup of coffee or a glass of beer. In this regard, we would hardly be doing justice to good taverns if we failed to describe the manner in which they are able to offer a *guarantee on the customer's investment*.

Patrons walk into a tavern. Should they find it empty or otherwise unappealing, they may turn and leave without spending a dime, or they may buy a token draught and then depart. If they enjoy themselves, however, they may stay longer and buy a second, perhaps even a third, drink. During the consumption of these, they have been provided with a cool place in summer or a warm one in winter. The patrons have company and conversation; a restroom should they need it; and overall, a homey and comfortable place in which to relax. There is a direct correspondence between the quality of the experience the place has to offer and the amount of money the individual will spend in it. And the investment, always relatively small, stops at precisely that point where rewards diminish or duty calls. A good third place tavern remains one of the best deals available in the public domain . . . if you can find one.

CHAPTER 12

The Sexes and the Third Place

THE CHARACTERIZATION of the third place contained within the first section of this volume is sexually neutral. Men and women stand to benefit in equal measure from participation in the core settings of informal public life. Yet, a neutered depiction of the third place ignores much of the reality surrounding it and obscures the important fact that the most and the best among third places are the haunts of men or women, but not both. The joys of the third place are largely those of same-sex association, and their effect has been to maintain separate men's and women's worlds more than to promote a unisex one.

Sexual segregation accounts for the origins of the third place and remains the basis for much of the appeal and benefits this institution has to offer. During Europe's Middle Ages, married women typically gathered at the washhouses; their husbands at the cabarets.[1] In New York City a century ago, working men congregated in the local taverns while their wives sat and chatted on their front stoops. The beauty parlor has no doubt been as much a social institution for women as the barber shop has been for men. Today, observes Philippe Ariès, the third place habit and the bonds of community life are strongest in the land of the "stubborn male." He is referring to the Mediterranean regions where adult males most successfully resist the "domestic pull" and reserve time each day for the company of other males.[2]

Third Places for Women

"A third place! God! I don't even have a *second* place!" Such is the reaction that some housewives have given to the topic at hand. The idea

230

that a husband might need a third place when she is largely confined to one place may produce a wholly understandable feeling of resentment on the woman's part. Other wives may object to the idea of a third place, insisting that home and the family life it offers are adequate to the social and psychological needs of both husband and wife. Others recognize the limitation of the home and the pluses of third place association but resent the fact that males seem to have them while females do not. It was in that latter spirit that a young wife composed and made me a gift of the following verse from which, to my regret, she withheld her name:

> There is something about the number 3
>   that is mystical and magic
> It can also be quite humorous
>   and sometimes even tragic.
> For it's "3 strikes and you're out!"
>   as every ballplayer knows
> And news of deaths arrive in 3's
>   (or so the saying goes)
>
> There are 3 coins in the fountain
>   3 persons in the Trinity
> 3 chances sell for one dollar
>   and so on, to infinity
> The 3rd rail runs the subway train
>   at a very rapid pace
> So it should come as no surprise to us
>   that a man needs his "Third Place."
>
> For a man likes to get his hand around
>   a brimming glass of brew
> And he aches to tell his buddies
>   a tall old tale or two,
> He longs to see a friendly face
>   that doesn't judge or mock
> Where a man can throw all pretense off
>   and make the rafters rock.
> There's no one there to fault him
>   if he lets his ashes fall
> And he'll jolly well enjoy it
>   should there be a friendly brawl.

> Now there's nothing wrong with this
>   in fact I'm really for it
> But there's one thing that bothers me
>   I really can't ignore it.
> If a man must have a Third Place
>   then is it not just as true
> That sure as she "came from Adam's rib"
>   a woman needs a Third Place too!

And, surely, some third place needs this woman, too! The poet, this female Robert Service, understands only too well the male dominance of the third place tradition. The stereotypical hangouts in American culture are overwhelmingly male—from the cracker-barrel circle to the western saloon, from the hotel coffee counter to the pool hall and lodge hall, third places seem to be mainly a male phenomenon.

Men's dominance of the third place tradition is not difficult to understand. The first and most obvious reason for it stems from the mothering role. Unlike men's third places, which are set apart not only from women but also from the entire family, gatherings of women have almost always included their children. C. S. Lewis felt, in this regard, that the world of women "was never as emphatically feminine as that of their menfolk was masculine."[3] With the need to keep an eye on the children, women's gatherings have not afforded the abandonment of men's. Being eternally "on duty," women have been far less inclined to drink alcoholic beverages, get rowdy, or stray far from the domestic setting and its responsibilities.

In many cultures, the pattern of male dominance is accompanied by a male prejudice against socializing among wives. As Alexander Rysman discovered, "a patriarchal society resents female solidarity."[4] Rysman came to this conclusion after examining the evolving connotation of the word *gossip* in English-speaking cultures. Gossip, in its noun usage, originally meant godparent and emerged as a contraction of the Old English "God sib." The term later came to be restricted to a *female* friend of the family and, henceforth, to take on the pejorative connotation now associated with it.

By the nineteenth-century, the term *gossip* came to refer to idle talk as well as to those who engaged in it—but only those of the feminine sex. "The male meaning, 'tippling companion,' carries a feeling of warmth and good companionship while the female application is more hostile. Women 'run about' and women 'tattle.' " Some observers have found the proscription against women socializing with nonfamily members to be strong within Chicano communities. There, the feeling is that women who get together can "make trouble" for men and, "for the 'gossip' to develop social ties outside of the institutions of male dominance becomes the major sin."[5]

Studies in deviance reveal that the husband with low self-esteem typically becomes infuriated at the very idea of his wife talking to "outsiders." It is a common characteristic of husbands and fathers who beat their wives, batter their children, or commit incest. The more normal and far more common attitude among American husbands, however, would seem to be one of insensitive disinterest, a posture that corresponds with their inability to understand the unhappy isolation of housewives.

Another reason for less third place participation on the part of women has to do with the costs (however modest) incurred in third place association. A recent history of London club life takes note of the fact that, although there have been several women's clubs in past years, these have not thrived. In comparison with the men's, they were less cheerful and anything but glamorous places. They were more likely to host suffragettes than debutantes but in any case, they suffered a niggardly crowd. "Women," the author observed, "grudge spending money on food and drink for themselves."[6] Women are used to having the men pay; women have had less money than men. Too, the woman is aware of domestic budgets and family needs, and of stretching limited dollars to meet them. Even today, it is more of an "occasion" when two or more wives go out and buy drinks or lunch for themselves than it would be for their husbands.

Finally, the separation of the sexes into male and female worlds does not require that each gender have a place of retreat. It has only been necessary that one have a place in which to "escape" the other. That the male should have been the one to have a place apart is no mystery. Most societies (arguably, all of them) have been dominated by males; survival of the whole has depended far more on male cooperation and camaraderie than on that of females; child raising confined the woman, not the man.

Worthy of note is the fact that, with relatively few exceptions, women have not complained about this state of affairs. They did object when the English coffeehouses excluded them, as the alehouses never had.[7] They mounted a strong campaign against the American saloon but only at a particular historic juncture. When industrial work was of such an onerous nature as to literally drive men to drink, and when the reputation and survival of an entire family depended upon the meager earnings of a single male breadwinner (with no social welfare programs to serve as safety nets), women felt they *had* to object to the saloon. They did so with the same grim determination mothers of most species exhibit in protecting themselves and their young.

Currently, many feminists are setting their sights on the exclusive male clubs formed within the world of business, and with reason. Within those circles deals are closed, important contacts are made, and careers are advanced—all to the exclusion of women. The men may argue the joys of all-male relaxation all they wish, but they contaminate relaxation with business in the "good old boy" fashion. All in all, however, the history of female reaction to male third places has been peaceful if not enthusiastic. By implication, women were not usually bereft of association with one another. Unfortunately for our immediate purposes, not much attention has been paid to the forms that feminine association took or to the places in which it occurred.

An exception is found in the research of the Frenchwoman Lucienne Roubin, who was able to account for almost every square foot of "female" and "male" space in the villages of the French province of Provence.[8] In so doing, she accounted for *all* the space within the villages and around them, for none of the territory was neutral ground. There is, perhaps, no other study that so clearly documents the fact that life was once lived in two worlds—a man's and a woman's—and that all real estate was carved up accordingly.

Within those rural French villages, the town square was "the very heart" of male space. Women crossed it and skirted its edges on market day, but they did not presume to stop and talk or to sit with the men or other women. The outlying fields were also the territory of the men who worked them. Important to the functioning of the community as a whole and to the integration of its various occupational groups were the evening meetings of the men in the wine cellars of the village homes. No other places were as obviously and exclusively male as these subterranean nooks to which the men retired in the evenings. The cellars were moderate in temperature—cool in the summer and cozy enough during the winter months.

With the exception of those nocturnal male invasions of the wine cellars, the house was the domain of the woman. Neither the husband nor any other male claimed a special room or corner of his own within it. The woman's world, Roubin noted, was closely circumscribed but carefully defended and completely dominated by her. Usurpation of space by men abounded up to the edges of the female domain, but beyond those borders, women behaved and functioned as sovereigns, conscious of and strengthened by the decisive weight of the contribution they were making.[9]

Women also presided over the garden plots just as men did over the outlying fields. They also got together with one another in the evenings in a fashion paralleling the habits of the men of the village. Whereas the men used the wine cellars, the women used the stables. They met as often as the men, but with an interesting difference in the pattern of assembly. The groups of women were more fragmented than those of the men; they found it necessary to reorganize and reconstitute membership with the coming of each winter. In contrast, the men's groups had great continuity and were not plagued by the many "falling out" incidents that characterized female association. Households that were united one year might easily suffer a chilliness of relations the next. Once a women's group was formed, however, it was as active and exclusive, as well-attended and strict in its admittance policies as those of the men.

Roubin's unusual analysis also shed light on the meaning of village festivals. More than anything else, those occasions permitted the coming together of the sexes. No holiday or festival of ours can even suggest the spirit and collective gaiety engendered by such events. One may observe, perhaps, a few lingering carryovers from the more segregated patterns of bygone times. Women are still more likely to visit male-dominated taverns during Saturday night (the celebrating time of the week) than at other times. And men and women not married to one another are more likely to hug, kiss, or dance with each other during festive occasions.

Third places exclusively for women or dominated by women have not been much in evidence in the United States. Though women have had, and continue to have, an advantage over men in the spare time available to them, they have used this time to cultivate other forms of association. Women are reported to be far more likely than men to have a best friend, and that friend is most likely to be another woman.[10] Women now have also become greater joiners than men. They hold more memberships in formally organized voluntary associations.[11] Women use golf and tennis facilities more than men.[12] During daytime hours, the lounging areas of the tennis academies as well as the courts are typically dominated by women.

Women also appear to have made a greater adaptation to the limited form of interaction afforded by the telephone. Many males remain uncomfortable with telephone communication, especially with those prolonged conversations that women enjoy. Yet, for all the convenience of the telephone, it is doubtful that today's women enjoy phone calls as much as yesterday's women enjoyed having people around.

Teas, tennis, and telephoning compensate the modern wife's exile from community, but not adequately. While men were building a community life around work, the commuter ride, regular business lunches, and businessmen's associations, women found themselves deprived of community and the kind of easy informal relations they had enjoyed earlier in life. As the sociologist Philip Slater once expressed it in a magazine article, marriage "cheats today's young women." It does so, he observed, by depriving them of community life. By taking up residence in the typical American suburb, the woman loses contact with the crowd, group, or gang, which used to assemble daily and automatically when she was in school. Before industrialization, Slater reminds us, people lived a community life and to be deprived of it was a punishment, an exile. Today the combination of graduation and marriage means exile for the woman who is not working outside the home.[13]

A West Coast psychiatrist received a great deal of attention not long ago by first lecturing and then producing a book on the subject of *Passive Men, Wild Women*.[14] He had struck a common chord, articulating a malady of broad proportions. The husband puts his time and energy into his work, spending himself dealing with people and their problems. By the time he comes home, he's "had it to the eyeballs" and wants to hide from everyone, his wife and her problems included. He takes retreat in the form of television, cocktails, magazines, and newspapers. He's active at work, but passive at home—and that's what

makes women "wild." The housewife with too few, if any, other adult
contacts during her day counts on her husband's return. An unaccom-
modating social environment sets her up to expect too much from her
husband; the same social environment renders him a disappointment.

Suzanne Gordon has looked deeply into the anatomy of loneliness
and found it nowhere more prevalent than among suburban housewives.[15] Gordon perceives that what she calls "spontaneous contact"
(informal association) is possible and would dispel loneliness. Yet, few
women permit it on their part or others. Ms. Gordon suggests two
reason why most American housewives reject informal contact. First,
they project their own need for association upon others and fear being
swamped or smothered by it. Second, they do not know how to set
limits on or control this kind of association. Their concerns are real. If
one lets neighbors drop into one's home unbidden and unannounced, to
what corner does one retreat when the time or inclination to associate
with them is not there? The suburban woman's need for "neutral
ground" (see Chapter 2) is almost universally unmet.

With considerable enthusiasm, the author of an article in a recent
women's scholarly periodical described the emergence of a neighborhood "self-help network" and the physical base from which it operated.[16] Adjacent to the neighborhood playground lived a woman who
opened her home to all comers. From that home, the mothers could
keep an eye on their children. The children were allowed to play in this
home as well, and the mothers soon instituted a coffee klatch. The
place was quite literally taken over: "As children wandered in and out
looking for their mothers, the overall impression was one of noise,
bustle, and sometimes confusion, but most importantly one of informal support and mutual enjoyment."

What is striking about situations like this is that something as important as that which this lady and her home afforded is left to chance, *and
the chances are none too good!* It is the rare and unusual woman who can
and will open her home in this manner. None of the other women
reciprocated. They held on to their control of informal association.
They entered and left this woman's home as they pleased but kept their
own homes off limits to informal neighborhood socializing.

The housewife is victim of the overzoned, nothing-but-other-
private-homes environment into which the bulk of new families locate
and that are remote from the other institutions of society. But, as

Suzanne Gordon also noted, a hostile physical environment is not the only problem. Gordon realizes how much courtship, mate selection, and the course of a marriage has ceased to be of concern to almost everyone but the couple themselves. The modern twosome is no longer "swayed by religious, financial, community, and family considerations."[17] Rejecting all pressures from outsiders in the choice of a mate, and few with respect to their social lives, the couple is also denied the built-in support from kin and community which once compensated for the lesser degree of privacy they had. What the community cannot control, it tends to lose interest in. Many are lonely in today's society and rightly sense that nobody cares.

It is precisely the isolation and immunity of modern marriage from other institutions and influences that make the location and surrounding environment of the couple's home a matter of paramount importance. Freed from the connections and wider concerns in which courtship and marriage once evolved, today's couples need a residential environment that facilitates informal association of the kind people can control and regulate to suit their situations, but most of all is available. What exists now is quite the opposite.

The recent women's movement began a few generations ago when millions of wives found themselves dumped in suburban housing tracts where they suffered an unexpected and undeserved exile from community life. The movement gained momentum when their daughters, who had grown up surrounded by their parents' unhappiness and the cabin fever of family life too much contained within itself, resolved to avoid a similar trap. The movement is a determined one, and it is based as much on lost connections as new ambitions.

The Disappearance of Male Places

The third place is a designation befitting the industrial society in which the workplace and the home are separate and in which those two places have become preemptive. The third place, currently a poor third, was once number one.

Among primitive societies, the institution of the men's house was widespread and its existence has been recorded in Asia, Africa, the Americas, and the islands of the Pacific. It survived in France until the beginning of the twentieth century.[18] Among the natives of Dutch

New Guinea, it was called the *Rumslam*; the *Kwod* by the people of the Torres Straits; the *Pangah* (meaning Head House) in primitive Borneo; the *Pabafunan* among the Igorot of northern Luzon; the *Maraes* by the Samoans; the *Khotla* in Bechuana country; the *Bweni* among the Bondei of German East Africa; the *Baito* by the Brazilian Bororo; the *Kivas* among the Pueblo Indians, and so on throughout the primitive world. Typically, the men's house was the largest, most ornate and prominent structure in the village. It served as town hall, council chamber, sleeping resort for bachelors, guest house for male visitors, trophy hall, and club. Women and children seldom visited there.

The men's house had special meaning for the boys of the tribe. Admittance to it signified the attainment of manhood. Following a rite of passage (a frightening and painful ordeal that tested manliness), the boy became a man and a member of the club at the same time. His transition to adulthood was also a transition from the world of his mother to that of his father or uncle. Following the rite of passage, the boy left forever the care of his mother. He departed the world of women and entered the world of men.

The evolution of male bonding may be traced from these primitive men's houses to the men's clubs familiar to our society.[19] The earliest urban clubs or circles were adaptations to both increasing population size and the emergence of social stratification. As with the men's houses of old, the membership of the men's club "zealously fended off any intrusion by females."[20] Later, however, most lodges and fraternal orders would come to depend for their survival upon support and assistance from members' wives. Among the working classes, as has so often been noted, the inn, pub, tavern, or saloon have served as poor men's clubs or working men's clubs. In these, the support of wives is not crucial, and the men's tavern remains more a distinct piece of male territory than the men's lodge.

Male bonding and male territory are both declining in American society. In the private and public sectors, few places remain that communicate a clear impression of masculinity. At home and in the world beyond, the places where males once met in seclusion from their women are fast disappearing. The average home no longer includes a male sanctum. Now rightly regarded as a single place, the residential site formerly included several distinct regions. When a much larger proportion of the population lived on farms and in small towns, people

had considerably more living and working space than increasing urbanization would later allow. The luxury of space and the preponderance of
occupations involving manual labor and worker-owned tools and
equipment resulted in the construction of a variety of niches and
outbuildings to which men, along with their sons and male neighbors,
would retreat from the household proper. There men felt comfortable
in their soiled work clothing. To sit in the parlor required that one
bathe and change clothes. Commonly, men would "wind down" their
days seated in a work area amid male companions rather than with their
women in the kitchen or parlor.

As country and small town life gave way to city dwelling, outbuildings were no longer common. Men then sought a place of retreat in the
basements of their homes. Beneath the wiring and pipes, under ex-
posed and unattractive ceiling joists, they retained a portion of the
basement for their tinkering. And, since the basement could normally
be entered from the outside without going through the house proper, a
crony or two could easily drop by without disturbing the other members of the family or requiring them to be presentable to "company." A
garage separate from the house with forward space for a workbench
and a few chairs often served as well.

But those small bits of male acreage were also destined to be fore-
closed. Technology persisted in its course and with it came an improved furnace, much smaller and cleaner and not nearly as ugly as its
predecessors. That innovation, along with do-it-yourself floor tiling
and inexpensive wall paneling, lent new possibilities to the old basement. Those included a spacious area in which to entertain couples or a
family recreation area, the latter representing a popular response to
growing pressures to make the home more competitive with attractions
outside of it.

There was a finality about the loss of that quarter of the basement.
The home had become a single heterosexualized setting where men had
to wear better clothes, clean up their vocabularies, and practice their
new manners—all this without respite or hope of escape.

Territories that men claimed beyond their homes were largely a
function of locale, social standing, and population size. Circumstances
simply imposed variety on the universality of all-male associational
settings. Men of all stations had their taverns; those ranged from lowly
joints to refined versions with oak paneling and smartly uniformed

bartenders. The city man found his retreats in the pool hall or golf club, while the small town man frequently took flight to the hunting and fishing shacks that once dotted the wooded regions of the nation.

Typically, those shacks allowed men to cast off the pretenses imposed by their occupations, wives, and towns bent on improving themselves. Here they returned to basics—a man's breakfast in the morning, a day of fishing or hunting, good tobacco, a bottle of the best liquor, and the uncomplicated joys of all-male company.

The shacks were furnished with castaway chairs or old car seats. The cots had bare mattresses, and orange crates nailed to the walls held a collection of cracked and mismatched dishes. Windows were curtain-less or covered with nothing more attractive than flour sack material. A cheap airtight stove supplied the heat. Such hovels were cleaned rarely and then, perhaps, by sprinkling heated water over the floor so that sweeping might remove more dirt than it raised. In repeating outings to such settings, men retained the ability to make do without the trap-pings of a civilized environment and without need of being looked after. It was in such places, also, that they retained the habits of male cooperation, which city living and bureaucratized work settings tend to eradicate.

Few such places exist any more. They have been replaced to a lesser extent by lakeside cottages with lawns and other suburban trappings and to a greater extent by recreational vehicles in which both men and women enjoy almost all the conveniences of home. And, as things changed on land, so did they at sea. The old-timers at a local yacht club well remember the boats of their fathers with hard bench seats and a simple pail for body wastes. Some had a simple drop-down table, which converted the cabin into a mess. The interiors of today's boats, in contrast, are gaily colored, comfortable, and highly appointed. They are preferred not only by the new wave of female sailors but also by today's males, who seem every bit as much converted to the new delicacy in their surroundings.

In the cities, the Depression and its long aftermath facilitated female invasion of men's golf and drinking clubs. Confronted with financial collapse, these institutions began opening their doors to women. Golf clubs became country clubs, with the ultimate result that women now spend more time than men in what was once all-male territory. In one drinking club after another, the hard decision to remodel was made. To remodel really meant to cater to a new clientele, a distaff one. Out went spittoons and sawdust on the floor. Nude paintings and male conversation pieces began to disappear, as did the old mahogany bars and, for the most part, natural lighting. These were replaced by indirect lighting, padded formica, additional table seating, carpeting, and the substitution of gentler blends for much of the bourbon and rye whiskey, which had once been the staples. The Bowery look gave way to the subdued and cushioned parlor type of bar, long on comfort, if short on character. The "symphony of browns," which had dominated the all-male bar, gave way to vivid golds, greens, and reds, as what had been saloons and taverns became lounges.

Fraternal organizations and businessmen's clubs offer about all that remains of what was once a strong tradition of group singing among American men. What remains pales by comparison to what used to be. Barbershop quartet and college fraternity singing are remembered in stereotype. In addition, however, men often sang on the occasions of their picnics, tavern assemblies, and other outings. Those of German descent, I recall, would often gather in the woods or at a local park in the evening to enjoy a *zigeuner* (after the German word for gypsy). They would harmonize until voice and keg were spent.

Men must feel close to one another to sing or dance together, and the absence of these joyous expressions of unity among males today probably marks, more certainly than anything else, the disappearance of the places and occasions that promote solidarity among them.

The fate of the pool hall is particularly informing. To a major extent it has been, like the bar, transported into the home. Writing on the state of domestic architecture at the turn of the century, Charles Hooper offered the opinion that the home billiard room was the invention of women who wanted to keep their husbands in tow.[21] Undoubtedly, however, men favored the idea as well, since so many regard the acquisition of one to be a distinct "point of arrival" in a culture given to status achievements and such acquisitions as serve to mark the success of life-style strivings. Too, the typical owner expects to capture some of the masculine aura of the pool hall or the atmosphere of the friendly tavern under his own roof when he "has the boys over" for an evening.

The men discovered, however, that the atmosphere of the pool hall cannot be purchased as easily as the basic equipment of the game. At parties, too many want to play; nobody gets to play enough; female guests must be allowed their turn; skill differentials are either irritating or embarrassing, depending upon the player's skill or lack of it. Other than at parties, the table is not used. Friends are not available to the extent assumed (especially without their wives) nor, in truth, does the owner's family situation allow for frequent invasions of the home.

Playing pool with one or two members of the family soon becomes boring, and the pool player finds himself in a bind. A significant portion of the home has been given over to a pool table; a considerable chunk of money has been invested. The owner is morally constrained not to visit public pool halls anymore. Pool has been brought home and the husband with it, but his friends and the culture of a male place have been left behind.

The game of poker has also been brought into the home. Men used to play this game in the back rooms of saloons, primarily, and those surroundings were markedly different from the cardplaying space now borrowed from the family. Gone are the tables with cigarette- and cigar-burnt edges, the low, green-shaded lights, the girlie calendar from the beer company, the background music of bar talk, the saloon chairs, the kibitzers, and the blue clouds of smoke rising to the high ceilings. Gone, in short, is the male atmosphere. Poker is now played mostly in borrowed and alien space, which belongs to the family. Players are on notice throughout the evening not to abuse the hosting institution by injecting foul smoke or foul language.

Cigar smoke and four-letter words were part of an extensive pattern of male behavior, which served the function of securing male territory once it was gained. Male circles transmitted styles and mannerisms from one generation to the next that had the effect of signaling an all-male presence. A common thread running through most of them was that of "male coarseness" and its unsuitability to mixed company. These mannerisms signaled the animal in man and a rejection of the veneers of civilization.

With the decline in the number and availability of all-male places in our society, there has emerged a new delicacy among men. It is now possible for the middle-class male to go through life consciously or unconsciously avoiding territory where men behave in the fashion described. This is especially true among careerists, who trim and tailor their social lives according to the dictates of the professional drive. The new delicacy does not necessarily render them more considerate of women, but it does diminish their inclination and capacity to enjoy the uninhibited camaraderies of traditional male groups.

The coarseness or vulgarity traditional among gatherings of the male of the species served not only the function of warding off women, but also that of strengthening bonds between men. Does male vulgarity subside or get set aside as men gain respect for one another? No, in fact, it's quite the opposite. The better they know one another, the worse it usually gets. Men who keep their conversation on a purified level, when given the choice, are not likely to be at ease with one another and are not likely to be good friends.

In slipping into a distinctly masculine style of talking and acting, men call out in one another the accumulated male experiences of their past; a common heritage surfaces. An almost immediate intimacy is engendered. Through adoption of the uniquely male demeanor, men the world over have shown themselves to be "regular guys" and have secured the trust of their fellow men by so doing. "Perfessor" and "Pill-Pusher" alike have entered the hunting camps of working men under keen and critical scrutiny, often to be told, as the second "dead soldier" is set up for target practice, "Hey, Doc, you're all right!" "All right," of course, means that a basic male demeanor has resurfaced; that the stuff of masculine commonality has remained intact beneath a temporarily discarded uniform of social and occupational involvement. The underlying male style is a common-denominator phenomenon that allows men to unite quickly and across class lines. For that reason it has been a key to the survival of society, especially in times of local and national emergencies, which call for massive collective action.

Why are male third places declining? Why has all-male territory within the society diminished so rapidly? The current women's movement can take no blame or credit since the cause cannot follow the effect. All-male territory and sustained all-male association were largely eliminated before the recent surge of feminine militancy. Most of what has been lost was lost well before the consciousness revolution, and it was not seen to be a loss during the critical period.

The family sociologist Gail Fullerton offers a concise analysis of what happened. "Our forebearers," she writes, "lived in two complimentary worlds: the man's world and the woman's world. We also spend our lives in two worlds: the mass society, where we earn a living and pay taxes, and the private world of the conjugal family where we love and hate and live."[22] Fullerton marks the point of transition between 1890 and 1920, the juncture at which the "new middle class" began to supersede the old. The older category were owner-executives—geographically stable men who presided over small family-owned companies. Of them, Fullerton notes: "These were men who had close and continuing relationships with a wide circle of friends and relatives and who found their deepest belonging in the exclusively masculine fellowship of a lodge or private club. They were often fond of their wives, but seldom communicated with them as equals."[23] The new middle class were few in number in 1890, but by 1920 their ranks had expanded rapidly and would continue to do so. These were professionals and salaried managers—men with transferrable skills who would move frequently, both "up the ladder" and across the land. These men "sought to make marriage as rewarding as possible, which meant that as the 'new' middle class grew, more men began to want greater intimacy with their wives, both at the emotional and sexual level."[24]

Men's attention turned away from male bonding and the third place settings in which it had been celebrated on a daily basis. A new appreciation of one's mate and a different marital relationship were being cultivated. In the face of repeated moves and the consequent loss of other stable ties, the husband came to rely upon his wife as a female sidekick whose growing presence in his life supplanted the lost continuity of male relationships. A new marital intimacy took shape around the fact that the spouse had become the man's one hope for a durable relationship in life.

The same transitional period witnessed a considerable relaxation of Puritan morality. A new sexual frontier opened, and husband and wife explored it together. With increasing numbers of men and women entering coeducational colleges, the equality of the sexes advanced rapidly. College-educated men were comfortable with women and promoted the new togetherness with enthusiasm. They took their women on hunting, fishing, and boating trips, into pool halls and taverns and other such settings in which men had earlier taken refuge from the opposite sex. To the enlightened young man of the times, there was little doubt but that the rest of the world would be as charmed by the presence of his female companion as was he. He became the prideful tour guide who escorted his lady into the diminishing localities of former all-male territory. The old-timers may have shaken their heads in dismay ("Only a college feller is stupid enough to take his wife on a huntin' trip!"), but the times were on the young man's side.

The new interest that the middle-class husband took in his wife contributed mightily to his own domestication. Whereas industrialization separated the place of work from the place of residence and took the father out of the home, he is not nearly as removed from domestic responsibility as many feminists and child developmentalists suggest. While parenting *is* largely mothering, Margaret Mead's observations are also true: "In all the known history of civilization, never have fathers taken as much care of their little children as in the United States today. Nor have mothers had as much companionship from their chosen mates in the kitchen and in the nursery."[25] The problem is not with a husband and father who is shirking his duty. The problem stems from the loss of that concerned and helpful contingent of *other* adults who helped raise children and who had earlier lent continuous social support to the nuclear but far from isolated family unit of the past.

Perhaps it was inevitable that Americans would come to see the loss of durable same-sex relations in a positive light and glorify companionate marriage as superior to the marital relationships of earlier generations. It is always easier to put a positive interpretation on things than actually improve them.

The Status of Togetherness

With the government providing suburban housing with no money down to 13.5 million returning veterans after World War II, the ideal of companionate marriage was afforded an optimal physical setting. In the quiet suburbs, in homes remote from in-laws and people who knew them as youngsters, the couple could realize the dream of a togetherness marriage. Marriages could be fashioned around sweethearts' dreams, all the while insulated from the intrusions of outsiders, who were thought to have "plagued" marriage in earlier times.

And how has togetherness fared? Indications are that the excessive confinement of husband and wife with each other, with too little close, frequent, and informal contact with other adults, is an unstable condition that struggles hard to survive its own deficiencies. A massive and growing body of evidence suggests that the ideal is basically flawed.

Since the 1950s, the stresses and strains of an overly-insulated togetherness have encouraged millions of people to seek alternatives. By 1981, almost two million American couples were cohabiting outside of marriage.[26] As early as the mid-60s, somewhere between two and five percent of the nation's married couples were regularly involved in mate-swapping; at either figure, millions were involved.[27] Currently, the rate of increase of single-person households is projected to be twice as great as that for all households in the United States.[28] The percent of people in their early twenties who are remaining single is rising sharply; whether they are postponing marriage or rejecting it altogether is not yet clear. College-educated women, those able to exercise the greater amount of choice about getting married, are the group of American women least likely ever to marry.[29]

The United States leads the industrialized nations of the world with a divorce rate that has doubled since 1960. The breakup of officially-sanctioned togetherness has occurred with such frequency that one observer could report, truthfully if somewhat facetiously, that America's contribution to the institution of marriage is divorce. Indeed, the failures at marriage in our society have become so frequent as to suggest a normal condition. Accordingly, many experts now prefer to call divorce a solution rather than a problem and prefer to look upon divorce not as the disorganization of personal and marital relationships but as family reorganization. Perhaps the new view eases some of the old pain.

Many experts, in confronting the failure of togetherness marriage, encourage more togetherness. In a sense, they are correct in doing so. Research reveals, for instance, that the average American couple spends only twenty minutes *per week* in direct communication with one another (and for this the modern-day Jiggs is expected to forgo his lively conversations down at Dinty Moore's place!).[30] Research also shows that couples in their thirties spend only thirty to forty hours *per year* in sexual activity. Companionate marriage imposes more togetherness than many couples are capable of either utilizing or enjoying while inhibiting stimulating contacts with other adults. Many marriages are not surviving and many more are shored up by that popular in-house escape from togetherness—the TV set.

Much is written and spoken against the institution of marriage, and not only by radical feminists who regard it as the formalization of female servitude to the male. Others are searching for alternatives to monogamous marriage as it has evolved in our society, often expressing a missionary's zeal for life-styles that but a couple of decades ago would have been regarded as bizarre and immoral. Many regard the language and the reasoning of these experimenters as artlessly self-indulgent as they flaunt tradition in their quest for personhood or individual fulfillment. When society's arrangements don't work well for people, individualism is promoted in all its glory, even though the arguments and the language put forth may be anything but glorious. Nor indeed, does my own way of putting it have any elegance: Marriage cannot afford all the togetherness presently imposed upon it; rather, each partner needs regular connections with other adults, particularly those of the same sex.

The Role of the Third Place in Sex Relations

Most third places are sexually segregated, some exclusively so, while in others separation by sex is a matter of degree. Far more often than not, these institutions of joyful and animated relaxation erect barriers between the sexes and promote the ancient division of social life into men's and women's worlds. The ultimate effect, however, is not divisive. Sexually segregated third places support the heterosexual relationships of mates in several important ways.

Among those who currently enjoy it, third place association reduces the dangerous insularity of modern marriage, a condition once described by the late Margaret Mead:

each spouse is supposed to be all things to the other. They're supposed to be good in bed, and good out of it. Women are supposed to be good cooks, good mothers, good wives, good skiers, good conversationalists, good accountants. Neither person is supposed to find any sustenance from anybody else.[31]

Regular association with enjoyable people in relaxed social gatherings reduces the pressure Mead described. The third place makes a substantial contribution to the individual's contentment with life; contented people are not likely to disturb, much less destroy, their basic relation ships. Those with fuller lives expect less from marriage and enjoy it more.

Third place association adds to the quantity of life's satisfactions and lends much that cannot be derived from marriage and family life. There is joy in raising the roof, letting one's hair down, or taking off one's shoes in the company of one's own sex. Social relaxation is greater without the low-level stress that attends the mixing of the sexes. The average individual is never quite as comfortable in the presence of the opposite sex as when in the company of friends of his or her own sex. The woman entirely devoted to her husband and children is, nonetheless, most likely to feel relaxed in the company of female friends.

It was for this reason that many Englishmen and Englishwomen who knew how to relax objected to their country's Sex Discrimination Act, which eliminated the Ladies' Only bars. Ben Davis gave the argument: "Why, indeed, should a pub not offer, where the demand exists, opportunity for either sex to escape, for a brief space, from the company of the other? Such a respite from one, at least, of the stresses of life is beneficial rather than harmful to anyone."[32]

Both husband and wife benefit, also, from the social support and connectedness that attends third place association. A woman well connected to a network of friends is not as much at the mercy of her husband as one who is not. The same, of course, applies to the man. To be a person outside of marriage as well as in; to have a degree of autonomy from the marital relationship; to exist as one who cannot be taken for granted—such qualities are beneficial to a marriage that would run the full course. Having a vital marriage *and* time "with the girls" or "with the boys" are key ingredients in the recipe for a full and satisfying existence. It is not a matter of having one's cake and eating it, too. It is a matter of keeping the cake from turning to stale crumbs.

Same-sex association encourages interest in the opposite sex. Men are never so much sex objects as when discussed in female groups, and women never so much as when the topics of all-male conversation. Among other things (and certainly not least among them), women are sex objects to most men and it is important that they remain that. But it is ridiculous to charge that women are only that in the mind of any normal male. Male groups influence their members to view women as sex objects but they do not typically encourage males to treat real persons as such. With what used to be a far more refined vocabulary, women's groups have offered a similar encouragement. Same-sex groups and gatherings encourage an interest in the opposite sex while at the same time offering a retreat, respite, and contrast from heterosexual involvement.

Herein, I suspect, lies the major contribution that the third place makes to the intimate life of the couple. As many sexologists understand, sexual contact represents a spark of intensely erotic interest that bridges a gap between partners. The gap results from conflicts, tensions, antagonisms, or barriers that tend to keep potential partners apart.[33] The principle is a simple one: no gaps, no sparks. It is tension that imbues sexual activity with emotion, drama, and meaning, and when those qualities are present sexual preferences are shaped.

Eroticism is almost always absent in all-male groups. There are no tensions. Lounging or rambling about in single-spirited camaraderie, men are as relaxed as one will find them in the wakened state. They are too much at ease and in tune with one another to engender those tensions necessary to erotic interest.

Heterosexual interest everywhere coexists with patterns of male bonding; where men are at ease and comfortable with one another, homosexual relationships are minimal. Where competition between men is great and institutionalized patterns of male bonding are weak or nonexistent, homosexuality becomes far more common.

In societies where young boys and girls are allowed sexual access to one another, the principle of the gap and the necessity for tensions may seem to be refuted. The barriers between boy and girl appear to have been totally eliminated. Yet it is just such cases that confirm the principle most of all.

Among the African Mbuti, for example, youth are encouraged to discover sexual intercourse early in life. They may couple with whom they please; no obstacles are placed in their way by the adult community. What happens, though, is that the girls (who are expected to take the initiative) never choose young men whom they can take for granted. They introduce uncertainty and inject tension at the outset. They begin by physically beating the boy of their choice, often to the point of inflicting serious injury and scarring him for life.

In our society, boys normally take the initiative, and the result is similar. The "easy" girl is not alluring. She's a "last resort," if resorted to at all. The literature and drama of grand passion depend on conflicts, barriers, misunderstandings, initial friction even to the point of intense dislike. Passion needs obstacles that fire the emotions and set up the consummation. The time the lovers are kept apart occupies all but the final scene or last page. Grand passion subsides with consummation.

Romance drama centers on courtship, not marriage's long haul. In real life people must cope with an enormously long postnuptial period during which the inherent eroticism of courtship gives way to the far duller (erotically) routine of marriage. Until fairly recently, widespread patterns of male segregation and the existence of other intimate ties served to minimize the time the couple had together and the extent of their dependency upon one another. Earlier marriages were built less on the partners' immersion in one another and more on the means for connecting with community that the marital union made possible. As the family sociologist Gail Fullerton observes, "the contemporary couple are more likely to mourn the passing of romance than to seize the opportunity to build a marriage. Either or both may begin covertly looking for a new romance. Or they may settle resignedly into a joyless existence. . . ."[34]

The desire of recent generations to prolong the honeymoon is understandable. The desire for passion lives on but the barriers that long served to fan passion's flames are gone. Nothing works as well and nothing ever will, but couples try. An entire industry, of sorts, has emerged out of the quest after passion. It involves water beds and mirrors, lush carpeting and the Playboy channel, Gothic sex novels and Jacuzzis, and, of course, a never-ending series of instruction manuals.

Commenting on the death of same-sex intimacy in our time, Stuart Miller finds it not surprising "that most Americans will tell you their spouses are their best friends, although many more men will so declare than women."[35] This heretofore unprecedented monopolization of individuals by their spouses contaminates potential relationships outside marriage with guilt and apprehension. As a result, Miller states, "When a man, for example, wants to go out at night with the boys, he doesn't just go; he tells them that first he must ask his wife whether their social schedule will allow it. There is no implied free social time for him other than that negotiated and granted by his wife."[36] Indeed, many males fail to get permission even when the social schedule allows it. A visiting fireman recently bragged to me about his marriage. He said:

You know it occurred to me that I'm the only guy among the husbands I know who can go out and play pool when my wife is *in* town. The rest of them call me now and then to go out for a few beers and to shoot some pool. I can predict it every time. They are free to do what they want only when wifey is gone. Jeez, whatta way to live.

In a remarkable upsetting of the older order of things, women now have more freedom to cultivate friendships than do men within the world of middle-class marriages. Moreover, women's heightened status and earning power are increasing their independence. Wives can walk out on their husbands more easily these days and, when they do, men not only lose their mates, but, often, their only close friend as well. Eventually the togetherness relationship between man and wife, rich as it once may have been, is apt to suffer from claustrophobia. The husband becomes a dull, overly familiar, less interesting person. The exclusiveness of the relationship comes to have a corrosive effect upon the couple's sex life: erotic attraction depends upon those differences that sexual contact serves to bridge. When the differences are diluted, individuals lose their sexual edge and their relationship becomes boring. A noted sexologist puts it this way:

> The male bond manages to deliver its considerable force to heterosexuality. Its homosexual component is ordinarily much too far from anything erotic to offer sexual competition to heterosexuality. But by supplying relief—in a sense, putting gas back in the tank—it satiates male needs and refreshes a man's appetite for a forceful return to heterosexual contacts. Male bonding is thus a "refueling operation." Many women intuitively understand this . . . and though they may miss their men who are "off with the boys," they use the time to recuperate, correctly sensing that they are the ultimate benefactors of men's diversions from them. Their hunch is right, as is the hunch of other women who feel a pensive disquietude with men who have no close male ties.[37]

When men have deep relations with other men, as another writer put it, their married sex lives are better.[38]

Masculinity and femininity refer to styles of appearance, conduct, outlook, and attitude that make the sexes interesting and appealing to one another. These are nurtured and replenished in same-sex association. Marriage that denies the full measure of same-sex adult association will yield endless rows of isolated homes where community used to be and will plague the joys of marital companionship with tedium.

Boys and Girls Together

A man cannot become "one of the girls" nor a woman "one of the boys." On occasion I have seen the woman who seems to believe that her entrance into all-male company makes no difference. The caution light that flashes is not seen by her. The change in mood is subtle; the restrictions imposed on conversation are not noticed. The men may do their best to make her feel at home but there is "strange wheat in the garden" and the company is instantly alerted. People are strongly disinclined to abandon their sexual identities, nor do they allow others to abandon theirs. The intruder into the opposite sex group effectively destroys what he or she may seek to share.

There are limits to the sexual integration of third places. Clearly, the admittance, even the welcoming of both sexes to an establishment, is rarely tantamount to sexual integration. Many a male haunt forced by circumstances to admit women remains very much a male haunt.

The immunity that most third places have against takeover by the opposite gender is scarcely appreciated by men, especially when a male citadel is first breached by females. Indeed, all seems lost! In part, this pessimism stems from the great conservatism of attitude, which most men hold toward their third places. A man may live in a home that is redecorated frequently; another may be ultraprogressive in his politics or ultraliberal in his sex relations; yet another may change employers just to gain a different work atmosphere. All, however, expect their third places to remain intact and unchanged. The slightest alterations are interpreted as signs of deterioration. The club will fold if members are allowed to eat without the necktie rule being observed! The new bar-counter has no character, no charm; the damned formica and fake leather are part of the whole plastic world! The patron who expects a short beer chaser with his shot of whiskey now has to *ask* for it! What happened to the good old days?

Small wonder, then, that the admittance of women seems to spell "The End" in those invaded retreats once exclusively male. The invasions, however, are rarely as devastating as feared, for full-scale integration of the sexes rarely follows a new admittance policy.

In the late sixties a club with which I'm familiar bowed to pressure from the members' wives and not only admitted them but also underwent total remodeling to make them comfortable. The old tavern look gave way to something akin to a modern airport cocktail lounge. Only the card room remained off limits to women. The billiards room was dispensed with. As many members feared, the women flocked in—for a brief time. But the place was suitably large, and groups of men were always able to find space away from the women. There, discussions retained their male flavor. On their own, the women weren't regular enough in attendance to achieve what the men had. The male member knew that he could enter at any time and find friends waiting (one sure test of a good third place and the feature that draws regulars like a magnet whenever free time allows); women could not.

Once the novelty wore off and the women had ample opportunity to find out what went on in their husbands' club, they became infrequent visitors. The club hasn't been sexually integrated in the manner many of its members had feared. *Accommodation* rather than *integration* would seem the more appropriate term in cases such as this. More often than not, in men's informal gathering places as in their fraternal lodges, there is an accommodation that usually leaves everyone satisfied without the deadly effect of total integration of interaction and activity.

Perhaps the closest thing to total integration that the average middle-class American experiences is the version often forced at private invitational dinner parties. Commonly, a boy-girl-boy-girl seating arrangement is imposed upon the guests. As a woman of C. S. Lewis' acquaintance put it, "Never let two men sit together or they'll be no fun."[39] Given a choice, it seems, at least one of the sexes prefers not to "integrate"—hence, they must be forced.

Forced integration at a table is doubtlessly more successful now than in Victorian times. A young American girl who visited her English uncle during the middle of the last century reported on the manner of accommodation with which English males consented to integration at dinner.[40] "On my right hand," she recorded, "I had Mr. Landon, who is deaf in his left ear; and on my left, Mr. Charlton, who informed me that he was deaf in his right ear." There was no rudeness; everyone was pleasant and agreeable. However, table talk was almost entirely addressed to the adventures of recent hunts and the problems with poachers. Afterward, the men retired to play cards, leaving the women to look on if they cared to do so."

In contemporary American life, men are far more likely to engage women in conversation on topics of common interest, even though they may hold no more interest than the discussion of a television show. The English remain much more the masters of accommodation without surrendering the richer flavors of male association. A friend ran full against their devices not long ago. She was and remains an incurable "car nut." Among the English, with whom she longed to "talk automobiles," her social engagements were always frustrating. Whenever she would attempt to broach the subject with an Englishman, he would promptly direct her to that part of the house where the ladies were gathered and relegate her to all-female company.

The manner of English accommodation was also evident during the course of extensive pub observations in one of the northern cities.[41] There, the vault (the northern term for the public bar) is virtually off limits to women—not legally, but in fact. The pub's best room is favored by women, and when they go there they most often talk among themselves. Typically, a working man will go with his wife to the pub on Saturday night, drop her off at the best room, and go to the vault. Periodically, he will have a waiter check on her needs and, in adherence to local custom, he will join her in the best room for the last hour before the pub closes. He spends the greater part of his Saturday night with his male friends and the last hour with the ladies in the best room, where the sexes eventually mix.

The continental male may be even more masterful at accommodating women in sociable settings than the Englishman. Surely, the *bier garten* and *gasthaus* have been models of third place sexual coexistence. The world traveler Harry Franck was obviously charmed by the mature and civilized ways of the Bavarians:

> The justly criticized features of our saloons are quite unknown in the Bavarian *Gasthauser.* In the first place, they are patronized by both sexes and all classes, with a consequent improvement in character. On Sunday evening, after his sermon, the village priest or pastor, the latter accompanied by his wife, drops in for a pint before retiring to his well-earned rest. Rowdyism, foul language, obscenity either of word or action are rare as in the family circle. Never having been branded society's black

sheep, the Bavarian beerhall is quite as respected and self-respecting a member of the community as any other business house. It is the village club for both sexes, with an atmosphere quite as ladylike as, if somewhat less effeminate, than a sewing-circle.[42]

The Englishwoman Violet Hunt was equally impressed with the lack of barriers and offenses to women on the Continent. Yet, when one reads her description of the third places within the German culture, it seems there were barriers. The men would sit with one another and drink and smoke and talk until the sun sank low in the sky. The women sat nearby but apart. They knitted or did needlework, watched the children, carried the lunch, and kept an eye on the time.[43]

In the little dining and drinking places in that region of the world, there is again a democratic spirit that bids welcome to all strata and both sexes. But what does one see in a commanding part of the room? A *Stammtisch*, a special table, usually a round one, for the "friends of the house." And who sits there? Men only. They come to it regularly on weeknights, while their wives and children remain home.

Accommodation is to be expected where physical segregation of the sexes is not acceptable but where men's and women's interests are different. In the immediate presence of women, men begin to talk like them; in the immediate presence of women, men become increasingly aware that they are performing. Relaxation is more difficult. The difference in interests between men and women and the reduced inhibition of same-sex association accounts for and justifies the "little polarizations" always found in third places shared by both sexes.

Sexual mixing is not a universal threat to the same-sex association upon which third places depend. In the looseness of structure, which is just as characteristic of these places, enforced integration at the level of immediate proximity and interaction is not possible.

Couples and Third Places

It is within the marital relationship that third place association is most often a troublesome matter. Many married people have no third place because their spouses want them home or because they themselves consider it appropriate to forego third place association for the responsibilities of marriage. Among middle-class Americans there are no clear norms as to what manner or degree of outside social life a husband or wife should be "allowed," along with a tendency for the husband to feel guilty about his "nights out with the boys."

Marital accountability has not enjoyed the attitude that has come to be applied to parent-child relationships. By the time half of American mothers had entered the labor force, there emerged the concept of "quality time" with children. A lot of time that mothers must spend apart from their children is compensated for by the "quality" time they enjoy when together. The idea is sound, even though quality time cannot compensate for all the advantages of "quantity time."

The idea of quality time has not been applied, however, to husband-wife relationships (even though it is basic to courtship and romance). Already too much a part-time activity, child raising becomes even more so; but there is to be nothing "part-time" about married life. Children in their years of dependence have more freedom to range on their own than do adult spouses. Adulthood and the independence that might be expected to accompany maturity purchases little freedom from the perpetual accountability to one's mate. The idea that the key to a more successful togetherness may lie in the time apart or in a contrast of associations is virtually unheard of in our land. Many of those who choose to cohabit rather than marry, I suspect, prefer to hang on to that measure of independence that the American version of marriage does not permit.

Beyond the problem of a marital relationship that excessively restricts outside contact for both husband and wife, there is the matter of the suitability of a couple, *as a couple*, to third place association. Apart from the quality of the relationship when contained in privacy, how does it appear in public? Apart from domestic and sexual compatibility, how compatible are the spouses when it comes to "dual presentations" in the presence of outsiders? Do the husband and wife make a good team socially? Do others find them interesting, enjoyable, and easy to be around? Are they a "fun couple"?

Perceptive people often note the difference in their friends or acquaintances when the spouse is present and when he or she is not. They are struck by the wondrous transformation when the spouse is not present. A husband may regard his wife, along with all other women, as "dumb" or "childlike." He may be exceedingly "touchy" and respond to everything she says with belligerence. He may level a steady stream of criticism at her in an attempt to bolster his self-esteem.

Women often seem hyperconcerned about the impressions their husbands make in the company of others. They may correct their husbands, excuse or apologize for their shortcomings; they may critically monitor everything their husbands have to say. The male at middle age is noted for his passivity under this form of oppression. He doesn't try to be witty, interesting, or to enjoy himself when his wife is around. He nods his head; he bides his time. For such men, the third place apart from the woman and her chronic disapproval may be doubly precious. Jiggs would resort to any device in order to escape Maggie and rejoin the boys at Dinty Moore's Saloon. For these men, the third place may offer the opportunity to restore their dignity.

The oppressive tongue is never more disruptive than in the third place. Conversation there, to recall a major point, is the main activity, and it is conversation of the best quality. Those who discover its essential charm simultaneously discover the worth of individuals beyond their duties and productive roles. The form that such conversation takes depends upon an uninhibited play of personalities. It is easily dampened by husbands or wives who invoke their special license to correct, criticize, and thereby discredit their spouses in public. An earlier etiquette discouraged marital bickering in public but it is now quite common, as is the tasteless doting over one another that many couples exhibit during casual social get-togethers. Perhaps this is to be expected of couples whose informal contact with other adults is irregular and infrequent. Marital relationships and episodes are not taboo subjects in third place conversation, but their discussion requires grace, tact, and subtlety.

It would seem that third places accommodate whatever relationship a couple has wrought. For the individual bound to a marriage from which frequent respites are imperative, the third place allows relaxation in the company of those able to appreciate what the spouse does not. A third place may also accommodate couples who are interesting and enjoyable. Yet, even the involvement of "fun" couples in such settings is more likely to be an occasional event than a regular one.

We are brought back to the major theme of this discussion: third places serve to separate the sexes, not to absorb them into equal and undifferentiated participation. Upon further examination of this characteristic of the Great Good Place, one can appreciate that it could hardly be otherwise. Sex identities are never forgotten and either same-sex association or mixed association will dominate any establishment that regularly hosts sociable gatherings. Where the sexes are balanced and interspersed and give their attention primarily to one another, erotic interest will dominate. Such places may be alluring in their own right but they are not third places.

Perhaps the best current illustration of the principle may be found in the integrated bar or cocktail lounge. A past generation of wives discouraged attendance at bars because of the "evil" that strong drink does; the present generation, however, dislikes them for a different reason. Men's bars have given way to those of mixed company in which men and women "get cozy" with one another. This is the major reason why today's married women don't want their husbands to visit bars without them.

If third places serve primarily to allow people regular association with members of the same sex, what are the opportunities for the couple to share social settings with others and how do those other situations differ from the third place? There are clues in the common and traditional patterns of couples' outings, which include night-clubbing, dining out with friends, the movies, the theater, pub-crawling with compatible couples, and invitations to home entertaining. Taking such instances as representative, as they would seem to be, one may note at least two differences between the social engagements of couples and those of the third place.

First, there is a greater *structure* to activities that attract the couple. Dinner out, the theater, night club entertainment, dancing—all these are highly structured. The course of action is never in doubt; the couple is not pressed to decide what to do or where to go once the evening is "in motion." When couples are confronted with a problem (the place is closed or the desired movie isn't showing), it causes more difficulty than it would among a same-sex group. Alternative courses of action seem fewer and harder to agree upon. Couples appear to rely more on the kinds of structured activities that third places do not offer. Only in adolescence do males and females "hang out" fairly well together. At that age, they seem to use the hours of unstructured time to get familiar with the worlds and ways of the opposite sex.

One may note, also, that when the couple presents itself to other adults outside the home, the tendency is for them to dress up. Their outings are, at least in this way, more special than visits to a third place.

And, as we dress up, we normally become more conscious of our behavior—men act more like gentlemen, women more like ladies. In deference to his or her mate, the individual strives to act a bit better than usual even as he or she takes the trouble to look a bit better than usual. Whenever individuals go out as couples, there is this tendency to "upgrade" themselves.

If they are to relax with others to a degree comparable with same-sex association in the third place, the couple will usually require the privacy and security of their home. When close friends are invited over, and especially later in the evening when overtaken by pleasant fatigue, the couple may approach that level of relaxation normal for third place association.

But for all the togetherness we have imposed upon ourselves, the ultimate in social relaxation is, for most people, still found in same-sex groups without monitoring spouses in attendance and need to tailor the talk in deference to the opposite sex.

Cohabitation

Living together outside of marriage, widespread and accepted now, represents neither moral degradation nor social enlightenment as much as apprehension about marriage. Based on the experiences of close friends, an unhappy home life with their parents, and the unpredictability of marriage, young people harbor a reasoned fear of going to the altar.

Cohabitation is far from an ideal arrangement in a society that continues to value marriage despite its problems. It does not connect people to community life as well as marriage, and it is an arrangement often fraught with uncertainty about its own future. The disadvantages for the woman are familiar. She is more likely to do the housework while sharing equally in the rent. And, as the pages of the calendar are turned, the woman loses her appeal more quickly than the man.

The cost of cohabitation for the male involves a more subtle accounting than for the female. Males haven't changed their outlook as much as females; most have always assumed a positive (if not downright *eager*) attitude about sleeping with their sweethearts before marriage. Until recent times, however, few women have consented. Bachelorhood was lived in male company and the resulting solidarity of young men was the product of it. Once a young man's favorite consents to sleep with him and do so regularly, the gang loses a member. As wedding bells once broke up those old gangs of maturing men, cohabitation now prevents them from forming.

Seasoned military men are perhaps more aware than most of the effects of widespread cohabitation. They talk nostalgically of the "good old days" when there was a vital and dependable barracks life—when "you could leave your watch or your wallet lying on a footlocker and find it there when you came back"—when the men looked after one another on base and off—when they went to town together at night or on the weekends. They talk of the camaraderie of that earlier time, convinced that it "made men and made the military." They talk disparagingly of the new breed, of the "six-packers," as they often call them. The six-packers are so named because of their habit of signing off base, stopping for a six-pack, and hurrying home to the females who share off-base housing with them. Among the six-packers, male bonding holds little attraction.

What the male gains in bed and dodges in responsibility by cohabiting, he pays for in an increasing dependence upon the female and a decreasing connectedness to a wider support group. He sacrifices the third place and the support it once offered in exchange for a first place built upon soft and shifting sand. Meanwhile, the kind of woman with whom he shares lodging remains untethered by babies and alert to the possibility that marriage may not ensue in the relationship. More than wives, cohabiting women are inclined to seek and nurture the company of women in similar situations. Female solidarity grows even as that of males declines.

The tradition of male-bonding is probably as old as human social life and it has been widely recognized. One of its many consequences was that of a male advantage in forming strong same-sex relationships. Third places, of course, were important both in the formation and sustenance of strong male ties. It is no coincidence that male camaraderie and third places are declining together in our society. It has already happened among most middle-class males and seems certain to plague working-class men as well.

It should not surprise me to see the male advantage in forming same-sex relationships, both more quickly and easily and with greater social diversity than women, lost entirely. Nor would it surprise me if "sisterhood" should one day set the better example.

CHAPTER 13

Shutting Out Youth

A SMALL GROUP of us sat at poolside helping ourselves to the potent slush at the bottom of an ice chest, which had been filled with frozen daiquiris when the festivities began. Our annual luau had reached its mellow stage. The last remaining ort of suckling pig had disappeared, and the men were congratulating themselves on another smashing social and gustatorial success. It had been more than pleasant, this sometimes raucous but mostly cozy *al fresco* affair, this crowning event in the year's progression of monthly dinner parties. "Only one thing wrong," I intruded, my mind having wandered back to the parties staged by my parents and their friends. "What's that?" asked a colleague. "The kids would have enjoyed this," I said, and then I got the looks reserved for people who say weird things.

As if it had been yesterday, I could visualize the fall outings of the Booster's Club or the Volunteer Fire Department. There were fifty-gallon cooking pots in which chicken and beef stewed in their juices. There was a long galvanized tank, the kind farmers use to water their livestock, filled with cracked ice and scores of long-necked bottles of beer, and among them, just for us kids, bottles of Orange Crush, cream soda, and root beer.

Everyone was friendly and generous. One might never have guessed it, but many staid townspeople did know how to have fun after all. By nightfall they were attempting to balance beer bottles on their noses, hit a target with a thrown axe, or climb a ladder leaning against nothing but thin air. The kids went to sleep in Mom's or Dad's arms before being laid out on a car seat and covered with a blanket. Right up to the point where we conked out, we were in on it all.

These glimpses of childhood happily integrated with adulthood belong to a time when adults did not feel that having a good time meant getting away from their children and when baby-sitting did not involve fifty- or sixty-pound "babies." Subsequent generations of adults have put a good deal of distance between themselves and youth, and in a relatively short span of time.

"Things are different now," we tell ourselves, and clearly they are. We have driven many wedges between youth and adults. We had already taken the schools out of the neighborhoods, enforced child labor laws beyond the point of protecting children, and rejected the kind of apprenticeship programs that serve well in other societies. More recently, 999 out of every 1,000 homes have installed television and much of the time that parents and children once spent together is lost to the "tube."[1] Conditions of employment, which effectively take Dad out of the parenting role, now claim Mom also, with no adjustments made for her mothering responsibilities. Pervasive zoning laws and poor planning have eliminated from new neighborhoods places where youth and adults once encountered one another frequently, casually, informally. The exile of youth from the world of adults still proceeds apace as if nothing can be done to reverse the process.

Something will be done, of course, and probably fairly soon. As the increasingly costly consequences of segregating youth from adults are finally forced upon the consciousness of the decision-makers, one may be certain that remedies will follow. Meantime, many continue to misread the signals. For example, the failures in child rearing associated with permissiveness are usually more easily explained. Many postwar youngsters have gone awry because their parents did not give sufficient time and attention to their children and there was no one else around to take up the slack. It's not so much new-fashioned ideology as old-fashioned neglect. Parents seem to care about their kids as much as ever and, with good reason, probably *worry* about them more than in the past. But mental anguish doesn't get the job done. Increasingly, Mom and Dad are away from a home located in an area where no one monitors the kids' activities or spends time with them. The devil's workshop is as likely to be found in a lifeless neighborhood as in idle hands.

Communities Without Youth

Residential areas have become the settings of isolated family life and when people find no reason to walk down the street from their homes, they begin to seek community and communion elsewhere. For many, the workplace has become the most available substitute. There, at least, are people with similar interests and life-styles with whom to associate. Among them may be many potential friends, and contact with them is easy, far easier than with neighbors. The urge to socialize finds its opportunities and these soon crystallize into on-the-job rituals. Birthdays are roundly observed, complete with cake, coffee, cards, and presents. Luncheon get-togethers are frequent as co-workers try out new places to eat and exchange gossip not safely discussed in the work setting. Coffee breaks, office parties, company-sponsored bowling leagues and the like become part of the rhythm of the workplace and go a long way toward compensating for the loss of community in the residential neighborhood.

Many employees find the office more pleasant than the home. The surroundings are comfortable and other people clean up after them. Problems typically encountered at work are not as onerous and depressing as family problems. The best conversations of the day take place at work. There are more people around; work is where the action is. And, for a great many Americans the job offers a substitute community. But unlike the residential community of the past, it is one in which there is no place for children. By contenting themselves with whatever forms of social involvement work offers, many parents effectively drive another wedge between the generations.

The family is failing a function long associated with it—that of connecting its younger members to a host of friends, relatives, and neighbors who were once a part of the child's world and who contributed much to his or her development. Today's legacy to youth is one of isolation. The American child spends far less time with real people and far more time watching television, listening to the stereo, and talking on the phone.

There is another kind of community with which people increasingly content themselves and about which many social scientists are openly enthusiastic. It is variously known as the "personal community," the "liberated community," or the "network." It is not defined in terms of location but in terms of the accumulated associations of a single individual. One's friends, acquaintances, and contacts, however scattered, constitute his or her network.

Each of us has his or her own "personal community," and its apologists make the network sound like an advanced form of society rather than an artifact of atomization. Those who have networks, we are told, are cosmopolitan. Their interests and relationships transcend the local neighborhood. The "networker" is "liberated" from local gossip and prejudice and is "free" to choose his or her friends on more rational and more personal bases than that of mere geographic proximity. Unlike the unfortunate members of the poor and working classes, the networker need not form relationships with the neighbors fate has put next door and across the way. (The jerk in the next office is somehow vastly superior to the one who lives next door.)

Community is a collective reality that does not depend upon the inclusion or exclusion of any given individual; to define it as a personal phenomenon is to pervert the concept. The concept of the personal community is catching on, however, and for at least two reasons. First, it permits us to retain the myth of a viable community form amid the atomization of life attending our chaotic urban sprawl. Second, networking is a useful aspect of careerism—individuals, as centers and overlords of their own communities, can tailor them to maximize their success in the career. It has personal appeal.

Networks, as presently conceived and promoted, are anti-child. That danger, coupled with the popularity of the concept, demand that it be examined on its own terms.

One might initially note that community, thus conceived, is grossly elitist. Networks are most available to the young- and middle-aged adult, the better-educated, the affluent, those who own new cars, and those most liberated from family responsibilities. The easy transportation, which the network enthusiasts admit is essential, does not exist for children, the elderly, and those who cannot afford decent cars. Further, how easy is transportation in cities choking on auto traffic?

It must be granted that the network, though not a true form of community, *is* the form that best fits the disastrous spatial organization of the typical American city. Urban planning assumes perfect mobility among the people, just as does the concept of the liberated community. One is easily convinced that if General Motors or Exxon were to plan our urban centers and do so with their characteristic concern for maximizing the sale of their products, our cities would look pretty much as they already do.

But what of youth and networks? It would seem that a parent's network offers no more of a community in which to raise children than the workplace from which children are more formally barred. That, I think, is the fundamental problem, but let's hear from the network experts. Locating one of the more thorough and reputable network studies, I restricted my second reading to those passages concerning children.[2] They were scattered, for like most studies of networks, this one contained no focused discussion of children. Here are the basic findings: Children restrict the activities of their parents—of mothers far more than fathers. Working women with two or more children have difficulty making and keeping friends. The advent of a child depletes the energy a parent could otherwise devote to friends. Childless couples can live closer to a city's entertainment centers and have nicer homes. A woman's mood in her home is enhanced by the presence of her spouse but depressed by the presence of her children. Childless adults enjoy better moods and better morale than those with children. Being a woman *and* a parent is an especially deadly combination in terms of the demands other people make on her. The more children one has, the less he or she will be able to enjoy relationships with colleagues.

The message is clear. Children are not compatible with a fuller realization of personal or liberated communities. And the message has been received. Voluntary or intentional childlessness, a fairly recent American ideal, has already been embraced by well over 10 percent of the married population.[3] Marriage and family textbooks are moving away from the word *childless* in favor of *childfree*, a term more appropriate to the undesirability of children in our present culture.

One liberated female, active in the feminist movement, suggested that we might be able to get our children by purchasing them from the poor people of foreign countries. Perhaps children could be raised on ranches in one of our large western states and shipped East when "heifer-sized." There could be mass bar mitzvahs and confirmations to cap off the annual roundups.

Two forms of community have emerged following the sterilization of the residential neighborhood, the workplace and the network. Both are hostile to children and have no place for them. How viable, in the long run, is a society that cannot unite the generations in an integrated community?

"No place to go, nothing to do"

Bill Levitt's remarkable project offers a clear example of the manner in which youth are shut out of participation in the modern community. Thanks to the painstaking observations of Herbert Gans, Levittown's story is, quite literally, an open book.[4] Gans's focus was upon the first three thousand families to occupy Levittown—an experiment in suburban living for the common person that prospered almost immediately. During the period of Gans's observations and inquiries in the late 1950s, the adult citizens of Levittown were "bullish" on their community, viewing it as a vital and attractive place to live.

Two of every three sixth-graders also liked the area, but the overwhelming majority of teenagers felt that Levittown was "Endsville." The community, like so many of America's suburban developments, was designed for young parents with small children. The adolescents were overlooked, and the sterility and oppressiveness of the place soon manifested itself in hostility towards adults and vandalism against adult property. Many parents entrenched themselves behind the view that, while not at school or work, the kids should be at home. That perspective on youth enforced the parental role as moral guardian but it discounted the exuberance of adolescents in quest of a wider world.

Like adolescents everywhere, Levittown youth desired the companionship of peers when the school day was over. But for them, at a time in life when the herd instinct is particularly strong, the yen for adventure great, and the desire to escape the boredom of the household is almost overwhelming, the kids were effectively told to stay put. Their choices were few. They could watch television, take a nap, or do their homework. The few places at which adolescents could congregate included the development's swimming pool, shopping center, and bowling alley, but, for most, these were a long way off. In Levittown the problem of distance was compounded. Few of the adolescents had cars and there was no other form of transportation. The long, curved streets usually necessitated walking two miles for every one the crow flies.

Even that minority of high school seniors who were positive about Levittown had nothing but negative comments about the available gathering places. The movies and bowling alley cost too much money, and the only place in which the kids could be by themselves was at the swimming pool and then only when adults weren't using it. Even there, however, they were not allowed to make noise or to smoke. The lack of public facilities resulted in a glut of parties given at homes, which, the teenagers reported, soon became boring. Boys and girls complained about the lack of neighborhood stores, and when they congregated on street corners despite the fact that there were no stores there, they tended to get into trouble. A group of teenagers would soon be making enough noise to prompt calls to the police. As one teenage girl put it, "I feel like a hood to be getting chased by the police for absolutely nothing."

Levittown was designed as though deliberately to frustrate its teenagers. At home, the bedrooms had enough space for studying and sleeping but were too small for entertaining friends. The schools were not intended for after-hours use. When dances were held there, the administration complained about scuffed floors and damage to fixtures. Shopping areas were designed for adult consumers and located far from the youngsters' homes. The bowling alley was a later addition, and when it opened the teenagers came in such numbers as to upset the shopping center's merchants. Youth ultimately found their only hangouts in the luncheonettes that opened on the fringes of the development despite the efforts of the developer and local planning office to keep them away.

Though most parents finally realized that Levittown's facilities were insufficient for older children and that some should be created, none were. The parents could not agree among themselves what might be appropriate or safe. Some viewed teenagers as responsible people overall and capable of managing their affairs with a minimum of help and supervision. Others felt that adults should exercise total control in guiding adolescents into the responsibilities of adulthood. The latter inclined to the view that home, work, and school were the only acceptable places for teenagers.

The adults of Levittown maintained a world in which youth were so shut out that no one seemed to know them. During Gans's study many bizarre rumors about the adolescents and their behavior floated among the adults and were widely believed. One rumor had it that forty-four of the high school senior girls were pregnant. Gans checked. There were two who were pregnant, and one of them was about to get married. The estrangement of the generations that made such rumors believable also brought hostility. Levittown's youth grew to dislike adults generally, engaged in considerable vandalism, and began consuming considerable amounts of alcohol.

Beware the Schedulers

In a small seacoast town in Florida, a house for scouting was founded in the mid-1950s, affording a place where Girl Scouts and Boy Scouts could hold their meetings. In the early sixties, the place was converted to a youth center available to all and open morning through evening. Ping pong and pool tables provided most of the focused activity for the nine- to seventeen-year-olds who made regular use of the facility. In 1970 an outdoor, lighted basketball court was added and immediately became popular.

After its conversion to general use the center became the rendezvous point for the teenagers of the community. Each morning when school was not in session, a crowd of local youngsters awaited its opening. After the basketball court was added, the center attracted youngsters even when the building wasn't open. And, after the addition of the basketball court, many adults also began to take an interest in the place. Soon, children and adults were playing against one another in regular basketball skirmishes.

Youngsters hurried home from school and then to the center in order to get the first game on a pool or ping pong table. A loyal audience of other children, usually younger, watched others play those games and were as regular in attendance as the players. Transient youth, those vacationing or visiting relatives, also found the place appealing. The locals, expectedly, had come to think of the center as "their turf" but not to the extent of hassling a new kid. The place offered free, unstructured, walk-in recreation and it was always occupied when open. The center was where the action was for the youthful population, and there was always some action.

In the judgment of those who served as the center's supervisors, the place had a positive effect on youthful character. Though admitting

that while "some of the boys became men, others seemed to be enjoying an endless adolescence," the supervisors insisted that the association afforded by the center had a "therapeutic effect" on misguided
youth. The center was a place where all were accepted and "where a
young fellow, in front of his peers, could show his stuff."

By the 1980s, the center had ceased to be a third place for the youth
of the community. Only the basketball players hang on now, for only
the basketball court remains available for the enjoyment of all comers.
What had been an open, inclusive, come-when-you-want-to, wholesome youth hangout was transformed into something quite different.
During the seventies, the building's facilities were gradually closed to
general and unstructured use. Instead, classes were being offered to
ladies willing to pay to exercise in the company of others or to children
whose mothers had hopes that they might excel in dance or make it to
the Olympics. The place came to resemble the typical community
center, misnamed in today's society and off limits to youngsters with
time on their hands and no appealing place to spend it. The youth of
the community bitterly resented those programs and the select few but
powerful people who were taking their place away from them. But they
could do no more than choke on their feelings of anger and frustration.
This world, after all, belongs to the adults.

It has been observed that the American middle class will make no
great contributions in music, the arts, or in letters; that their sole talent
is for organization. It may now be seen that one of the most profound
and sweeping changes in the lives of the nation's children stems from
the adult intrusion of this dubious talent into the whole range of
youthful activity. The organizers and schedule-setters are attacking the
world of children with an aggressiveness and scope that threatens to
destroy childhood altogether. Already, children's games have been almost totally transformed into adult-dominated "children's sports." It
should come as no surprise that unstructured youth hangouts should
fall victim as well. The era of the "organization child" as *Time* referred
to him, is full upon us.[5] "From the moment he enters nursery school at
the age of three," observes Norman Lobsenz, the child's life "is tightly
scheduled for the next fifteen years. Boys and girls go solemnly from
dancing class to judo class, from swimming school to riding school,
doing all the things that should be pleasures as part of a workmanlike
routine."[6]

In recent years the psychiatric profession has detected a substantial jump in the incidence of depression among children, an intriguing finding in that children have always seemed immune from depression.[7] But was it children who were immune or was it childhood? When kids were free to wander around their neighborhoods, to follow their own interests, to be creative in their own fashion, and to match activities to their own moods rather than to adult-imposed schedules, the antidotes to depression may well have been built into the structure of the childhood years. Today, youngsters find little release from the fetish imposed upon them. As their young lives are continually warped and molded to fit schedules based upon adult values and motivations, is it not to be expected that they should manifest such adult reactions as depression and chronic boredom?

Other unsavory consequences attach to the excessive organization of children's lives. In our zeal to keep kids "off the streets" and contain them within safer places, we contribute to the further deterioration of our public space. As we shuttle our children from one safe and certified adult to another, the streets continue to deteriorate in accordance with the negative view held toward them. Some of this is necessary at present, but the long-range goal of the municipality should be inspired by Zechariah's Jerusalem where "the streets of the city shall be filled with boys and girls playing in the streets thereof." When that is accomplished, the public domain will be safe for adults as well, and we will have cleansed our communal ground of the scum that blights it.

Also evident in the manner in which the schedulers and organizers control the activities of youth is a narrowing of concern as to whose youth are being provided for. Time was when parents and community leaders provided activities and events for all children in the community. Now, much of the concern seems to involve sheltering one's own children from association with the nebulous peer group or youth culture.

Organizing and scheduling are powerful weapons. The middle class, which is the managing class, uncritically accepts the superiority of organized activity—no proof or evidence seems necessary. That the youth center in that little Florida town now serves only a tenth of the youngsters it once served only a tenth of the time seems to concern no one. Organized time is better than unorganized time; scheduled activities are vastly superior to unscheduled ones. It is this middle-class credo that allows the influential few to pirate facilities from the many. It is this blind belief that allows those who already have the advantage in private means and facilities to move in and take over a lion's share of the public facilities as well. In that little Florida town, the usurpation of the community center by the schedulers and organizers meant that the children who needed the place most were barred forever.

Ethnic Ties Dissolved

The best third places for children are those with adults around. But to find those disappearing locales in which people of all ages are still having fun together, one must visit some of the ethnic enclaves where generational ties are maintained against that powerful dissolving agent known as the American way of life. The various ethnic groups that came to America characteristically banded together in communities of mutual assistance in order to survive and become established in the new land. Out of the need for those people to get to know and become comfortable with one another and to discover their common problems, centrally located gathering places were among the first structures built. The different groups varied in the manner in which they relaxed and celebrated with one another and in the degree of resistance to outsiders, but the formation and eventual dissolution of once close-knit communities follows a similar pattern whether the people are of Hispanic, Germanic, Hellenic, Italic, or other ethnic extraction. The example afforded by a Slavic enclave on our Eastern seaboard reveals this pattern clearly.

The Polya Club, identified by one outside observer as a "large community hall," was constructed as the core structure among a cluster of modest cabins by a colony of Russian émigreés in the mid-1930s. At the time it was built, many considered it too large for the six-hundred-odd people the facility was designed to serve. Within twenty years, however, an additional wing had to be added. To the original dance hall, restaurant, bar, and game room, a spacious lounge was appended as a waiting room for dinner guests.

The game room was equipped with tables and chairs only but was heavily used by all ages for playing cards and checkers. These games were enthusiastically pursued to the exclusion of almost all others because they promoted conversation. They offered a talkative and outgoing people ample opportunities for "shooting the breeze." For that reason cards were preferred over checkers and the latter was resorted to only when there were too few people at a table to have a good card game. Poker, by an overwhelming margin, was the most popular card game. That single game, played by all, was a great integrator. Children learned it as soon as they were old enough to shuffle a pack of cards.

Though the children enjoyed the run of the place, they were usually seen tagging along with their fathers, who had brought them to the club. Boys attended more frequently than girls, but rarely by themselves. Dad took his son to the Polya Club; it was something both looked forward to and a matter of pride for both. Two or more boys might meet and play cards or checkers or, since the man who presided over it was so fascinating and amiable, the boys often gathered in the barroom. Always dressed to the nines and rather colorfully, the bartender charmed people of all ages. He spoke to everyone and to children in a special way, which made them feel important. The boys behaved particularly well in his domain, not wanting to be called on their manners by one so much esteemed. For those youngsters unable to control their restless nature, he would produce a paddleball from under the bar and direct them to a wall just outside.

The most exciting times for the children took place on Friday, Saturday, and Sunday evenings. From early evening until about one in the morning a campfire was kept going by the side of a large natural pond just outside. This small lake was so pleasant a site that it had determined the location of the club. At fireside some of the club members would play the *balalaikas* [Russian guitars] they had brought with them while everyone sang old Russian folk songs. Children would stay by their parents' side until it was time for their mothers to take them home and put them to bed.

On those same evenings that the campfire burned outside, a dance band held forth within, and when a polka was struck, the dance floor was filled to capacity. Members and several guests (all were welcome) danced with great energy and not just in a contained area but on every square foot of the heavy plank flooring. Would-be wallflowers were dragged into participation, and the average man danced with at least a half-dozen partners each night. Newcomers were greeted upon arrival; kisses from women, hugs (and sometimes kisses) from the men were bestowed on all. It was a time and place to embrace one's fellow human, physically and with feeling. Nowhere did couples stand quietly and talk to one another on the periphery of the dance floor as dour-faced Americans do in their more sophisticated ballrooms. Everyone was swept up in the boiling current created by two hundred bouncing torsos and twice as many stamping feet. Well, not everyone's feet were stamping. Now and then a young lady of tender years would be danced about with shiney new shoes a long way from the floor.

Children who went with their parents to the Polya Club as recently as the 1960s carry with them values and memories that changing conditions will not wholly erase. But for the most recent generations it is gone. The building is still there but children are no longer allowed into it. Club membership peaked in the mid-1960s at about thirteen hundred dues-payers but underwent a sharp decline thereafter. By 1980 it had dwindled to about a hundred. The mystical murals and tapestries depicting Russian peasants, the Russian countryside, and the orthodox churches of the old country have been replaced by American harbor scenes. The game room now has an electronic bowling game, a few video games, and a jukebox. The price of drinks, once the lowest around thanks to a subsidy from membership dues, is now as high as in other places. There are no more campfire gatherings or guitar playing or group singing. Those who frequent the place exhibit little animation. They come in, find a place to sit, and stay rooted there until they leave. The bartender is still friendly but he talks now to people who are strangers, to people with whom there is no relationship, and the conversations are brief and without spirit.

Children can no longer be found at the Polya Club. They are not welcome. This place where yesterday's fathers were proud to bring their children is now a joint where fathers go to get away from their children. The clientele, which used to be about equal parts male and female, especially during the peak hours, is predominantly male today.

"What happened?" asked a saddened young man upon his return to what had been the most wonderful setting of his childhood. A surviving charter member of the club, to whom he had directed the question, summed it up: "Well, the younger men began getting jobs far away, even out of state, and couldn't even make it here on weekends. And while they were away, other people moved in—Irish, or English, or something else—and eventually the older members started dying off and nobody wanted to keep up the place. It's not the same now. We used to go there and everyone would listen to accordion music and the balalaikas and, boy, we had a great time. Today, the guys just go there to drink and listen to trashy music on the juke box. They just don't know how to have fun."

The Youth Bar

Two decades ago, the political leadership of the country succumbed to the interesting notion that the age of majority is reached at about the same point in life no matter what area of human development is at issue. The result was a significant lowering of the drinking age. In the period from 1970 through 1975, twenty-eight of the fifty states reduced the legal drinking age, most of them by a full three years, from twenty-one to eighteen. Those who had cautioned that age changes should be introduced slowly, carefully, and with close monitoring of the effects, were subsequently proven right. More recently, drinking ages have again been raised in many states.

Not long after the age of requirement was sharply lowered, youth bars (places catering especially to youthful drinkers) became the vogue and the general character of these places may be expected to survive even though the law was reversed. Not only did the youth bar serve a much narrower spectrum of age, it also offered a far different quality of tavern experience than that which formerly held appeal for young, middle-aged, and elderly adults alike.

With the youth bar phenomenon, the admittance of the young male to the licensed premises of his locale ceased to be a rite of passage into adulthood. Traditionally the tavern had been an important agency in linking the generations and in encouraging a young man to set aside the lesser habits of his adolescence. At age twenty-one, a young man was first permitted to enter the company of seasoned tavern-goers, the majority of whom were considerably older than himself. Entry into the tavern marked a transition away from the teenage culture of his recent past. The following reminiscences of an age-mate of the author's illustrate it well:

When I was a young fellow the drinking age was twenty-one and I began going to bars during my junior year in college. My roommate was older and he took me along with him to Schultie's, which was his favorite spot. Most nights I was the youngest guy in the place. It wasn't noisy but it wasn't all that quiet either. It always had a decent crowd and talking was their thing. There was no wandering off to play pinball machines or pool. Schultie's didn't have those things. We just sat at the bar and talked and it wasn't that silly kind of conversation we used to engage in at the campus Rendezvous. You learned darn quick that the women in Schultie's wouldn't put up with the wise cracks and teasing that the coeds seemed to like. In talking with the guys at the bar, you were impressed with your own lack of experience. You hadn't worked as much, traveled as much, or lived as much as the older guys. You wanted to be accepted, of course, so you thought hard before you opened your mouth and, mostly, you listened. But when you did talk and were taken seriously, it was a sign of acceptance. Made you feel good.

Going to an adult bar, far from having the dangerous effects that so many pillars and pillaresses of the community were prone to assume, altered this man's drinking habits for the better. He said:

> I also discovered how to drink at Schultie's. I already knew how to chug-a-lug. I knew how to get puking drunk and passed-out drunk but I didn't know how to drink a couple of enjoyable beers and go home clear-headed. My first couple of beers at Schultie's went down quick. I never let go of the bottle until it was drained. The older fellows would let their beers sit off to the side for several minutes at a time. When the talk was lively, they seemed to forget the beer altogether. They'd sip a little during the lulls and there weren't many lulls. Those guys taught me how to relax, or at least they tried.

In the adult tavern, many a young man learned to detach himself physically from his bottle or glass with quickly diminishing separation anxiety—learned, that is, to drink less like an infant and more like an adult. They also learned that those who overdid their drinking had low status, that the obnoxious drunk was thrown out, and that the pernicious drinking of the pale malt worm at the end of the bar earned that unfortunate person nothing more than solitude.

In our survey of the public bars in a small city (visited during the era of reduced drinking ages), 36 percent of the places were dominated by youthful drinkers and two-thirds of all the youthful drinkers observed were in bars where all the customers were young. Generally, youth gravitated toward their own places and within them, the cult of youth tended to perpetuate itself. Meanwhile, many of the other taverns had the aura of dying institutions. What might have been their "new blood" was being siphoned off into the more aggressively managed youth bars.

One consequence of the youth bar has been to persuade many that bars, generally, are primarily for young people and singles. Young women who patronize the newer coeducational drinking establishments before marriage are apt to object strongly to their husbands continuing the bar habit after marriage. And, beyond the wife's concern that bars are places where husbands stray and may be lost, both males and females are more likely to experience the tavern culture as a passing phase in the life cycle and not as a harmless and convivial retreat for people of all ages or as a reliable source of companionship and lively conversation. What was an adult fraternity is now more likely to be regarded as one of fading youth's last playpens, a thing to be set aside with Frisbees and soccer cleats.

The reduced drinking age created a new tavern clientele and one that changed the character of America's drinking establishments. This youthful patronage, not yet tied down with family responsibilities or tethered by the marital bond and seemingly susceptible to any silly gimmick designed to increase sales was targeted in earnest. Bars that catered to the youthful trade were soon among the largest and most lucrative drinking establishments to be found in those states where drinking ages had been lowered. The industry may have hurt itself in the long run. Certainly, much damage was done to the American drinking establishment's potential as a third place.

Especially for Children

Adults have always maintained much of their control over youth by confining them spatially. Until urbanization and industrialization altered the structure of society, family and community provided the space, monitored the space, and *shared* the space in which youngsters grew up. The necessary monitoring of youth was accomplished so casually and informally that it was seldom a conscious matter. With urbanization and industrialization, however, new conditions of work demanded that adults be freed of their offspring in order to maximize productivity during the long hours of the workday. Children had to be gotten out of the way.

Mandatory schooling of increasing duration became the major solution to the problem of containing and monitoring children. The law demanded not that all educable children be educated, only that they be submitted for monitoring by other adults. In today's schools no less than earlier ones, the abiding concern is with accounting for the location of bodies and not the development of minds. Scholastic progress is checked sporadically but the location of the bodies is accounted for several times daily.

The belief that schools are designed primarily to serve youth is not the only myth surrounding the containment of the young. Other places are created especially for children, though the primary motivation is to remove them from areas where adults don't want to have them around. Most of these continue to be created despite colossal rates of failure and despite the fact that their designated users (children) do not want them. Examples abound in all Western industrial cities.

In the early 1970s, the West German government sponsored studies of the effectiveness of the play areas in that country's "new towns."[8] Compared with children in the older cities, it was found that those in the new towns felt "isolated, regimented, and bored." The children in the new towns were found to derive more satisfaction from playing around trash cans and water puddles, in hanging around shops and busy streets, or in poking around the debris at construction sites than they did in their designated play areas. Children prefer to be where the action is and resent being insulated from the hustle and bustle of daily life. Rejecting the scenic paths that the planners had laid out to connect the children's homes with their schools, they would "detour" through supermarkets and busy streets. When the report on this failure of the new towns was released, the Ministry of Housing was observed to be "wrestling with the implications of the study." They probably would have preferred the study had never been done.

The planners of Welwyn, an English "garden city," reported that "like dogs, the other source of complaint," the children of the community "roam wherever the leader of the pack takes them."[9] The "better" areas for play did not get nearly as much use as those near the roads, even though the areas in which the planners hoped to contain the children were "baited with swings and seesaws." The children of Welwyn, "being unaware of planning principles," were not playing where they were supposed to.

The author of a book-length report on growing up in an Australian city found that the adolescents of Sydney spent the great bulk of their leisure time in places adults also frequented.[10] Particular attention was focused upon "places specially set up for adolescents," and it was found that youth generally shunned them. The majority of Sydney's teen-agers had a regular set of friends, peer groups usually consisting of seven to twelve members, and these youngsters were particularly dis-dainful of the youth clubs and milk bars created especially for them. "Fun parlors" and penny arcades found little support among children of any age.

Jane Jacobs reports on similar findings here at home.[11] Of such enclosed park enclaves for children as one finds in Pittsburgh's Chatham Village, Los Angeles' Baldwin Hills Village, or smaller courtyard colonies in New York and Baltimore, Miss Jacobs observes that "no child of enterprise or spirit will willingly stay in such a boring place after he reaches the age of six. Most want out earlier." Typically, adolescents are forbidden entry to these enclosed parks. They are reserved for the little tots, docile and decorative, and not yet old enough to want to alter an environment that is already "perfect."

In the systematic observation of the activities of residents within a ninety-five-block area of Baltimore, another researcher discovered that 54 percent of the recreational activity was taking place in streets, alleys, yards, sidewalks, steps, and porches and that only 3 percent was going on in the parks and playgrounds.[12] Another reporter found that the children of Radburn, New Jersey, like those in Park Forest in south Chicago, were playing in the parking lots and avoiding the green areas provided especially for them behind the buildings and away from the streets.[13] The writer was alerted to the failure of many special play areas because of his prior interest in photographing their use by chil-dren. He always seemed to show up at the wrong time; the children were never there when he and his camera were. After several such attempts, the message was clear: the youngsters were virtually *never* to be found there and had little interest in such uninteresting places.

When my children were of the swing and teeter-totter age, I used to take them to a play area during visits to relatives. Though we lived hundreds of miles away, it was as though the little park had been created just for our use. During the years we visited the park we always had it to ourselves. The place also had a building (which I never saw open) atop of which was a large sign proclaiming it to be a community center. In the same sense that the relative vacuum at the eye of a hurricane is a center, so, apparently, was this. The park was wanting for children even though the area in which it was located was not.

Whenever anyone takes the trouble to monitor the use that is made (or *not* made) of places created especially for children, the results usually indicate that the basic idea may be wrong. Certainly it is clear that youth should have alternative outlets for recreation and association and that these alternatives should be readily available. Indeed, the most extensive study of recreational opportunities in the United States made that very point.

In the late 1950s, President Eisenhower appointed the Outdoor Recreation Resources Review Commission, which completed its study after four years of effort and produced a twenty-seven-volume report and a one-volume summary. One of its most important conclusions was that recreation *not* be primarily associated with recreational areas![14] The kind of recreation that is most important is that which is part of everyday life. Questions were posed and criticisms raised to which government and developers, alas, have turned a deaf ear. Are children of necessity driven to school and thus sheltered from the environment or can they walk or bicycle to school and encounter the environment along the way? Are there streams for fishing in the afternoons or have they all been buried in concrete culverts? Has a stand of woods been preserved in the neighborhood for a picnic, a stroll, or for the imaginative and adventuresome play of young children, or have the developers taken it all?

On the wall of a community center I recently encountered was an item of youthful graffiti that read: BEAM ME UP, SCOTTY. THIS PLACE SUCKS! The play on a familiar "Star Trek" line was probably borrowed from a bumper sticker or a line in some movie, but it could not have found a better context than on a wall of that community center. An ideal location and physical setting had been sacrificed, so it seemed, to the goal of easy maintenance. The place was seldom open for use and then only by small, select groups of people. When youth abuse a facility with graffiti or do other damage, adults are inclined to wonder what's wrong with these kids. Rarely do adults ask themselves what's wrong with the facility.

Basic Training at the Mall

When shopping malls began to spread throughout the urban landscape, their developers and managers registered surprise that teenagers began to invade them almost as soon as they opened. That anyone should have found this youthful invasion surprising attests to the lack of attention Americans pay to the ecology of child development. Anyone with the slightest concern would have been aware that tract housing and negatively zoned residential areas had allowed the kids nothing; that there was no other place for them to go. By now the pattern is well established. Adolescents spend more time in shopping malls than they do in any place beyond home and school.

The affinity between the teenagers and the shopping centers was once a matter of major concern to mall management. Unlike younger children, adolescents have traditionally acted on the environment and could not be counted on to leave the mall environment just as they found it. The vast, totally, and carefully appointed commercial worlds in which people are lulled into a buying mood might easily have been fouled by hordes of undisciplined and adventuresome teenagers. Also, the prospects of theft loomed larger with the inclusion of the teenager mall visitor. One would not have been surprised had management employed every available tactic to discourage the appearance of the adolescent crowd.

But there is nothing like the promise of increased profits to spur interest in youth that is typically lacking elsewhere in the community. Studies were commissioned to investigate the possible compatibility of the teenager with the shopping center. For mall developers and managers, the news was good. As a guide for mall managers explained, teenagers should not only be tolerated but *encouraged* to visit the malls since "the vast majority support the same set of values as does shopping center management."[15] The shared outlook on life that makes blood brothers of the teenager and the mall manager is that one's ultimate purpose is "to make money and buy products, and that just about everything else in life is to be used to serve those ends."[16] People are not

Born to Shop as a young lady's bumper sticker proclaims; they learn it early and continuously. From that kindergarten of consumerism, the televised children's commercial, one advances to the "university of suburban materialism," the shopping mall.

Actually, that institution offers a double major. The dual degree is in consumership and *passivity*. The malls do not "graduate" Tom Sawyers and Huck Finns. A half-century ago, youngsters of mall age were building and equipping shacks or clubhouses for their recreational use. They were hopping freight trains for the adventure of it. They spent entire days in the woodlands, hunting and fishing and adding vegetables to their catches to make cowboy stews. They were throwing cabbages at adult males in order to "get the chase." They were organizing their own athletic teams and resolving their disputes by putting on the gloves. The meeting and watching and walking around that comprise the basic activity of today's mall rats would have bored them beyond endurance. Can it be that today's youth are being conditioned *not* to assert and establish themselves in a problematic environment but to passively attune themselves to one that is arranged for them?

It has been suggested, moreover, that shopping malls offer a warmth and structure that is missing in many contemporary American homes.[17] The ersatz caring ("We do it all for you!") compensates for the loss of old-fashioned motherhood. Control over mall visitor behavior is as gentle as it is firm. Mall management will tolerate no gross misbehavior; still, it offers such a *pleasant* place. The gloom of a cold and rainy day does not extend into the mall, nor do the wilting effects of excessive heat and humidity. The controlled atmosphere is most conducive to the displays of appearance-conscious youngsters. There are no gusts of wind to disarrange feature-cut and blow-dried hairdos; no drafts to spoil the poses of youthful sophistication. And what a soothing retreat from the world's cares is found there, for no reminders of things unpleasant are allowed to contaminate the lulling atmosphere of the shopping center. In order to avail themselves of that which the mall has to offer, adolescents need only behave themselves and adapt to "the ways of a large-scale artificial environment."[18] Mom and Dad are more than willing to give their blessing. Indeed what parents would not approve of a place where their children are watched over by responsible adults; parents are virtually guaranteed that while there, the youngsters cannot get into trouble.

The shopping mall offers basic training in consumerism and the passive acceptance of highly controlled environment; it helps preserve the myth that America is a child-centered culture. Writers and parents alike insist that the nation's kids *do* have a place to go—the mall. That it's not much of a place in terms of excitement, interest, or human development is easily overlooked. Youngsters do not interact with adults at shopping centers; rather, both manage a peaceful coexistence. Lower-class youngsters are effectively screened out, and mall rats are segregated by both age and social class. Mall allure fades in the face of alternatives. Where beach cultures exist, for example, roaming the malls is considered a boring and juvenile pastime by anyone sixteen years of age or older. Adolescents, generally, quickly outgrow the mall, and in their late teens remain addicted only to its clothing stores and record shops.

As a place for youthful congregation the mall isn't close enough to the homes of adolescents. It is not open as early as it should be, nor as late. It offers far too few activities and opportunities for development. It promotes values of a less than admirable sort. It attracts youth in direct proportion to the extent that alternate hangouts have been purged from the landscape. As a place for youth to spend their idle hours, it is better than nothing, but not much.

Until a few years ago, many local television stations performed a nightly public service. Between programs an enquiring voice would say: "It's eleven o'clock. Do you know where your children are?" What more appropriate message to beam across the neighborhoods devoid of places for youth to congregate and in which youth-adult contact is confined to the insularity of the home. By eleven o'clock, of course, the malls had already closed and there was good reason to be concerned about the youngsters. An earlier generation of parents might not have been fond of the corner store in which their kids hung out like idle bums. But the adults knew where the kids were, and the kids had a place to go.

CHAPTER 14

Toward Better Times . . . and Places

WORLD WAR II marks the historical juncture after which informal public life began to decline in the United States. After that war, in both the land of the victor and the land of the vanquished, people retreated into their homes on a scale not seen before. The Germans took refuge in the woefully small unit of the family because their whole social order had been destroyed by the war and nothing else remained. Americans proved unwilling or unable to preserve or create an urban habitat sufficient to the requirements of community life and we, too, sought refuge in homes and fenced yards as the larger world about us lost its homelike qualities.

A tendency toward isolation, as many careful scholars have documented, has always been evident among Americans. But so has our gregariousness. The small town revealed it all. There were those who took fullest advantage of a habitat that permitted the individual to know and enjoy many people, and there were those who declined the opportunity. But since the war, even the most gregarious among us have been frustrated. It is as though a concerted effort is being made to shut down the informal public life of the society.

Available information suggests that we've probably lost half of the casual gathering places that existed at midcentury—places that hosted the easy and informal, yet socially binding, association that is the bedrock of community life. Old neighborhoods and their cafés, taverns, and corner stores have fallen to urban renewal, freeway expansion, and planning that discounts the importance of congenial and unified residential areas. Meantime, the newer residential neighborhoods have developed under negative zoning codes, which prohibit all such establishments of the type capable of hosting the informal gathering of local populations.

Paralleling the decline in the core settings of informal public life is a more generalized loss of interest in public facilities. It has been noted that the greatest difference between the present generations of Americans and that which framed the Constitution centers on this issue. Whereas our colonial forbears were deeply preoccupied with the public good, we have ceased to be concerned. The average citizen's interest in public or community affairs been aptly described as "diluted" and "superficial."[1] The individual's present relationship to the collective is as empty as it is equitable: community does nothing for them and they do nothing for community. And we continue to shape the environment as if to preserve that perilous arrangement. Segregation, isolation, compartmentalization, and sterilization seem to be the guiding principles of urban growth and urban renewal.

An unsuitable habitat fuels the desire to escape it. Private acreage, offering as much "splendid isolation" as one can afford, looks doubly good when viewed against the deteriorated condition of the public domain. But will an unsuitable human habitat also, eventually, fuel the desire to change it? Will we ever solve the problem of place in America? Patrick Goldring, who painted one of the bleakest pictures of contemporary urban life I've encountered, and who pointed to massive evidence in doing so, was nonetheless convinced that community will ultimately emerge victorious. He wrote:

> I believe the human instinct towards real community and dignity will survive any processing and will assert itself in a crisis. Sooner or later there will be a check in the seemingly inexorable movement towards ant-like inhumanity, organizing for organizing's sake.[2]

It is heartening to realize that as historians gauge time, the "mess that is man-made America" is of recent manufacture. The average individual has not yet caught on to the problems of place and still tends to blame other factors for the hardships imposed by bad urban design. The spatial organization of modern life imposes great difficulties on marriage and family life, to take a major example, but parents and spouses are still inclined to blame personalities and relationships for the problems inherent in an unfavorable human habitat. Also, we have, until recently, been able to compensate for the limited vision of the urban planner. Most of the informal public life we managed in the past represented the triumph of the space user over the space planner—we simply took over establishments and spaces created for other purposes. What is revolutionary about our new environment is not its freeway mazes or its hulking rectangular skyscrapers with their smoked-glass skins, but its unprecedented resistance to user modification.

But as the planner's hand becomes a heavier one, tolerance for its abuses diminishes. The establishment that dictates space use invites more confrontation with the public even as it exhausts its strategies for foisting upon human communities what the people do not want. America's upcoming generations will learn more than we about adaptation of the human organism to its habitat and about adaptation of the environment to the needs of the organism. It is an education that will be forced upon them.

The lessons to be learned are not taught by those who write articles or books but by the experiences of trying to enjoy life amid a badly designed environment. It's already happening. Some of the best urban habitats to be found anywhere in the United States are those preserved or restored through grass-roots efforts in reaction against the brutality and banality of urban-renewal programs. Like Goldring, I have faith that the human instinct for community will eventually prevail, even though I agree with James Bryce that the government of cities is the one conspicuous failure of the United States.

Many lessons will and are being learned that will eventually set an informed public will against the forces that have made a shambles of public life. As an epilogue to the subject I've treated, and from the vantage point afforded by the ground covered in researching it, I anticipate an eventual change in the American outlook and attitude in at least three areas. Each will favor the development and rediscovery of an informal public life, of community itself.

A Return to Convenience

"Even if I had a third place, I wouldn't have the time to enjoy it." This is a common response among those who appreciate the merits of third place involvement but who are inclined to relegate these pleasant little institutions of social relaxation to a simpler past and its slower pace of life. The thought of devoting additional time and effort to the establishment of a third place, or a community life more generally, can be a discouraging one. Time and energy are commodities that too many of us have too little of to spare.

Eventually Americans will learn that the fast and hectic pace of urban life is not due to modernity but to bad urban planning. Life is so badly staged in our time that people are encouraged to abandon the most basic kinds of commitments in order to cope with its resulting complexities. Attempting to hold together the pieces of one's existence across a landscape that spreads and scatters them is difficult, even for those who travel light and alone.

One of the most laughably erroneous characterizations of contemporary American society is that it is a "convenience culture." Convenience is a persistent theme in our lives and in advertising media only because there is such a crying need for it. But only by confusing trivial conveniences with essential ones could we delude ourselves. In a genuinely convenient culture, the necessities of life are close by one's dwelling. They are within easy walking distance. In a convenience culture, one's European guests would not remark, as ours do, "My God, you have to get in the car for *everything*!"

Having sacrificed every measure of real convenience to bad urban planning, we gain a false reputation for convenience by trying to compensate in little matters. Unfortunately, such conveniences as plastic credit cards, vending machine coffee, electric can openers, prepackaged frozen dinners, and the like do nothing to solve the basic problems of an inconvenient society. The time they save is paid for in a diminished capacity for taste, discrimination, and discipline, and in the loss of important social rituals.

For most people, work is no longer drudgery. Work has a coherence and a simplicity about it and, at work, what one needs on a regular basis is close at hand. If those same qualities were obtained in the residential areas, if living were as important as production, life would be far simpler and fuller for almost everyone. In the United States, the spheres of productive activity are reasonably well arranged, but those of community and family life are terribly deranged. The world of work remains intact amid the spread, sprawl, and scatterization that plague the off-work hours. Correspondingly, many find that work is easy but life is hard.

Having the necessities within easy walking distance is the defining characteristic, the common denominator, of vital neighborhoods.[3] Convenience does not emerge where local residents make little more use of the neighborhood than to eat, sleep, and watch television—all within their homes. But in localities where an easy walk secures post-age stamps, dry cleaning, groceries, a magazine, or a sweet roll and a cup of coffee, there will be life beyond private dwellings.

It is convenient to be able to buy the forgotten loaf of bread or gallon of milk *without* having to drive, park, walk, stand in line at a checkout counter, walk, and then drive some more. It is convenient not to have to get into the car each time one feels the urge to be in a different environment or setting. It is convenient, also, if nondriving members of the family can be sent to buy groceries or to mail packages or to return borrowed items. Modern neighborhoods are so poorly connected to essential facilities that children can no longer be sent on useful errands. Children with too little to do can't help out. Parents who've been on the run too much during the day have to do more running. Children have too few opportunities to feel and be useful. Children can no longer learn from relationships with those people with whom errands used to bring them in contact. In many a middle-class family, the youngster doesn't become useful until he or she is old enough to drive a car and do some of the running about necessary to maintain a household. At that point in his or her life, however, the youthful motorist begins to contribute to everyone else's inconvenience by adding to the increasing flow of automobile traffic that is choking our cities.

In using *nearby* facilities, in visiting them afoot and regularly, the residents of an area effectively create a casual social environment and reap its benefits. The pedestrian mode of transportation invites human contact that automobile transportation precludes. People get to know their merchants and their neighbors; from among the many, the compatible few are able to discover one another. Neighborhoods, like small towns, have never been "big happy families." Rather, the key to their amenities is that they facilitate the discovery and easy association of people destined to become special to one another. Widows and spinsters find their companions for shopping, lunching, and bridge. Amateur mechanics and carpenters discover their fellow hobbyists, get involved in one another's projects, and become useful as well as enjoyable to one another. Via the local grapevine, the poker players, horse-shoe tossers, and clubbers of golf balls learn of one another's existence and are free to take it from there. From among the many, a contingent of casual friends emerges. For some there will be the great gift—a deep and abiding friendship in the form of one who also lives close by and is *available*. For all, there is a control valve. One can have as much engagement and involvement with the neighborhood as one wishes. Those who prefer none may have it just that way.

Such an environment is well described as *casual* because the elements of accident and informality are strong within it. In the strollways of a casual environment much of what one needs and enjoys in life comes easily and incidentally. Without having to plan or schedule or prepare, those who move about in a familiar and casual environment have positive social experiences. They bump into friends; they receive daily doses of novelty, diversion, and social support. On an ordinary day, people privileged to have a decent tavern in their neighborhood may enjoy a much better "party" than the office folks can manage with a month of planning.

And people are helpful in neighborhoods where casual contact has made them aware of one another's situations. Baby cribs, bicycles, children's clothing, and the like are passed along by those who no longer need them. The man about to buy an expensive lawn mower gets a more reliable assessment of the machine from the neighbor who owns one than from the stranger who is trying to sell it to him. Neighborhood residents who know a family will cast a caring eye on its youngest members. In this scrutiny there is protection for the children and, often, a bit of help in raising them.

The casual environment meets many needs without incurring the effort, and, often, the inefficiency of rational planning; it also meets needs beyond the individual's capacity to recognize them. Most individuals, particularly those cut off from community life, suffer what some psychologists call cognitive bias. The fundamental idea is that individuals, in their ignorance, *think* they know all their needs and how to satisfy them. This is not true. Life lived amid a variety of other people in a casual habitat supplies much of what people need without their ever being aware of it.

I gave a specific illustration earlier in the discussion of friends "by the set." Out of regular involvement in a third place, the individual comes to be friends with virtually the entire company that gathers there. The individual is warmed and enriched by the breadth of these relationships. The fragmented world becomes more whole and the broader contact with life, thus gained, adds to one's wisdom and self-assurance. Elsewhere, individuals tend to select their friends more narrowly and strategically, usually keeping within the confines of occupation and social class. The benefits of broader association are lost. Casual neighborhoods supply friends and acquaintances beyond the individual's choices and the reasons for making them. Individuals benefit despite themselves.

The casual environment, finally, is the natural habitat of the third place. Third place settings are really no more than a physical manifestation of people's desire to associate with those in an area once they get to know them. The same measure of diversity that satisfies needs locally and thus brings people into contact with one another also welcomes third places. The basic flaw of the American suburb is its lack of diversity, and that flaw may prove fatal to it. Some planners, at least, have seen the implications. If suburbia is to survive, concludes a Long Island planner, it will have to reflect more of the diversity characteristic of older cities and small towns; this "willingness to create and accept diversity will be the measure of whether suburbia remains vital."[4]

A recent study conducted in Los Angeles suggests that Americans would be receptive to more diversity in their residential areas than current zoning allows.[5] A sample of residents, which included upper-, middle-, and low-income families revealed that drugstores, markets, libraries, and post offices were strongly desired by all. More surprisingly, it was only among low-income blacks that the idea of a bar in the neighborhood was disapproved by a majority. The study also revealed that the most important thing about living in a neighborhood was the human contact it afforded. Sociability was rated first; friendliness second. Personal and property safety were ranked eighth; quiet was tenth and last. Convenience ranked above safety.

The sterilized or purified neighborhoods that contain nothing but houses emerged in great number as the nation became overreliant on the automobile. "Nothing neighborhoods" came into being only because the car was counted upon to satisfy every need and desire ·hat the home could not. Eventually our overreliance on the automobile caused a deterioration in the quality of our lives that few can ignore. Since the early- or mid-seventies, Americans have begun to develop an ambivalent attitude toward automobiles. The freeways, which are the lifelines to sterilized neighborhoods, are getting clogged, as are the lesser arteries. The air is turning foul with the hundred million pounds of carbon monoxide that cars pump into it every year. The loss of life from auto accidents touches every citizen closely. The cost of automobiles is outrageous.

As consumer groups press for greater automobile safety; as more of the old neighborhoods are razed to permit highway expansion; as citizen's groups demand more crackdowns on drunk drivers; and as the cost of cars begins to rival that of homes, the American people will continue to make sacrifices, willingly and otherwise, to automobile transportation. Eventually, however, they will realize that an ever-increasing number of sacrifices and an ever-diminishing quality of life are the prices paid for a system that is fundamentally unsound. When the greatest of our conveniences is understood to have become, through excessive reliance upon it, the basis of a terribly fragmented and inconvenient life, the situation will begin to change.

As a final comment on convenience and the corresponding need to resurrect the neighborhood as a casual environment, I should acknowledge occasional research that claims to show, on the basis of surveys, that people living in a given residential area do not want a shared existence because they lack consensus on virtually all matters of social and personal concern. Social scientists, I can only conclude, are as prone to setting the cart before the horse as anyone else. Consensus, if we are to call it that, *follows* interaction and involvement more often than it precedes it. Individuals, like neighborhoods, evolve and develop. When people are thrown together, they discover much to like, to get attached to, to add to their lives, and to change their minds about. When they are kept apart (which is what the sterilized development does to them) what does their level of consensus matter?

The Limits of Self-Help

Self-help books have become popular in the United States. Bookstores, even many drugstores, have separate sections for them. They are the inspirational literature of people without community. They offer advice and assurances to people too socially isolated to resist them.

Self-help literature can be useful to people who live in a fragmented society and lack the many trustworthy sources of daily support and direction available in unified societies. On the other hand, this litera- ture tends to glorify the condition which creates the market for it. It teaches that the good life, or well-being, or contentment is never a collective achievement but an individual one. Just as surely as it is the individual who pays for the "You're OK" advice, it is the individual who becomes the center of all things and who is "in charge" of his or her well-being. The literature obscures the extent to which the individual's enjoyment of life, and the quality of his experiences, and the breadth of his experiences are greatly influenced by the quality of group life which surrounds him. Community membership is often presented, not as a means to contentment or fulfillment, but as an impediment to "self- actualization."

The literature on self-help contributes to the abuses of the concepts of individualism and individual freedom which are greatly praised but rarely understood in this country. Most of our recently acquired free- doms, as Gail Fullerton observes, are the "freedoms of amputation."[6] She elaborates:

> Cut off from the primary groups that nurtured their forbearers and gave them a sense of identity, large numbers of Americans are looking for someone to tell them who they are or who they should be. Depending on their means and level of sophistication, they may enroll in courses that promise to develop "personality" or enter some form of therapy. But most are seeking an acceptable label or the secret to gaining power over others, rather than seeking to know themselves.

Incessant and excessive promotion of the individual and the idea that the good life is an individual accomplishment discourages collective effort, discounts collective effort, and obscures the fact that many good and necessary things can only result from collective effort. The reader is easily led to believe that every failure of collective effort is a great rousing victory for personal liberty.

We recently perused a book by an author of some standing in the self- help tradition. In it were set down the "ten hallmarks of well-being."

Each was phrased in the first person singular. Each suggested that well-being or the failure to achieve it is largely up to the individual. The hallmarks were put forth as declarative statements (e.g., "I am pleased with my growth and development." "My life has meaning and direction." "I have many friends." etc.), and each affirmative response takes the reader a step closer to well-being. I scored 100 percent, and I shared the criteria with several other people who also scored 100 percent. We seem to epitomize well-being. (I wonder why we're such a moody bunch.) W. C. Fields would probably have attacked the matter this way: "Doing well? How can I be doing well? I'm living in Philadelphia!" How many people within the typical American urban environment can be said to exemplify well-being?

It is well to encourage the individual to assume responsibility for his or her life and to advise accordingly. But it is a disservice to suggest that happiness, contentment, or the good life are wholly within the grasp of individual psychic and social manipulation. It is naïve to believe that one's well-being or contentment in life is independent of that of one's neighbors or coworkers. Among creatures essentially social in nature and whose condition is deeply affected by the quality of group life, personal well-being has definite limits. The encouragement to *personal* well-being in the magnitude and direction we see today suggests the lack of a collective well-being but will not compensate for it.

Since World War II, Americans have become more affluent; they are also more separate from a community life than ever before. One condition has promoted the other, for money creates the illusion that one does not need people. That select group of consumers who are young, well-educated, liberal in general outlook, and living away from their parents, and who used to be called "upward mobiles" by the marketing specialists who studied them, have blossomed into the more familiar Yuppies. The Yuppies are being tracked by many people. Some of us are interested to see how much well-being a six-figure annual income can buy for an enterprising couple. Most Yuppies were children in the purified and sterilized suburbs inhabited by their parents. Not surprisingly, they grew up as representatives of the values that prevailed there and pursued life-styles predicated upon materialism and self-absorption.[7] When one considers the money required, there seems relatively little to envy about the way most Yuppies live.

Encouragement to self-help and promotion of the idea that well-being is up to the individual also defuse the political potential inherent in an unsuitable urban habitat. If people more fully understood that many of their problems were neither of their own making nor amenable to self-help but stemmed from the "mess that is man-made America," personal problems would soon become political issues. There would be pressure on those who create the unsuitable habitat to begin to effect environmental remedies.

The ideology of self-help literature and therapies is one of adaptation; of deemphasizing the basic problems in favor of individualized survival modes. Its strongest appeal lies in its promise of immediate remedy, but the remedy is personal and more likely to obscure root causes than to attack them. The long-nurtured American fondness for individual solutions to problems must, however, eventually confront its limits. As the urban condition in America goes from bad to worse, those who suffer it will increasingly realize the limits of self-help. And, once they do, a whole new set of expectations will reemerge with respect to public space and public life. The days of the "private citizen"—that wholly American contradiction in terms—will give way to the publicly-concerned or civic-minded individual with whom our hope lies.

The Power of Place

The tyrannical force of the physical environment is revealing itself slowly to Americans. We've long enjoyed a good measure of immunity from the determinism of place and space. We've been blessed with an abundance of space to use, abuse, and leave behind. High national rates of geographical mobility suggest that most of us, in frequent changes of residence, escape the long-range consequences of living in a deficient habitat. Frequent moves also excuse our failure to get deeply involved in a specific locale or to be concerned about its deficiencies. Even our social scientists tend to treat the human relationships they otherwise study so carefully as if they float somewhere above the terra firma. Those relationships are, in fact, grounded, contained, and forced onto available physical staging, which affects their quality.

In that latter regard, it has been heartening to see environmental psychology rise in status vis-à-vis that discipline's other specialities. Roger Barker, a prominent environmental psychologist, once stated the position with wonderful simplicity. Asked how he would explain human behavior, Barker suggested that he merely needed to know where the individual in question was located—if the person is in church, he "acts church." If he's in a post office, he "acts post office."[8]

The implications are, of course, tremendous. Experiences occur in places conducive to them, or they do not occur at all. When certain kinds of places disappear, certain experiences also disappear. So also the breadth of experience may be sharply curtailed by an inadequate habitat. I thought of this a few years back when an add-on or do-it-yourself necklace became popular. A woman bought the chain and added her choices among the fairly expensive beads as she could afford them. I saw many necklaces in those days with few beads on them. Somewhere in my reading at the time, I encountered a writer's metaphor on the content of daily life. Individual lives, he or she said, are built up by stringing together those situations and their settings to which one returns each day. The embarrassingly few beads around many necks seemed to me emblematic of the paucity of places or settings that the contemporary urbanite visits daily. I thought, too, how many "beads" of daily experience were on the necklace of those who had lived in small towns compared to their counterparts in the automobile suburb. Boredom plagues the average American more frequently. There are too few beads on the chain of daily experience.

Beyond any question, the most recounted anecdote in architectural circles is that concerning Winston Churchill's conduct following the bombing of one of Parliament's buildings by the Nazis during the Second World War. Churchill is reported to have gone to the membership and asked them not what features and frills they wanted in the restoration, but whether they wished to effect any changes in the way they conducted their affairs. When he learned that they intended no changes in procedure, he announced that the building would be restored just as it had been. Humans first shape their environment, Churchill reasoned, and then the environment shapes and controls them. The environment, as I've said, is a tyrannical force but, increasingly, human beings are the real tyrants, for the environment is increasingly fashioned by them.

I recently spoke to an audience of fifty to sixty people on the subject of the informal public life. I asked the group if Americans living in the suburbs had the freedom to put on their sweaters in the early evening and visit their friends at the neighborhood tavern. A resounding yes was given by the group. I asked if the younger children could go with coins in hand to the corner store and pick out some gum or candy or a comic book. Another resounding yes. Finally, I asked if the older children could stop in at the malt shop after school. Yes was the response of the audience, who seemed far more informed about America's freedoms than her environment. I'd hoped someone would realize that none of these people can go to a place that isn't there or have an experience that is no longer possible.

The environment in which we live out our lives is not a cafeteria containing an endless variety of passively arrayed settings and experiences. It is an active, dictatorial force that adds experiences or subtracts them according to the way it has been shaped. When Americans begin to grasp that lesson, the path to the planners' offices will be more heavily trod than that to the psychiatrists' couches. And when that lesson is learned, community may again be possible and celebrated each day in a rich new spawning of third places. If there is one message I wish to leave with those who despair of suburbia's lifeless streets, of the plastic places along our "strips," or of the congested and inhospitable mess that is "downtown," it is: *It doesn't have to be like this!*

Notes

Chapter 1. *The Problem of Place in America*

1. Richard N. Goodwin, "The American Condition," *The New Yorker* (28 January 1974), 38.

2. Kenneth Harris, *Travelling Tongues* (London: John Murrary, 1949), 80.

3. Victor Gruen, *Centers for Urban Environment* (New York: Van Nostrand Reinhold Co., 1973), 217.

4. Philip E. Slater, "Must Marriage Cheat Today's Young Women?" *Redbook Magazine* (February 1971).

5. Suzanne Gordon, *Lonely in America* (New York: Simon & Schuster, 1976).

6. *Ibid.*, 105.

7. Richard Sennett, "The Brutality of Modern Families," in *Marriages and Families*, ed. Helena Z. Lopata. (New York: D. Van Nostrand Company, 1973), 81.

8. David Riesman, "The Suburban Dislocation," *The Annals of the American Academy of Political and Social Science* (November 1957), 142.

9. Dolores Hayden, *Redesigning the American Dream* (New York: W. W. Norton & Company, 1984), Chapter 2.

10. See Sennett (*op. cit.*) and Aries, Philippe. "The Family and the City." *Daedalus*, Spring, 1977. Pp. 227–237 for succinct statements of the two views.

11. Sennett, *op. cit.*, 84.

12. Philippe Aries, "The Family and the City," *Daedalus* (Spring 1977), 227.

13. Goodwin, *op. cit.*, 38.

14. P. F. Kluge, "Closing Time," *Wall Street Journal* (27 May 1982).

15. Frank L. Ferguson, *Efficient Drug Store Management* (New York: Fairchild Publications, 1969), 202.

16. Urie Bronfenbrenner, "The American Family: An Ecological Perspective," in *The American Family: Current Perspectives* (Cambridge, Mass.: Harvard University Press, Audiovisual Division, 1979), (audio cassette).

17. Claudia Wallis, "Stress: Can We Cope?" *Time* (6 June 1983).

18. *Ibid.*

19. *Ibid.*

20. *Ibid.*

21. Richard Goodwin, "The American Condition," *New Yorker* (4 February 1970) 75.

22. Thomas M. Kando, *Leisure and Popular Culture in Transition*, 2d ed. (St. Louis: The C.V. Mosby Company, 1980).

23. *Ibid.*, 101.

24. Generally, the Mediteranean cultures.

25. Lyn H. Lofland, *A World of Strangers* (Prospect Heights, Ill.: Waveland Press, Inc., 1973), 117.

26. Sometimes the phrase employed is "the mess that is man-made America." Planners appear to use it as much as anyone else.

Chapter 2. The Character of Third Places

1. Joseph Addison, *The Spectator*, no. 9 (Saturday, 10 March 1711).

2. Joseph Wechsberg, "The Viennese Coffee House: A Romantic Institution," *Gourmet* 12:16, 1966.

3. Carl Bode, *The Young Mencken* (New York: The Dial Press, 1973), 197.

4. Richard Sennett, *The Fall of Public Man* (New York: Alfred A. Knopf, 1977), 311.

5. Jane Jacobs, *The Death and Life of Great American Cities* (New York: Random House, 1961), 55.

6. *Ibid.*

7. O.E.D. Noun definition no. 2.

8. Robert J. Allen, *The Clubs of Augustan London* (Hamden, Conn.: Archon Books, 1967), 14.

9. Georg Simmel, in *On Individual and Social Forms*, ed. Donald N. Levine (Chicago: The University of Chicago Press, 1971), Chapter 9.

10. Richard West, "The Power of 21," *New York* (5 October 1981), 33.

11. Michael Daly, "Break Point," *New York* (5 October 1981), 45.

12. Tibor Scitovsky, *The Joyless Economy* (New York: Oxford University Press, 1976), Chapter 11.

13. Ralph Waldo Emerson, *Essays and Journals* (New York: Doubleday, 1968), 158.

14. Richard Goodwin, "The American Condition," *The New Yorker* (28 January 1974), 36.

15. William Wordsworth, "The Art of Conversation," in *Wordsworthian and Other Studies*, ed. Ernest de Selincourt. (New York: Russell & Russell, 1964), 181–206.

16. *Ibid.*

17. Henry Sedgwick, *The Art of Happiness* (New York: Bobbs-Merrill, 1930), Chapter 17.

18. Brian Jackson, *Working Class Community* (London: Routledge & Kegan Paul, 1968), Chapter 4.

19. "The English Department," *Playground Daily News* (25 November 1982).

20. John Timbs, *Clubs and Club Life in London* (Detroit: Gale Research Company, 1967 Reprint), 214–215.

21. Ralph Waldo Emerson, *Uncollected Lectures* (New York: William Edwin Rudge, 1932), 36.

22. *Op. cit.*

23. Laurence Wylie, *Village in the Vaucluse* (New York: Harper & Row, 1957), Chapter 11.

24. *Op. cit.*

25. *Op. cit.*

26. Henry Miller, *Remember to Remember* (London: The Grey Walls Press, 1952), 12.

27. Elijah Anderson, *A Place on the Corner* (Chicago: The University of Chicago Press, 1976).

28. Maurice Gorham, *Back to the Local* (London: Percival Marshall, 1949), 41.

29. Johan Huizinga, *Homo Ludens: A Study of the Play Elements in Culture* (London: Routledge and Kegan Paul, Ltd., 1949), Chapter 1.

30. *Ibid.*, 12.

31. David Seamon, *A Geography of the Lifeworld* (New York: St. Martin's Press, 1979), Chapter 10.

32. Personal correspondence.

33. Matthew Dumont, "Tavern Culture: The Sustenance of Homeless Men," *American Journal of Orthopsychiatry*, 1967, vol. 37, 938–945.

Chapter 3. The Personal Benefits

1. Tibor Scitovsky, *op. cit.*

2. *Ibid.*

3. Pete Hamill, "A Hangout Is a Place . . ." *Mademoiselle* (November 1969).

4. Mass Observation, *The Pub and the People: A Worktown Study* (London: Victor Gollanca Ltd., 1943).

5. Marshall B. Clinard. "The public drinking house and society" in *Society, Culture, and Drinking Patterns*, David Pittman and Charles Snyder (eds.) (New York: John Wiley and Sons, Inc., 1967.)

6. *Op. cit.*, 238–239.

7. Seldon Bacon, "Alcohol and Complex Society," in *Society, Culture, and Drinking Patterns*, eds. David Pittman and Charles Snyder (New York: John Wiley and Sons, Inc., 1962).

8. John Mortimer, "Rumpole and the Man of God," in *The Trials of Rumpole*.

9. Kenneth Rexroth, "The Decline of Humor in America," *The Nation*, 1975, vol. 84, 374–376.

10. Ralph Waldo Emerson, essay on "Experience."

11. Mike Feinsilber and William B. Mead, *American Averages* (Garden City, New York: Dolphin Books, 1980), 60.

12. Ray Oldenburg, unpublished observations of seventy-eight Midwestern taverns, 1981.

13. Jacob Levine, "Humour as a Form of Therapy: Introduction to Symposium," in *It's a Funny Thing, Humour*, eds. Anthony J. Chapman and Hugh C. Foot (New York: Pergamon Press, 1977).

14. John R. Atkin, "A Designed Locale for Laughter to Reinforce Community Bonds," in Chapman and Foot, *Ibid*.

15. Georg Simmel, in *On Individual and Social Form*, ed. Donald N. Levine (Chicago: The University of Chicago Press, 1971).

16. George Malko, "The Biltmore for Men Only," *Holiday Magazine* (January 1969), 16.

17. Ralph Waldo Emerson, "Friendship," in *Ralph Waldo Emerson: Essays and Journals* (Garden City, New York: Doubleday and Company, 1968), 161.

18. See the discussion of neutral ground in Chapter 2.

19. Harry Carmichael, *Most Deadly Hate* (New York: E.P. Dutton & Company, 1974).

20. Thomas S. Langner and Stanley T. Michael, *Life Stress and Mental Health* (New York: The Free Press of Clencoe, 1963), 284–287.

21. *Ibid*.

22. Claude Fischer, *To Dwell Among Friends* (Chicago: The University of Chicago Press, 1982).

Chapter 4. The Greater Good

1. Manuela Hoelterhoff, "Life Amid the Ruins of East Germany's Porcelain City." *Wall Street Journal* (22 September 1983).

2. Laszlo Varga, *Human Rights in Hungary* (Gainesville: Danubian Research and Information Center, 1967).

3. Irving Wallace *et al.* "When Coffee was Banned in Sweden," *Parade Magazine* (12 September 1982), 24.

4. Carl Bridenbaugh and Jesse Bridenbaugh, *Rebels and Gentlemen* (New York: Oxford University Press), 1962, 21.

5. Sam Bass Warner, Jr., *The Private City* (Philadelphia: University of Pennsylvania Press, 1968), 19–20.

6. *Ibid.*

7. Fred Holmes, *Side Roads* (Madison, Wisconsin: The State Historical Society, 1949), 75.

8. Allan Nevins, *Grover Cleveland: A Study in Courage* (New York: Dodd, Mead & Company, 1966), 73.

9. Warner, *op. cit.*, 21.

10. Victor Gruen, *The Heart of Our Cities* (New York: Simon & Schuster, 1964), 106.

11. Kirby Winston, "The Impact of Television: The Communication of Social Disorganization," in *Cities in Transition*, eds. Frank Coppa and Philip Dolee (Chicago: Nelson Hall, 1947), 177.

12. James MacGregor Burns, "Is the Primary System a Mistake?" *Family Weekly* (26 February 1984).

13. *Op. cit.*

14. *Ibid.*

15. Robert Goldston, *Suburbia: Civic Denial* (New York: The Macmillan Company, 1970), 140.

16. David Mathews, "Civic Intelligence," *Social Education* (November/December 1985), 678–681.

17. Alexis de Tocqueville, *Democracy in America* (New York: Alfred A. Knopf, 1963), vol. 1, 196.

18. Newell Sims, ed. *The Rural Community* (New York: Charles Scribner's Sons, 1920), 626.

19. *Ibid.*, 628.

20. *Ibid.*, 628–9.

21. *Ibid.*, 631.

22. *Ibid.*, 533–48.

23. *Ibid.*, 512.

24. *Ibid.*, 513.

25. *Ibid.*, 632.

26. *Bridenbaugh, op. cit.*, 21.

27. *Ibid.*, 22.

28. Mass Observation, *op. cit.* Chapter 6.

29. *Ibid.*

30. Anderson, Elijah. *op. cit.*

31. *Ibid.*, 55.

32. *Ibid.*, 1.

33. Bill Gilbert and Lisa Twyman, "Violence: Out of Hand in the Stands," in *Sports in Contemporary Society*, ed. D. Stanley Eitzen (New York: St. Martin's Press, 2d ed., 1984).

34. Grady Clay, "The Street as Teacher," in *Public Streets for Public Use*, ed. Anne Vernex Mouden (New York: Van Nostrand Reinhold Company, 1987), 109.

35. Oscar Newman, *Defensible Space* (New York: The Macmillan Company, 1972), Chapter 4.

36. *Ibid.*

37. Scitovsky, *op. cit.*, Chapter 11.

Chapter 5. The German-American Lager Beer Gardens

1. Fred L. Holmes, *Side Roads: Excursions into Wisconsin's Past* (Madison, Wisconsin: The State Historical Society, 1949).

2. The quotation is by Samuel Johnson, *The Idler*, no. 58, 1759.

3. Wisconsin State Historical Society, Madison, "Germans in America" Collection. Milwaukee, December 1946, letter 325, 179.

4. Junius Henre Browne, *The Great Metropolis: A Mirror of New York* (Hartford, Connecticut: American Publishing Company, 1970), 161.

5. Alvin F. Harlow, *The Serene Cincinnatians* (New York: E.P. Dutton & Co., Inc.), 201.

6. *Ibid.*, 191–2.

7. Violet Hunt, *The Desirable Alien: At Home in Germany* (London: Chatton and Windus, 1908), 76–7.

8. *Ibid.*, 79.

9. *Ibid.*, 78.

10. Browne, *op. cit.*, 162.

11. *Ibid.*, 166.

12. Holmes, *op. cit.*, 67.

13. *Ibid.*

14. Kathleen Neils Conzen, *Immigrant Milwaukee, 1836–1860: Accommodation and Community in a Frontier City* (Cambridge, Mass.: Harvard University Press, 1976), 157–158.

15. Richard O'Connor, *The German-Americans: An Informal History* (Boston: Little, Brown and Company, 1968), 290.

16. *Ibid.*, 288.

17. Browne, *op. cit.*, 165–6.

18. Harlow, *op. cit.*, 184.

19. *Ibid.*, 188.

20. *Ibid.*, 192.

21. O'Connor, *op. cit.*, 297.

22. Holmes, *op. cit.*, 56–66.

23. *Ibid.*, 69.

24. *Ibid.*

25. Browne, *op. cit.*, 160.

26. *Ibid.*

27. *Ibid.*, 159.

28. Descriptions of the elaborate beer and palm gardens may be found in the works of Conzen, Holmes, O'Connor, Browne, and Harlow, all of whom are cited above.

29. Carl Wittke, *We Who Build America: The Saga of the Immigrant* (Cleveland: The Press of Western Reserve University, 1939), 204–205.

30. Perry R. Duis, *The Saloon: Public Drinking in Chicago and Boston, 1880–1920* (Chicago: The University of Illinois Press, 1983), 153–154.

31. Karl Theodor Griesinger, "A Historian's Forebodings," in *This Was America*, ed. Oscar Handlin (New York: Harper and Row, Publishers, 1949), 252–69.

32. *Ibid.*, 262.

33. O'Connor, *op. cit.*, 293.

Chapter 6. Main Street

1. Robert Traver, *Troubleshooter* (New York: The Viking Press, 1943), 207.

2. Kirkpatrick Sale, *Human Scale* (New York: Coward, McCann and Geoghegan, 1980), Part III, Chapter 4.

3. Leopold Kohr, *The Overdeveloped Nations* (New York: Schocken, 1977), 14–19.

4. Roger Barker *et al.*, *Midwest and its Children* (Hamden, Connecticut: Archon Books, 1971).

5. Robert Bechtel, *Enclosing Behavior* (Dowden: Hutchinson and Ross, 1977), Chapter 9.

6. T. R. Young, *New Sources of the Self* (New York: Pergamon Press, 1972), 37.

7. Personal correspondence, 1980.

8. "How Shopping Malls Are Changing Life in U.S." *U.S. News and World Report* (18 June 1973), 43–6.

9. Richard V. Francaviglia, "Main Street, U.S.A.: The Creation of a Popular Image." *Landscape* (Spring/Summer 1977), 18–22.

10. Ralph Keyes, "I Like Colonel Sanders," *Newsweek* (27 August 1973), 8–9.

11. Eugene van Cleef, *Cities in Action* (New York: Pergamon Press, 1970), Chapter 17.

12. Arnold Rogow, *The Dying of Light* (New York: G. P. Putnam & Sons, 1975), 226.

13. *Ibid.*

14. David Halberstam, "One Man's America." *Parade Magazine* (31 October 1982), 4.

15. Orrin E. Klapp, *Overload and Boredom: Essays on the Quality of Life in the Information Society* (New York: Greenwood Press, 1986), 31.

Chapter 7. The English Pub

1. Robert Goldston, *London: The Civic Spirit* (New York: Macmillan, 1969).

2. John Timbs, *Clubs and Club Life in London* (Detroit: Gale Research Company, 1967), 2–3.

3. Mass Observation, *The Pub and the People: A Worktown Study* (London: Victor Gollancz Ltd. 1943), 17.

4. Frank J. Dobie, *A Texan in England* (Boston: Little, Brown, and Company, 1944), 251–2.

5. Ben Davis, *The Traditional English Pub: A Way of Drinking* (London: Architectural Press, 1981), 3.

6. Maurice Gorham, *Back to the Local* (London: Percival Marschall, 1949), 9.

7. Maurice Gorham and H.M. Dunnett, *Inside the Pub* (London: The Architectural Press, 1950), 71.

8. Ben Davis, *op. cit.*, 73.

9. *Ibid.*, 74.

10. Nathaniel Gubbins, "The Pubs," *Holiday Magazine* (July 1947), 71.

11. Mass Observation, *op. cit.*, 105.

12. Ernest Barker, ed. *The Character of England* (Oxford: The Clarendon Press, 1963), 459.

13. Gubbins, *op. cit.*, 71.

14. Richard Burgheim, "McSorley's Old Ale House," *Holiday Magazine* (May 1970), 84 ff.

15. Raymond Postgate, "English Drinking Habits," *Holiday Magazine* (February 1963), 87 ff.

16. Kenneth L. Roberts, *Why Europe Leaves Home* (New York: Bobbs-Merrill, 1922), 274.

17. Postgate, *op. cit.*, 34.

18. Gorham, 1949. *op. cit.*, 34.

19. Roberts, *op. cit.*, 273.

20. Davis, *op. cit.*, 79.

21. Gorham, 1949. *op. cit.*, 94–6.

22. Mass Observation, *op. cit.*, 94–6.

23. Barry Newman, "Good Times or Bad, There'll Always be an English Pub," *The Wall Street Journal*.

24. *Mass Observation*, *op. cit.*, 33.

25. Davis, *op. cit.*, 63–4.

26. Lewis Melville and Aubrey Hammond, *The London Scene* (London: Baber & Gwyer, 1926), 33.

27. Gorham, *op. cit.*, 85.

28. Davis, *op. cit.*, 62.

29. Gorham, *op. cit.*, 909.

30. Gwyn Thomas, "Tranquility and Warm Beer," *Holiday Magazine* (May 1964), 168.

Chapter 8. The French Café

1. Paul Cohen-Portheim, *The Spirit of London* (Philadelphia: J.B. Lippincott Company, 1935), 89.

2. Joseph Wechsberg, "The long, sweet day of the sidewalk cafe," *Holiday Magazine*, (August 1967), 50.

3. Sanche de Gramont, *The French: Portrait of a People* (New York: G.P. Putnam's Sons, 1969), 462.

4. John Gunther, *Twelve Cities* (New York: Harper & Row, 1967), 70.

5. Lebert H. Weir, *Europe at Play* (New York: A.S. Barnes & Co., 1937), 437–8.

6. Paul-Henry Chombart de Lauwe, *Des Hommes et des Villes* (Paris: Payot, 1965), 28–9.

7. Fernando Diaz-Plaja, *The Frenchman and the Seven Deadly Sins* (New York: Charles Scribner's Sons), 147.

8. Wechsberg, *op. cit.*, 50.

9. Gramont, *op. cit.*, 462.

10. Florence Gilliam, *France: A Tribute by an American Woman* (New York: E.P. Dutton & Co., 1945), 42.

11. Wechsberg, *op. cit.*, 50.

12. Bernard Rudofsky, *Streets for People: A Primer for Americans* (Garden City, New York: Doubleday & Company, 1959), 313.

13. Wechsberg, *op. cit.*, 87.

14. Edward T. Hall, *The Hidden Dimension* (Garden City, New York: Doubleday & Company, 1969), 145.

15. Jean Fourastie, *The Causes of Wealth*. Translated and edited by Theodore Caplow (Glencoe, Illinois: The Free Press, 1960), 182–3.

16. *Ibid.*, 193.

17. *Ibid.*, 194.

18. *Ibid.*, 195.

19. Gramont, *op. cit.*, 452.

20. David E. Wright and Robert E. Snow, "Consumption as Ritual in the High Technology Society," ed. Ray B. Browne in *Rituals and Ceremonies in Popular Culture* (Bowling Green: Bowling Green University Popular Press, 1980), 326–7.

21. Laurence Wylie, *Village in the Vaucluse* (New York: Harper & Row, 1957), Chapter 11.

22. *Ibid.*

23. Diaz-Plaja, *op. cit.*

24. Robert T. Anderson and Barbara Gallatin Anderson, *Bus Stop for Paris: The Transformation of a French Village* (New York: Doubleday & Company, 1965), 237 ff.

25. Francois Nourissier, *Cartier-Bresson's France* (New York: The Viking Press, 1971), 199–200.

26. *Ibid.*, 200.

27. Gyula Halasz Brassai, *Le Paris Secret des Annes 30* (Garden City, New York: Doubleday and Company, 1966).

28. For an informative discussion of these nonalcoholic equivalents, see Al Hines, "What the Teetotal Traveler Drinks at the Sidewalk Cafe," *Holiday Magazine* (January 1969), 82.

29. Fourastie, *op. cit.*

30. *Ibid.*, 17–8.

31. *Ibid.*, 18.

32. *Ibid.*, 170.

33. *Ibid.*

34. *Ibid.*, 210.

35. *Ibid.*, 164.

36. Wechsberg, *op. cit.*, 87.

37. Gramont, *op. cit.*, 380.

Chapter 9. The American Tavern

1. "Bars and Cocktail Lounges," *Small Business Reporter* (San Francisco: Bank of America, 1977), vol. 11, no. 9.

2. Gerald Carson, "The Saloon," *American Heritage: The Magazine of History* (April 1963), 25.

3. Paul Frederick Kluge, "Closing Time," *Wall Street Journal* (27 May 1982), 1 and 31.

4. Mike Feinsilber and William B. Mead, *American Averages* (Garden City, New York, 1980), 313.

5. Tibor Scitovsky, *The Joyless Economy* (New York: Oxford University Press, 1976), 241.

6. Marc Kessler and Christopher Gomberg, "Observations of Barroom Drinking: Methodology and Preliminary Results," *Quarterly Journal of Studies on Alcohol*, vol.35, 1974, 1392–1396.

7. Cara E. Richards, "City Taverns," *Human Organization*, (Winter 1963–64), vol. 22, 260–8.

8. Anthony E. Thomas, "Class and Sociability Among Urban Workers: A Study of the Bar as a Social Club," *Medical Anthropology*, 1978.

9. Feinsilber and Mead, *op. cit.*, 319.

10. Richards, *op. cit.*

11. Arthur Blumberg *et al.*, "The Teacher Bar." *The Educational Forum* (Fall 1982), 111–25. Also, Edward Pajak, "Cathartic and Socialization Functions of 'Teachers Bars'." Presented at the annual meeting of the American Educational Research Association, Boston (April 1980).

12. "From Corner Tavern to Disco: Selling the Good Life," *Entrepreneur Magazine*, (July 1980), 7–30.

13. Kluge, *op. cit.*

14. *Ibid.*

15. *Ibid.*

16. *Ibid.*

17. *Ibid.*

18. *Ibid.*

19. "From Corner Tavern to Disco" *op. cit.*, 17.

Chapter 10. Classic Coffeehouses

1. Gerald Carson, *The Old Country Store* (New York: E.P. Dutton and Son, 1965). Also, Phyllis Fenner, "Grandfather's Country Store," *The Atlantic Monthly* (December 1945).

2. Described in Chapter Six, "Main Street."

3. Kenneth Davids, *Coffee* (San Francisco: 1010 Productions, 1976), 169.

4. Raymond Calkins, *Substitutes for the Saloon* (Boston: Houghton Mifflin Company, 1919).

5. Davids, *op. cit.*, 170.

6. Thomas A. Erhard, "Coffee House," in *The World Book Encyclopedia*, 1980 ed.

7. Aytoun Ellis, *The Penny Universities* (London: Secker and Warburg, 1956), see the title page.

8. *Ibid.*, 45.

9. *Ibid.*, 44.

10. *Ibid.*

11. *Ibid.*, 88.

12. The "Women's Petition" is reproduced in *Old English Coffee Houses* (London: Rodale Press, 1954).

13. *Ibid.*, 11.

14. Ellis, *op. cit.*, 117 ff.

15. *Ibid.*, Chapter 12.

16. *Ibid.*, 168.

17. T. W. MacCallum, *The Vienna that's not in the Baedeker* (New York: Robert M. McBride and Company, 1931), 27.

18. *Ibid.*, 30.

19. Joseph Wechsberg, "The Viennese Coffeehouse: A Romantic Institution," *Gourmet* (December 1966).

20. MacCallum, *op. cit.*, 42.

21. *Ibid.*, 41.

22. Joseph Wechsberg, *The Vienna I Knew* (New York: Doubleday and Company, 1979). The author's mother is reported to have objected to one of the coffeehouses in their native Ostrau because it "seemed the paradise of independent husbands."

Chapter 11. A Hostile Habitat

1. Philippe Aries, "The Family and the City," *Daedalus* (Spring 1977), 227–35.

2. David T. Bazelon, "The New Factor in American Society," in *Environment and Change: The Next Fifty Years*, ed. W. E. Ewald, Jr. (Bloomington, Illinois: Indiana University Press, 1968), 264–286.

3. Wolf Von Eckardt, *Back to the Drawing Board* (Washington, D.C.: New Republic Books, 1978), 15.

4. Robert Theobald, "Planning *with* People," in Ewald, *op. cit.*, 182–185.

5. Lionel Brett, *Architecture in a Crowded World: Vision and Reality in Planning* (New York: Schocken Books, 1971).

6. J. Ross McKeever, ed. *Community Builders Handbook* (Washington, D.C.: Urban Land Institute, 1968).

7. Ray Bradbury, "Beyond 1984: The People Machines," in ed. Taylor, *Cities: The Forces that Shape Them* (New York: Rizzoli, 1982), 167.

8. *Ibid.*

9. Patrick Goldring, *The Broilerhouse Society* (New York: Weybright & Talley, 1969).

10. *Ibid.*

11. *Ibid.*, 14–5.

12. *Ibid.*, 64–5.

13. Victor Gruen, "New Forms of Community," in ed. Laurence B. Holland *Who Designs America?* (New York: Anchor Books, 1965).

14. *Ibid.*, 172–3.

15. Dolores Hayden, *Redesigning the American Dream* (New York: W.W. Norton & Company, 1984), 38.

16. *Ibid.*

17. Mike Feinsilber and W. B. Mead, *American Averages* (Garden City, New York: Dolphin Books, 1980), 192.

18. Peter Blake, *God's Own Junkyard: The Planned Deterioration of America's Landscape* (New York: Holt, Rinehart, and Winston, 1954).

19. Ian McHarg, *The Fitness of Man's Environment* (Washington, D.C.: Smithsonian Institute Press, 1968), 211.

20. Seymour M. Gold, *Recreation Planning and Design* (New York: McGraw-Hill, 1980).

21. Victor Gruen, *Centers for the Urban Environment* (New York: Van Nostrand Reinhold Company, 1973), 85 ff.

22. Mike Royko, "Neighborhood on the Way Back," *Chicago Daily News* (26 November 1973).

23. Adolf Ciborowski, in his introduction to Robert B. Carson, *What Ever Happened to the Trolley?* (Washington, D.C.: University of American Press, 1978).

24. Jane Addams, *The Spirit of Youth and the City Streets* (New York: The Macmillan Company, 1923), 8.

25. *Ibid.*, 7.

26. Nathan Silver, *Lost New York* (New York: Houghton Mifflin Company, 1967), 227.

27. Paul Gray, "Another Look at Democracy in America," *Time* Essay (16 June 1986).

28. Robert Macy, "Entertainer bemoans high prices in Vegas," *The Pensacola News-Journal* (15 July 1982), 5D.

29. *Ibid.*

30. Jim Pettigrew, Jr. "The Vanishing Game of Snooker," *Atlanta Weekly* (12 October 1980), 15 ff.

31. I based the calculation on figures reported in Andrew A. Rooney, *A Few Minutes with Andy Rooney* (New York: Atheneum, 1981), 58–59.

32. *Southern Beverage Journal*, Feb. 1982, p 39.

33. *Ibid*, p. 39.

34. *Ibid*, 23.

35. Kazem Motamed-Nejad, "The Story-Teller and Mass Media in Iran," in eds. Heinz-Dietrich Fischer and Stafen Melnik, *Entertainment: A Cross-Cultural Examination* (New York: Hastings House, 1979), 43–62.

Chapter 12. The Sexes and the Third Place

1. Philippe Ariès, "The Family and the City," *Daedalus* (Spring 1977), 277–35.

2. *Ibid.*

3. C. S. Lewis, *The Four Loves* (New York: Harcourt Brace Jovanovich, 1960), 95.

4. Alexander Rysman, "How the 'Gossip' became a Woman," *Journal of Communication*, 1977, vol. 27:1, 176–80.

5. *Ibid.*

6. Anthony LeJeune, *The Gentlemen's Clubs of London* (New York: Mayflower Books, 1979), 14.

7. See Chapter 10.

8. Lucienne Roubin, "Male Space and Female Space within the Provencial Community," in *Rural Society in France, Selections from the Annales Economies, Societies, Civilization* (Baltimore: The Johns Hopkins University Press, Robert Foster (ed.) 1977), 152–80.

9. *Ibid.*

10. Lillian Rubin, *Intimate Strangers* (New York: Harper & Row, 1983).

11. Murray Hausknecht, *The Joiners* (New York: The Bedminster Press, 1962), 31.

12. Charles Winick, *The New People* (New York: Pegasus, 1968), 136.

13. Philip E. Slater, "Must Marriage Cheat Today's Young Women?" *Redbook* (February 1971), 57.

14. Pierre Mornell, *Passive Men, Wild Women* (New York: Simon & Schuster, 1976).

15. Suzanne Gordon, *Lonely in America* (New York: Simon & Schuster, 1976).

16. Rosalie G. Genovese, "A Women's Self-Help Network as a Response to Service Needs in the Suburbs," *Signs* (Spring, 1980), vol. 5, no. 3, 248–256.

17. Gordon, *op. cit.*

18. Hutton Webster, *Primitive Secret Societies* (New York: Octagon, 1968), Reprint of 1932 ed. Chapter 1.

19. Roubin, *op. cit.*

20. *Ibid.*

21. Charles E. Hooper, *The Country House* (New York: Doubleday, Page & Co., 1905).

22. Gail Fullerton, *Survival in Marriage* (Hinsdale, Illinois: Dryden, 1977), 215.

23. *Ibid.*

24. *Ibid.*

25. Margaret Mead, "The American Family" in ed. Huston Smith, *The Search for America* (Englewood-Cliffs, New Jersey: Prentice-Hall, 1959), 119.

26. Bert N. Adams, *The Family* (New York: Harcourt, Brace, Jovanovich, 1971), 4th ed., 354.

27. *Ibid.*, 360.

28. Paul C. Glick, "How American Families are Changing," *American Demographics* (January 1984), 21–25.

29. *Ibid.*

30. Reference is to the comic strip entitled "Bringing Up Father."

31. Mead, *op. cit.*

32. Ben Davis, *The Traditional English Pub* (London: The Architectural Press, 1981), 99.

33. C. A. Tripp, *The Homosexual Matrix* (New York: McGraw-Hill, 1975), Chapter 4.

34. Fullerton, *op. cit.*, 60.

35. Stuart Miller, *Men and Friendship* (Boston: Houghton-Mifflin Co., 1983), 26–7.

36. *Ibid.*

37. Tripp, *op. cit.*

38. Miller, *op. cit.*

39. Lewis, *op. cit.*, 109.

40. J. F. C. Harrison, *The Early Victorians* (New York: Praeger, 1971), 94.

41. Mass Observation, *The Pub and the People* (London: Victor Gollancz, Ltd., 1984).

42. Harry A. Franck, *Vagabonding through Changing Germany* (New York: Harper & Bros., 1920), 281.

43. Violet Hunt, *The Desirable Alien* (London: Chatto & Windus, 1913).

Chapter 13. Shutting Out Youth

1. Urie Bronfenbrenner, *Two Worlds of Childhood* (New York: Russell Sage Foundation, 1970). Chapter 4, "The Unmaking of the American Child."

2. Claude S. Fischer, *To Dwell Among Friends: Personal Networks in Town and City* (Chicago: The University of Chicago Press, 1982).

3. Denzel E. Benson, "The Intentionally Childless Couple," *USA Today* (January 1979), vol. 107; 45 and 56.

4. Herbert J. Gans, *The Levittowners* (New York: Pantheon Books, 1967).

5. Norman M. Lobsenz, *Is Anybody Happy?* (New York: Doubleday and Company, 1962), 78.

6. *Ibid.*

7. Marie Winn, *Children without Childhood* (New York: Penguin Books, 1984). Chapter 4, "The End of Play."

8. Lawrence Fellows, "Psychologists' Report Finds New Towns in West Germany Boring to Children," *New York Times* (9 May 1971).

9. William H. Whyte, *The Last Landscape* (New York: Doubleday and Company, 1968), 262.

10. W. F. Connell and E.E. Skilbeck, *Growing Up in an Australian City: A Study of Adolescents in Sidney* (Melbourne, Australia: ACER, 1957), Chapter 11.

11. Jane Jacobs, *The Death and Life of Great American Cities* (New York: Vintage Books, 1961), 79 ff.

12. Sidney Brower, "Streetfront and Sidewalk," *Landscape Architecture* (July, 1973), 364–9.

13. Whyte, *op. cit.*, Chapter 15.

14. Charles E. Little, *Challenge of the Land* (New York: Pergamon Press, 1968), 10–12.

15. William S. Kowinski, *The Malling of America* (New York: William Morrow and Company, 1985), 350.

16. *Ibid.*

17. *Ibid.*, 352.

18. *Ibid.*, Chapter 36.

Chapter 14. Toward Better Times . . . and Places

1. The adjectives are those recently employed by *Newsweek* writers in describing the values of the "best and brightest" of the baby boom. See "A Return to the Suburbs," *Newsweek*, (21 July 1986).

2. Patrick Goldring, *The Broilerhouse Society* (New York: Heybright and Talley, 1969), 216.

3. A description of the basic necessities a neighborhood should contain may be found in Wolf Von Eckardt, *Back to the Drawing Board!* (Washington, D.C.: New Republic Books, 1978), Chapter 27.

4. Lee Koppelman, cited in William S. Kowinski, "Suburbia: End of the Golden Age," *New York Times Magazine* (16 March 1980).

5. Tridib Banerjee and William C. Baer, *Beyond the Neighborhood Unit* (New York: Plenum Press, 1984).

6. Gail Fullerton, *Survival in Marriage* (Hinsdale, Illinois: The Dryden Press, 1977), 44–5.

7. "A Return to the Suburbs," *op. cit.*

8. Edwin P. Willems, "Behavioral Ecology," in ed. Daniel Stokols, *Perspectives on Environment and Behavior* (New York: Plenum Press, 1977), 50.

Bibliography

Adams, Bert N. *The Family*. New York: Harcourt, Brace, Jovanovich, 1971.

Addams, Jane. *The Spirit of Youth and the City Streets*. New York: The Macmillan Company, 1923.

Addison, Joseph. *The Spectator*, no. 9. In *The Spectator*, edited by Donald F. Bond. London: The Clarendon Press, 1965.

Allen, Robert J. *The Clubs of Augustan London*. Hamden, Connecticut: Archon Books, 1967.

Anderson, Elijah. *A Place on the Corner*. Chicago: The University of Chicago Press, 1976.

Anderson, Robert T., and Barbara Gallatin Anderson. *Bus Stop for Paris: The Transformation of a French Village*. New York: Doubleday and Company, 1965.

Argyris, Chris. *Argyris on Organizations: Prescriptions/Predictions*. New York: Amacum, 1976. Cassette series.

Ariès, Philippe. "The Family and the City," *Daedalus* (Spring 1977).

Atkin, John R. "A Designed Locale for Laughter to Reinforce Community Bonds." In *It's a Funny Thing, Humour*, edited by Anthony J. Chapman and Hugh C. Foot. New York: Pergamon Press, 1977.

Bacon, Seldon. "Alcohol and Complex Society." In *Society, Culture and Drinking Patterns*, edited by David Pitman and Charles Snyder. New York: John Wiley and Sons, 1962.

Banerjee, Tridib, and William C. Baer. *Beyond the Neighborhood Unit*. New York: Plenum Press, 1984.

Barker, Ernest. *The Character of England*. Oxford: The Clarendon Press, 1963.

Barker, Roger, *et al. Midwest and Its Children*. Hamden, Connecticut: Archon Books, 1971.

Bazelon, David T. "The New Factor in American Society." In *Environment and Change: The Next Fifty Years*, edited by W. E. Ewald, Jr. Bloomington, Indiana: Indiana University Press, 1968.

Bechtel, Robert. *Enclosing Behavior.* Dowden: Hutchinson and Ross, 1977.

Benson, Denzel E. "The Intentionally Childless Couple." *USA Today* (January 1979).

Blake, Peter. *God's Own Junkyard: The Planned Deterioration of America's Landscape.* New York: Holt, Rinehart, and Winston, 1964.

Blumberg, Arthur, *et al.* "The Teacher Bar." *The Educational Forum* (Fall 1982).

Bode, Carl. *The Young Mencken.* New York: The Dial Press, 1973.

Bradbury, Ray. "Beyond 1984: The People Machines." In *Cities: The Forces that Shape Them*, edited by Lisa Taylor. New York: Rizzoli, 1982.

Brassai, Gyula Halasz. *Le Paris Secret Des Annees 30.* Garden City, New York: Doubleday and Company, 1966.

Brett, Lionel. *Architecture in a Crowded World: Vision and Reality in Planning.* New York: Schocken Books, 1971.

Bridenbaugh, Carl and Jesse Bridenbaugh. *Rebels and Gentlemen.* New York: Oxford University Press, 1962.

Bronfenbrenner, Urie. *Two Worlds of Childhood.* New York: Russell Sage Foundation, 1970.

_____. "The American Family: An Ecological Perspective. In *The American Family: Current Perspectives.* Cambridge, Mass.: The Harvard University Press, Audiovisual Division. 1979. Cassette series.

Brower, Sidney. "Streetfront and Sidewalk." *Landscape Architecture* (July 1973).

Burgheim, Richard. "McSorley's Old Ale House," *Holiday Magazine* (February 1963).

Burns, James MacGregor. "Is the Primary System a Mistake?" *Family Weekly* (26 February 1984).

Calkins, Raymond. *Substitutes for the Saloon.* Boston: Houghton Mifflin Company, 1919.

Carmichael, Harry. *Most Deadly Hate.* New York: E.P. Dutton and Company, 1974.

Carson, Gerald. "The Saloon." *American Heritage: The Magazine of History* (April 1963).

_____. *The Old Country Store.* New York: E.P. Dutton and Son, 1965.

Chombart de Lauwe, Paul-Henry. *Des Hommes et des Villes.* Paris: Payot, 1965.

Ciborowski, Adolf. Introduction to Carson, Robert B. *What Ever Happened to the Trolley?* Washington, D.C.: University of America Press, 1978.

Clay, Grady. "The Street as Teacher." In *Public Streets for Public Use*, edited by Anne Vernez Moudon. New York: Van Nostrand Reinhold Company, 1987.

Clinard, Marshall B. "The Public Drinking House and Society." In *Society, Culture and Drinking Patterns*, edited by David Pittman and Charles Snyder. New York: John Wiley and Sons, 1962.

Cohen-Portheim, Paul. *The Spirit of London.* Philadelphia: J.B. Lippincott Company, 1935.

Colmey, John. "The Coffeehouse: Grounds for a New Renaissance." *The Minnesota Daily* (16 May 1980).

Connell, W.F. and E.E. Skilbeck. *Growing Up in an Australian City: A Study of Adolescents in Sidney.* Melbourne, Australia: ACER, 1957.

Conzen, Kathleen N. *Immigrant Milwaukee, 1836–1860.* Cambridge, Mass.: Harvard University Press, 1976.

Daly, Michael. "Break Point." *New York* (5 October 1981).

Davids, Kenneth. *Coffee.* San Francisco: 101 Productions, 1976.

Davis, Ben. *The Traditional English Pub.* London: The Architectural Press, 1981.

Diaz-Plaja, Fernando. *The Frenchman and the Seven Deadly Sins.* New York: Charles Scribner's Sons, 1972.

Dobie, Frank. *A Texan in England.* Boston: Little, Brown and Company, 1944.

Duis, Perry R. *The Saloon: Public Drinking in Chicago and Boston, 1880–1920.* Chicago: The University of Illinois Press, 1983.

Dumont, Matthew. "Tavern Culture: The Sustenance of Homeless Men." *American Journal of Orthopsychiatry* 37, 1967.

Ellis, Aytoun. *The Penny Universities.* London: Secker and Warburg, 1956.

Emerson, Ralph Waldo. *Uncollected Lectures.* New York: William Edwin Rudge, 1932.

————. *Essays and Journals.* New York: Doubleday and Company, 1968.

Entrepeneur Magazine. "From Corner Tavern to Disco: Selling the Good Life." (July 1980).

Erhard, Thomas A. "Coffee House." In *The World Book Encyclopedia.* 1980 ed.

Feinsilber, Mike, and William Mead. *American Averages.* Garden City, New York: Dolphin Books, 1980.

Feiss, Carl. "Taking Stock: A Resume of Planning Accomplishments in the United States." In *Environment and Change: The Next Fifty Years,* edited by William R. Ewald. Bloomington, Indiana: Indiana University Press, 1968.

Fellows, Lawrence. "Psychologists' Report Finds New Towns in West Germany Boring to Children." *New York Times* (9 May 1971).

Ferguson, Frank. *Efficient Drug Store Management.* New York: Fairchild Publications, 1969.

Fischer, Claude. *To Dwell Among Friends.* Chicago: The University of Chicago Press, 1982.

Fourastie, Jean. *The Causes of Wealth.* Glencoe: The Free Press, 1960.

Francaviglia, Richard V. "Main Street U.S.A.: The Creation of a Popular Image." *Landscape* (Spring/Summer 1977).

Franck, Harry A. *Vagabonding Through Changing Germany.* New York: Harper and Brothers, 1920.

Fullerton, Gail. *Survival in Marriage*. Hinsdale, Illinois: Dryden, 1977.

Gans, Herbert. *The Levittowners*. New York: Pantheon Books, 1967.

Genovese, Rosalie G. "A Women's Self-Help Network as a Response to Service Needs in the Suburbs." *Signs* 5, no. 3 (Spring 1980).

"Germans in America" Collection. Wisconsin State Historical Society, Madison.

Gilbert, Bil, and Lisa Twyman. "Violence: Out of Hand in the Stands." In *Sport in Contemporary Society*, edited by D. Stanley Eitzen. New York: St. Martin's Press, 2d ed., 1984.

Gilliam, Florence. *France: A Tribute by an American Woman*. New York: E.P. Dutton & Co., 1945.

Glick, Paul C. "How American Families Are Changing." *American Demographics* (January 1984).

Gold, Seymour M. *Recreation Planning and Design*. New York: McGraw-Hill, 1980.

Goldring, Patrick. *The Broilerhouse Society*. New York: Weybright & Talley, 1969.

Goldston, Robert. London: *The Civic Spirit*. New York: Macmillan. 1969.

_____. *Suburbia: Civic Denial*. New York: Macmillan. 1970.

Goodwin, Richard. "The American Condition." *The New Yorker* (January 21, January 28, and 4 February 1974).

Gordon, Suzanne. *Lonely in America*. New York: Simon & Schuster, 1976.

Gorham, Maurice. *Back to the Local*. London: Percival Marshall, 1979.

_____, and H. Dunnett. *Inside the Pub*. London: The Architectural Press, 1950.

Gramont, Sanche de. *The French: Portrait of a People*. New York: G.P. Putnam's Sons, 1969.

Gray, Paul. "Another Look at Democracy in America" *Time* Essay (16 June 1986).

Griesinger, Karl Theodor. "A Historian's Forebodings." In *This Was America*, edited by Oscar Handlin. New York: Harper and Row, 1949.

Gruen, Victor. *The Heart of Our Cities*. New York: Simon & Schuster, 1967.

_____. "New Forms of Community." In *Who Designs America?*, edited by Laurence B. Holland. New York: Anchor Books, 1965.

_____. *Centers for the Urban Environment*. New York: Van Nostrand Reinhold Co., 1973.

Gubbins, Nathaniel. "The Pubs." *Holiday Magazine* (July 1947).

Gunther, John. *Twelve Cities*. New York: Harper & Row, 1967.

Halberstram, David. "One Man's America." *Parade Magazine* (31 October 1982).

Hall, Edward T., *The Hidden Dimension*. Garden City, New York: Doubleday and Company, 1969.

Hamill, Pete. "A Hangout Is a Place . . ." *Mademoiselle Magazine* (November 1969).

Harlow, Alvin F. *The Serene Cincinnatians*. New York: E.P. Dutton & Co., 1959.

Harris, Kenneth. *Travelling Tongues*. London: John Murray, 1949.

Harrison, J. F. C. *The Early Victorians*. New York: Praeger, 1971.

Hausknecht, Murray. *The Joiners*. New York: The Bedminster Press, 1962.

Hayden, Dolores. *Redesigning the American Dream*. New York: W.W. Norton & Company, 1984.

Hester, Randolph T., Jr. *Neighborhood Space*. Stroudsburg, Pennsylvania: Dowden, Hutchinson and Ross, 1975.

Hines, Al. "What the Teetotal Traveler Drinks at the Sidewalk Cafe." *Holiday Magazine* (January 1969).

Hoelterhoff, Manuela. "Life Amid the Ruins of East Germany's Porcelain City." *The Wall Street Journal* (22 September 1983).

Holmes, Fred. *Side Roads*. Madison: The Wisconsin State Historical Society, 1949.

Hooper, Charles E. *The Country House*. New York: Doubleday, Page and Company, 1905.

Huizinga, Johan. *Homo Ludens: A Study of the Play Elements in Culture*. London: Routledge and Kegan Paul, 1949.

Hunt, Violet. *The Desirable Alien*. London: Chatoo and Windus, 1913.

The Idler. no. 58, 1759.

Jackson, Brian. *Working Class Community*. London: Routledge & Kegan Paul, 1968.

Jacobs, Jane. *The Death and Life of Great American Cities*. New York: Random House, 1961.

Kando, Thomas M. *Leisure and Popular Culture in Transition*. St. Louis: The C.V. Mosby Company, 1980.

Kanigel, Robert. "Stay-Put Americans." *Human Behavior* (May 1979).

Kessler, Marc and Christopher Gomberg. "Observations of Barroom Drinking: Methodology and Preliminary Results." *Quarterly Journal of Studies on Alcohol* 35 (1974).

Keyes, Ralph. "I Like Colonel Sanders." *Newsweek* (27 August 1973).

Kirby, Winston. "The Impact on Television: The Communication of Social Disorganization." In *Cities in Transition*, edited by Frank Coppa and Philip Dolee. Chicago: Nelson Hall, 1947.

Klapp, Orrin E. *Heroes, Villains, and Fools*. Englewood Cliffs, New Jersey: Prentice-Hall, 1962.

Kluge, P.F. "Closing Time." *Wall Street Journal* (27 May 1982).

Kohr, Leopold. *The Overdeveloped Nations*. New York: Shocken, 1977.

Koppelman, Lee. In "Suburbia: End of the Golden Age," edited by William S. Kowinski. *The New York Times Magazine* (16 March 1980).

Kowinski, William S. "Suburbia: End of the Golden Age." *The New York Times Magazine*. (16 March 1980).

_____. *The Malling of America*. New York: William Morrow and Company, 1985.

Langner, Thomas S. and Stanley T. Michael. *Life Stress and Mental Health*. New York: The Free Press of Glencoe, 1963.

LeJeune, Anthony. *The Gentlemen's Clubs of London*. New York: Mayflower Books, 1979.

Levine, Jacob. "Humour as a Form of Therapy: Introduction to Symposium." In *It's a Funny Thing, Humour*, edited by Anthony J. Chapman and Hugh C. Foot. New York: Pergamon Press, 1977.

Lewis, C. S. *The Four Loves*. New York: Harcourt Brace Jovanovich, 1960.

Little, Charles E. *Challenge of the Land*. New York: Pergamon Press, 1968.

Lobsenz, Norman M. *Is Anybody Happy?* New York: Doubleday and Company, 1962.

Lofland, Lyn G. *A World of Strangers*. Prospect Heights, Illinois: Waveland Press, 1973.

Long, Huey B. "Taverns and Coffee Houses: Adult Educational Institutions in Colonial America." *Lifelong Learning: The Adult Years* (January 1981).

MacCallum, T.W. *The Vienna That's Not in the Baedeker*. New York: Robert M. McBride and Company, 1931.

Macy, Robert. "Entertainer bemoans high prices in Vegas." *The Pensacola News-Journal* (15 July 1982).

Malko, George. The Biltmore for Men Only." *Holiday Magazine* (January 1969).

Mass Observation. *The Pub and the People: A Worktown Study*. London: Victor Gollancz Ltd., 1943.

Mathews, David. "Civic Intelligence." *Social Education* (November/December 1985).

McHarg, Ian. *The Fitness of Man's Environment*. Washington, D.C.: Smithsonian Institute Press, 1968.

McKeever, J. Ross, ed. *Community Builders Handbook*. Washington, D.C.: Urban Land Institute Press, 1968.

Mead, Margaret. "The American Family." In *The Search for America*, edited by Huston Smith. Englewood Cliffs, New Jersey: Prentice-Hall, 1959.

Melville, Lewis and Aubrey Hammond. *The London Scene*. London: Baber & Bwyer, 1926.

Michner, James A. "Australia." *Holiday Magazine* (November 1950).

Miller, Henry. *Remember to Remember*. London: The Grey Walls Press, 1952.

Miller, Stuart. *Men and Friendship*. Boston: Houghton-Mifflin, 1983.

Monckton, H.A. *A History of the English Public House*. London: The Bodley Head, Ltd., 1969.

Mooney, Sean and George Green. *Practical Guide to Running a Pub*. Chicago: Nelson-Hall, 1979.

Mornell, Pierre. *Passive Men, Wild Women*. New York: Simon & Schuster, 1976.

Mortimer, John. "Rumpole and the Man of God." In *The Trials of Rumpole*. New York: Penguin Books, 1981.

Motamed-Nejad, Kazem. "The Story-Teller and Mass Media in Iran." In *Entertainment: A Cross-Cultural Examination*, edited by Fischer Heinz-Dietrich and Stefan Melnik, New York: Hastings House, 1979.

Nevins, Allan. *Grover Cleveland: A Study in Courage*. New York: Dodd, Mead and Company, 1966.

Newman, Barry. "Good Times or Bad, There'll Always be an English Pub." *Wall Street Journal* (16 November 1981).

Newman, Oscar. *Defensible Space*. New York: The Macmillan Company, 1972.

Nourissier, Francois. *Cartier-Bresson's France*. New York: The Viking Press, 1971.

O'Connor, Richard. *The German-Americans: An Informal History*. Boston: Little, Brown and Company, 1968.

Pajak, Edward. "Cathartic and Socialization Functions of 'Teacher Bars.' " Presented at the annual meeting of the American Educational Research Association, Boston, April 1980.

Pettigrew, Jim, Jr. "The Vanishing Game of Snooker." *Atlanta Weekly* (12 October 1980).

Playground Daily News. "The English Department" (25 November 1982).

Postgate, Raymond. "English Drinking Habits." *Holiday Magazine* (February 1963).

Rexroth, Kenneth. "The Decline of Humor in America." *The Nation* 84, 1975.

Richards, Cara E. "City Taverns." *Human Organization* 22 (Winter, 1963–64).

Riesman, David. "The Suburban Dislocation." *The Annals of the American Academy of Political and Social Science* (November 1957).

Roberts, Kenneth L. *Why Europeans Leave Home*. New York: Bobbs-Merrill, 1922.

Rogow, Arnold. *The Dying of Light*. New York: G.P. Putnam's Sons, 1975.

Ronay, Egon. *Pub Guide*. London: British Tourist Authority Publication, 1976.

Rooney, Andrew A. *A Few Minutes with Andy Rooney*. New York: Atheneum, 1981.

Roubin, Lucienne. "Male Space and Female Space within the Provencial Community." In *Rural Society in France*, edited by Robert Foster. Baltimore: *Selections from the Annales Economies, Societies, Civilization*. 1977.

Royko, Mike. "Neighborhood on the Way Back." *Chicago Daily News* (26 November 1973).

Rubin, Lillian. *Intimate Strangers*. New York: Harper & Row, 1983.

Rudofsky, Bernard. *Streets for People: A Primer for Americans*. Garden City, New York: Doubleday and Company, 1969.

Rysman, Alexander. "How the 'Gossip' Became a Woman." *Journal of Communication* 27, no. 1 (1977).

Sale, Kirkpatrick. *Human Scale*. New York: Coward, McCann and Geoghegan, 1980.

Sampson, Anthony. *Anatomy of Britain*. New York: Harper & Row, 1962.

Scitovsky, Tibor. *The Joyless Economy*. New York: Oxford University Press, 1976.

Seamon, David. *A Geography of the Lifeworld*. New York: St. Martin's Press, 1979.

Sedgwick, Henry. *The Art of Happiness*. New York: Bobbs-Merrill, 1930.

Sennett, Richard. "The Brutality of Modern Families." In *Marriages and Families*, edited by Helena Z. Lopata. New York: W. E. Norton and Company, 1973.

_____. *The Fall of Public Man*. New York: Alfred A. Knopf, 1977.

Silver, Nathan. *Lost New York:* New York: Houghton Mifflin Company, 1967.

Simmel, Georg. *On Individual and Social Form*, edited by Donald N. Levine. Chicago: The University of Chicago Press, 1971.

Sims, Newell, ed. *The Rural Community*. New York: Charles Scribner's Sons. 1920.

Slater, Philip E. "Must Marriage Cheat Today's Young Women?" *Redbook Magazine* (February 1971).

Small Business Reporter. "Bars and Cocktail Lounges." San Francisco: Bank of America, vol. 11, no. 9 (1977).

Stevenson, John. *British Society: 1914–45*. London: Penguin Books, 1984.

Swift, Jonathan. "Hints Towards an Essay on Conversation." In *English Essays: Volume 27*, edited by Charles W. Eliot. New York: P.F. Collier & Son Corporation, 1937.

Theobald, Robert. "Planning with People." In *Environment and Change: The Next Fifty Years*, edited by W. W. Ewald, Jr. Bloomington, Indiana: Indiana University Press, 1968.

Thomas, Anthony E. "Class and Sociability Among Urban Workers: A Study of the Bar as a Social Club." *Medical Anthropology* 2, no. 4 (Fall 1978).

Thomas, Gwyn. "Tranquility and Warm Beer." *Holiday Magazine* (May 1964).

Timbs, John. *Clubs and Club Life in London*. Detroit: Gale Research Company. Reprint (1967).

Time Magazine. "Mobile Society Puts Down Roots" (12 June 1978).

Tocqueville, Alexis de. *Democracy in America*. New York: Alfred A. Knopf, 1963.

Traver, Robert. *Troubleshooter*. New York: The Viking Press, 1943.

Tripp, C.A. *The Homosexual Matrix*. New York: McGraw-Hill, 1975.

van Cleef, Eugene. *Cities in Action*. New York: Pergamon Press, 1970.

Varga, Laszlo. *Human Rights in Hungary*. Gainesville, Florida: Danubian Research and Information Center, 1967.

Von Eckardt, Wolf. *Back to the Drawing Board.* Washington, D.C.: New Republic Books, 1978).

Wallace, Irving, *et al.* "When Coffee was Banned in Sweden." *Parade Magazine* (12 September 1982.

Wallis, Claudia. "Stress: Can We Cope?" *Time Magazine* (6 June 1983).

Warner, Sam Bass, Jr. *The Private City.* Philadelphia: University of Pennsylvania Press, 1968.

Webster, Hutton. *Primitive Secret Societies.* New York: Octagon, reprint, 1968.

Wechsberg, Joseph. "The Viennese Coffee House: A Romantic Institution." *Gourmet Magazine* 12, no. 16 (1966).

————. "The long, sweet day of the Sidewalk Cafe." *Holiday Magazine* (August 1967).

————. *The Vienna I Knew.* New York: Doubleday and Company, 1979.

Weir, L. H. *Europe at Play.* New York: A.S. Barnes & Company, 1937.

West, Richard. "The Power of 21." *New York* (5 October 1981).

Whyte, William H. *The Last Landscape.* New York: Doubleday and Company, 1968.

Willems, Edwin P. "Behavioral Ecology." In *Perspectives on Environment and Behavior,* edited by Daniel Stokols. New York: Plenum Press, 1977.

Winick, Charles. *The New People.* New York: Pegasus, 1968.

Winn, Marie. *Children without Childhood.* New York: Penguin Books, 1984.

Wittke, Carl. *We Who Build America: The Saga of the Immigrant.* Cleveland: The Press of Case Western Reserve University, 1964.

Women's Petition, The. In *Old English Coffee Houses.* London: Rodale Press, 1954.

Wordsworth, William. "The Art of Conversation." In *Wordsworthian and Other Studies,* edited by Ernest de Selincourt. New York: Russell & Russell, 1964.

Wright, David E. and Robert E. Snow. "Consumption as Ritual in High Technology Society." In *Rituals and Ceremonies in Popular Culture,* edited by Ray Browne. Bowling Green: Bowling Green University Popular Press, 1980.

Wylie, Laurence. *Village in the Vaucluse.* New York: Harper & Row, 1957.

Young, T.R. *New Sources of the Self.* New York: Pergamon Press, 1972.

All correspondence with the author should be addressed to: Ray Oldenburg, The University of West Florida, Pensacola, Florida 32514.

Index